FEAST OR FAMINE

FEAST OR FAMINE

Food, Farming, and Farm Politics in America

ED EDWIN

CHARTERHOUSE
New York

To my mother

Jennyce Cecelia Edwin

Preface and Acknowledgments

A second world food shortage in less than ten years returns us to the question of whether America's farms can maintain our eating standard at prices we can afford. Yet most of us know little about the challenges and risks of farming; we have become accustomed to buying the foods we want when we want them.

I began researching agriculture during the world food panic of the mid-1960s. What struck me most forcibly were the rapid changes taking place on American farms. It occurred to me that an up-to-date survey of how American farmers operate and of trends suggesting what will happen in the years ahead would be useful, a presentation based on the best technical data available for lay persons concerned with public issues but with slight knowledge of agriculture.

My research has necessarily been multidisciplinary, and has led me into specialized areas where my background was limited. As I have done as a news reporter for some years, I have tried to marshal the salient factors for the reader without a technical background. The effort reminds me of a remark made by a distinguished science correspondent who was on a panel at a meeting of the American Association for the Advancement of Science.

"I don't know why I'm up here," he said, "because I'm not an expert in anything—unless it's in being an amateur."

In this effort, I have received much assistance from individuals and organizations; they have been generous with briefing time, in responding to queries, in supplying documents and reprints, and in keeping me informed through news releases. I wish that I could have contacted many others in the confidence that they would have been similarly responsive, so I wish to thank as a group farmers, extension agents, state commissioners of agriculture, universities and their affiliated experiment stations, government and international agency experts, foundations, other voluntary organizations, other agribusinessmen, and political leaders. And their media aides and other staff members have often been especially helpful.

Any deficiencies in this treatment are, of course, my responsibility.

The total number of persons queried is much larger than the number cited in the text, and I would like to acknowledge the help from some of these others, particularly those who responded to my requests time and again, provided me materials yielding deeper insights, or arranged interviews. Several members of the Office of Communication in the U.S. Department of Agriculture have been helpful, and I wish to thank particularly Larry B. Marton for his assistance since the mid-1960s. At the United Nations, Lila Goldin, Norman R. Michie, and George Mulgrue of the Food and Agriculture Organization; Stephen Whitehouse, Glenda Adams, and Edward H. Omotoso of the Center for Economic and Social Information; Morris Huberman and Ulla Olin of the UN Development Program; Lalit M. Thapalyal of the World Health Organization; W. J. Knight of the International Labor Organization; and Kenneth B. Kelly of the press room have aided me in finding the kind of information I needed.

Also of assistance were James Singer when he was at the Beltsville, Maryland experimental station and later the Department of Health, Education and Welfare; Sam Belk and Jerry E. Rosenthal at the Agency International Development (AID); and Herbert A. Kassner of the Corp of Engineers, Lower Mississippi Valley Division. Among university agricultural program specialists were R. S. Fosbrink at Purdue; James Graham and Tom Sork at Fort Collins, Colorado; and Lee Thompson at Ames, Iowa.

Keeping me posted at the state level were Brevard Crihfield and Herbert L. Wiltsee of the Council of State Governments; at the World Bank, David C. Fulton and Donald J. Pryor; at the American Association for the Advancement of Science, Thelma C. Heatwole; at the Rockefeller Foundation, Henry Romney; Walter E. Ashley when he was at the Ford Foundation; at the AFL-CIO, Al Zack; and at the Conference Board, Joseph L. Narr.

John R. Rague at Negative Population Growth and the Association for Voluntary Sterilization and Donald Higgins of the latter were notably helpful in arranging for interviews and special materials when the dimensions of the world population surge became apparent, as was James Walls, first at the Population Council and then IPPF–Western Hemisphere. George A. Barbour and Emanuel T. Ellenis arranged several briefings in Nova Scotia.

Among representatives of businesses that contributed were Sidney Shore of Sidney Shore Associates, Robert G. Randolph of the Chevron Oil Corporation, George Neily of Deere, Will R. Yolen of Hill and Knowlton, Leon Thiel of Manning, Selvage & Lee, Richard Whelan of IBM, Donald B. Walker of Archer-Daniels Midland, and G. Marshall Abbey of Baxter Laboratories. Melvyn H. Bloom of Murden and Company, Elaine Schwartz at the San Francisco Produce Market, and Howard W. Mattson of the Institute of Food Technologists.

I have also appreciated briefings, symposia papers, and/or guidance in personal communications from John S. Aird, China expert with the Census Bureau; H. R. Albrecht, director of the Institute of Tropical Agriculture in Nigeria; Durwood L. Allen, wildlife ecologist at Purdue; Hugh C. Barton, economic consultant in Puerto Rico; Alan D. Berg, nutritionist with the Brookings Institution; James P. Brazzel and W. M. Ring of the U.S. Plant Protection and Quarantine Program; Lester R. Brown, now with the Overseas Development Council; Harrison S. Brown, geochemist at the California Institute of Technology; Mary S. Calderone of the Sex Information and Education Council of the U.S. (SIECUS); Robert F. Chandler, director of the International Rice Research Institute (IRRI) in the Philippines; Sripiti Chandrasekhar when he was Indian Minister of Public Health and Family

Planning, as well as his countrypersons, Pralhad S. Jahever, medical developer of new birth-control devices, and V. Rahmathulla of a Madras clinic; Dorris C. Clark at the National Seed Storage Laboratory; Kenneth B. Clark, the psychologist; Calvin S. Cronin, editor-in-chief of *Chemical Engineering;* Richard A. Donnelly of *Barron's* "Commodities Corner"; Jose Figueres, former president of Costa Rica; Ronald Freedman of the University of Michigan Population Studies Center; U. J. Grant of the International Center for Tropical Agriculture in Colombia; Katayun H. Gould, family researcher at the Jane Addams Graduate School for social Work in Illinois; the late Dr. Alan F. Guttmacher of World Population—Planned Parenthood; Dick Hansen, Jr., a western farm writer; Oscar Harkavy, family planning expert at the Ford Foundation; W. Averell Harriman, diplomat; J. M. Hejl of the U.S. Veterinary Services; Carl Hodges, director of the Environmental Research Laboratory at the University of Arizona and his associate, Wayne Collins; W. David Hopper of the International Development Research Center in Toronto; Louis B. Howard, head of the National Association of State Universities and Land Grant Colleges; Peter Jordan, who heads the schistosomiasis project on St. Lucia, West Indies; William D. Jackson, biologist at Bowling Green University in Ohio; Alberto Lleras Carmargo, former president of Colombia; Shao-wen Ling, FAO aquaculturist; Akter Hameed Kahn when he was Deputy Minister of Agriculture of Pakistan; David E. Lilienthal of the Development and Resources corporation and his aide, Warren G. Fugitt; Robert B. Livingston at the University of California at San Diego; Charles E. Logsdon, of the Institute of Agricultural Sciences, University of Alaska, geochronologist at the University of Arizona; the late Tom Mboya when he was Minister of Economic Planning and Development for Kenya; Miloš Macura of the UN Population Division; Leonardo J. Mata, chief microbiologist at the Instituto de Nutrition de Centro America and Panama (INCAP); Richard J. McConnell, head of the Department of Economics at Montana State Univeristy; T. B. McMullen of the National Center for Air Pollution Control; George C. Mehren and Kenneth Mueller during different periods at the Agribusiness Council; Paul H. Mussen, director of the Institute of Human Development at Berkeley and his associate, Vivien March; M. R. Peterson of the Federal

Crop Insurance Corporation; U.J. Pittman, plant expert at the Canadian Department of Agriculture; Malcolm Potts, when he was medical director of the International Planned Parenthood Federation; A. Philip Randolph, the labor leader; R. T. Ravenholt of the AID Office of Population; Oswald A. Roels of the Lamont-Doherty Geological Observato; J. Mayone Stycos, family planning specialist at Cornell; Hobart Taylor, formerly of the Export-Import Bank; L. M. K. Wasti of the King Edward Medical College in Lahore, Pakistan; Edwin J. Wellhausen, director of the Centro de Mejoramiento de Maiz y Trigo (CIMMYT) in Mexico and his associate, Gregardio Martínez; and Sterling Wortman, a vice president of the Rockefeller Foundation, and Lewis M. Roberts, its associate director of agricultural sciences, and Virgil C. Scott, associate director of biomedical sciences.

Years ago, several Columbia University professors encouraged me to research in some of these directions, notably Andrew W. Cordier when he was dean of the School of International Affairs; William E. Leuchtenburg, Dewitt Clinton Professor of American History; the late Philip E. Mosely when he was director of the Russian Institute; David B. Truman when he was head of the Department of Public Law and Government; Ralph J. Watkins who specialized in international trade and finance; and Louis M. Starr, director of the Columbia Oral History Research Office.

Henry Hall Wilson, Jr., and Herbert G. Klein, as presidential aides in succeeding administrations, were particularly helpful.

In my field, my interest was kept alive through assignments or use of my work especially by Elmer W. Lower of ABC News, Walter Cronkite of CBS News, and Russell C. Tornabene of NBC News.

Other organizations whose staff members have assisted me include the Agency for International Development, U.S. Department of the Interior, Council on Environmental Quality, the National Academy of Sciences–National Research Council, the New York Academy of Sciences, International Planned Parenthood Federation, Population Reference Bureau, the Asian Development Bank, and the Federation of Rocky Mountain States.

A number of newsmen recommended local contacts, especially Roy F. Heatly, a TV news director in California, and William D. James of the Great Falls (Montana) *Tribune*. Several other friends, including George H. Hyde of New Jersey, Robert Hecht and Paul Lutzeier of Michigan, Milka Markovich Wigfield of Minnesota, and my brothers Russell L. Edwin of Montana and Howard W. Edwin of California, provided me articles and other information which otherwise would not have come to my attention. My father, Edward S. Edwin, a physician, gave me counsel on certain health aspects, as did Howard B. Shookhoff, a New York internist and tropical medicine specialist.

I think, too, there should be a special word for my regular postal carrier, Steve Sipola, who delivered the frequent large bundles with unfailing good cheer.

Most especially, I thank my wife, Jane, who, while "living" with this project so long, ferreted out many of the facts required, screened bibliographical references, and critiqued the early manuscript.

Contents

Prologue: The Incessant Peril   1

Part I   Agricultural Inputs—Nature's and Man's   41

CHAPTER 1   The Plant—Another Kind of Creature   47

CHAPTER 2   The Soilsphere—Its Formation
and Its Inhabitants   58

CHAPTER 3   The Capricious Forces—Climate
and Weather   79

CHAPTER 4   The Most Ancient Survivors—Insects
and Other Pests   96

CHAPTER 5   Energy and Power—Solar, Mechanical,
and Chemical   121

CHAPTER 6   Intensive Agriculture, the Biosphere,
and Earthwatch   134

Part II   The Cornucopia of Agriculture   153

CHAPTER 7   The Imperative of Nutrition   155
CHAPTER 8   Important American Crops   197
CHAPTER 9   Of Mammal, Fowl, and Fish   231

Part III   The Farm—Rhetoric and Realities   261

CHAPTER 10   Evolution of Farming   263
CHAPTER 11   The Politics of Agriculture   291

Epilogue: The Future of Agriculture   333

Index   349

City people have forgotten agriculture, and they had better realize that no civilization has survived without it. They need to understand it, to be benevolent toward it, because they need it. No country becomes strong without it or remains strong without it. Apparently when you are too successful in a society, you turn around and destroy it.

—EMIL M. MRAK
Chancellor Emeritus,
University of California at Davis
May 8, 1972

Prologue / The Incessant Peril

No one knows when or where the next great famine will occur, its extent and severity, or the reasons why it will come. Fifteen years ago, widespread starvation seemed improbable. The world appeared to have the natural and technical resources to prevent it, there had been no major episode for some time, and Americans were eating better while paying the lowest share of their incomes for food of any people in history.

Since that time, there have been famines on three continents, a massive harvest failure threatening for the first time an industrialized nation neither at war nor recovering from war, a rampant blight raising new doubts about the future of American farmers' marvelous productivity, a deterioration of an agricultural environment spanning almost the width of a continent, and a sharp decline in the world fish catch. In addition, the rate of increase in global population overtook the rate of increase in food output, markedly so in the poorest and most densely inhabited regions: the stork was outrunning the plow. The shortages induced a worldwide inflation of food prices, and in 1973 America's eating standards declined for the first time in a quarter of a century.

These events and trends were grim reminders to the apostles

of economic development that factories, dams, highways, bridges, and airfields by themselves do not prevent starvation. "When tillage begins," Daniel Webster said, "other arts follow. The farmers, therefore, are the founders of human civilization." He could have added that when tillage is neglected or disrupted, civilization crumbles, for the first imperative of survival is food.

The weather—droughts, floods, frost, hail, hurricanes, typhoons, tornadoes, and tidal waves—causes most food shortages. Other direct natural causes are volcanic eruptions, earthquakes, deterioration of the soil, decline of water quality, diseases, and pests. Further, if population growth exceeds the capabilities of a society to provide and store food, people go hungry. Maldistribution, often caused by transportation breakdowns or marketing inequities, can lead to localized hunger, and poor people as a group can starve simply because they lack money for enough food.

Nutritional standards can also decline after "modernizers" or commercial farmers replace traditional food crops with "cash" plantings such as cotton, rubber, coffee, or sugar. After such an economic "advance," the Marquesas Islanders in the South Pacific, for example, earned more money with which to buy clothing, household wares, and liquor; but because fewer nutritious foodstuffs were available in their markets, their health degenerated. When the farm-labor force decreases or becomes less productive, fewer food crops may be cultivated. Such a decrease can occur when immigrant workers are vulnerable to a disease in a new environment or, conversely, when they introduce a disease among a local populace.

Hunger as a Weapon

Wars, revolutions, and riots are more often than not followed by hunger; and food shortages can cause violence in the first place. Since ancient times, food sources have been targets in combat. The Mongols ranged through India, China, Mesopotamia, and as far west as Europe in search of more plentiful food supplies; the Medes and Persians left their Iranian plateau to seize the fertile fields of Babylonia and Sumer; the Goths pillaged the estates of the dissolving Roman Empire; and both Napoleon and Hitler coveted the grain belts of Russia and the Ukraine.

Since no nation can survive, much less make war, without a steady supply of food, military maneuvers were frequently planned to destroy the food supply or deny the enemy access to it. On the Nile Delta in the eleventh century, four thousand raiding Berber horsemen ripped dikes, gutted canals, laid waste the harvests, and terrorized the food producers in the countryside; nine centuries later, a Nazi governor of the Netherlands tried to bring on a civilian famine by destroying the dikes. After the Japanese occupied the Burmese rice paddies and blockaded the Bay of Bengal during World War II, the British had to decide whether to ship food or arms over the two rail lines across the subcontinent. Weapons took priority, and estimates of deaths by starvation in Calcutta ran from 1 million to 3.5 million. In 1972 the United States blocked supplies going to North Vietnam by sea; it was estimated that 38 percent of seaborne cargo to Hanoi was food—mostly rice and wheat. According to a National Security Study Memorandum quoted by the *New York Times*, "the importance of food imports [to North Vietnam] can hardly be overstated." Also, herbicides were dropped on crops in hostile territory.

The Nazis used starvation to commit genocide, both in concentration camps and when they sealed off the Warsaw ghetto. (Much of our knowledge about starvation comes from the painstaking, horrifying records kept by Jewish doctors before they, too, died.) And the Ibos of Biafra accused the central Nigerians of halting food supplies during their secessionist war, with the specific aim of exterminating them as a group.

It is instructive to note, in this context, that two of the more effective American black leaders to emerge in this century polemicized with hunger metaphors. Harlem Congressman Adam Clayton Powell, Jr., declaimed, "We have had enough of our bellies scraping against our backbones," and Malcolm X accused "the white slavemaster" of "giving us crumbs, never loaves." (Indeed, the genocide rhetoric among the more extreme black militants even accused the whites of instituting family-planning programs for that purpose.)

Historically, governments have been fearful of spokesmen

emerging from the hungry masses, though often such natural rebels have not themselves been of the impoverished classes, and the Establishment's leaders have gone beyond political and economic counteractions. They have at times even executed these men in a public display, as an object lesson.

A History of Famine

Starvation, one of the Four Horsemen of the Apocalypse, is always accompanied by another, pestilence, and often brings forth the other two, war and death. An eminent physiologist, Ancel Keyes, has written on the insidiousness of starvation:

> Most important, social consciousness evaporates, petty thievery and dishonesty are rampant, and political ideals and cohesion give way to demagoguery, corruption, and dictatorship. This unhappy picture well describes the chronic situation among large sectors of the population of the world today.

The earliest written reference to famine, which dates to about 3500 B.C., was found in Egypt. Apparently, hunger was a bane of ancient Egypt. "Each man has become a thief to his neighbor," a monarch lamented, and old writings relate how parents subsisted by eating their children and how men waylaid mothers to snatch babies from their arms. Chronicles of the seven-year famine, during which the Nile failed to overflow to deposit moisture and nutrients, report that butchers, concealing themselves behind latticed windows in upper stories of buildings, snagged unwary pedestrians with meat hooks, slaughtered them, and sold them in pre-cooked pieces. By the second year of another famine, peasants with land had exchanged it for food and taken jobs, thereby changing the entire system of land tenure and serfdom; many eventually preferred suicide to a life without their own land.

Tales of famine in the Roman Empire are equally ghastly. One famine was accompanied by such widespread disease that even the vultures avoided the accumulating bodies. During twenty years of chronic famine in the fifth century, thousands flung themselves into the Tiber River.

At first, the Romans were devoted agriculturists, advancing the knowledge of plants, irrigation, fertilizing, and implements. Although they produced surpluses of some items, including oil and wine, they were not self-sufficient in grain, so they demanded that Carthage export its grain to Italy and refrain from competing in the oil and wine markets. As negotiations faltered, Cato, the leader of the landowners' party, persuaded the government that the Carthaginians were a menace, and the Third Punic War ensued. Symbolically if perversely, the victorious Romans dragged a plow through the leveled, empty city saying, "Those who live by the plow, must perish by the plow." The sword was deemed mightier than the plowshare, and the term "Carthaginian peace" entered the language.

At home, the Roman elite became careless about domestic agriculture. Early Rome had many freeholding farmers, but most of their farms were consolidated into country estates worked by slaves (as in Athens) and owned by wealthy people who lived in the city and visited them for pleasure and to collect rents. Neither the slaves nor the owners dedicated themselves to the land, and by the second century, olives, of which there had been a surplus, were in such short supply that the government banned further shipments and began importing. Though the privileged feasted more sumptuously, chronic starvation spread among the lower classes. The former smallholders and free farmhands, when no longer needed on the estates, fled to the cities for employment, and feeding them became a critical problem. The emperor, fearing rebellion, decreed a dole of bread a hereditary right—an early example of "bread politics." In the fourth century, Rome directed provincial governments to provide their own grain as well as their own defense, a policy that led to secessions, a reduction of grain exports to the capital during the invasions, and, eventually, the breakup of the Empire.

During the Dark and Middle Ages, the common folk lived off the land without producing surpluses, and Roman agricultural techniques were preserved mainly in the monasteries. It was a time of general hunger and frequent, brief, localized famines, often precipitated by the warfare that was chronic until around

A.D. 1100. Harvests declined, nutrition was poor, some plant diseases affected human beings, and agricultural organization stagnated. The typical system of community farming destroyed incentive, for the peasants worked manorial and monastic lands in common tillage, plowing, sowing, and reaping at specified times. They could introduce new crops only by changing the system, and habitually no agreement on such changes could be reached. From the eighth to the fourteenth centuries, episodic famines caused men to eat anything and everything after they had slaughtered their animals; they searched for acorns like prehistoric men and ate bread that was nine-tenths bark and straw.

The year 943 witnessed in Limoges, France, what has become known as the "ergot famine," considered by some historians as the major European food disaster up to the time. Ergotism is a fungus that makes rye black and sweet—and so toxic that anyone eating it goes into a seizure of shrieking and writhing climaxed by convulsions, gangrene, and collapse. Although Roman scholars had warned against eating infested rye, medieval Europeans generally were unaware of their admonitions.

Whatever else improved as the Europeans emerged from the Dark Ages, the nourishment of the masses did not. From the tenth century to the Renaissance, chroniclers recorded some four hundred widespread famines. In fourteenth-century France, one writer remarked that "the merchants nor others dared venture out of the town to look after their concerns or to take any journey, for they were attacked and killed whatever road they took." By the eighteenth century, most people survived on herb soups, bread substitutes, chestnuts, olives, native fruit, and roots. At times, bark made up much of their diet. In 1700, in France, several provincial governors officially reported that the country was gradually starving to death, and within fifteen years a third of the population—about six million people—had died of starvation. In 1769 another 5 percent perished.

Tastes and food habits did not help conditions. Though people in rural areas had resorted to all manner of things to eat, the Parisians relied on wheat bread; they scorned potatoes and macaroni, complained of the smell of maize flour, and insisted that oats were fit only for horses. Nor were they interested in market gardening—the raising of vegetables and fruits for sale or barter. In 1780 Antoine Auguste Parmentier, a botanist, tried to promote the potato as at least a supplemental food, and the American ambassador, Benjamin Franklin, did the same for corn, but neither attempt succeeded.

The most severe drought in years struck France in 1789, drying millstreams and stilling water wheels. There was a bread shortage, prices soared, and the people were sure that the royal household was hoarding supplies. In October fifty thousand armed citzens marched to Versailles, where Marie Antoinette secured her niche in history with the advice, "Let them eat cake!", but they found no bread (cake, in the parlance of the time, may have meant well-refined bread, not a confectionery). The revolutionary leaders, however, on gaining power, did assign top priority to the distribution of bread. Yet, in time the post-Revolution nouveaux riches grew forgetful, ate festively, and hunger remained widespread.

Although Napoleon did not really minimize the importance of agriculture, he failed to monitor his grain harvests well, and food supplies were not always adequate. When Russia sided with his enemies, he lost his source of cheap grain and decided to invade. The Russians, correctly suspecting that he intended to seize their harvests, effected a scorched-earth policy in their retreat of 1812; and as the French army withdrew, it suffered the greatest grain disaster in the history of warfare. "Bread is an army's greatest ally," says a Russian proverb. "The soldier marches no further than his stomach." And the Russians followed a similar scorched-earth strategy 125 years later against Hitler.

The British experienced over two hundred famines from the tenth to the mid-nineteenth centuries. Parents often sold themselves or their children to slavemasters in return for provisions; in prisons, inmates literally tore newcomers apart, and cannibalism was also frequent on the outside. In the eighteenth century, conditions were such that the satirist and clergyman Jonathan Swift was moved to write *A Modest Proposal*, in which he recommended that the English leaders contract with the rich for the fattening of the children of the poor as future dinner fare; he further infuriated the Establishment by suggesting recipes.

When food growing gave way to sheep grazing, displaced English smallholders emigrated to the industrial slums, where their diets were less substantial than on their farms. As late as the middle of the last century, nearly one-third of the English subsisted on potatoes and occasional corn, while another third got along on wheat or oat bread and occasional pork. The remaining third probably ate well, as usual.

The Irish potato famine, which occurred little more than 125 years ago, had the severest national impact of any recorded famine and, incidentally, also altered American demography and politics. The Irish, the only Europeans to adopt the potato whole-heartedly, had seeded their fields to it almost entirely by the middle of the seventeenth century—an early case of monoculture or one-crop farming. The high-yield tuber enabled poor couples to marry young and support large families, and the population jumped in 150 years from 2 million to over 8 million.

In 1822 a blight damaged the harvest, and the fungus persisted until 1845, when it wiped out the crops upon which three-fourths of the people relied. By the spring of 1847, in one work-house alone, 2,500 were dying every week, and in that year total deaths were estimated at from 250,000 to 350,000 or between 2.5 and 4 percent of the population. A flu epidemic struck, and the peasants, now pressed by debts, tried to organize revolts, but their leaders were imprisoned, exiled, or executed. A quarter of a million Irishmen set out in that year for the United States, but so many fell ill with what they called "famine fever" that only half that number were able to embark from Liverpool, and whole families died on the voyage. The blight raged through 1849, leaving a total of about 1 million—about 12 percent of the population—dead. Crop failures, starvation, disease, emigration, and suppression set off a depopulating trend that continued until 1917. The population dropped to around 4 million before it stabilized, and Ireland, a Roman Catholic country, has since had one of the lowest birthrates in the world.

In imperial Germany, the food-producing class was despised by the townspeople, though the country lacked sufficiency in grain and relied on imports from Russia. For five years prior to World War I, the Germans built a strategic buffer against a one-year war by importing half of the Russian barley harvest and much other grain. Yet, by the war's third year, Germany was suffering a bread disaster that was to traumatize it for years.

After the armistice, government policy sought to reorient attitudes by fostering a back-to-the-land movement, but agriculture lagged in the interwar German economy. In October 1933, Hitler addressed himself to food supplies. "The peasant not only assures the nation of its daily bread," he declaimed, "he is the guarantor of its future and provides a people with force, health, equilibrium, and endurance." Nevertheless, Hitler mechanized his armies but not his farmers; six years later, his minister of agriculture conceded that fewer than 2 percent of the farmers owned tractors. Hitler's 1939 pact with the Russians was conceived largely to remedy German grain deficiencies; yet he subsequently became convinced that he could succeed where Napoleon had failed, and deployed his forces into the Russian grain belt in 1941. The Russians fell back, leaving the land barren before the oncoming Nazi army. Domestically, Hitler stiffened the determination of the farmers and rekindled fears of another food disaster by claiming that the English planes had dropped larvae of the Colorado potato beetle on German fields. After World War II, subsistence rations of relief grain, largely American, kept the Germans and other Europeans from starving.

The earliest Russian famine on record occurred in the year 1024; accompanied by pestilence and war, it was, like many other Russian disasters, considered divine punishment. At least seven famines took place in each century from the twelfth to the sixteenth, and when a plague accompanied another food shortage in 1600, at least half a million perished. The latter half of the nineteenth century witnessed eleven famines, about half of the most serious food hardships outside India during the period. Accounts record how the people devoured grass, mice, carrion, and sawdust during these episodes, and how merchants sold pies of human flesh. In an average year in some of the fertile black-soil regions, nearly two-thirds of the peasants were unable to raise enough food for themselves, and although czarist policy legally obligated each community to maintain an emergency store of grain (whose deficiencies were to be met by the central government), these arrangements usually failed when needed most.

Following the Bolshevik Revolution, an extensive drought reduced the food stocks of from 20 to 24 million people, of whom an estimated 1.25 to 5 million died. At the time, 85 percent of the population was rural, and despite the West European conception of Russia as a vast granary, the peasants did little more than subsistence farming and cropped the lowest yields in Europe; grain exports came chiefly from the large estates. One local writer of the time lamented, "Never did five years pass without famine. The town was famous throughout all Russia as a grain mart—but not more than a hundred persons in the whole town ate their fill of grain." At the time and since, anticommunists have ascribed the famine to failures of the Soviets, but in *The Famine in Soviet Russia 1919–1923,* H. H. Fisher, the former chief historian of the Historical Department of the American Relief Administration, wrote:

> The failure of the rain to fall in 1920 and 1921 cannot be attributed to the madness of Bolshevism, nor to the intervention of Providence to punish the blasphemous Communists for their sins. It is equally necessary, on the other hand, to show that the causes which made this famine worse than others of recent times were not wholly, or even largely, the result of the blockade of Russia or the intervention of the Allies.

Weather alone would have ruined the harvests.

In 1932, 1933, and again in 1947, grain procurement and export policies were largely responsible for widespread and severe hunger; actually, Soviet economic policies at times accommodated hunger as part of the price of development. Collectivization from 1932 to 1934, forced procurements, and the subsequent destruction of livestock by peasants caused the deaths of an estimated 5 million to 6 million people (some estimates run higher, but census analyses do not support them). With grain production off by 12 percent of the 1926–30 average, and potato output off by 5 percent, what has been characterized as a ruthless procurement policy left the peasants with a third to a fourth less food grain than in the earlier period. The government exported enough grain to provide 1,000 calories daily for two years for its 17 million citizens. In 1963 *Pravda* quoted Nikita Khrushchev's criticism of Stalin's grain policies. "Their method was like this," he said. "They sold grain abroad, while in some regions people were swollen with hunger and even dying for lack of bread."

Subsequent agricultural difficulties eroded confidence in Khrushchev, however, and contributed to his ouster. Appreciable crop shortfalls, especially in feed, caused farmers to slaughter so many of their hogs that herds reportedly fell from 70 million to 40 million head—over 40 percent—and bread turned gray because the flour was being watered down.

No people, with the possible exception of the Indians, have suffered so much starvation as the Chinese. Nearly every year since their earliest recorded famine in 108 B.C., food shortages have hit one or more provinces, and known episodes total over 1,800. Children were often exchanged for food, and cannibalism was reported during a number of famines. From 1333 to 1337, four million persons reportedly died in one region; the Black Death that would later sweep Europe may have originated in China at this time. What may have been the worst famine in history occurred during the great drought of 1876 to 1879, when there was scarcely any moisture in an area of almost a third of a million square miles—about the size of California, Oregon, and Washington combined. Taking into account related disease and violence, this famine claimed between 9 million and 13 million lives, and huge ditches dug for corpse disposal were recalled for decades as the "10,000-man holes."

Hunger was so endemic in China that during the crop failures following World War I, the International Red Cross initially rejected an appeal for food on the ground that famine was a perpetual condition in the country rather than an emergency. Fortunately, the decision was reversed, and all but about 500,000 of some 20 million starving people were saved. Journalist-historian Theodore H. White recalls an episode in China after World War II:

> My notes tell me that I am reporting only what I saw or verified; yet even to me it seems unreal: dogs eating human bodies by the road, peasants seeking dead human flesh under cover of darkness, endless deserted villages . . . babies abandoned to cry and die on every highway . . . trees on the road have been peeled of their bark. Peasants dry and powder the elm bark and then cook it. They also eat leaves, straw, roots, cottonseed, and water reed. . . . When they die, they just lie down. . . .

Western doctors who have visited China since 1972 report that the people generally look well nourished, that whatever starvation may have occurred during the "bamboo curtain" period apparently was brought under control. The chairman of a local revolutionary committee mainly concerned with agriculture told a *Wall Street Journal* reporter, "Before the liberation . . . we had grain for only half a year; after that, we ate husks and roots. There were 46 households then, and seven families died of starvation between 1929 and 1949." In the aftermath of the 1972 weather adversities, Peking apparently averted starvation through grain and soybean imports.

The Indian subcontinent experiences a drought about once every five years, but, except for such oblique references as "the flesh of a son was preferred to his love," ancient accounts reveal little of the tribulation endured during Indian famines. In Kashmir from A.D. 917 to 918, so many bodies covered the Jhelum River that it appeared to be a great open burial ground, and in 1677, after torrential rains fell on Hyderabad, famine often left no more than two or three survivors in each village. During the drought in Bengal from 1769 to 1770, death estimates ranged from 3 million to 10 million—a tenth to a third of the populace. From 1870 to 1900, long before the contemporary population spurt, hunger deaths may have been as high as 20 million. As recently as 1967, parents were reportedly selling their children for about 70 cents, which they spent on food for the rest of the family.

Indian famines, however, were sometimes caused by maldistribution. In 1877, while an estimated 4 million people were dying, cereals were being exported. Present provincial governments closely regulate wheat shipments, and some may withhold surpluses while a neighboring province has shortages. When the huge wheat shipments arrived during the world food panic of the mid-1960s, they often remained piled in ports, exposed to rats and other pests, while many rural families lacked food.

Although Latin America does not have a reputation for chronic famine, some historians suggest that farming disasters contributed to the mysterious disappearances of the Mayan, Toltec, and Olmec civilizations. The most notable chronic famine area is probably the Brazilian Northeast, the Seratâo, where for centuries the people have barely subsisted. During the nineteenth century, the Seratâoans went through ten harsh winters and seven major droughts, and the worst drought in a dozen years ended only in 1971. In 1972, following a drought in Central America, an earthquake destroyed Managua, the capital of Nicaragua, and disrupted some of the countryside; it was estimated that over one-fourth of the nation's nearly 2 million people would need food donations for some time. And during the 1973 Southern Hemisphere winter, double the normal amount of rain poured on Buenos Aires Province in Argentina, a flatland area larger than Italy. Six months later, much of the 2.4 million farm acres were still under water, 50 percent of the crop was lost, and what grew on ground not fully flooded cost four times as much to harvest.

Records of famine in Africa, except for Egypt, are sketchy, but we know that much of the Saraha was under cultivation twice, until apparently climatic changes made agriculture no longer possible. Recent revolutionary strife, particularly in Nigeria and the Congo, caused hunger by interfering with traditional food-distribution channels, but conditions returned more or less to normal after pacification. At this writing, the greatest recorded famine threat in Black Africa has struck eighteen countries and possibly over 30 million people, and in some areas is in its eighth year. The UN Food and Agriculture Organization (FAO) estimated that between 5 million and 10 million people were in danger of dying either from hunger or thirst in the most severely struck region, the Sahel, a semi-arid zone extending about 2,000 miles along the southern edge of the Sahara and embracing an area larger than the continental United States. The Sahelian countries are Chad, Mali, Mauritania, Niger, Senegal, and the Upper Volta.

The people subsisted mostly by tilling and herding until grain output was reduced by half and livestock losses were from 25 to 80 percent, depending on the country. Between 1969 and 1973, Mauritanian herdsmen, among the hardest hit, lost at least three-fourths of their cattle, more than half their sheep and goats, and a third of their camels. Hungry families in some localities ate their seed grain and therefore could not plant the following wet season, but moisture was again sparse for the 1974 crop. The nomadic desert people, their remaining herds starving, disregarded national frontiers and continued their push into lands traditionally reserved for farmers and into cities in search of food.

Disease spread among the livestock; and chicken pox, flu, jaundice, typhoid, tuberculosis, measles, cholera, and diphtheria broke out in these floating populations, which were also anemic. Refugee camps were set up, where conditions were reported as abominable. The need of traditionally self-reliant tribesmen to beg for handouts in strange terrain caused emotional disturbances, and suicides were reported among groups in which suicide had been virtually unknown. Even in normal times, only 50 percent of the children survive to the age of five, but when diphtheria struck children in one area, parents asked relief authorities not to send drugs; diphtheria was less tortuous a way of dying than slow starvation. Or they sacrificed their weakest children by giving relief food to the others. Their action appeared perilously close to "disguised infanticide."

The drought spread, affecting, in various degrees, Cameroon, Central African Republic, Ivory Coast, Nigeria, Somalia, Sudan, and Togo. In Nigeria, just south of Sahel, the 1974 peanut crop dropped to 300,000 tons from 800,000 tons the year before, and by February, the regional marketing board had been able to buy only 21,000 tons from local farmers compared with 366,000 tons at the same time in 1973. "The farmers are afraid to get rid of a crop they may be forced to eat to stay alive," one observer said. But there was also smuggling into Chad and Niger, where prices were higher than the controlled levels in Nigeria. Most of the peanut-processing plants, built under development programs, were expected to close. In Ethiopia, the situation was confused; the central government assertedly had not received reports of famine in two provinces from local officials and subsequently suspended one governor. It was also reported that, while thousands of peasants starved, the country exported food and left some unused in storage. In March 1974 a study released by the Carnegie Endowment for International Peace charged that "a pattern of neglect and inertia" on the part of the U.S. Agency for International Development (AID) and the FAO caused relief supplies to arrive too late to save over 100,000 lives, that " an administrative and bureaucratic disaster was added to the natural calamity."

The earliest settlements in North America were threatened, and sometimes wiped out, by famine. A Norse colony founded by Eric the Red in Greenland in 986 failed because the summers,

though warm, were too brief to supply enough cereals and vegetables, and husbanding was limited to the sheltered fjord slopes.
Excavations in the 1930s, uncovering bodies well preserved by
the Arctic climate, revealed that few of the colonizers had lived
beyond the age of twenty; they were dwarfed in stature and apparently seriously crippled by rickets.

The first settlement in the United States was nearly wiped out
by starvation. In Jamestown, Virginia, only 60 of 500 settlers
survived the winter of 1609–10; and, after rebuilding the population to about 4,000 by 1617, starvation and sickness reduced it
again, to 1,275 by 1624, as the colonists' seed grains failed. After
two Indian prisoners taught the colonists to grow corn, it became
their staple. The Pilgrims, too, nearly starved on the rocky soil
of Plymouth, until they learned from a friendly Indian, variously
known as Tisquantum and Squanto, to plant corn and fertilize
each mount with a fish (which releases nitrogen as it decomposes).
Their successful 1621 harvest inspired the Pilgrims to revive the
celebration of the English yeomen known as "harvest home," but
which the Pilgrims established as our first Thanksgiving. Critical
food shortages endangered the South during the Civil War because agriculture in the region was devoted mainly to cotton and
tobacco—cash crops. Grain-conversion attempts were too late, and
General William Tecumseh Sherman not only laid waste a broad
swatch of countryside on his march to the sea, but he also refused
to permit rail shipments of food to hungry civilians. The North
and West had concentrated on food crops and had surpluses for
export to a needy England, a trade relationship which probably
restrained the British from allying with the Confederate states.

Although no food shortages have endangered the United
States since the Civil War, 90 percent of Americans lived below
or near what was considered poverty level at the beginning of
this century. At the depth of the Great Depression, Franklin D.
Roosevelt described one-third of the nation as "ill-fed." A drought
followed by eroding winds created the Dust Bowl in the mid-
1930s which, combined with the depression, caused widespread
hunger, social dislocation, and mass migration. Even today, according to conservative estimates, 10 percent of the population is
still poorly nourished because of poverty. But hunger in the
United States is caused primarily by maldistribution or, more

precisely, insufficient purchasing power, not by the absence of good food. Even during World War II, when enormous amounts of food were needed overseas, the United States had enough food for the home front under an equitable rationing system.

Five Portents

The United Nations proclaimed the 1960s the First Development Decade, but it turned out to be a decade of disappointment and a time of deterioration of the human condition. Over half of the world's population remained undernourished or malnourished, and the number still rises. What went wrong? Years ago, Brillat-Savarin, author of *The Physiology of Taste,* observed, "The destiny of nations depends on how they eat." Had we forgotten? Or did we err in the assumption that famine had been conquered?

In his last year in office, President Eisenhower observed sanguinely, "There have been no major famines in the free world during the past decade, and to my knowledge this cannot be said of any prior decade." Within a year of Eisenhower's assertion, President Kennedy saw indications of instability; in his first foreign-aid message to Congress, he warned that the surging populations of Latin America were likely to erode living standards. In 1964 the President's assistant for National Security Affairs, Walt W. Rostow, counseled Lyndon B. Johnson that, by 1975, famines of such unprecedented scope would occur that they would strain the food-producing capabilities of the unaffected areas of the world. Johnson, in his State of the Union address the following year, termed "hunger and malnutrition . . . the most grave health problem in the world," and, in the address the next year, he pledged the United States to "lead the world in a war against hunger. . . . Next to the pursuit of peace, the really greatest challenge to the human family is the race between food supply and population increase. That race tonight is being lost."

Asia: The First Portent

In Johnson's administration, the United States seemed admirably suited to become a "breadbasket for the world." Our farms produced huge and diverse harvests; and though there were occasional shortages of, and higher prices on, some items, our national food supply offered ample surpluses to meet the demands of war, reconstruction, and famine overseas.

The drought in Asia in 1966 and 1967, however, demonstrated that the potential of American agriculture to cover farming failures abroad was not limitless. As the dry weather persisted, one billion people—an unprecedented number—verged on starvation. Census analysts, moreover, discovered that, over the prior decade, the populations of the Third World—the lesser developed regions of Asia, Africa, and Latin America—had increased beyond most demographers' highest projections. The rate of world population increase exceeded that of world food output, and within the Third World the difference in rates of increase was marked; in most of it, there was a per capita decline in food output of from 4 to 5 percent. World population had already reached 3.5 billion, a total that two decades earlier had been projected for the end of the century. Said B. R. Sen, the FAO director-general, "Any remaining complacency about the food and agriculture situation must surely have been dispelled by the events of the past year. . . . When many millions of people are already inadequately nourished, there is little if any margin against the effects of a bad season."

"We were in a state of panic," said an official of the Agency for International Development (AID) in Washington. Orville L. Freeman, then secretary of agriculture, startled an Overseas Press Club forum in New York by disclosing that American grain surpluses were gone and predicting a "social catastrophe that would claim lives not in the hundreds of thousands or millions as in the past, but in the hundreds of millions—more than all of the wars in history." Speaking before a Chicago Board of Trade agribusiness conference in 1967, Vice-President Hubert H. Humphrey implored, "Oh, how I wish that those whose consciences cry out for peace would concentrate on food for the hungry!" (This remark, made as anti-Vietnam protests were mounting, was omitted from the official transcript of the conference.) Richard M. Nixon, then in private life, told the Conference Board, an organization of leading businessmen, "The race against hunger is part of the overriding race of the last third of the twentieth century. . . . The frightening fact is that the poor are multiplying twice as fast as the rich."

Agro-industry was mobilized for greater manufacture of fertilizers, pesticides, and implements, and the respected business weekly, *Barron's,* reported that experts considered the United States and Canada "the only hope for averting widespread starvation in the coming years." In Chicago, speculators traded commodities futures frenetically and in unprecedented volume; neither World War II, the Korean outbreak, nor President Kennedy's assassination sparked such bedlam. A scare book was inevitable, and two agriculturists, William and Paul Paddock, wrote *Famine 1975! America's Decision: Who Will Survive?,* in which they warned:

> No matter how one may adjust present statistics, and allow for future increases in the American wheat crop, for future shipments of rice and corn to India, and for a possible increase of India's own production of grains, today's trends show it well beyond the resources of the United States to keep famine out of India during the 1970s.

They predicted a situation so critical by 1975—it would be "the time of famines," they said—that it would require the application of the military principle of "triage," according to which field commanders with limited medical services and supplies must decide which of the wounded men can be saved with available resources and which should be left to die for the sake of the others. Among the nations the authors predicted would be starving, those classified as "can't be saved" were India, the United Arab Republic, Haiti, and possibly the Philippines. In 1967, the polemical Stanford biologist Paul R. Ehrlich, who was coming out with another pessimistic work, *The Population Bomb,* was asked if he agreed. "Yes," he replied, "unpalatable as it is, I support the 'triage' approach."

The crisis had already affected farm policies and farmers throughout the nation. In 1966 the secretary of agriculture made two increases in wheat-acreage allotments totaling 30 percent, bringing the total authorized plantings to over 68 million acres. He said, "We expect wheat prices, even with the larger acreages, to be well above support levels next year because of the strong commercial demand at home, continued export expansion, and large food assistance requirements." In 1967, in the greatest flotilla assembled since D-day, the United States shipped one-fourth of its wheat harvest to the Indian subcontinent.

Underlying the rapid expansion of American agriculture was the assumption that the mostly illiterate and reputedly obdurate Third World farmers could not (or would not) adopt superior technologies and methods, or, if they did do so, it would not be done quickly enough to close the food gap. The drive to raise American grain output was in full sway when Lester R. Brown, then chief of the International Agricultural Development Service of the Department of Agriculture, presented a paper titled "New Directions in World Agriculture" to a 1968 Washington conference on hunger. Little publicized at the time, perhaps because Brown was not yet widely recognized as a spearhead theoretician and frequent traveler in the Third World, his analysis suggested that projections of world food supplies were "out of date [because] we may be on the threshold of an agricultural revolution in many of the hungry, densely populated countries of the less developed world. . . . Many of the studies undertaken in recent years . . . have not allowed for the possibility of sharply increased yields due to new technology." After hearing Brown's analysis, a department official exclaimed, "Wow! What a reversal!" The FAO was not in immediate accord, and an incredulous spokesman asked, "What caused Les Brown to go 'hawkish' on the world food crisis?"

Brown revisited Asia for another assessment, and in an interview after his return in March he said that his "New Directions" speech now appeared "conservative." In the past, he pointed out, experts thought that India would never fulfill its agricultural goals because it never did, but the outlook had changed. "I think the agricultural revolution underway," he said, "is going to force us to recalculate the future."

What had happened?

In some areas, the perpetually wary village farmers had observed how new varieties of wheat, rice, and corn, recently developed in tropical-research institutes in Mexico and the Philippines, gave far higher yields than traditional plants. Simultaneously, local grain prices had risen, offering not only the more affluent farmers but also subsistence farmers a chance for higher incomes, if they could raise more than their family needs. Secretary Freeman, bordering on hyperbole in a 1968 memo to President Johnson, wrote, "The new miracle rice . . . is being adopted at a speed which exceeds anything in history. . . . A whole new day in tropical agriculture seems possible."

This "green revolution," as it came to be called, began with the 1967 plantings, about the time that *Famine 1975!* reached bookstores, and India and Pakistan led all nations in the proportion of farmlands converted to the new wheats. W. David Hopper, a Canadian agricultural economist who worked variously for the Ford and Rockefeller Foundations in India for about twenty years and lived part of the time in a village, recalled villagers' attitudes during an extensive interview. "The underestimation of the receptivity of village farmers to improved practices did occur," he said. "They have intuition, a country wisdom, which enabled them to obtain better yields from new varieties than did the experimental plot scientists." Commenting optimistically on the Indian farmer's willingness to convert to new varieties, Roger Revelle, head of population studies at Harvard, said, "He may not be able to read, but I never saw one who couldn't count." Addeke H. Boerma, the new FAO director-general, stated in 1968, "The world has trembled on the brink of a serious food disaster, but changing human attitudes combined with other developments now permit a cautious optimism about the future."

Coinciding with the adoption of superior technology was the return of favorable weather to Asia, bringing forth bumper crops—often record crops—of wheat, rice, corn, and soybeans. In the late 1960s, world food output increased at an annual rate of 5 to 6 percent—double that of population growth—and so much of the increase was in the poorer countries that India, Pakistan, the Philippines, and China reduced imports. In fact, a rice glut was building up in Asia. In the United States, grain surpluses reaccumulated, and there was fear of excess soybeans. As prices paid to wheat farmers, for example, plunged to the lowest levels since the depression—$1.19 a bushel—Secretary of Agriculture Clifford M. Hardin, pointing out that the green revolution had caused "dislocations" in world agricultural trade, ordered acreage cutbacks.

Clifton R. Wharton, Jr., president of Michigan State University and widely experienced in Third-World social and economic matters, in 1969 spurred further examination of what had happened in the opinion-molding journal *Foreign Affairs*. He noted in an article in April that some felt that "the race between food and population is over, [that] the new agricultural technology constitutes a cornucopia for the developing world. . . . Others see this development as opening a Pandora's box; its very success will produce a number of new problems which are far more subtle and difficult than those faced during the development of a new technology." Concluding that the green revolution "offers an unparallelled opportunity to break the chains of rural poverty in important parts of the world," he postulated that any increases in production would "automatically produce a whole new set of second-generation problems which must be faced if development is to be sustained and accelerated."

Yet exuberance prevailed over cautious optimism. By 1972, India had both wheat and rice for export, was able to provide food assistance to Bangladesh during and after its war of independence, and Minister for Food and Agriculture Annasaheb Shind told newsmen that at the rate of increase being achieved in grain output, India would "outstrip the United States in seven or eight years." In the interim, however, Americans had a disturbing agricultural period, partly without precedent.

Weather and a Ravaging American Blight: The Second Portent

Although the hybrid midwestern corn plants had been free of major disease for nearly a quarter of a century, unusual moisture over the monocultured fields in 1970 created a congenial micro-environment for the southern corn-leaf blight. The fungus broke out of its native region and fanned across the corn belt. Early estimates that it would destroy a fourth of the corn were too fearful, but the loss of 15 percent of the financially most valuable American harvest was nonetheless serious. For 1971, the federal government authorized expanded plantings, yet a shortage of seeds of resistant varieties was at first a further concern. But normal weather returned, the blight did not recur, and farmers reaped another burdening surplus. Nevertheless, the question began nagging as to whether extensive monoculturing might not leave American crops more vulnerable to diseases and pests than was supposed.

The next year, the government reduced acreage allotments, and then erratic weather unsettled the northern and central Atlantic states, the corn-soybean belt, and the wheat fields of the Great Plains. The spring of 1972 arrived late—if it really came at all—and delayed plantings. In June, Agnes, one of the most ferocious tropical storms ever, raged across southern croplands, crisscrossed the seaboard states, and roared into western Pennsylvania and upstate New York. Continuous downpours left some 28 trillion gallons of water in eight states, and the Pennsylvania flood plains—the river-valley flatlands that are the repositories of seasonal overflows—were inundated when the Susquehanna River spilled over its dikes. The total damage has been estimated at over $4 billion—the greatest natural disaster in American history.

Then in 1973, one of the great floods of the century occurred, as the Mississippi River and its tributaries overflowed from Illinois to the deltas of Louisiana. An estimated 13 million acres in eight states were below water in the spring, and total damage was more than $1 billion. Thousands of farmers were forced to delay or abandon their seeding, which contributed to the rise in the price especially of soybeans, the major American source of high-protein feed, and so helped inflate meat costs. In addition, not only did the flooding wash over many catfish farms, enabling that "livestock" to escape, but it led the U.S. Corps of Engineers to open diversionary spillways in order to save New Orleans, an action which brought fresh water into the brackish and saline waters of the Louisiana coastal marsh. Commercially important fish dispersed. The ensuing fish shortages inflated seafood prices, and hundreds in the seafood industry were laid off.

Elsewhere during this period, the worst drought in recent times settled over the Southwest, extending from Oklahoma into Southern California and Baja. The area around Magnum, Oklahoma, for example, received only one inch more rainfall in 1971 than during the drought preceding the Dust Bowl, and wheat yields fell from an average of 23 bushels an acre in good years to only 1.2 bushels. In the Midwest, particularly in southern Illinois and Indiana, as the East recovered from hurricane Agnes, torrential winds and monsoonlike rains upset the harvesting. In November, winter blustered over the prairies, where record crops still stood, and in three major soybean states—Illinois, Iowa, and Indiana—one-fifth to one-half of the harvest remained in the fields. The early snowfall also kept about 14 percent of the anticipated Iowa harvest of 1.2 billion bushels of corn in the fields. Frigid weather persisted over much important farmland and affected crops in storage as well as in the field and livestock. Low temperatures stimulated consumer demand for natural and propane gas and for fuel oil, all of which are needed for grain elevators. In Iowa, the most stricken state, more than 500 of its 1,200 elevators were shut down, and tens of millions of bushels of corn piled up in bins and spilled over into the streets of small towns. The higher moisture content of the grain, which resulted from the wet autumn harvest, necessitated more drying, a further complication. An aide to the governor said, "We figure the elevators would have to run full blast for two weeks at the rate of five hundred bushels an hour to catch up with the time that we've lost," and added that it would take at least a month to dry the grain.

In the beef-producing areas of northwestern Texas, Oklahoma, and eastern New Mexico, cattle died at double the normal seasonal rate. About 2 million head were in feedlots in those areas, and another 1.25 million were grazing; from November to mid-January, the cold spell killed about 150,000.

Obviously, much of the damage caused by these and other adversities was to agricultural land, crops, planting schedules, livestock, machinery, and buildings. Yet, in early 1974, the secretary of agriculture did not have a national assessment, breaking out the specifics either in terms of crop and livestock (which should include the loss of prospective output when crops could not be planted or livestock properly cared for) or in terms of dollar value—a disturbing revelation in light of the need to know how much setback these episodes can cause during a period of tight world food supplies. Although the department has an extensive field staff gathering data and a centralized collating establishment, an official of the Statistical Reporting Service, in response to queries, pleaded a lack of personnel. One indication of damage, however, is a report on emergency loans from the Farm Home Administration for the 1973 fiscal year. What were classified as "major disasters" hit 22 states; nearly 130,000 emergency loans were granted compared with fewer than 13,000 the year before, and they totaled over $500 million compared with not quite $109 million the previous year. In July 1973, the President asked Congress for an additional $1.8 billion for disaster relief and reconstruction funds necessitated by Agnes.

As for the Mississippi damage, the lower Mississippi district Corps of Engineers offered the following "probable estimates" of farming losses: 50 to 100 million bushels of wheat, 40 million bushels of soybeans, 15 to 25 million pounds of rice, and 50 to 100 million pounds of meat, as well as 750,000 bales of cotton. The warning was timed adequately to permit the evacuation of livestock, but to where? Many stockmen sold their animals too soon to get top prices, and those that saved their stock found feed prices exorbitant after the disaster. The damage to machinery was also heavy; much of it rusted.

And in early 1974, the Mississippi threatened another flood of the century. After the 1973 floodtide receded, many levees failed to dry out, remaining soggy and weakened. "Once again the river is disturbingly above normal as we approach the highwater season," Major General Charles C. Noble, district engineer for the lower Mississippi, reported. The January levels were, in fact, higher than at the same time one year earlier, and the snows, whose melt would swell the river further, were heavy across the plains and into the Rocky Mountains.

Yet, despite the adversities, the 1973 American harvests reached record or near-record levels—fortunately so, for the third portent had materialized.

Disaster in Soviet Agriculture: The Third Portent

Until 1972 in the Soviet Union, an economically advanced, industrialized nation had never in a period of peace (except immediately after a war) suffered harvest failures of such scope that they endangered the national food supply. The Soviets have had periodic difficulties in agriculture, but their progress has nonetheless been considerable, and they have increased their exports. Unlike American agriculture, however, Soviet farming has been unable to rebound quickly from adversities—a problem perhaps compounded by policy and managerial mistakes. Food supply was no longer the highest priority in economic and social planning in 1972, but after repeated bouts of bad weather, priorities were reordered.

In the post-Khrushchev era, Soviet agriculture recovered, people's diets improved, and the demand for further advances increased. But in 1972 a series of weather difficulties began, and throughout the year it was variously too cold, too hot, too dry, or too wet. The potato harvest around Moscow and vegetables in several areas were nearly wiped out, and according to Communist Party chief Leonid Brezhnev, the grain harvest fell 22 million tons short of the goal. In addition, it was estimated that from 20 to 25 percent of the grain was too moist to keep well. The shortage, in turn, jeopardized the Soviet livestock program, which had been expanded to raise protein consumption.

The government launched campaigns to have bread and flour, while moving aggressively, but rather surreptitiously, to buy buffer supplies abroad. With consummate skill that awed their capitalist counterparts, Soviet traders contracted for nearly half a billion bushels of grain—encompassing the largest wheat purchase ever made by a single country, from the United States and mostly at bargain prices; the grain commitment constituted 20 percent of all grain stocks held by the United States as of mid-1972. They also bought what they could from Canada and other sources. These massive Soviet imports, combined with the needs of other importing nations, caused world grain supplies to become tight, and demand was similarly high for soybeans for feed. Demand for wheat persisted, and futures reached a high of nearly $6.00 a bushel in January 1974, corn a record $3.49 in February, and Maine potatoes, once $2.00 a hundred pounds, $19.05 in April, while soybeans rose to a record of over $12.00 per bushel in 1973, quadruple of what they once had been, after which they dropped back somewhat.

This pressure was soon reflected in American supermarkets, as food prices soared to levels averaging 15 to 17 percent above those of 1972. This inflation brought about the sharpest drop in

American per-capita food consumption in 15 years in 1973—
about 1.5 percent—and the lowest level of consumption in four
years. The 6 percent drop in meat consumption was the most
precipitous since 1948. The Soviet-American grain deal aroused
intense controversy, particularly as evidence accumulated that
American agricultural attachés had reported the extent of the
Soviet harvest failure to forewarn the Nixon Administration's
negotiators. Yet the government paid nearly one-third of a billion
dollars in export subsidies to the grain dealers, whereas the Russians would have paid the full price if necessary. And many American farmers sold their harvests when prices were low because of
lack of knowledge. Several congressional investigations are still
underway, trying to determine whether there was wrongdoing
in terms either of conflict of interest or whether the Administration was so eager to further the cause of détente that it ignored
the agricultural intelligence available to it. At a news conference
Nixon conceded that the United States had been "snookered,"
and Treasury Secretary George P. Shulz said the country had
been "burned," particularly because "it seems now that the price
of a loaf of bread in Moscow is cheaper than it is in the Safeway
here." Furthermore, the grain transfer snarled the American
transport system—to move the Soviet grain purchase required,
it was said, 10,000 miles of freight cars.

American wheat export subsidies were discontinued, an export
reporting system was organized, and the secretary of agriculture
lifted all acreage restrictions—American farmers were encouraged "to plant fence to fence." In an article in the *New York
Times Magazine,* Joseph Albright concluded, "The best expla-
nation of the mishandling of the grain deal is more prosaic than
nefarious": a series of misjudgments and oversights had caused it
rather than conspiracy.

In the Soviet Union, Brezhnev held his constituency, and the
1973 farm year was the best in Soviet history. Farmers also had
more cattle and hogs than two years before. To sustain the momentum, the Soviet government allocated about 27 percent of
all capital investments for the economy to agriculture, two and
a half times that of the previous year. The Kremlin, from the
beginning of the grain negotiations, intended to meet its livestock production goal for 1975 and to avert the massive slaughter

that occurred in 1963, which lowered protein standards for several years. Besides, the government had a nutritional goal of increasing protein consumption by one-fourth. Doubtless also in the policy-makers' minds were the 1970 Polish riots protesting shortages of food and other consumer items.

Environmental Intrusion in the Sahel: The Fourth Portent

Though the Sahelian tragedy was attributed directly to drought, projects "modernizing" agriculture left the fragile environment of the arid lands more susceptible to encroachment by the desert. Wells with pumps provided much more water, and herdsmen let their stock increase, sometimes doubling their numbers. When the water table lowered, the animals overgrazed the remaining pasture and even uprooted trees for feed. By 1974, the Sahara was taking over at an annual rate of 30 miles—and 100 miles at some points. Meanwhile, climatologists reported that a drought climate seemed to have shifted southward, perhaps permanently; it stretched a latitude around the earth from Nicaragua through Africa into India.

An FAO expert team feared that "a natural, irreversible process of desertification had begun," and found that more cropping and husbandry, new water schemes, and livestock vaccination campaigns might aggravate environmental stresses if planning does not provide for new balances:

> There are numerous instances in which drilling for water directly led to the degradation of vast areas as a result of overgrazing. Lowland development for agriculture may deprive livestock of invaluable reserves of fodder on which they can survive during feed shortage periods. As a result there is an ever more serious conflict between farmers and stockraisers. . . .
>
> The spectacular numerical increase in livestock numbers following vaccination campaigns and trypanocide and worming treatments has not always been balanced by sound policies of livestock management patterns.

It was not until March 1973 that the governments of West Africa made a declaration of disaster, however. Antoine Dakouré, the

Upper Volta minister of agriculture, said the peasants would "need a long time to recuperate the strength they've lost, to recover their work capacity and then to restore their working capital—the soil . . . . it's not only this last drought that ruined it; there's been a succession of droughts and no protection for the soil."

A Disrupted Hydrosphere: The Fifth Portent

A warning that the increased use of more efficient fishing technology was disturbing the aquatic environment came in 1969 when, for the first time in a decade, the world catch dropped slightly. But hope returned the following year when the catch reached a record 134.5 billion pounds, and 1971 was nearly as high. In 1972, however, the catch plunged nearly 10 percent from these records, to 123.0 billion pounds; the lowest in five years, and the 1973 catch remained low.

The drop was due largely to the disappearance of the huge anchovy fishery off Peru, which had rocketed the country into first place in fishing during the mid-1960s. Peru also became the largest producer of fishmeal, a major source of high-protein feed supplement for animals, and it accounted for half of the year-to-year increase in the American consumption of feed. The anchovies are sensitive to what fishermen mockingly call, *El Niño de Navidad,* or "Christmas child," a current of warm water that flows down the coast of Peru from the Equator around Christmas. It is usually pushed farther out to sea by the frigid Humboldt Current coming in from the South Pacific, but every few years (the local people say every seventh year) *El Niño* overwhelms the Humboldt Current, the change of currents carries away or affects the growth of the plankton, the anchovies' food, the waters turn warm, and the fish become sluggish, scattering, breeding poorly, and dying.

Traditional fishing methods took only limited catches, and enough anchovies survived to repopulate the fishery. But in 1972, modernized fishermen located the sluggish fish with electronic sounders and decimated the remaining population. The 1973 catch fell so drastically that the government banned further exploitation temporarily. It was estimated that by 1974, some 8 billion pounds of fish remained compared with the normal 60 billion pounds, as normal oceanic conditions returned. The shortage of Peruvian fishmeal heightened demand for the other high-protein feed, soybean meal, and so became a contributing factor to higher meat prices throughout the world. Though the government authorized renewed fishing, the catch was limited to a billion pounds, about a fourth of a normal good year's haul. But even fishmeal from this amount could mean less pressure on feed-grain prices, according to Irwin Kellner, an economist at the Manufacturers Hanover Trust Company, and partially accounted for lower soybean prices.

That a huge population can be fished out had been shown years earlier by the disappearance of California sardines. Now, off America's eastern shores, three popular species—cod, haddock, and halibut—are considered endangered. The New England cod catch in 1880 was said to be a record 294 million pounds; in 1972, it was around 39 million pounds. That year, the Icelandic herring catch fell to 132.3 million pounds from 1.7 billion pounds in 1965. Other fish that are in trouble, if not yet endangered, are striped bass of the Atlantic, yellow-fin tuna of the Pacific, and the bluefin tuna and salmon off both American coasts.

It was forecast that the 1974 Alaskan salmon catch would be the poorest since 1899. In 1899 American lobstermen in small boats, using only hand equipment, brought in 30.5 million pounds; in 1972 a modernized fleet working 100 miles offshore brought in less, 29.3 million pounds, and the once-frequent 25-pounders are now rare. Among sea mammals, several species of whale appear headed toward extinction.

It is not known how seriously pollution is affecting ocean fisheries, but scientists believe that, combined with overfishing, it could be calamitous. Some marine biologists now doubt that catches can be more than doubled, and then only by exploiting species not commonly eaten, such as hake, whiting, and the Arctic krill on which whales feed. They also caution against exploiting other species too extensively, for they are part of the food chain of the fish we eat. About 80 percent of the world's creatures live in the oceans, and marine organisms as a whole supply 70 percent of the world's oxygen. Some scientists fear that, if what they characterize as plunder of the deep continues, all biological life might be endangered by the next century.

The Green Revolution in Retrospect

By 1973, bad weather returned to much of Asia, and once again pockets of famine proliferated. Experts on climate and agriculture, brought together by the Rockefeller Foundation in early 1974, reported a southern shift of monsoon rains could probably be blamed for severe droughts in Asia, Africa, and parts of Latin America. For the first six decades of this century, rainfall increased gradually in parts of India, for example, but since 1960, droughts have been frequent (though not usually as severe as in the last century, they are more injurious because of the huge population spurt). The FAO reported glumly that in 1972 food output had fallen behind the rate of population growth again, and it foresaw no acceleration in the annual rate of increase in food output of 1 to 2 percent in the Third World. In Asia, per capita food production dropped 3 percent; in Latin America, 2 percent; and in the Near East, 1 percent. Less than a year after predictions of a rice glut in Asia and wheat self-sufficiency in India, shortages and food riots spread on the subcontinent. The failure of the monsoons in India, affecting some 200 million people—about a third of the population—was more severe than during the mid-1960s food panic, and the 10 million tons of buffer stocks were exhausted in six months. Indonesia, Malaysia, Thailand, Afghanistan, and Cambodia suffered droughts, while the Philippines experienced its worst floods in this century, sweeping away much of its rice crop in the north. Flooding in Pakistan was believed the worst in its history, as it broke down irrigation and water-control systems and destroyed or damaged about one-fourth of the rice crop and an amount of stored wheat equivalent to about 13 percent of a normal harvest. Parts of northern China, according to Hsinhua, the official press agency, had their worst drought in almost a hundred years; southern China was buffeted by floods, hail, and winds.

The momentum of the green revolution, moreover, had slowed.

It had never been so widespread as publicity suggested, and even experts who suggested that the tropical breakthroughs had bought perhaps twenty to thirty years' time for backing them up were overly optimistic. New plantings of the high-yield seed were narrowing, since the more progressive farmers with sufficient financing had already adopted it, and in many areas the quality of the seed was deteriorating as a result of mixing. Because of the extensive adoption of a few varieties of the seed over a wide Asian belt in which many varieties had previously been cultivated, harvests were vulnerable, and some varieties could not adapt to a wide enough range of weather conditions. The "miracle" rices were not working out on so large a scale as the improved wheat either; they encountered consumer resistance to taste, texture, or color.

Fertilizer was not being applied in the recommended amounts as a result of failure of distribution services to expand and a worldwide shortage of nitrogenous and phosphatic fertilizers that developed in 1973. India, which had looked forward to improved harvests with the return of favorable weather, reduced its 1974 harvest estimate by 2 to 4 percent; some authorities believed that its farmers might reduce applications of chemical nutrients from 3.5 million tons in 1973 to 2.5 million tons in 1974, which could slash grain output by 10 million tons.

Robert S. McNamara, the president of the World Bank (International Bank for Reconstruction and Development), once compared the green revolution to the Industrial Revolution in historical significance, and Wharton's premonition that the breakthroughs might mean not so much cornucopia as Pandora's box was being borne out as its benefits failed to help many of the people. Those that were bypassed began migrating into the cities in search of jobs, but employment opportunities have not kept pace with the need, and the in-migrants clustered in urban "behavioral sinks," the prime example of which is probably Calcutta. Richard Critchfield, a *Washington Star* newsman who investigated the Asian upheavals under a grant from the Alicia Patterson Fund, reported that among the bypassed in some areas there was a "sense of apocalypse" that "comes very close to being a true Malthusian breakdown."

India, in 1973, took control of wheat distribution from the private traders in an attempt to keep prices low and stable, but by March 1974 they had risen 36 percent from that time a year before. Furthermore, the government, whose bureaucracy floundered, was able to procure little more than half of the wheat required for its "fair price" shops in the major cities, and fears of food shortages deepened among the people. Their mood became violent, and in 1974 food riots and hoarding became widespread in India. In February, the government of Gujarat, where food riots had flared for weeks, fell, and the central government moved in. Public distribution systems in other states—Beihar, Kerala, and Maharashtra—verged on collapse, and in March the central government returned wheat distribution to private channels.

The only three nations still net food exporters—the United States, Canada, and Australia, J. George Harrar, president-emeritus of the Rockefeller Foundation, told the 1974 meeting of the American Association for the Advancement of Science (AAAS) "represent the buffer between the rest of the world and annual deficits in available supplies." Present technology and resources, he said, can no longer keep up with the expanding world population.

Finally, the world energy crisis became an enormously complicating factor, particularly because it threatened to intensify the fertilizer shortage and inflate prices further. In January 1974 an Iowa fertilizer dealers' conference was told that the year would begin "with an empty wagon." The Department of Agriculture projected a million-ton shortage of nitrogen, a projection close to that of Edwin D. Wheeler, president of the Fertilizer Institute; moreover, Wheeler warned, 1974 crop forecasts might be much too optimistic—particularly for corn which uses over half the American output of nitrogen fertilizer. Wheeler was also concerned over a prospective shortage of railroad hopper cars; Fertilizer Institute members spend $500 million annually on freight. A shortage of hopper cars, for shipping as well as receiving, has long been the bane of many farmers, particularly grain growers. In 1950 the price of urea, a major ingredient of nitrogen fertilizer, was $50 a ton; by 1974, some buyers were paying $250 a ton. During the late 1960s, an oversupply of fertilizer dropped world prices to their lowest levels, but in 1971 demand began growing so rapidly that it overtook supply. In the United States, nitrogen fertilizer manufacturers were considering converting their feed-stock plants from natural gas to coal, which, however, would be more expensive.

Still another shortage developed in the United States in baling wire and twine, critical items for the fourth most valuable field crop, hay. The African drought cut supplies of sisal; and Japan, a major supplier of wire, nearly all of which is imported, reduced production in 1973.

These mounting shortages, beginning with crops and live-stock themselves, inevitably brought rises in the price of food. Thailand, traditionally Asia's leading rice exporter, put pressure on world prices when it had to import rice (its output had dropped by a fifth); the Indonesian drought tripled local rice prices; and India could afford to buy only 4 million of the 7 million tons of grains needed in 1973. Strange tradeoffs began to occur. Moscow, in an unusually favorable position because of good harvest prospects for the new year combined with its huge 1973 purchases at bargain prices, offered India a loan, to be repaid in kind, a move that could be characterized as "food for politics" or "food diplomacy," particularly because American supplies were committed. In early 1974 the Indonesians approached the Thais, one of whose senior officials chided, "We will do our best to help you—even though you were not able to help us with a single barrel when we asked you for oil." There were rumors, officially denied, that before the new Soviet harvest prospects brightened, the United States was hinting to the Arabian oil states that they could buy no American grain unless they loosened the oil embargo.

In the United States, while the 1973 consumer price index rose 8.8 percent, the food component rose 20 percent; broken down, meat prices rose 26.4 percent, cereal and bakery products 28.2 percent, and dairy products 22.5 percent. These were the largest rises since the aftermath of World War II; they reversed the better-eating trend, not only in the United States, but among families everywhere. The subsidized American school-lunch program faced deep cuts because of the costs—a September 1973 Senate study estimated that 800,000 pupils would no longer receive the nutritious meals. Food-relief programs overseas were also cut back.

When the world feed shortage became acute in mid-1973, the United States abruptly imposed export controls on soybeans by cutting the July and August contracts by 50 percent and banning new orders, an action that infuriated several importers, notably Japan and France. In effect, they accused the United States of double-crossing them, for American trade negotiators had pressed for reductions in agricultural import barriers and domestic subsidies (particularly the European Common Market) to encourage the purchasing of more American farm commodities at their lower prices. Two months later, in September, the United States lifted the controls. But by 1974, as an American grain shortfall threatened, lobbying mounted for export controls, and Europeans feared they would be reimposed; they also were concerned that the American cutting back of contracts would lead other exporting nations into unfair trade practices.

Wheat reached an all-time high of over $6 a bushel—durum, a wheat used for spaghettis and noodles, drew $9 in early 1974—and the Department of Agriculture's projection of a mid-year reserve of around 220 million bushels was sharply reduced to 178 million. Bill O. Mead, chairman of the American Bakers Association, predicted that a loaf of bread, then selling for 45¢, would soon cost $1, and the association president, Robert Wager, said, "People may have to stand in line for a loaf of bread at much higher prices the way they now wait in line to buy gasoline." Morton Soslin, editor of *Milling and Baking News*, respected for its independent reporting, characterized the statement as "probably an exaggeration but not an unrealizable price." Loath to impose export quotas again, the administration requested some overseas buyers, notably the USSR, to slow down the rate of imports until after the May-June harvesting in Texas and Oklahoma, and on January 24 the President suspended restrictions on wheat imports for five months, mainly to allow Canadian grain to have a "stabilizing effect" on American prices.

Regional food shortages and rising prices have brought about food smuggling and violence. In Argentina, President Juan D. Perón's price controls encouraged widespread smuggling into Chile, Bolivia, Brazil, Uruguay, and Paraguay, where prices were higher in 1973 and 1974. The Argentinian finance minister reported that 400,000 tons of soybeans—more than half of the 1973 crop—were shipped as contraband into Brazil, and the "disappearance" of 3 million chickens contributed to a poultry shortage. In Bolivia the government decreed a doubling of basic food prices to halt smuggling, and thousands of peasants blockaded roads near a major agricultural center in order to keep the food from being sold in cities. The government deployed ground and air forces to "clean out" the barricades.

Then, on January 29, 1974, Soviet Deputy Minister of Foreign Trade Vladimir S. Alkhinov told a New York news conference that his country would consider selling grain to the United States for stock replenishment. Wheat at the time was selling at nearly two and a half times what the Russians had paid only a year before. The following week, the Department of Agriculture held more meetings on the "wheat situation" than anyone could remember, according to their chief economist, Don Paarlberg.

In 1961, the world had food reserves to feed itself for 95 days; 10 years later, it had enough for 51 days, and in 1973, for only 29 days. The following table shows how the pressures mounted on world wheat and feed grain supplies during that period, as wheat consumption increased more rapidly than output, then fell behind, only to outpace production again; while feed grains had a somewhat different pattern.

In 1973, world wheat consumption was estimated at 90.2 percent of total supply, including surplus carryovers, and feed grains at 91.8 percent compared with 76.8 percent and 80.4 percent in 1960.

Average Annual Percent Increases in Wheat and Feed Grain Output and Consumption

Period	Number of Years	Wheat		Feed Grains	
		Output Rise	Consumption Rise	Output Rise	Consumption Rise
1960-65	5	1.8%	2.6%	1.1%	2.1%
1965-69	4	3.9	2.8	4.4	3.9
1969-73	4	3.8	4.4	3.1	3.2

SOURCE: Massey-Ferguson, Ltd., annual report, 1973.

All sides agreed that 1974 would be a test year, since American
farmers intended to seed all available cropland. But complicating the situation further is the deficiency in gathering, much less
evaluating, intelligence on food supplies and prospects. "Recent
research indicates that world food intelligence is not as good as
some previously thought," the Rockefeller Foundation conference on "Weather and Climate Change, Food Production and
Interstate Conflict" reported in 1974. "The issue is not how the
U.S.S.R. purchased so much grain at such low prices. Rather, the
issue is why such an inadequate response to the unprecedented
concomitant failure of crops in so many places in 1972. Complacency, failure to respond promptly, can be added sources of
general vulnerability. . . . The problem is how to improve data
and world-wide food intelligence capabilities." The two best data
collection capabilities, the report said, are those of the U.S.
Department of Agriculture and the Canadian Wheat Board. Yet
even though much was known about the Soviet crop shortfall
in August 1972, the extent of the Soviet importing was known in
September, and the likelihood of harvest failures about the same
time, the United States maintained planting controls on wheat
and feed grains into 1973.

The FAO warned of the possibility of trade wars over farm
products, in which the poorer countries would "come off worst."
In its *1973 State of Food and Agriculture* report, Director-General
Boerma wrote:

> The world food situation in 1973 is more difficult than at
> any time since the years immediately following the devasta-
> tion of the Second World War. . . . Cereal stocks have
> dropped to the lowest level in 20 years. . . . Prices are rocket-
> ing, and the world's biggest agricultural producer [the
> United States] has had to introduce export allocations for
> certain products. . . . Per capita food production in the de-
> veloping countries as a whole has now fallen back to the
> level of 1961–65. . . . There is thus little if any margin
> against the possibility of another widespread harvest fail-
> ure and the world has become dangerously dependent on
> current production . . . the world [is] almost entirely depend-
> ent on a single season's weather for its basic food supplies.

This was the outlook in early 1974, despite a record world harvest of grains in 1973, estimated at nearly 900 million metric tons (some 50 million tons over the disaster year of 1972, and 30 million over the record year of 1971). This is not to say that the benefits of the green revolution ceased; if there had not been one in India, grain output during the 1973 drought would have been 15 to 20 percent lower. But improved technology and practices could not be adopted rapidly enough to keep pace with population growth. In 1973, it should be noted, world population grew by about 75 million.

In 1967 F. F. Hill, a Ford Foundation agriculturist, talked about the green revolution:

> Agricultural development is never a smooth, even process. It's not like taking a piece of bread and spreading a hunk of butter evenly over it. . . . "Miracle rice" was a miracle in West Pakistan; if you went there, you would agree. But if you went to East Pakistan [now Bangladesh], you'd probably ask, "Where is it?"

In 1968 Swedish economist and author Gunnar Myrdal was asked about the green revolution and the prospects for eradicating hunger. He replied:

> I am open to the possibility of an agricultural revolution. But I say to my friends at Harvard and in Washington that you are living in a sort of euphoria.
>
> I'm not blind to the possibility of doing great things with technology. But if you don't change the relationship between land and man, it will benefit mostly the upper classes. It may leave the underclasses worse off than before.
>
> Don't believe only in technology.

Part I / Agricultural Inputs— Nature's and Man's

Take care to learn before and to observe
The winds, and changing temper of the air,
The soil, the native genius of the place,
What fruit it bears and what it will refuse.

—VIRGIL, *The Georgics*

No animal accepts its environment. It adapts it, making whatever changes it can to survive, protect its young, and perhaps live more comfortably. Although man credits his forebears with being the first to intervene in nature by cultivating the soil, there is some doubt about this. In 1861 Dr. Gideon Lincecum, a Texas physician, claimed that ants invented agriculture. In response to a skeptical query from Charles Darwin, he wrote:

> Around the mount . . . the ant clears all the ground of all obstructions, levels and smooths the surface. . . . Within this paved area, not a green thing is allowed to grow, except a single species of grain-bearing grass. . . . The insect tends and cultivates it with constant care . . . and watches the ripeness; then it harvests the crop.

Giving further credence to Lincecum's theory was the knowledge that ants store provisions for the winter, including wild grass seed called "ant rice," and evolve pastoral societies, some of whose members tend and feed beetles which they press for their milk. Did man learn to farm by observing ants? After myrmecology, the study of ants, came into being, this question was re-examined. In 1937 entomologist Ferdinand Goetsch concluded that ants sowed only accidentally, by leaving grains on the soil in the course of building. Goetsch's view has been generally accepted.

Human beings made the greatest discovery in history: the growth of food plants can be manipulated by intervening in natural cycles to increase the quantity, quality, and reliability of harvests. Once early cultivators began to understand that, they could to a degree, decide what, where, and how much to plant. They sought further ways to overcome the constraints, or parameters, of nature and blended what agriculturists call *inputs* with those of nature. Man intervened in the soil cycle first by cultivating and then by fertilizing, in the hydrological cycle by irrigating, in the biological cycle through plant selection and pest control, and in the power cycle by conceiving new means of harnessing energy.

Taming the Wilderness

To tame the wilderness means to develop and exploit the environment in order to make it suitable for human settlement—and the most important phase is encouraging the land to produce a food supply. The first set of inputs is natural—seed, soil, water, air, sun, and other forms of life and physical processes that are involved in plant growth. The second set is man's contributions and interventions, which can be characterized as the manipulation of the natural inputs.

Until about ten millennia ago, man searched for food as wild animals do, and relied a great deal on nuts, fruits, vegetables, and, when he could get them, meat and fish. The earliest food producers were not strictly speaking farmers; though they gathered, hunted, and fished, they neither cultivated nor husbanded. But they did harvest, and to be successful at it they had to learn to pick before seeds or fruits were dropped, blown, or brushed from the plant, and to dig tubers at the proper time. They had, moreover, to compete with animals, birds, insects, and other wild creatures for the ripening fruit. Man's migrations suggest that sumptuous diets were not easily come by.

We know little about any transitional period that must have preceded the invention of agriculture, but the constant stimulus must have been the possibility of famine. Cultivation probably came after people observed that naturally dispersed seed sprouted more vigorously under some soil conditions than under others.

The first cultivators did not work the river valleys, as was once thought, but took to the adjoining hillsides and higher tablelands, perhaps out of fear of the flood plains. They first domesticated wheat and barley, then rye and oats. Later they grew millet, vetch (a climber with edible seeds and fodder leaves), peas, and lentils. Wheat was especially important to them because it could be stored and ground. They also domesticated animals. Attachment to the land was gradual, and the early grain growers were migratory people, possibly because of depleted soil or population pressures.

Primitive farmers learned to choose plant varieties that had survived over centuries of natural selection and had adapted to their locales without much further management. They also observed that varieties whose seed clung so tenaciously to the stems or stalks that shaking, beating, or trampling was necessary to separate the seed from the plant were the most resistant to harsh weather. (E. H. Jacob, in his fascinating *6,000 Years of Bread*, speculates that woman rather than man gained this crucial insight. In the probable division of labor, men were preoccupied with expeditions into the wild; women, remaining near the settlement, watched plant germination more closely.)

These discoveries mark the first agricultural revolution. Norman E. Borlaug, plant breeder and Nobel Peace Laureate who is also known as the father of the green revolution, calls the ancients "the most highly successful group of plant and animal breeders that the world has ever known," and says that Neolithic man "laid the groundwork on which all modern agriculture and animal husbandry and indeed all of the world's subsequent civilizations have developed."

Observing also that soil becomes sterile, early cultivators perceived the necessity of moving on to other land and leaving used soil fallow for regeneration. This method of farming, known as "slash-and-burn" because those have been the usual means of clearing land, is still practiced in parts of Africa and Latin America. Early farmers adapted cultivation to flood plains, where seasonal overflows replenish nutrients—an approach typified today by rice paddies in Asia. They learned, too, that crops planted among trees—a mixed cultivation—had more protection against the harsh elements. With experience, they enlarged clearings and planted them to a single crop, a monoculturing, which led to plantation agriculture, and they devised new ways to store food for lean seasons.

As cultivators learned more, they discovered the value of rotating crops and of laying human and animal excrement and marl, a crumbly deposit of clay and calcium carbonate, to prevent soil exhaustion. But although they selected the most productive plant varieties, they did not learn to choose the best specimens within a variety until a few centuries ago. In this respect, herdsmen were in advance of cultivators, for they sensed quickly the value of mating superior parents to bear superior offspring.

Agricultural advances mean increasing "yield," the quantity and quality of food obtained from a crop relative to the value of the inputs, which in combination are called a "package." Yields are usually expressed in terms per acre (or hectare), but may be expressed in terms of fruit per tree, seeds per stem, or money received for money invested.

In sum, man learned that not all the apparent limitations in the soil, plants, and air were absolute; they could be made less restrictive under his care. Only the weather defied the early farmers, though they sought to control it, too, through entreaties and sacrifices to their gods.

The Age of Science increased agricultural technology, but the basic areas of intervention in natural cycles did not change. In periods of farming history, one advance or another—the chemical boom, for example—was considered the spearhead of an agricultural revolution, but, as the discussion of chemicals in another chapter illustrates, we must systematically pursue improvements in all directions. René Dubos, a Rockefeller University biologist, says that this interplay between human beings and the rest of nature has "commonly taken the form of a true symbiosis," a biological relationship somewhat altering each "in a way that is beneficial to both."

1

The Plant—Another Kind of Creature

Plants, like animals, breathe, drink, eat, reproduce, and die. A seed is a dormant plant, which under proper conditions awakens, or germinates. As it absorbs moisture, it swells, a process activating the embryonic plant's enzymes, which in turn enables it to utilize food reserves within the seed. Roots push deeply and widely into the soil to anchor the seedling and to forage for water and minerals, which they absorb through thousands of tiny hairs and conduct to the stems and leaves. Once the leaves sprout, the plant becomes independent of the seed for nutrition; it relies on the soil and the atmosphere for the raw materials from which it manufactures its own food. Moisture and minerals are required in the right quantities and at specific times. When minerals are too sparse, the plant starves; an excess of minerals can also be injurious.

Plant roots, as well as the leaves and stems, take part in respiration; they have openings called *lenticels*, through which they breathe in oxygen from the soil. Root systems vary in size, and some roots may lengthen several inches a day. When corn is "knee high," its roots may have penetrated nearly 2 feet, and by late summer as deep as 6 feet. Alfalfa tap roots usually penetrate

6 to 10 feet, but may go as deep as 20 feet. Researchers found that a rye plant grown in a cubic foot of soil for four months developed 385 miles of roots with 2,550 square feet of surface, and 66,000 miles of root hairs with a surface of 4,320 square feet.

Despite obvious differences between plant and animal physiologies, some vegetative processes perform the same functions as those of animal organs. The plant lacks a brain and pituitary gland, but it produces a growth-regulating hormone called *auxin.* Auxin flows throughout the plant, instructing the leaves to move and face the sun, directing enlargement of the cells, advising when blossoming time has come, and deciding if a leaf or fruit should hold or fall.

In a sense, auxin is the master liaison agent between the plant and the sun, whose radiation is turned into chemical energy in photosynthesis. This process is essentially the fabrication of complex organic materials, largely sugars, from carbon dioxide, water, and inorganic salts, which are stored in the stems and roots; we know it in the forms of sap, resin, or milky latex. Plants vary in the amount of light they need, and the leaves seldom shade one another completely; rather, they space themselves around the stem for maximum access to light. Any plant that does not get sufficient radiation becomes weak and spindly, and its growth pattern becomes distorted as it strains for more light.

Photosynthesis is capable of turning some 20 percent of absorbed solar radiation into chemical energy—a performance that plant physiologist Bessel Kok characterizes as "a pretty good achievement for a conversion machine of such fragile nature using a source of energy as fleeting as light." This is not to say, however, that farmers achieve such a high conversion index with their crops; they may reach only one-tenth of this potential. During the growing season of corn, for example, over 2 billion kilocalories of energy reach every acre, but only 1.26 percent is converted into plants, and only 0.4 percent of the total into corn grain. If scientists can discover ways of increasing this conversion rate by even a fraction, they will raise yields appreciably without need for further use of energy.

Plants also respond to care in ways not fully explained by science, suggesting that the phrase "green thumb" has some validity. Malayan women offer their milk symbolically by going into rice fields nude to the waist, and some Indonesians believe rice plants grow differently depending on whether men or women seed them. Several investigators have caused controversy by hypothesizing that plants are responsive to sound and grow more robustly in an ambience of pleasant music or encouraging words, but react traumatically to certain noises or even to the death of a nearby creature. Traditionally, scientists have dismissed such views as folkloric or magical, but we have been learning recently in various fields that such suppositions are not necessarily wide of the mark. Even plant breeder Norman E. Borlaug says, "Wheat talks to you."

Nevertheless, as the world population-food problem has become more acute, the crucial fact of photosynthesis has drawn more attention, which is likely to intensify during the energy crisis. Says Dutch crop specialist C. T. de Wita:

> How many people can live on earth if photosynthesis is the limiting process? To answer this question, the potential photosynthetic capability of green crop surface has to be estimated and related to the energy requirements of man.
>
> Up to this point in man's history, photosynthesis is the only source of food on earth and its capacity may ultimately determine the number of people who can live on this planet without starvation.

Improving the Plant

Plant improvement did not become a science until 1865, when Gregor Mendel, an Austrian monk, postulated the basic laws of heredity. In this century, biological engineers have created many new varieties, including the highly yielding hybrid corn, wheat that can grow in harsh climates, grains with higher protein content, and plants resistant to some diseases and pests. But the geneticists' mission is never-ending, for the new technologies and practices that constitute intensive agriculture jostle environmental balances, and realignments are necessary.

Geneticists most often emphasize yield, but the potential of a plant is restrained by pests and weather. So increasing pest resistance or weather tolerance may be more important to ultimate yield than creating a plant that bears more lushly. Indeed, a plant yielding more grain, fruit, or leaves, unless heightened resistance is also bred into it, may simply attract more of its natural predators. Furthermore, the uniform ripening of a crop, the thickness of a fruit's skin, or the distance of a snap bean from the ground, may be altered to facilitate mechanized harvesting. In the marketplace, taste, texture, appearance, and suitability for processing may be desirable. And when better nutrition can be bred into a staple, the diets of poor people can be improved quickly without changing food preferences or distribution systems.

While some types of wheat may grow as high as five or six feet under generous moisture conditions and with fertilizing, the height is not necessarily an advantage—the stalks lodge, or fall over, making combining difficult and increasing susceptibility to disease. During the thirties, Japanese scientists discovered the genetic key to growing a stiff, short-stemmed plant that they called Norin 10, and after World War II some of its seeds were brought to Washington State University. There, geneticists created a variety suited to the humidity of the Pacific Northwest called Gaines, and it became a parent of the new tropical varieties that contributed to the green revolution. Mexican farmers, who traditionally averaged only eleven bushels per acre, adopted the new varieties, and by 1964 were obtaining yields of nearly sixty bushels.

What differentiates our cultivated plants from their wild ancestors is their structure, particularly the enlarged size of their fruit or seed, which accounts for the increased yield. Geneticists are still developing more gigantism; in India, the geneticist Dilbagh S. Athwal bred new wheat with grain heads far larger than the usual—once characterized "like big sausages" and he later was experimentally producing stalks with multiple heads. Another major difference is in the mechanisms of disseminating the seed. Wild plants tend to shatter, while we need plants that tend to hold their seed, so we can harvest. Plants that survive in the wild are often bitter if not toxic, a protection, while man has sought more sweetness, whether in succulent fruits or in corn. And we have shortened or lengthened the growing period for different climates or to work against birth periods of pests. But some of these changes have meant the new varieties need more protective help from man.

Resistances

A breakthrough in breeding immunity to pests into plants occurred early in this century when southern farmers were distressed by cotton wilt, a fungus disease that survived indefinitely in the soil and stopped up root systems. William A. Orton, a plant pathologist who was studying the problem, learned that a South Carolina farmer had observed that some plants had survived in the infested fields, and had saved their seeds. The farmer's observation encouraged Orton to look for resistance among other cotton varieties. He found that, though virtually all were susceptible, there were considerable differences in resistance, and sometimes one or a handful of plants in a field were immune. These observations led to the insight that selective crossbreeding among immune plants of different varieties might produce an immune variety. Since then, geneticists have selectively crossbred most of our major crops, not only for resistance to disease but for other purposes as well. We now have, for example, drought-resistant corn, frost-resistant strawberries, and a new hybrid onion that withstands prolonged storage.

Nevertheless, the possibility of unanticipated losses remains real, as cases in the 1968 annual report of the Federal Crop Insurance Corporation showed. "Each year in the Crop Insurance experience," said the agency "there are also many 'never before' stories of losses." An example was an aphid or greenbug attack on grain sorghum on the southwestern and some central plains, "which threw a major scare into grain sorghum production prospects." A Texas report stated:

> Never before in the history of grain sorghum production had this insect been a serious threat to the crop. Farmers were advised by entomologists that the insects would not damage the grain sorghum enough to use control measures. However, the greenbugs continued to increase in number

and damaged or practically destroyed thousands of acres of grain sorghum.

But, in 1972, the Texas Agricultural Experiment Station released two greenbug-resistant sorghum breeding stocks, and recommended that they be crossed with good commercial varieties. P. L. Adkisson, head of agricultural studies at Texas A&M University, writes, "New hybrid varieties of our most important food and feed grains must be developed that will produce higher yields and be able to withstand insect and disease attack with limited chemical protection."

The Nutritional Challenge and Opaque 2

During the 1950s, Edwin T. Mertz, a biochemist at Cornell University, engaged in a frustrating search for a gene that would improve the protein content of the most widely used American crop, corn; in 1963, another scientist, Oliver E. Nelson, joined him. After examining many seeds, including mutant types, they found a single recessive gene that contributed more of the two essential amino acids that are limited in ordinary corn, lysine, especially, and tryptophan. They called the gene Opaque 2 because it lacked translucency; and the new variety of corn, which may take its name from the gene but is also called high-lysine corn, has twice the protein quality of ordinary corn.

Scientists believe that the gene has been around for over five thousand years. It was first discovered in 1935, but it was viewed simply as an oddity, and its nutritional potential remained unknown. "It was strange," Mertz said, "because these mutant genes had just been lying around in the 'tool chest,' in the 'breeder's handbag.' I don't think you can call [our discovery] serendipity, because in that case you're searching for one thing and find another. We were searching for this one. But we had no scientific basis for predicting that one type of corn would have the attribute. It was the Edison technique of searching—just a search."

High-lysine corn is being provided experimentally to poor families in several parts of the world; in Latin America, it has been ground up for corn bread and tortillas. These traditionally low-protein foods then have the same nutritional value as skim milk, but, in Guatemala for example, most poor children do not get skim milk, whereas corn makes up one- to two-thirds of the average caloric intake. In Cali, Colombia, a seven-year-old boy with an advanced case of malnutrition was put on a diet in which 80 percent of his protein came from high-lysine corn and 20 percent came from vegetables and fruits. He not only survived but began growing at the same rate as other children in his age and weight brackets.

In the United States, limited commercial use has been made of high-lysine corn for livestock, particularly swine. Experiments showed that pigs gained 4.3 times as much weight in a given period as those fed on standard corn. In Guatemala, pigs fed high-lysine corn grew five times as fast as those eating the local variety. Properly supplemented, the new corn is also suitable for poultry, but it is not useful for ruminant animals—cattle, sheep, and goats—whose peculiar double stomachs synthesize their own protein. (Another mutant found by Mertz and Nelson, Floury 2, is higher in methionine—another amino acid—and is superior for chickens, but little better than the regular corn for swine.)

"These exciting findings," the President's Science Advisory Committee reported in 1967, "point out the increased feasibility of attacking the problem of quality of proteins in cereals by the manipulation of germ plasm." And they spurred work on wheat and rice. "The whole investigation has broken wide open," said V. A. Johnson, a wheat specialist at the University of Nebraska who has spent over twenty years trying to raise wheat protein levels to 20 percent. The Department of Agriculture has estimated that if the protein content of corn alone could be improved by 25 percent, 5 million tons of protein would be added to the world supply. Experiments are now underway in more than thirty countries to help resolve the world protein problem through genetics.

The immediate problem with high-lysine corn was that it cost more than ordinary corn, mainly because it yielded around 30 percent less. But some seed companies in the corn belt are promoting it, and in 1972 one of them claimed its high-lysine seed yielded only 10 percent less than regular commercial corn, a difference more than compensated for by its better protein content. (George F. Sprague, a corn expert at the federal experiment station in Beltsville, Maryland, points out that such new varieties are often accepted at first as a specialty crop and later become commercially attractive.)

Broader worldwide use of high-lysine corn was restricted also by its inability to produce its highest yield over a wide range of locations—actually, corns have been one of the most location- and environment-specific crops grown. Because different pests and diseases occur in the different micro-environments, either broad resistance or a variety created for that limited locale has been needed. The soft, starchy nature of Opaque 2 not only resulted in lower yield on a weight basis—10 to 15 percent—but the soft grains appeared more vulnerable to disease and insect attack in both the field and in storage. In Mexico in 1972, at the International Maize and Wheat Improvement Center, breeders created an Opaque-2 variety with a hard endosperm, which displayed good yield potential; seed was shipped quickly to fifteen other countries for testing.

Man-made Species

While geneticists were creating new varieties within a plant species, they were fascinated with the notion of creating an entirely new species, and they have recently succeeded in crossing wheat and rye. The grain is called Triticale (a contraction for the Latin names of its parents). Originally developed by Spanish and Swedish scientists, it was first treated as a curiosity, but during the last decade, American, Canadian, Mexican, and Russian scientists became more interested. Experimentally, Triticale has out-yielded wheat grown under comparable conditions by 50 percent, and some plants have heads as long as ten to twelve inches. Its protein content is as much as 18 percent, with a high lysine level, and its flour bakes into a flat, rye-type bread with a tasty, nutty flavor. The varieties also showed variations in growing seasons, height, and disease susceptibility. But Triticale has major deficiencies: its grains shrivel, reducing yield; it has poor milling qualities; and it is sterile. B. Charles Jenkins, who experimented with it in Canada during the late 1960s, discussed its unconventional appearance:

> One fact should be emphasized, that this is an entirely new grain, and not wheat or rye, but rather a combination of the two types. People often think that the grains are less attractive than those of wheat because of the slight wrinkling, but I maintain that this is a characteristic that will have to be accepted, rather than trying to approach the smoothness of wheat.

Although it had been predicted that Triticale would displace corn as feed, growers have yet to make its yield competitive.

Other approaches to create new varieties, if not new species, include radiation and cell fusion, which may shorten the time necessary for genetic engineering.

Radiation has induced mutations with impressive results. By 1970, at least sixty-five new varieties created by radiation had been released to growers, and nearly two-thirds of those varieties had been created in the preceding five years.

A new, fast-moving field of experimentation is the fusion of cells of different varieties and species. As Peter S. Carlson of the Brookhaven National Laboratory in New York puts it, the technique "bypasses conventional sexual mechanisms," and it enables scientists to breed and screen the equivalent of acres of crops in small dishes without planting seeds. Triticale, the only manmade species, was created by conventional mating, and the cross was facilitated by the parent plants' being similar biologically. Cell fusion has been successful with two species of tobacco, but scientists are experimenting with crossing such dissimilar food plants as wheat and soybean, perhaps combining the drought-resistant properties of the former and the use of nitrogen in the air of the latter. Also under investigation are rice, potatoes, tomatoes, carrots, asparagus, and eggplants. Science fiction writers may conceive such results as orange-bearing seaweed; scientists will probably use the new technique to improve protein content, increase resistances, and raise yields. According to Lewis M. Roberts of the Rockefeller Foundation, in 1970 it would have been difficult to find fifteen researchers throughout the world concentrating on cell fusion; now there are many more. But, says Carlson, "Fusion is another trick in the geneticists' bag of tricks—another positive input. It will not replace traditional genetic engineering."

There is another type of fusion, grafting, that has long been used by citrus growers, although it is not strictly speaking crossbreeding. Most citrus trees grow in two parts: the roots and trunk make up the rootstock, and the upper parts the scion. Their juncture is known as a bud onion, appearing as a horizontal line around the trunk of a mature tree. One type of fruit can be grown on the rootstock of another variety by slicing a bud from a twig, placing it into a slit which has been cut a few inches above the ground in the seedling of another type, and bandaging the juncture. When a new shoot emerges from the bud, the upper trunk of the young tree is cut, leaving the transplanted scion growing on the rootstock. In California, nearly all lemon trees are raised on orange roots, and, indeed, a natural Christmas tree can be grown, displaying lemons, limes, grapefruit, tangerines, kumquats, and oranges all at once.

But creating new varieties and species, and successful new methods of growing, are likely to remain, for the most part, long, tedious procedures, as H. H. Cramer, an agriculturist at Purdue, emphasized in a 1968 interview:

> There are lots of things that you cannot solve by a windfall of money and crash programs. Perhaps you can solve things in the physical sciences. But when you're dealing with crops and seasons, it takes maybe 15 to 20 years. . . . Few advances are as spectacular as high-lysine corn.
>
> Take hybrids. In 1878 [botanist William James] Beale at Michigan first crossed to produce hybrid vigor. Calculate the percentage per year to raise corn yields since that time, and it is less than 2 percent; that is, spreading it over the number of years that the principle was known.

The National Seed Storage Laboratory

Intense concern over preserving genetic stocks has been aroused by the growing number of endangered varieties. Traditionally, plant breeders tossed aside seeds that seemed without value. They frequently found, when they needed them again, that they had deteriorated or disappeared or that their native regions were in hostile countries. So in 1956, Congress funded a national seed storage laboratory, which was established in Fort Collins, Colorado, three years later. The total capacity of the laboratory is 300,000 seed samples; by 1971 it held over 82,000 and 6,000 to 7,000 samples are being added yearly. The majority of seeds are for food crops, especially vegetables, but also stored are seeds for some forest and ornamental trees and for crops within potential medical uses. Recently, greater emphasis has been placed on seeds that may have genes producing resistances.

Any qualified breeder or seed experimenter is eligible for seed at no cost if it is unavailable from other sources; usually 50 to 100 seeds are given away on request. The laboratory considers the ideal sample for storage to be about 10,000 seeds, but a minimum of 2,000 is necessary. To test the viability of the seeds—their capability to germinate and grow—technicians plant a few from each sample at least every five years, oftener if the sample is of low quality. Seeds have varying life expectancies—some quite short and others long—but eventually all must be replaced. Until then, they are stored in a cold, dry room (around 35 to 40 degrees F.), which lengthens their life by depressing their rate of respiration.

Producing improved seed is the mission of the plant breeders of the seed companies, who are especially pressed when acreages are quickly expanded or when resistant varieties are needed after a major blight. There are hundreds of seed producers—the American Seed Growers' Association lists among its members 475 companies in North America—and in 1974 one company, DeKalb, offered 88 varieties of hybrid corn and 15 varieties of sorghums. The federal government encourages development through the Plant Variety Protection arrangement, granting a sort of patent for new varieties for 17 years to prevent competitors from multiplying the new seed.

2

The Soilsphere—Its Formation and Its Inhabitants

Futurists have written optimistically about "harvesting" the seas, converting petroleum into protein, farming hydroponically (the growing of plants in liquid nutrient solutions rather than soils), and other approaches to food production which would require little if any soil. But by far the most important source of our nourishment—of about 98 percent of it, in fact—is the land, and this is likely to remain so. Ironically, the scientific study of soils was developed relatively recently. Little was really known about American soils until after 1899, when the Department of Agriculture began conducting and publishing soil surveys. The theories of European soil researchers, who were more advanced than the Americans, were not generally circulated in this country until 1915, except perhaps where they were coincidental to to the theories of chemists, geologists, or botanists.

For the plant, soil has two main purposes: It is a mooring for roots, holding the plant upright and in place, and it provides water and nutrients and stores them until they are needed. But, as Charles E. Kellog, who has perhaps mapped more soils than anyone, notes in *The Soils That Support Us*, they "are not simple storage bins."

Soil fecundity awed and mystified early man. Some believed that the sky—the air, the sun, the rains, and the dew—had a masculine fertilizing ability, while the earth nurtured like the womb. The Greeks believed that the earth was one of Zeus's wives, and, according to mythology, when she took the first plowman, Jason, as a lover, Zeus struck him down with a thunderbolt. The joining of man and earth was considered sacred, and Hesiod instructed Greek plowmen to sow in the nude, as clothing would desecrate the relationship.

One of the earliest studies of soils was made around 2000 B.C. in China by an engineer named Yu, who grouped them according to structure and color. But while Athenian philosophers and scientists puzzled over astronomy, mathematics and food, they rarely poked into land or experimented with plants (except for Aristotle and Theophrastus who perceived an interrelationship between soil fertility and plant nutrition). Cato the Elder, Varro, Pliny the Elder, and Columella also sensed the interrelationship, and Columella wrote an extraordinary work, *Husbandry*, which discussed different soils and their most efficient management; it long remained the most authoritative exposition on the subject.

As societies "matured," the leaders tended to separate themselves from the direct care of the soil and assigned land management to the "lower" classes. While the privileged rejoiced in bountiful and imaginative cuisines, food production remained a crude occupation. The repository of information about the soil was largely the oral tradition of "simple" folk who live on and from the land.

After 1600, experimentation revived. In 1629, a Dutchman named Jon Baptiste Van Helmont inadvertently dramatized how little was known. He watched a willow tree grow lushly for years in soil to which nothing was added but rainwater, and since only two ounces of soil disappeared, he concluded that water is the chief source of plant nutrition. This led an English scientist, John Woodward, to reason that plants should do well in pure water. To test the hypothesis, he planted peas variously in rainwater, water from the Thames River, and water from a mudhole. The first barely survived, the second grew poorly, and the peas in the muddy water flourished. Reversing his position, he reported that the soil imparts the "spirit" or "soul" of life to vegetation, and that vegetables "are not formed of water, but of a certain peculiar terrestrial matter."

The Eastern Europeans, especially the Russians, with their great diversity of lands, climates, and plants, made great strides in soil study. (The Russians had the added advantage of having many virgin soils as well as those under the plow.) In the eighteenth century, M.V. Lomonosov discovered that soils are evolutionary, not static bodies. In 1863, V.V. Dokuchaev presented the first scientific classification and descriptions of major groups of soils and worked out methods of soil mapping in both the field and laboratory. His research showed that soils consist of horizons, or layers, and each soil reveals a profile of characteristics when sectionalized. Refining and amplifying his discoveries three years later, Dokuchaev proposed that the word "soil" be the scientific term for "those horizons of rock which daily or nearly daily change their relationship under the joint influence of water, air, and various forms of organisms living and dead."

The foundations were now laid for the study of soil genesis, or pedology, which involves the physical properties, meteorological phenomena, and biological processes that are the bases of soil formation.

The various influences in soil formation are minerals, chemicals, vegetation, and organisms, including man. Early in the nineteenth century, Albrecht von Thaer, the Prussian minister of agriculture, classified for the first time eleven different grain soils. This was a large step; since Roman times, only "heavy" and "light" growing soils had previously been recognized.

About this time, the English chemist Sir Humphrey Davy theorized on the interrelationships between chemistry and plant physiology, a line of thought that led to a historic breakthrough.

In the 1830s a young German professor of chemistry, Justus von Liebig, moved his laboratory from the university into the fields and shortly thereafter discovered that farmers "robbed" the soil rather than cultivating it. In his famous book, *Chemistry Applied to Agriculture and Physiology*, he pointed out that plants remove four essential nutrients—nitrogen, potassium, lime, and phosphoric acid—and contended that these nutrients could, and should, be replaced by added chemicals. He also formulated the "law of the minimum," which held that plant growth was directly proportional to the nutrient in most limited supply. For some years after, Liebig's Patent Manure was marketed. Another scientist, V. R. Williams, gave a biological refinement by describing the life cycle of soil as the withdrawal of nutrients by plants, which later give back leaves, stems, and roots to the topsoil, but the crucial role of micro-organisms could not be understood until investigations were made with the microscope after 1886.

In 1892 E. W. Hilgard, an American geologist specializing in soils, likened the soil to an "embroidery" on the surface of the earth, a fabric woven by the processes of weathering, plant growth, and cultivating practices. More theoreticians began viewing soil as a distinct sphere, worthy of the same recognition as the atmosphere, hydrosphere, and biosphere; but delineating the soilsphere is somewhat arbitrary, since it really represents slices from each of the others.

However, these early findings did not excite much interest in the soil, and the industrial revolution, rather than acting as a catalyst to a more enlightened attitude, accorded prestige to scientists and manufacturers while degrading the food-producing class. The farmer's hands were "dirty" and his clothing "soiled," and the pejoratives became code words of wider application, such as "dirt cheap" and a "dirty player."

Arable Land

Narrowly defined, arable land is plowable soil; more broadly, it is land on which farmers can grow crops. This distinction is important in categorizing soils for agricultural purposes, for there are arid lands that can be plowed but are unproductive without irrigation. When we consider the potential of land for growing food, our first criterion is tillable land, and our second is whatever additional inputs are required to render it productive. Ideal soil has a deep zone for rooting and for storing nutrients, water, and air, but farmers can deepen a shallow zone by plowing more deeply, by adding soil or compost to the top, or by planting such crops as alfalfa, whose penetrating roots break up lower layers.

Only three-tenths of the surface of the globe is land. Half of it has some agricultural use, about equally divided between possible cropping and only grazing. The potentially arable land is about double what has been cropped during recent years. But as time goes on, these estimates are likely to change as new technologies transform poor lands into productive ones or as we and nature make productive lands sterile. Arid but plowable soils, for example, may become useful through the creation of new crop varieties that thrive where others withered.

Two terms are applied—soil fertility and soil productivity— and they are not synonymous. Fertility is the sum of the properties of the soil supporting plant life, while productivity is the soil's capacity to produce one or more specified crops under certain kinds of cultivation. The latter is therefore an economic rather than an ecological concept: a soil that is productive for wheat without irrigation may not be so for corn or rice.

Nature's Input: Soil Genesis

Soil, like all living things, undergoes a cycle of birth, growth, aging and renewal, and death. Some soil scientists refer to parent material, immature soil, mature soil and old soil; immature and mature soils are the most fertile, and old soil may be said to be weathered out, with no further release of nutrients. Five factors influence the genesis of soil—parent material, climate, relief (especially slope), the biosphere, and time.

Soil formation usually begins with the crumbling of mineral-holding rocks that mix with decayed foliage and roots, though some soils come from peat, which is mainly organic matter. The agents of crumbling are moisture which, reacting over the topography of the earth, grinds rock down; and heating and cooling, which shatters rock surfaces—especially the sudden cooling that occurs in some deserts.

A cross section of soil, or soil profile, reveals several layers, known as *horizons*, of which there are typically three, termed the A, B, and C horizons. The top, or A, horizon is enriched by decomposed organic matter, while lower horizons have more of the mineral matter from the parent material. Soil is finally composed of minerals, water, air (gases), and organic matter; an ideal garden or lawn soil is 45 percent mineral, 25 percent water, 25 percent air, and 5 percent organic.

About one-half of soil consists of pore space, through which water and gases pass. The rate of water movement through the soil depends on the number and size of soil pores. While sandy soil is heavy, because it is only around 30 percent pore space, water usually moves through it quickly because the pores are large. The finely textured surface soils, such as clay, are over 50 percent pore space, but the pores are smaller, so that water and air move through it with difficulty, and a good deal of moisture is retained—clayey soil may contain as much as 30 pounds of water per 100 pounds of solid matter.

In a moist, well-drained soil, air usually fills the larger pores, called *aeration pores* or *macropores*, while the small pores, called *capillary* or *micropores*, hold water—it is known as "capillary water." The ability of soil to transport water and air is called *permeability*. For cropping there must be enough total pore space of the proper size ranges to hold enough water and air to satisfy the roots between rainfall or irrigation. After a heavy, prolonged rain, pores may be saturated for a few hours; but after a dry day or so, some water drains down in response to gravity—"gravitational water"—and the larger pores again fill with air.

Solid particles make up 40 to 70 percent of total soil volume, depending on the type of horizon, and are divided into groups, or *separates*, on the basis of size, irrespective of their chemical composition, color, weight, or other properties. The relative proportions of sand, whose particles are comparatively large; silt, whose particles are smaller; and clay, with its tiny particles, determine the coarseness or fineness of the soil, known as its *texture*, which governs the rate and extent of many important physical and chemical reactions. The separates are classified into very coarse sand, coarse sand, medium sand, fine sand, very fine sand, silt, and clay. Since water retention in soil is a function of the total surface area of its component particles, the finer the separate, the more water the soil can hold. Clay has thousands of times more surface per gram than silt, and as much as a million times more particle surface than very coarse sand, and may contain as many as 30 pounds of water per 100 pounds of soil.

No soil consists of only one type of separate; most are blends of the majority of types, so soils are classed according to proportions of the different separates. The separates impart their qualities to one another, but not to the same degree; clay, for instance, imparts more of its properties to the mixture than the others do. Pores, by allowing water to pass through them, facilitate the removal of soluble compounds. They also permit the transit of oxygen for the respiration of plant roots, the diffusion of carbon dioxide out of the soil, and the penetration of roots. And they provide a habitat for micro-organisms.

While texture refers to the size of soil particles, their arrangement, or aggregation, is termed *structure*. Structure modifies the influence of texture relative to moisture and air movement, nutrient movement, root growth, and the activity of micro-organisms.

Moisture and Temperature

A natural irrigation system is built into good soil. Under ideal conditions, moisture is admitted into the soil and, in proper proportions, supplied to the plant, stored, and disposed of when in excess. What is not admitted into the soil flows away on the surface as runoff. Some moisture returns to the air through evaporation, and some that is absorbed by the plants is emitted from their leaves in the process of transpiration—a combined process known as *evapotranspiration*. Moisture that is taken in but not used immediately or kept in reserve percolates down to the water table, which is the point below which the ground is saturated with water, or to an aquifer, which is an underground reservoir, or it may reach a nonporous rock surface and flow as an underground stream until it emerges as a spring or bog or joins a larger stream flowing back to the sea.

The downward percolation of surplus water opens pore space in the upper levels for the air needed to sustain plants and the micro-organisms that contribute to soil fertility. When moisture is needed near the surface and there is some in reserve lower, it will percolate back upward through the soil. The less moisture soil contains, the more vigorously it retains what is left. After a favorable rainfall on soil that is good for corn, about one-half of the pore space will contain water. But the proportion varies greatly among different soils and even among various horizons of the same ground. The ideal growing soil combines the good drainage and meandering aeration provided by sand with the capacity to store moisture that is typical of clay.

Under certain conditions, parts of the soil's natural irrigation system can operate harmfully. The weight of the heavy rainfall typical of the tropics causes an excessively rapid downflow, which carries nutrients away from the surface—a process called *leaching* that reduces fertility. However, in soils that cannot filter water down as fast as they receive it, the air supply is restricted, waterlogging occurs, and plants may contract root rot. Or water in lower horizons of soil may become saline, and when dryness toward the upper horizons stimulates an upward percolation, injurious quantities of salts may be carried into the topsoil. (Salinity can be detected often by the formation of a white film on the surface.)

While some runoff is desirable because it exposes fresher soils, excessive runoff erodes the land, steepening the hillsides, carving gorges or arroyos, hewing stone outcroppings, and leaving what we know as *badlands*. The process of evaporation cools the earth and helps moderate sunlight that is too strong and direct for plants and micro-organisms, but very rapid evaporation after heavy rains under a blazing sun can bake the surface hard, and in the process the surface contracts, buckles, and breaks until it looks like an expanse of concave slabs and is about as unplowable. In a desert, the little rain that falls is likely to burst from the clouds and strike the soil forcefully, seeping rapidly to depths below the root zone and running off simultaneously. Another serious condition is *compacting*, which destroys the porousness of the earth—a phenomenon that can be observed in the ruts of a dirt road, which do not permit vegetation to grow long after the road has gone out of use.

The amount of effective rainfall—that is, moisture that can be utilized or stored until needed—depends on the rate of evapotranspiration and organic decomposition in the topsoil, and these rates depend on temperature. The solar radiation that is absorbed by the soil rather than reflected by it heats it; and as temperature rises, the speed of chemical reactions involving water accelerates exponentially—perhaps two or three times for a rise of 10 degrees C. Light soils absorb 80 percent of radiation, while dark soils absorb only 30 percent. The density, height, and color of vegetation also affect the degree of absorption. (Of all radiation, 47 percent is absorbed by the earth, 19 percent by the atmosphere, and 34 percent is reflected.) Heat absorbed during the day is generally lost at night when the soil radiates heat back into space, but cooling also depends upon the thermal properties of the soil and on the turbulence of the wind. The temperature of the soil is also controlled to a great degree by the capacity of the soil to retain moisture; sandy soils, for example, heat more rapidly than clay. In the average satisfactory moisture cycle, moisture is depleted during the summer when plants draw on stored water, and by November, the soil is wilted, ready to be revived by the return of rains or early snowmelts.

The more mobile a nutrient is in the soil water, the more readily it moves toward the root system. But because capillary water and dissolved nutrients can move only a limited distance in any event, the roots must continually spread in the ground. The root hairs soon permeate an entire soil body, foraging mainly toward clay particles or following the paths left by earlier roots or by organisms. And there must be enough total pore space of proper size to hold enough water and air to satisfy the roots between moisture renewals. For when moisture is low, root growth is reduced, and nutrient absorption is therefore less. And a low oxygen supply around the roots also retards growth and affects the absorption of salts.

In a sense, soil normally functions as a bank does, loaning nutrients to foster vegetation, which the plant repays in kind through decomposition. Plants require at least sixteen nutrients, the principal ones of which—macro-nutrients—are carbon, oxygen, hydrogen, nitrogen, phosphorous, potassium, sulfur, and calcium. It also needs small amounts of other—micro-nutrients—including iron, manganese, magnesium, zinc, copper, boron, chlorine, and usually molybdenum.

Soil-borne Organisms

Humus, which is the dark substance in soil resulting from the partial decomposition of animal and vegetable matter, is a source of plant nutrition, and multitudinous members of the animal and plant realms join in producing it.

For fertile soil formation and the recycling of nutrients, the soil and climate must provide a suitable habitat for the micro-organisms. For example, some need oxygen while converting nutrients in organic matter into the soluble forms needed by higher plants; others thrive in the retained water.

The smallest and most numerous group of animals in the soil are the protozoa, which are really aquatic since they live in the water films around the soil particles and feed on bacteria, fungi, algae, and dead organisms. There is also the worm family, whose tiniest members are the microscopic nematodes; others are the familiar earthworms; the arthropods, such as lice, spiders, mites, and ants; the mollusks, such as snails and slugs; vertebrates, such as reptiles, moles, shrews, mice, gophers, badgers, and other larger animals; and birds. Aquatic creatures that burrow under rocks or press against embankments also affect formation of the soil.

The microflora are bacteria, fungi, actinomycetes, and algae; and the macroflora are the roots of higher plants. The bacteria, which are single-celled, are the most numerous; a single ton of soil may contain over a billion bacteria. The fungi weigh more, an average of 1,000 pounds per acre of soil. The actinomycetes are related to both fungi and bacteria, and are variously classified as fungilike bacteria or simply another group of bacteria.

Nitrogen, the key ingredient of protein, is essential to soil fertility and plant nutrition, but it must be captured, or fixed, from the air, of which about 80 percent is the colorless, odorless, inert gas—about 35,000 tons for every acre of land. It is in a free state in the atmosphere, useless to plant and animal life, and must combine with other elements, which it does not do easily. Certain of the micro-organisms—mainly two groups of bacteria—are able to seize nitrogen from the air for use in building their own cells, thereby changing it into a fixed form, which plants can draw upon later.

One is the rhizobia, which invade the root-hair openings of legumes, nestle in the plant cells, and form growths called *nodules*, in which they live and work in partnership with their host. Their colonies grow to a million or more bacteria, as they take the plant's sugar for energy, which they use to change free nitrogen into a form that the plant can assimilate and convert into amino acids. About 4 million tons of nitrogen is fixed this way annually in the United States. Among the important legumes enjoying this symbiotic relationship are soybeans, lentils, beans, peas, and peanuts. If a legume is well nodulated with efficient rhizobia, it may not respond to nitrogen fertilizing; if it is not, it must obtain its nitrogen from the soil or from applied fertilizer.

Methods have been developed for mixing legume seeds with the correct strain of bacteria culture before planting, either on the farm or by seed dealers or grain elevators. The procedure is called *seed innoculation*—which should not, however, be confused with pesticidal seed treatment; in fact, most seed disinfectants injure these beneficial bacteria.

Rhizobia, however, are selective; not only do they refuse to collaborate with cereal crops (the grasses), but individual strains colonize only specific varieties of legumes. Because of the prospect of a world nitrogen crisis, scientists are making rhizobia one of the most thoroughly researched bacteria in history as they work with some fifty collections. Their efficiency, says Deane F. Weber, a microbiologist with the U.S. Plant Nutrition Laboratory, "could be increased if we could change them genetically so they could fix more nitrogen symbiotically or non-symbiotically [in the soil]."

Symbiotic fixation normally provides about 100 pounds of nitrogen per acre, but there is a question as to whether the process is actually inhibited by high levels of nitrate fertilization; in any event, soybeans, for example, well nodulated with efficient rhizobia do not respond to it. One approach being investigated involves new forms of nitrogen fertilizer that demonstrably do not interfere with symbiotic fixation, or, conversely, finding strains of nitrogen-fixing bacteria that tolerate heavy nitrogen fertilization. Scientists are also trying to create new strains genetically that will fix nitrogen for non-legumes, especially the important grains, and to understand the fixing mechanisms, which involve an enzyme that might be synthesized, well enough to invent a machine that will fix nitrogen from the air. In 1973, investigators were heartened by the discovery of a rhizobium in New Guinea that fixes nitrogen for a non-legume, believed to be a variety of elm.

Some free-living bacteria also fix nitrogen in the soil, but relatively little research has been done on them. In fact, there is now doubt that they are all as free-living as theorized, since a strain was found in Brazil that colonizes grass roots. What is particularly needed, though, is better information on how non-legumes obtain their nitrogen.

Fertilizer

Plants also require sound diets, and while most land supplies some nutrients, others are often lacking and out of balance. Under natural conditions, soil tends to have its fertility replenished by the kind of vegetation that grows on it, but plants flourish where the soil initially offers the vital nutrients. As farmers seeded varieties not previously growing on their plots, they soon sensed that plants often grew better after the soil was fertilized. Some early cultivators discovered that burying a fish fostered more reliable and productive growth—though they did not immediately understand that the release of nitrogen was the reason—and farmers the world over observed how plants usually grew more robustly when excrement was added to the soil. Soon they gained insights into composting, and Roman farmers found that lime stimulates some crops.

But knowledge of plant nutrition advanced slowly until the Age of Science, with its developments in chemistry late in the eighteenth century. Chemists discovered that the three main elements of plant nutrition are nitrogen, potassium, and phosphorus; that proper fertilizing, the agricultural jargon for nutrition, consists of balances among major and minor nutrients; and that the timing of their availability is important. We now know that plants need at least 16 elements; the secondary nutrients are calcium, magnesium, and sulfur, and the micro-nutrients are iron, boron, manganese, copper, zinc, molybdenum, and chlorine. More than 40 other elements are found in plants, which may be beneficial but not essential. It is a rare soil that can supply all essential nutrients for long under intensive cultivation.

During the nineteenth century, scientists found that by burning the plant and analyzing the minerals and the ash, any nutritional deficiency would appear. But where to obtain the chemical replacements? In the United States around 1820, an influential southern reformer, Edmund Ruffin, popularized the use of marl, which is essentially a mixture of clay and carbonate lime, often in the form of fossil shells, and his advocacy led Virginia farmers to restore the fertility of many of their soils and cultivate successfully what had been wastelands. An early commercially marketed fertilizer was Peruvian guano, the dried excrement of seafowl, which was first shipped to Baltimore in 1849. Subsequently, other fertilizers were touted; some of them were helpful and cheaper than guano, while others were of slight value. The versatile scientist Wilbur Olin Atwater, who had organized the first American agriculture experiment station in 1875 in Connecticut and manifested a lifelong concern for nutrition, taught that the greatest reservoir, however, was the air itself, which is mostly nitrogen. Lime was available from many sources, and potassium was found in the form of potash, or wood ashes, and in burned seaweed.

Fertilizer became the spearhead of another agricultural advance, and in the United States from 1935 to 1939, liming probably was about double what it had been during the 1920s; during World War II, it more than tripled. At the beginning of this decade, world fertilizer consumption was increasing yearly by 8 to 9 percent, mostly nitrogen, followed by phosphate and potash. The proportions of these fertilizers are listed in that order for commercial brands, such as 5-10-5.

Soil scientists take surveys to determine what the soil offers, and what nutrients, if any, have been removed from the organic matter. For example, a 100-bushel corn crop may take 78 pounds of nitrogen from the soil, 36 pounds of phosphoric oxide, and 26 pounds of potassium oxide.

But fertilizing can be overdone. If the nitrogen is too highly concentrated, it may burn the plants, or run off as a pollutant. Organic food advocates hold that chemical fertilizing, like chemical pesticides, decreases the quality of the food, a view disputed by most plant biologists who say that a plant really cannot differentiate between an organic and synthetic nutrient; it converts both in the same way.

Classifying the Soils

The soils of the world are classified into thirty-nine great soil groups, then subdivided into families, series, types, and phases.

The United States has more than 70,000 types of soil, each of which peculiarly influences farming, and some agriculturists say that this diversity means the country has at least that many kinds of farms. Attempting to generalize about the values of the thirty-nine great soils is difficult because, under specified conditions, virtually all are useful for some sort of farming. Yet, no matter how potentially productive they may be, weather, local technological backwardness, or several other conditions may make them uneconomic or difficult to farm.

TABLE 2.1. WORLD LAND AREA IN DIFFERENT SOIL GROUPS

Soil Group	Total Area (billions of acres)	Percent of All Land	Percent of Group Potentially Arable	Grazable
Tundra	1.28	3.9	0	0
Desert	5.26	16.2	3.3	7.0
Chernozem and Brunizem	2.03	6.2	3.5	2.2
Noncalcic Brown	.72	2.2	.8	1.1
Podzol	4.85	14.9	2.4	3.8
Red-yellow Podzolic	.96	3.0	1.0	1.5
Latosol	6.18	19.0	8.1	5.4
Grumosol, Terra Rossa	.81	2.5	1.3	.11
Brown Forest, Rendzina	.25	.8	.2	.4
Ando	.06	.2	.1	.1
Lithosol	6.73	20.7	.6	3.1
Regosol	1.90	5.8	.5	1.1
Alluvial	1.47	4.5	2.4	1.3
TOTAL	32.50	100.0	24.2	15.60

SOURCE: *The World Food Problem—A Report of the President's Science Advisory Committee* (Washington, D.C.: U.S. Government Printing Office, May 1967), vol. 2, table 7-1, p. 423.

TABLE 2.2 THE GREAT SOIL GROUPS

Classification	Characteristics
Alluvial	Though covering comparatively little of the world, these soils produce about one-third of all our food. They accumulate in elongated river basins and on deltas, and only climate and seasonal flooding limit cultivation. When flood waters pull back slowly, they refertilize these soils by depositing miniscule rock particles.
Ando	Dark, mainly of volcanic ash, and often hilly and forested; under good management these soils can be moderately to highly productive.
Brown	Varying from light brown to gray or chalky, these soils are in layers from one to three feet below semi-arid grassland in cool to temperate climates. Farmers can cultivate them where they are level with economic irrigation.
Brown Forest	Rich in humus, these soils are dark brown to lighter color, 2 to 4 feet under forests in cool and temperature regions; if not too steep, stony, or in the Arctic, they are highly productive for many crops.
Brown Podzolic	With brown, acidy surfaces, these soils develop under forests in cool-temperate and temperate climates, and are suitable for cool-season crops if adequately fertilized and irrigated.
Brunizem	These are dark-brown soils, lying below humid grasslands in temperate and cool climates. Several grains, including corn and forage crops, yield well on them.
Calcisol	Because these soils spread over arid and semi-arid regions and contain a lot of powdery calcium carbonate, they have shallow layers for rotting. Farmers use them mainly for grazing where they are level, and they can often be irrigated successfully, unless they have hardpans (hard, unbroken, unporous layers below the soft soil).
Chernozem	Black, granular, rich in organic matter and calcium carbonate, these soils lie from 2 to 4 feet below grasslands in subhumid areas. Grains, especially corn, grow well on them.
Chestnut	Dark brown with calcium carbonate, these soils

Classification	Characteristics
	are also at 2 to 4 feet in semi-arid temperate grasslands. Except in dry years, they are good for grains and can be irrigated productively.
Desert	Vegetation on these light-gray or brownish-gray soils is typically sparse; they contain little organic matter, but, unless they are too stony or have hardpans, irrigation and fertilizing make them productive.
Gray-brown Podzolic	Created under forests of deciduous trees, these pale-brown acid soils with leached surfaces and clayey subsoils support many crops.
Gray Wooded	These soils are found in forested areas with cool to temperate climates, and farmers can raise short-season crops with fertilizing.
Ground-water Laterite	These are leached surface soils, gray or brown, lying over a fairly deep, doughy laterite, which hardens irreversibly when exposed in tropical climates with alternating wet and dry seasons. If cultivating practices prevent hardening, crops can be raised on this land.
Ground-Water Podzol	Ranging widely from humid climates near the Arctic to the tropics, these soils usually lie below forests, including palms. Their leached sandy surfaces cover dark-brown sandy subsoils above water tables that fluctuate from about 1 to 4 feet below. They can produce moderately but may require drainage and fertilization.
Grumosol	Appearing in warm to tropical climates with wet and dry seasons, these soils, black to brown, have surface clays that crack and mulch naturally when dry, creating a micro-relief known as *gilgai,* or small gully. Sorghum grows on them with heavy tillage and irrigation.
Half Bog	Developing mainly below tropical to cool-humid swamp forests, these soils are brown and peaty, and lie from 6 to 18 inches down in gray mineral ground. With drainage, farmers can grow locally adapted crops.
Humic Gley	These soils lie over gray or mottled mineral soils under grass or forest in warm to cool temperatures and humid to subhumid moisture.
Latosol	This reddish soil develops under tropical woodlands and savanna; it lies deep, is composed of

TABLE 2.2 THE GREAT SOIL GROUPS (*cont.*)

Classification	Characteristics
	highly weathered minerals, and is very permeable. Under sound management, many crops grow well on it, and some are still used under shifting cultivation.
Lithosol	Thin, usually stony, these soils often settle over rock in many climates, and produce scrubby vegetation, some of it usable for grazing. In a few areas, farmers have successfully terraced their plots with manual labor.
Low-Humic Gley	These are light-colored, clayey, or sandy soils, evolving where water tables are high during part of the year in humid-temperate to tropical climates, and mainly under forests or savanna. Crops grow well after drainage and fertilizing.
Noncalcic Brown	These soils form under thin forests in climates that are temperate to warm and subhumid with wet and dry seasons. Sloping areas are used for pasture and flatlands for irrigated cropping.
Podzol	These surface soils form under forests in cool-temperate or cool climates; they are light colored, acidic, and cover dark-brown subsoils. When sloping, stony, or shallow, they are often forested; but farmers can raise cool-season crops where they are level.
Reddish-brown	These soils are found in subhumid areas with warm to warm-temperate climates, and lie at depths of 18 to 30 inches with accumulations of calcium carbonate. Where level, grains grow well, and slopes produce good pasture.
Reddish-brown Lateritic	Thick surface soils, dark red or brown with clayey red subsoils, these are found under forests that are warm-temperate to subtropical and humid. The flatlands are productive under proper irrigation and fertilizing, and the slopes are good for forage.
Red Desert	These light, reddish-brown surface soils with red clayey soil beneath are commonly calcareous, and form under desert growth in climates that are temperate to warm to tropical. Unless underlain with hardpan, level areas are productive, especially when irrigated.
Reddish Chestnut	Reddish-brown with calcium carbonate, these

Classification	Characteristics
	soils are at 2 to 5 feet below grasslands in warm, subhumid areas. Flatlands are good for grains and cotton, and irregular slopes for grazing.
Reddish Prairie	Red-colored, these soils range over grasslands or savannas in warm to warm-temperate climates, and are intermediates of Brunizem and Reddish Chestnut. Grains and cotton grow well on them.
Red-yellow Podzolic	These are light-colored, acidy surface soils lying over clayey acidic, often quite deep, subsoils in forested areas in warm-temperate to tropical climes. Many crops thrive on the level areas, which are also highly responsive to irrigation and fertilizing, and hillsides may be heavily forested.
Regosol	Occurring in many regions and under many conditions of precipitation, temperature, and vegetation, these are generally sloping young soils formed variously from sand, silt, glacial drift, and the like. The more level areas produce well under irrigation.
Rendzina	These surface soils are gray to charcoal and lie over soft limestone or marl under grasses, sometimes mixed with trees, in climates that are subhumid and cool-temperate to warm. In humid areas, they can be used for intensive grazing, especially of sheep and goats, and on more level areas, unless stony, for cropping.
Sierozem	These are intermediate between the desert and brown soils, light or brownish-gray, grading into calcareous matter 1 to 2 feet below thin grass and desert shrub, in cool to warm climates. If free of salt deep down, farmers can cultivate level areas intensively with abundant water.
Solonchak	Heavy in soluble salts, these soils form in subhumid to arid areas under sparse vegetation tolerant of salinity. Nevertheless, with abundant water soundly drained, farmers can intensively crop this land.
Solonetz	Ranging from the subhumid to the semi-arid and from cool to tropical climates, these soils have light to dark surface layers lying over hard, alkaline, prismatic, clayey soil and commonly

TABLE 2.2 THE GREAT SOIL GROUPS *(cont.)*

Classification	Characteristics
	form within other soil areas in small areas from under an acre up to around 10 acres. They can be reclaimed by integrating them with surrounding soils.
Soloth	These soils have light-colored surface layers lying over more clayey subsoils of dark brown under grasses, which may be mixed with trees. They also appear in limited areas, from 2 to 10 acres, and can be consolidated into surrounding soils.
Sols Bruns Acides	These are brown, acidy soils of nearly uniform texture for 2 to 3 feet below forests in cool-temperate climates. Level areas, if fertilized, are suitable for many grains, vegetables, and forage.
Subarctic Brown Forest	Forming below trees, these soils are dark gray or brown, acidy, and cool when deeper than 18 inches. Though the surface is covered erratically by permafrost, short-season crops will grow in some areas, but they are used mostly for browse for Arctic animals.
Terra Rossa	These are reddish-brown, calcareous, friable loams (soils with about equal mixtures of sand and silt and somewhat less clay), generally lying over hard limestone; most are around the Mediterranean. Except where shallow, stony, or eroded, they are good for olives, grapes, and several other crops.
Tundra	Dark brown and peaty, most tundra soils are underlain with gley (a grayish or bluish soil) and penetrated by permafrost, too cold for crops. But they support low shrubbery and mosses in cold, humid areas; and where slopes face the sun, farmers can harvest a few short-season grasses and food crops.
Yellowish-brown Lateritic	These soils form in humid temperate to tropical areas, and are friable. Unless hilly or stony, they can be intensively cultivated with water control and fertilizing.

In *The Soils That Support Us,* Kellog classifies the great soil groups in the United States into "broad associations," each of which includes several soils that "make up a distinctive pattern, or broad landscape."

1. The light-colored leached soils—mostly Podzols with Lithosols, Bog, and Half Bog—in the northern forested areas.

2. Leached soils of the high mountains with thin soils on the slopes and various soils in the neighboring valleys—Podzolics, Lithosols, Brown, Chestnut, and Chernozem—in the West and Northwest.

3. The grayish-brown and brown leached soils of temperate forested regions of the Northeast, mid-Atlantic, and central Midwest—mostly Gray-brown Podzolic with Brown Podzolic in the eastern part, and Alluvial, Bog, and Half Bog in the southwestern part.

4. The red and yellow leached soils of the warm-temperature forested areas with poorly drained soils of the coastal plains and Alluvial soils of the lower Mississippi Valley—mostly Red-yellow Podzolic with Ground-water Podzol—which stretch from the mid- and south Atlantic coastline into Texas and from the Gulf coast northward into Iowa.

5. The red and grayish-brown leached soils of the northwestern forests with much hilly or stony land—Red and Gray-brown Podzolic and Lithosols with some Alluvial and other soils.

6. The dark-colored soils of the comparatively humid temperate grasslands and some nearly black, poorly drained soils and some light-colored soils on steep slopes—Alluvial and Gray-brown Podzolic, with a few other soils—which lie across the heartland of the Midwest.

7. The dark reddish-brown soils of the relatively humid warm-temperate grasslands with some black and some light-colored soils —Reddish Prairie, Rendzina, Red-yellow Podzolic, and Alluvial —in a belt from Kansas down through Oklahoma to the tip of Texas.

8. The dark-colored soils of the subhumid temperate grasslands —mostly Chernozem—from the Canadian border through the eastern Dakotas, Nebraska, Kansas, and western Minnesota.

9. The dark reddish-brown soils of subhumid warm-temperate grasslands, some of it hilly—mostly Reddish Chestnut with some Lithosols—largely in central and northwestern Texas, western Oklahoma, and southern Kansas.

10. Dark-colored to light-brown soils of the California valley

and coastal mountains—Chernozem, Chestnut, Reddish Chestnut, Desert, Alluvial, and Lithosols.

11. The dark-colored to light-brown soils of the Northwest, especially Washington—Chernozem, Prairie Chestnut, and Brown, with some Lithosols.

12. The brown to dark-brown soils of the semi-arid grasslands, with some hilly and sandy soils and badlands—mostly Chestnut and Brown soils, with some Lithosols—stretching from the North to the Central Plains, through eastern Montana, Wyoming, Colorado, the western Dakotas, Nebraska, and Kansas, into northern Texas.

13. The grayish soils of the arid West and Northwest with the soils of arid and semi-arid mountains and their slopes—mostly Sierozem or Gray Desert soils with much Lithosol and some Brown Chestnut and Alluvial—which make up nearly all of Nevada and Utah and are also found in southeastern Oregon and southern Idaho.

14. The grayish soils of the arid and semi-arid intermountain plateaus and valleys—also mostly Sierozem or Gray Desert and Brown, with some Lithosols—largely in eastern Utah and western Wyoming.

15. Reddish soils of the arid to semi-arid Southwest—Red Desert, Reddish-Brown, Noncalcic Brown, and Lithosols—which stretch from southern California through southwestern Texas.

16. The brown to reddish-brown soils of the semi-arid southern high mountain plateaus and valleys—Brown, Chestnut, Lithosol, and Desert—which are largely in Arizona.

3

The Capricious Forces—Climate and Weather

Though it operates within parameters set by other factors—sloping, drainage, technology, and pollution—climate, more than any other single factor, determines which plants will grow in which soil. Meteorologists have divided the climates of the world into five major zones. In order of size, they are the tropical zone (covering 37.7 percent of the earth), cool-temperate zone (22.1 percent), the warm-temperate subtropical zone (21 percent), the cool-temperate boreal zone (15 percent), and the polar and subpolar zones (4.2 percent).

The most vast—the tropical—covers more than half of all presently arable land. Most of this zone lies abreast of the equator, extending 20° to the north and south of it, and some is found at low altitudes beyond. There are few, if any, seasonal variations of temperature, which is generally high enough for continuous cropping, but uneven moisture supply frequently restricts cultivation. In some areas, excessive rains during the wet season leave the land gutted, and, during the dry season, the soil is scorched hard and salinated. Other land receives so little rain and lies over such low water tables that it is desert.

The cool-temperate zone, though it covers only one-third of all arable land and is not productive in winter, nonetheless has enormous importance. It produces the great exportable surpluses, particularly of grains and increasingly of soybeans. The growing season is long enough for farmers to plant a wide range of crops, and often two or more crops are planted to the same field during the same year, since certain cool-season species will mature during the spring and fall. The cool-temperate zone lies mostly in the Northern Hemisphere, largely between 35° and 55° of latitude, and includes the United States, the southern half of Canada, most of Europe, the southern Soviet provinces, and northern China. Temperatures and precipitations differ widely, but in more than half of this zone rain-fed farming is profitable. In the other half, supplementary irrigation is needed to broaden the choice of crops or, in places, to permit more than grazing.

Though the warm-temperate subtropical zone covers about the same total acreage as the temperate, only about 17 percent of it is arable. This climate covers two bands of land that lie between 20° and 35° of latitude in the Northern and Southern Hemispheres. During most of the year, temperatures are high enough for food crops, but soil fertility is often low, and many of the great deserts are in this zone.

The cold-temperate boreal zone extends from the northern limits of the cool-temperate zone toward the North Pole. It includes only 1.5 percent of all arable land, although it encompasses nearly a seventh of the world land mass. Arable land within this zone is mainly in small coastal enclaves where temperatures, moderated by the sea, rise sufficiently for forage and cool-season crops. The temperate season is brief, and the nights are cold, but the days are long around the summer solstice and intense solar radiation stimulates exuberant plant growth. Recent studies by Alaskan agriculturists suggest that more land is tillable in this and other parts of the subpolar region than was previously thought.

The polar and subpolar zones surround the two poles and also include high elevations at other latitudes, even near the Equator. Covering merely 4.3 percent of the land surface, these areas sustain little other than lichens, mosses, and tussock grasses. These are sufficient forage for caribou, musk oxen, and perhaps reindeer.

Based on the number of months that farmers can crop each year, there are thirty-three types of climate within these five great zones. Agronomists have regrouped them into seventeen agro-climatic regions, combining characteristics of soil and climate. For example, if either the temperatures are immoderate or the moisture sparse for four months of each year, the region is classified as an eight-month agro-climatic region. Of the approximately 8 billion acres of arable land on our planet, nearly one-sixth (1.2 billion acres) can produce crops throughout the year without irrigation, while a little over one-twentieth (430 million acres) can be cultivated for eight months. Nearly one-fourth receives enough moisture for six months, and in just over one-fourth, low temperatures prevent cropping during most, if not all, months.

Although most of us use the words *climate* and *weather* interchangeably, they are not synonymous. Weather refers to the various atmospheric phenomena, the most important of which are temperature and moisture; while climate is the average weather. For a certain crop within a specific area, average measures may be meaningless—especially the average temperature in temperate zones and the average rainfall in the tropics. On the American North Plains, daytime temperatures may simmer around 100° in summer and sink to 50° below zero during winter cold spells. By the same token, an average temperature for a twenty-four-hour day is uninstructive if it disguises searing middays and overnight frosts, which occur in some mountain valleys and on high plateaus.

Similarly, in the humid tropics, torrential rains during the wet seasons may restrict cropping, and in the arid tropics a short showery season does not appreciably alter desert conditions. Type of rainfall is also significant, for a drizzle of one-half inch of rain seeping into the soil is much more helpful to crops than a cloudburst. And, of course, weather defies climatic averages by varying from one year to another, bringing droughts to normally humid areas and floods to arid ones—which is why a Danish proverb holds that one should ask not how the harvest outlook is but how the weather has been.

Other climatic factors affect agriculture, too. Variations in pressure bring on winds which may influence the form of moisture and where it falls. Where there are high hills or mountains, the windward side is likely to receive more rain than the leeward. And the behavior patterns of air over land and sea masses have an even greater effect. Over much of Asia, for example, winds blow in from the seas for six months of the year, bringing on the monsoon rains; for the rest of the year, they blow from over the mountainous land and are likely to be dry.

The Sun

Both the length and quality of daylight are critical for plants. Day length is generally a function of latitude and season, in the equatorial band where it is virtually always about twelve hours. Over the polar regions, on the other hand, the sun never sets around the summer solstice and never rises around the winter solstice. At latitudes of 50°, there are about sixteen hours of daylight in summer and only half as much in winter. In the Northern Hemisphere, this latitude roughly traverses the American-Canadian border, mid-Europe, the Ukraine, and the Manchurian and Mongolian frontiers. It crosses much less land in the Southern Hemisphere, falling south of Africa and Australia but touching the tip of Argentina. The long summer days over so much fertile soil in the Northern Hemisphere compensate for the short growing season.

The quality of insolation, or radiation from the sun received by the earth, varies according to latitude, season, humidity, the density of cloud cover, soil conditions, and atmospheric pollutants; the intensity of solar energy also depends upon the angle at which its rays strike. Normally, the more humid the air, the less heat it transmits.

Moisture

The most common cause of low crop yields is poor water supply. In choosing to grow a crop, it is important to consider when the rains fall, how reliably, and in what form. Although plants usually need frequent moisture, they do not necessarily need it regularly; the intervals depend on the stage of growth and solar radiation. For example, when the fruit is swelling, a plant needs plenty of water; after the fruit has ripened, a lot of water may be injurious. Driving rain or hail may knock seed from the soil, batter seedlings to the ground, or bruise maturing fruits; heavy rainfall at harvest time may interfere with machinery.

In the United States, about 40 percent of rainfall is normally taken up by surface soil, 20 percent filters into aquifers and underground streams, 25 percent runs off quickly, and about 15 percent is lost through evapotranspiration. How much moisture is lost by a specific land area depends on the volume of rain, the rate of fall, the degree of humidity, the density of vegetative cover, the topography and condition of the soil, and the extent of urbanization.

Although rain is the chief source of moisture, other forms of moisture can at times—especially snowmelt and dew—be as important. An old Russian proverb says, "Corn is as comfortable under the snow as an old man in a fur coat." Although the soil becomes cold during winters in temperate zones, it rarely freezes under good snow cover, which blocks the penetration of frost and also keeps it from drying out too much. Snow is also a form of water storage, from which moisture is released gradually by the sun or warm breezes of springtime. If the surface layers of the soil have frozen, however, the warmth of the deeper layers must radiate upward to thaw them, otherwise the snowmelt may run off rather than filter down. The glacial snows of the highlands and mountain ranges may constitute another natural reservoir, for when they thaw, they feed water into lowland streams and rivers.

One form of moisture that is always unwelcome is hail, and in the United States, only Florida, southern Texas, and the West Coast are usually free of it. Other areas are pelted one to eight days a year, and the central Great Plains and western intermountain region are hit most often. Grain farmers are particularly afraid of hail just before and during harvest, when the laden stalks are so vulnerable that losses can be total.

Only 6 percent of all available water is not salty or otherwise unsuitable for agricultural use—a remarkably small amount when we think that 71 percent of the world's surface is water. Although Americans are so conditioned to the free availability of water that we practically throw it away (five gallons of purified water is used each time a toilet is flushed), the supply of water is limited. Dr. William G. Pollard, director of the Oak Ridge Universities (a group of southern universities working with the Atomic Energy

Commission), has concluded that the world might feed a population of up to 10 billion but for the fact that the means of supplying the necessary water "are simply not in sight."

In the United States, agriculture is the largest consumer of water, consumption meaning the use of water so that it does not immediately return to the ground or surface. For every gallon consumed in urban areas, farming uses nearly six. Agriculture uses at least half of the water consumed in thirteen of the seventeen water regions of the mainland states, and it sometimes uses nearly all of it. Most of the 121 billion gallons used agriculturally in 1971 went for irrigation, and it is projected that by the turn of the century this requirement will reach 153 billion gallons. Actually, we receive sufficient water through rainfall—thirty inches a year, or 4.2 trillion gallons—to meet greater needs, but the problem is managing it economically, efficiently, and equitably. For example, Alaska receives almost half as much precipitation as all the mainland states combined, and that constitutes the largest amount of unused water in the country.

Managing Moisture

Primitive people adapted to the natural availability of water by settling near rivers and lakes; gradually they learned to divert, store, and distribute water according to their needs. Irrigating was the greatest agricultural advance after the domestication of crops and animals.

Pre-Columbian Indians in the American Southwest understood water tables and planted their crops by streams where they knew the roots could reach underground moisture. They also built small dams to retain water and drainways to distribute it over their fields. The Mexican and Peruvian Indians, the Mesopotamians, the Egyptians, and ancient Asians also developed irrigation. About 4,000 years ago, Middle Bronze Age communities cleared hillsides of rocks and gravel and smoothed surface soils to increase runoff, which they channeled through contour ditches in low-lying fields. In the Indus Valley, archeologists have uncovered water-storage tanks that are 5,000 years old. The Romans built aqueducts, some of which are still in use.

One of the most sophisticated of the early systems was designed by the Nabataens in the middle of the Negev Desert between the second century B.C. and the second century A.D. The greatest farmers of their time, they conserved rainfall by diverting it from large areas into cisterns, and they practiced a kind of primitive cloud seeding. They did this by stacking flintstones to make channels that would cool the night winds; as the winds cooled over the channels, they shed dew, which trickled to become concentrated runoff and was guided toward small areas of deep, absorbent soils.

The decision a farmer faces in water management involves several questions: Should he irrigate at all, and if he should, when should he bring in the water? If it rains while he is irrigating, how much can he reduce the flow? Also, is the moisture application uniform? But irrigation is not for water alone; it may also be for cooling when the weather turns too hot for his crop.

Early systems of irrigation did not supply large areas and often failed to control salinity. Later schemes faltered because soil evaluations were faulty—some desert soils, for example, either were too salty or became saline under irrigation; others were too sandy, with rapid loss of moisture and nutrients. The rapid enlargement of projects began around 1880, and the United States has been a leader in big-scale irrigation.

The Mormons developed cooperative irrigation in much of Utah as well as in parts of Arizona, Colorado, Idaho, Nevada, and New Mexico. Their sound planning and cooperative effort proved that making the desert bloom was no quixotic vision. Farmers in the generously rain-fed regions could clear a plot, put up a dwelling, and in one season reap a harvest; desert farmers first had to collaborate in engineering designs and in the construction of reservoir dams, diversion canals, and drainage ditches. Their achievements led the way to converting such areas as the San Joaquin Valley of California and the Mexicali Valley in Baja into some of the most productive croplands in the world.

The best-known American scheme is under the Tennessee Valley Authority (TVA), whose main thrusts, however, were rural electrification and flood control. Actually, the direct agricultural significance of the TVA is arguable, for while it protected 110,-000 acres from flooding, its reservoirs inundated over 600,000 acres, much of it fertile farmland. In the West, the trend has been toward ever-larger dams, such as the 726-foot-high Hoover Dam which stores up to 31 million acre-feet of water in Lake Mead.

What so far is the ultimate in water management is the California State Water Project, which features canals as broad as large rivers, tunnels as wide as two-lane highways, nuclear reactors that power pumps to lift water 2,000 feet over the Tehachapi Mountains and controls to release water at up to twenty-four levels at temperatures cool enough for downstream spawning fish in the fall and warm enough for the farmers' crops in the spring. In the next century, when it will be operating at full capacity, the project will comprise 21 dams and reservoirs, 22 pumping plants, and 685 miles of canals, tunnels, and pipelines. It will prospectively open another quarter of a million acres to cultivation as well as relieve areas where aquifer levels have dropped. Constructed at a cost of around $11 billion, its capability of releasing water at varying temperatures and quantities prompted an engineer to quip, "It is the most expensive water faucet in history."

One of nature's systems for managing moisture is the *watershed*, the region or area drained by a stream, or, in an agricultural context, the area above the diversion or storage point for farm water supplies. The latest national inventory of conservation needs, published in 1971, revealed that nearly 9,000 watersheds needed protection and development. A naturally sound watershed conserves and directs the flows of water; when it is out of kilter it becomes destructive, causing erosion, silting, and flooding. In 1953 the federal government initiated a watershed management program under the Bureau of Land Management in the Department of Interior; tens of millions of acres are now affected. The projects involve dams, usually small ones, levees to restrain flood waters, and improvement of stream channels. Experiments have been conducted with new technologies, including the trapping of rainfall or snowmelt in nylon-reinforced mats acting like giant water bags; chemical treatment of ponds to prevent seepage by sealing the undersoils; draining water from potholes into aquifers; deep plowing to increase penetrability; and reducing the permeability of other soils with vegetation, sheeting, subterranean pavement, or chemical compounds.

What makes watershed management of special importance is the extent to which American agriculture relies entirely or mainly on natural moisture. It is called *dryland farming*, actually a misnomer since it is really rain-fed farming. Great Plains farmers practice dryland farming widely because it is more economical; it will continue to be so unless prices of farm products make more irrigation profitable. But dryland farming can be excessively costly in undesirable ecological side effects. A Montana dryland wheat rancher, Dick O'Day, has figured that by irrigating and planting to Gaines wheat, he could increase his harvest eightfold, but the price of wheat has been too low (at least until 1973) to compensate for piping in the water. Another factor is the greater recognition that high dams, huge reservoirs, and broad canals can also produce these undesirable side effects.

An early writer on this type of agriculture was Hardy Webster Campbell, a Vermonter who homesteaded in the Dakota Territory. He advised that the root bed be "plowed reasonably deep" and packed "fine and firm," so that it would retain more water. After the great drought of the 1880s, Campbell invented a subsoil packer for this function. In 1884, a dryland farming experiment station was established at Cheyenne Well, Colorado, and the drought spurred a global search for varieties tolerant to aridity.

Many areas of the earth cover large reservoirs and stream beds, which we can tap as we drill for oil; they are one of our greatest and yet least utilized natural resources. But exploitation of underground water is being studied more closely. It may be less expensive than the grandiose irrigation schemes, and there are also fewer feasible dam sites. Lying under the vast Gangetic Plain encompassing nearly a fourth of India is an aquifer larger than any surface lake in the world, nearly double the size of the Caspian Sea and over three times the area covered by all the Great Lakes. Aquifers have been located below the Sahara Desert, and some experts speculate that the Egyptians would have been better advised to develop their underground water than to build the Aswan High Dam.

Widespread areas with underground water exist in the United States, including much of the Atlantic seaboard from Rhode Island to the Carolinas, Alabama, Arkansas, and Louisiana in the South, and Kansas, Nebraska, Illinois, Michigan, and Wisconsin in the Midwest. In some semi-arid areas, such as eastern Colorado, pumps for deep wells are connected to sprinkler systems which are mounted on wheels and are a quarter of a mile long. By rotating around a well like the hand of a giant clock, the sprinkler can water as many as 125 acres. What has been described as one of the most outstanding water-bearing formations in the world lies under the desert of southern Idaho, a huge body of basalt fed from the surrounding Rocky Mountains. Geologists believe that as many as 250 million acre-feet of water may be stored there, about eight times as much as held by the largest man-made lake in the country, Lake Mead. Yet, in 1973, aquifer water was drawn to irrigate only about 640,000 acres of Idaho cropland— though trout farmers using springs from it produce 5 million to 7 million rainbows annually.

The drawback to heavy usage is the consumption of water more quickly than it is replenished; experimenters have developed ways of reducing evaporation on nearby soils and speeding seepage of rainfall to the water table. Near the sea, there may be an interface between fresh and salt or brackish water; this can result in the loss of fresh water to the salt water or to the inland encroachment of saline moisture. Israeli engineers have stabilized the interface by pumping fresh water back into aquifers that are being depleted, a sort of recycling and storage approach using the natural underground reservoir. When the freshwater presses toward the sea, they capture some of it for storage elsewhere. These techniques may become important if American water shortages continue, for it has been estimated that two-thirds of the United States is underlain with brackish water, including underground tidal rivers.

To increase usable water supplies, futurists have dreamed of desalination, "harvesting" fresh water from the oceans, salt seas, and brackish estuaries. So far, costs has been the barrier. In San Diego, California, for example, water traditionally cost 35 to 40 cents a gallon; railing it to the San Joaquin Valley raised its cost to $7 a gallon. In 1967, desalting in that area cost $1.40 a gallon, uneconomical for the city but more worthwhile for the valley farmers. Key West, Florida, and some other areas resolve the cost-effectiveness issue by installing dual water systems, in which desalinated water is used after conventional sources have been exhausted. The Egyptians around Alexandria need seven inches of rainfall annually, but receive six inches, so they pay a high price for the additional inch required. In American agriculture, desalination is beginning to have another useful application: restoring and maintaining the natural proportion of salt in normal fresh waters in both rivers and aquifers.

When UN Secretary-General Kurt Waldheim proclaimed 1975 as International Water Development Year, he suggested that a usable water supply will become a more acute problem than food supply. By the turn of the century, a water crisis more serious than the 1973 fuel crisis will have changed people's attitude toward "free" water. We will have to treat water much more carefully, monitoring it continuously to maintain quality standards.

Historical Cycles of Change

Though climate is defined as "average" weather, these averages have not been constant historically. Quite the contrary, and the world food problem has enlivened interest in climatology, the study of long-term weather conditions—a branch of meteorology once considered dull. American long-range forecasters refer to a twenty-year drought cycle; there was the Dust Bowl in the early thirties, a recurrence in the fifties, and some believe we are about due for another drought. They also recall that when the "forty-niners" trekked to California, they went through head-high grass where the land is now near-desert.

Even more ominous is a view that global climate is undergoing a considerable change. For nearly half of this century, mankind has enjoyed the most benign climate in at least a millennium—a respite from "the little ice age" that began in 1600, and for at least 700,000 years world mean temperatures have been as high only 5 percent of the time. This warming trend began about 1890 and peaked in 1945; since that time, mean temperature has dropped about 2.7 degrees F. This apparently slight drop, however, reduced Iceland's hay yield by one-fourth, caused a southward movement of ice floes impeding fishing in certain northern waters for the first time in this century, and cut the average growing season in England by two weeks. Hubert Lamb, a British meteorologist who heads Europe's main climatic research organization, believes this is "the longest unbroken trend downward in hundreds of years."

This change also alters the planetary system of integrated winds and rainfall, and may underlie not only the persistent Sahelian drought, but what is beginning to appear as a semipermanent swath of aridity from Central America, to the Middle East, and into India. The descending dry air has pushed farther south, and its pressure has blocked the moisture-laden monsoon winds from the otherwise arid grazing lands. The wet monsoons, in turn, have dropped their moisture instead in regions already with an excess of rainfall or into the sea. If this trend persists, expanding deserts, including the Sahara, southward, then the building of tree fences or irrigation systems will be to no avail. "If it continues," says Reid Bryson, director of the Institute of Environmental Studies at the University of Wisconsin, it "will affect the whole human occupation of the earth—like a billion people starving."

The American grain belt is likely to be less seriously affected. But James McQuigg, a climatologist at the University of Missouri, who has related crop yields of the past century to each year's weather, concludes that the great increases of the last fifteen years have been due at least as much to favorable temperatures and rainfall as to improved varieties and other technology. "The probability of getting another fifteen consecutive years that good," he says, "is about one in 10,000." *Fortune*, which reported extensively on these phenomena in February 1974 said, "From the evidence found in such things as sea-floor sediments, peat bogs, and tree rings, the earth's long-term climatological history has been as full of rallies and plunges as the stock market. . . . There's fair agreement among researchers that the earth is now heading very slowly into another major ice age such as the one that brought the glaciers deep into North America . . . 10,000 years ago."

Other climatologists are more sanguine. J. Murray Mitchell, Jr., of the National Oceanic and Atmospheric Administration, says, "We observe these trends in the Northern Hemisphere. . . .

But we can't find the central tendency of the trends or know how long they will last." He suggests that the cooling trend will be naturally reversed, possibly aided, paradoxically, by the "greenhouse effect" caused by carbon dioxide from the burning of fossil fuels. (Its molecules trap heat, converted from light by the earth and reradiated.)

Prediction and Control

One of man's earliest scientific endeavors was trying to predict the weather but, until recently, he still relied on cloud formations, bird flights, insect behavior, sunset colors, the stars, and feelings in his joints. Folklore is full of predictive counsel, toward which the World Meteorological Organization takes a benign if cautious view:

> Most weather traditions which have entered into the folklore of nations are in fact the results of generations of outdoor experience. They cannot be lightly rejected nor can they on the other hand be regarded as beyond suspicion. The wise farmer combines his own knowledge with the official advice and tries to make the best of both worlds.

Nor are our most modern forecasting techniques beyond suspicion, as sudden and unexpected hurricane disasters remind us. Often enough, a weather broadcaster incorrectly describes present conditions, and only the very trusting fully believe what they say. Some years ago, in fact, the president of a television network issued a directive that no forecast would be aired until the announcer had looked out the window.

Forecasts, especially the short-range forecasts provided airline pilots, have become increasingly accurate. The farmer, who really requires a forecast for an entire growing season or perhaps even a year, can nonetheless be helped by the meteorologist in his short-term planning, since the vagaries of the weather affect every phase of agriculture from preparing a seedbed to shipping a harvest. When meteorologists spot an air mass moving southward from the Arctic, for example, an alerted fruit grower in

Florida may run irrigation or fire heaters to counter it. Or if severe cold threatens, growers may lay on extra crews to harvest early.

There are both physical and statistical approaches to weather forecasting. The first requires an understanding of equations governing complex atmospheric processes, which can be applied to current conditions. It is called *hydrodynamic numerical modeling*, and it is the technique used by the government in its daily forecasts. The statistical method involves searching past weather records for patterns that may predictably repeat themselves.

The federal government became involved in forecasting for farmers in 1872, when Congress directed the meteorological branch of the Army Signal Corps to add "such additional stations, reports, and signals as may be necessary for the benefit of Agriculture and Commercial interests." The Corps began issuing a *Weekly Weather Chronicle*, and although it lapsed after nine years, it was revived in 1884 as the *Weather Crop Bulletin*, and has since been published under various names. Subsequently, the U.S. Weather Bureau was established. It is now known as the National Weather Service and is a part of the National Oceanographic and Atmospheric Administration of the Department of Commerce.

Today, weather experts and crop statisticians issue the *Weekly Weather & Crop Bulletin*, a summary of the national crop and livestock situation plus a weather forecast. These are based on reports by more than 13,000 weather observers, most of them volunteers, by county agricultural extension agents, and by state climatologists. Further information comes from radar-scanning balloons bearing radiosondes, ships at sea, ground observation stations, and weather satellites. The National Meteorological Center receives state reports, and specialists compile a national survey within twenty-four hours. Among factors covered are temperature, rainfall, percentage of the season's crop planted or harvested during the previous week, crop conditions in the field, quality of the harvest, drought or flood conditions, state of pasture, and condition of the livestock. The bulletin also features maps indicating crop moisture, precipitation, and temperature for the previous week; a thirty-day forecast; a projection of the average number of days that thunderstorms are expected; and the total "growing degree days." Timely articles on pests, irrigation, and shipping are included as well.

Across rural America, radio and television broadcast forecasts for up to five days, while newspapers publish weather outlooks for a month. For longer-range planning, there are studies based on weather records of nearly a century. Special needs of farmers are often provided for locally by private weather services. In the mid-1960s, the Department of Commerce set up the National Agricultural Weather Service Program, often called the Agricultural Weather Wire Service, which distributes forecasts in twenty-one states. Weather advisories and zone forecasts may be put out three times a day and a farm weather summary for the next thirty-six hours once a day. A recent Purdue University survey showed that farmers assigned the highest value to spring weather information and found weather advisories especially helpful when they were harvesting or haying, preparing the soil, and spraying. In Chico, California, when frost threatens the fruit-and-nut producers in seven surrounding counties, a radio station stays on the air all night to receive phone reports of changes in the wind, temperature, and cloud cover. The station's weather experts then construct a pattern of air movements, which enables them to estimate where and when the frost will strike.

The present goal of the weather services is to forecast reliably for two weeks, but the unexpected ravages of Hurricane Camille in a West Virginia valley in 1962 was an example of failure of local, short-term predicting. There were several parallel valleys in this region and, had the rain swept over them all, the fall in each would have been fairly light. But the downpour was concentrated on only one valley—an unlikely pattern—and the precipitation gauges were too far apart to signal the buildup of the deluge. A forecasting expert at the Massachusetts Institute of Technology, Frederick Sanders, concludes that it "can never be exact. We must forever see through a glass darkly."

More attention has been paid recently to the statistical approach to forecasting. Three Massachusetts Institute of Technology scientists, Donald B. DeVorkin, John T. Prohaska, and Hurd C. Willett, recently reported relationships between atmospheric pressures in some areas and temperatures in other areas one to twelve months later. They also claim to have found correlations between average temperatures in some areas and precipitation in others during the same month. By 1970, their five- to six-month predictions were more accurate than the thirty-day forecasts of the Weather Service and much better than those of the *Farmer's Almanac.*

The device with the greatest potential for improving forecasts is probably the weather satellite. For the first time, we are receiving photographs and measurements of atmospheric conditions which we previously could largely only guess at. It is too soon to tell, but even the satellites may be most valuable for forecasts of five to ten days, and the two-week goal remains for this decade. Improved forecasting will require computers at least a hundred times as fast as those in use to process the data we are now receiving. We must also increase our understanding of several crucial atmospheric processes and cover much more of the earth's area by satellite than the 20 percent being covered in 1970.

Weather Modification

It used to be known as "rainmaking," but the calling attracted charlatans and consequently lacked respectability. The term "weather control" was substituted, but that had an ominous nuance; now we call it "modification." Although most frequently applied to rain, weather-modification attempts have also been made to increase snowfall, suppress hail, disperse fog, dilute hurricanes and tornadoes, and abate lightning.

Flaming smudge pots have been used for years to circulate warm air just above the ground to prevent the descent of frosty air, and today wind machines are designed for the same purpose. Covering the ground with mulch, which consists of straw, leaves, manure, or similar matter, also protects against unseasonal cold. Irrigation alters weather by reducing the rate of temperature changes and increasing humidity; and plastic shelters, recycled moisture, and temperature control, which maintain a certain micro-climate, may make the traditional greenhouse the Model T of weather modification.

Broad-scale interference with weather cycles raises legal, social, and moral questions, for modification in one area may have unwanted effects in another. If Oklahoma waits for rain from clouds forming over Kansas, and Kansas drains them before they can reach Oklahoma, are rights violated? Should weather modification be used as a weapon of war, as the United States did in Southeast Asia during the late 1960s? Aside from these questions, will interference with the weather have ecological side effects? In some places, altered ecosystems have already created hospitable micro-environments for pests not normally prevalent, and we may not be aware of other such reactions for years.

The central practical question, however, remains: At best, is modification worthwhile? In 1973, the National Academy of Sciences pointed up the uncertainties:

> The panel now concludes on the basis of statistical analysis of well-designed field experiments that ice-nuclei seeding can sometimes lead to more precipitation, can sometimes lead to less precipitation, and at other times the nuclei have no effect, depending on the meteorological conditions.

The panel chairman, Thomas F. Malone of the University of Connecticut, reported that "progress has been made during the past few years," but much more slowly than had been hoped for.

The most successful work has been the seeding of winter clouds over mountains to stimulate greater snowfall, but efforts to stimulate heavier rainfall have faltered, apparently because of timing. Progress in altering severe storms has been made without legal or political repercussions because these storms are usually localized; far-reaching effects have not been obvious. Climatologists have reduced the force and size of hail and have modified thunderstorms that could evolve into systems spinning off tornadoes. And Project Stormfury has produced data, though meager, indicating that hurricane winds may be reducible.

According to the National Academy of Sciences, there are three goals of weather-modification activities that are clearly in the public interest. They include the establishment of moisture modification on a firm basis by 1980, the development of methods of mitigating weather hazards, and the determination of the extent to which man is inadvertently altering weather and climate.

4

The Most Ancient Survivors–Insects and Other Pests

Pests damage about one-fourth of the food grown in America, and one-third to well over one-half in much of the rest of the world. India, according to Chidambaram Subramaniam, the Industrial Development Minister, "is losing a minimum of 10 percent of grains during storage and by insects, rodents, fungi, and fire each year . . . a minimum of about 10 million tons—a little more than the amount by which we fall short of our needs." This is food enough for 50 million Indians for one year. The most injurious pests have been insects; as the Old Testament puts it, "The almond tree shall flourish and the grasshopper shall be a burden" (Ecclesiastes 12:4). Farmers evolved means of controlling them often with notable success, until the last decade when there were significant indications that we were retrogressing.

Insects

Insects dominated the earth over 300 million years before man emerged and 100 million years before the earliest known fossil mammals. The earliest fossil insect found is a springtail named

Colembola that was discovered in Scotland and lived about 370 million years ago in the middle Devonian period. As forestation spread, insects increased in response to the vastly increased food supply; they evolved with aggressive flexibility, learning early to seek the protective embrace of the environment. Recognizable modern species evolved about 25 million years ago, predating man by over 24 million years. When man emerged, he claimed a niche in an ecosystem in which insects were ensconced, and they competed for food. A typical insect eats 100 times its weight daily, a voraciousness that, if unchecked, would defoliate the earth; yet the insect, too, is a link in the food chain.

Entomologists estimate that there are at least 3 million, and perhaps as many as 10 million, species of insects, of which we have discovered nearly a million. There are more than three times as many insect species as there are species of all other animals combined, and at any instant about 100 billion individual insects are living. At least 2.5 million species of insects do not exist in the United States, of which about 6,000 are known to be damaging areas similar to parts of America. In all of North America there are about 80,000 known insect species; of those in the United States, about 10,000 are potentially injurious. About 1,115 species arrived as undesirable aliens, of which 212 do about half of the insect damage done to crops and horticultural plants. In the early 1970s, this comparative handful destroyed some $13 billion worth of crops annually and $1.2 billion in stored grain, even though $2 billion a year was spent on insect control.

The major American insect pests include several beetles that eat leaves, some true bugs (a suborder of insects) that inject toxins when sucking plant juices, loopers that ravage leaves, aphids that suck sap, leaf miners that tunnel and stunt growth, cutworms that slice plant stems, mealybugs that hide inside fruit trees, leafhoppers that suck sap from the underside of leaves and can inject toxins or transmit viral diseases, mites that are not really insects but arachnids like spiders, and both armored and soft scales that inhabit bark, stems, or leaves, and are so named because they are often covered by a waxy secretion or tough substance after attacking a plant.

The most spectacular damage to our food supply is probably done by the locust, of which there are 10,000 kinds. They build up periodically into huge populations that migrate en masse, leaving a swath of barren fields. In Africa and southwestern Asia, columns of desert locusts (*Schistocera gregaria*) migrate over 9 million square miles, covering some 60 countries.

Like armies, locusts travel "on their bellies," and a medium-size swarm may ravage 3,000 tons of food each day; a migrating swarm may enlarge to 1 billion individuals deployed over more than 200 square miles. The largest swarm on record, which flew over the Red Sea in 1889, covered an estimated 2,000 miles and weighed nearly half a million tons. In Ethiopia one summer, locusts ate over 100,000 tons of grains.

The Animal-Plant Health Inspection Service of the Department of Agriculture maintains a surveillance over infestations, which it terms severe if there are more than eight grasshoppers (they are locusts) or crickets per square yard of rangeland. Six to seven grasshoppers per square yard over a ten-acre area will eat as much in a season as one grazing animal.

Rodents and Other Animals

In many areas, rodents, especially rats, are major pests. AID specialist Nels Konnerup once reported from Asia, "In some grain fields where rat densities reach a high level, standing grain is literally trampled to the ground." Rats feed on grain, vegetables, and meat, and cause fires by gnawing at insulation of electric wires—it has been estimated that up to 25 percent of farm fires of unknown origin are caused by rats. They contaminate food with their droppings, urine, and fallen hair, and they carry salmonella, rat tapeworm, murine typhus, and bubonic plague. Food in storage, transport, or processing is especially vulnerable. The Center for Disease Control in Atlanta estimates that the American rat population is about 100 million and that each rat consumes $1 to $10 worth of food, feed, and other matter per year, bringing the total dollar value of damage up to $1 billion. When food supplies become more plentiful, the females bear and keep alive more young. The Norway rat (*Rattus norvegicus*), which is the most common and largest of American rats, produces litters of eight to twelve pups four to seven times a year.

Midwestern corn fields near bodies of water are prey to raccoons, and field mice have, on occasion, all but wiped out California avocado harvests. Rabbits, gophers, squirrels, and weasles, under certain conditions, can be damaging.

Birds

The worst pest in the bird world is the African Quelea-quelea, a member of the finch family. It is popularly known as the locust bird because it travels in swarms that seemingly descend from nowhere; when small grains ripen, it can leave wide fields barren. An estimated 3 billion locust birds are in Africa; they have no natural enemies, and no economic means of control has been devised.

The fear that such a bird might populate other areas is well founded; what some say is the most disliked bird in North America, the starling, which attacks fruit and transmits a disease through its droppings, is now the most numerous—in some areas, it outnumbers people two-to-one. The starling was imported from Europe in 1890 and released with dozens of other foreign species in the expectation that it would be beneficial, which it sometimes is. Other birds that can be damaging are blackbirds, crows, magpies, and sparrows.

Recently monk or Quaker parakeets (*Myiopsitta monachus*), of which 50,000 were brought in from South America as exotic pets, have escaped or been let loose, and they proved so adaptable that they have migrated into twenty-two states, from the Northeast to Virginia and to North Dakota. A native of Argentina, parakeets thrive also in Brazil, Bolivia, Paraguay, and Uruguay, where colonies have destroyed up to half of the corn, sorghum, millet, citrus, and sunflower seed harvests. Argentinians have tried unsuccessfully to eradicate them since 1947, and ornithologists warn that they are likely to spread to Florida and the Pacific Coast.

In Colorado and Wyoming, sheepmen believe that eagles kill lambs and have tried to wipe them out both by poisoning and shooting from the air. In 1971 a helicopter pilot testified before a Senate subcommittee that he and several other hunters had shot 770 bald and golden eagles (the former of which are federally protected). Biologists believe that the 2,000 bald eagles and 8,000 golden eagles still alive in the country present no threat to ranchers.

Plant Pests

A weed is a plant that is harmful to other plants or to animals that we consider beneficial. Weeds compete successfully with a desired plant for water, nutrients, and space, and they may be toxic to livestock. Yet a few of our most important food crops are either descendants of weeds or were, at one time, considered weeds themselves. Most home owners with lawns consider the dandelion a weed because it crowds out the desired grasses, but some people consider it pretty, and others eat its nutritious greens. For similar reasons, farmers in some parts of this country consider the sunflower a weed, but its seed has valuable food properties and is an important crop in several countries.

Some weeds develop root systems that penetrate as much as twenty feet deep, making control especially difficult. Noxious weeds can cause such birth defects in livestock as dwarfing, bone curvature, cleft palates, oversized tongues, and heads with a single eye under the nose. For years, ranchers blamed these deformities on poor breeding stock and killed the siring animals, but by 1971 the Poisonous Plant Research Laboratory at Utah State University identified three noxious plants as the cause of the deformities if eaten in small amounts during certain periods of pregnancy and lethal if eaten in large amounts. According to the laboratory director, Wayne Binns, poisonous plants in general kill 3 to 5 percent of range livestock annually in the western states.

Pest Control

What makes our food crops susceptible to ravaging, insect nutritionist Ken Hagan points out, is that insects generally have the same nutritional requirements as human beings (except calcium, since they have no bones). Early methods of pest control included erecting scarecrows, patroling the fields, plucking, brushing, making noise, and diverting, and some of these primitive methods are still effective locally. In the Middle East, farmers still erect screens to deflect the columns of locusts, dig and ignite fire trenches as swarms approach, and beat pans to frighten off any settling swarms. Noise is also used to frighten birds, rodents, and larger animals, especially when crops are ripening. In Africa, onslaughts of the driver ants (*Dorylus*) are blocked by channeled flood water, sometimes loosed by breaking small dams. Baiting is another simple method of diversion that is still in use: Insects that puncture citrus fruit are attracted to piles of sugar cane placed between rows of trees and picked off by farm workers.

Border Watches

In 1869 a Harvard naturalist brought a gypsy moth (*Porthetria dispar*) from Europe for experiments; it got away, and today it is one of the most ravaging and proliferating pests in the country. In 1972 it damaged or destroyed over 1 million acres of trees, most of them in New England.

The federal government was slow to offer assistance in controlling imported pests, and in the 1890s, Massachusetts instituted a quarantine plan in an effort to isolate infestations and bring them under control. California also took independent steps during the last century; after the invasion of the San Jose scale, an Asiatic insect, the state set up a system of plant inspection at ports of entry into the state and barred individuals from carrying in fresh fruit. Congress finally passed the Insect Pest Act of 1902, but it was not enforced. The following year, though, the Department of Agriculture started to inspect the plants it imported, and in 1909, its Bureau of Entomology worked out a voluntary inspection program among importers. Public attention was drawn to the problem in 1910 when the mayor of Tokyo gave 2,000 Japanese cherry trees to President Taft's wife; when the trees were found infested with fruit moths, they were burned. The Japanese sent another 2,000 trees in 1912; in that year the President signed the Plant Quarantine Act, which gave the federal government power to collaborate with state officials and inspectors, and expanded the quarantine system. Though plants are inspected at border crossings, much of the inspection work now takes place before the plants destined for shipment leave their native lands.

In recent years, inspection and quarantine have actually become more difficult. Some groups favoring the elimination of trade barriers consider inspection and quarantine delays to be disguised blocks to freer commerce, and the speed and volume of modern travel put pressure on the government to reduce these delays. Containerization, the mass packing of cargo into units of uniform size, makes it harder to get at cargo in transit, and containers may be shipped into the heart of the country before their contents become accessible to inspectors. The carrying vehicles and the outside of containers themselves may become infested, especially in the case of cargo jets, which may land in several pest zones within twenty-four hours.

The Pesticides

When it was discovered that certain chemicals controlled many pests, especially injurious insects, "the golden age of chemicals" began. The development of insecticides can be divided into three generations. The first poisons, such as arsenic and nicotine, controlled but did not eradicate. The first stomach poison used successfully on a large scale was Paris green, a highly toxic pigment containing arsenic trioxide and copper acetate, which was usually applied as a dust or mixed with baits; it halted an alarming advance of the Colorado potato beetle during the 1860s and was later found effective against the cankerworm on fruit trees and a few other insects. In the interwar period, many formulas were developed, based mainly on metallic compounds, botanical products, and petroleum oils; they did not usually cause serious ecological disruptions but neither were they too effective. Finally came the synthesized hydrocarbon insecticides that apparently eradicated pests and spearheaded an agricultural revolution; some agriculturists hailed them as the "ultimate weapon," since they had high initial toxicity and sufficient persistence to suppress new generations of pests and prevent in-migrations.

DDT (dichlorodiphenyl trichloroethaner) was first synthesized in 1874, but scientists did not discover its effectiveness as an insecticide until the early 1940s when it saved the Swiss potato crop from the Colorado potato beetle. During World War II in Italy, DDT arrested a typhus epidemic caused by lice, and after the war applications eradicated the malaria-transmitting mosquito in Sri Lanka (then Ceylon) and other countries. By 1968, American manufacturers were selling nearly 180 million pounds of DDT annually, a record volume for any insecticide; and by 1970, farmers around the world were applying a billion pounds of insecticides, herbicides, fungicides, and rodenticides every year. More than a third of them were used in the United States, a half of that on farms, where it was estimated they increased crop output by one-fourth.

There are two broad categories of insecticides: stomach poisons, used mainly against pests with chewing jaws; and contact poisons, which are sprayed or dusted directly on pests or spread where pests will brush against them. There are also repellents, which prevent attack by their odor or taste. Most of the third generation of insecticides, however, killed a broad spectrum of insects, the great majority of which were beneficial, and some were also persistent.

Some entomologists had been warning that resistant pest populations could emerge, that the chemicals might cause mutants. They also considered it possible that genes determining resistance exist randomly in insect populations prior to applications, and those individuals possessing resistance-determining genes (i.e., "the fittest") survive to repropagate with a largely resistant generation.

The early-warning episodes began in the 1950s, when California fruit growers adopted DDT, though it also destroyed the ladybird beetles. A scale epidemic erupted, and orchard owners were so desperate that they bid the price of ladybugs up to a dollar apiece. In 1956, after eight years of heavy pesticide applications in the Cañeta Valley of Peru, insects suddenly reappeared in great quantities, and the farmers applied more poison, but the new populations were resistant, destroying 50 percent of the harvest. A dozen years later, the experience was repeated in Central America, where it was not the poorly educated, low-income smallholders that made the mistake, but the educated, large-scale growers. Finally, in the Rio Grande Valley in 1962, the boll weevil developed resistance to DDT-type insecticides, and farmers switched to methyl parathion. Because this is not persistent, they applied it more often, and it killed the predators that attacked not only the weevil but also the bollworm and budworm. Previously only secondary pests, these became more damaging than the weevil, and in 1968 the budworm began resisting parathion —indeed, there was evidence that the pests had become addicted to the poisons and were thriving on them. Yields by 1970 were the lowest in twenty-five years, with losses of up to a third of harvests, and in parts of northeastern Mexico, the budworm almost totally destroyed the cotton industry.

Almonds, a specialty crop worth between $5 million and $10 million in sales in California in 1971, were infested by the navel orange worm the following year. The worms, which invaded from Arizona, affected up to 15 percent and perhaps over 30 percent of some groves, burrowing inside the nut where chemicals could not reach them. Leopoldo E. Caltagirone at the International Biological Controls Center observed with amusement that growers not previously interested in the natural approach had dropped by "in desperation."

The FAO has warned that "large areas . . . of Latin America and the Middle East are on the brink of disaster through the excessive use of pesticides on cotton and other high-yielding crops," and the stability of some governments has actually been threatened by the harvest failures. In 1972 the World Health Organization (WHO) reported that more than 230 species of insects could withstand one pesticide or another, including 38 species of malaria vectors, 19 elephantiasis vectors, the yellow fever mosquito, and the flea that carries bubonic plague. At least two varieties of California mosquitos, one of which can be an encephalitis vector infecting both humans and animals, are immune to all pesticides. One newly resistant crop attacker is also the primary carrier of some 150 plant diseases. FAO consultants also fear increases in cross-resistance—resistance to one group of insecticides assuring resistance to chemicals to which a pest has never been exposed—and one entomologist characterized the cotton industry "as being based on an 'insecticidal crutch,' which has broken with a resulting ecological anarchy."

In the Texas recommendations for insect control in 1953,

DDT was listed 120 times; the current recommendations list it only 4 times, all of which are minor uses where no alternative insecticides exist. At the Texas Agricultural Experiment Station at Pecos, entomologists produced cotton crops for three years with almost no insecticide; while the boll weevil did not exist there, the budworm did, but was controlled by native beneficials. "The continued development of insecticide-resistant strains of insects threatens to render obsolete much of our present control technology," says Perry L. Adkisson, chairman of the Department of Entomology at Texas A&M University.

After Rachel Carson's *Silent Spring* was published in 1962, the congressional Appropriations Subcommittee on Agriculture released a study asserting that chemicals touched less than 5 percent of all American acreage and less than .5 percent of land hospitable to wildlife. As late as 1969, the influential Dow-Jones publication *Barron's* characterized Carson as "a noted marine biologist with a marvelous command of her subject and a weakness for venturing beyond her depth." Like many visionaries, Carson was not necessarily correct in the details of her forecast, but she had accurately identified an emergent peril. A study at Clear Lake, California, where DDT was sprayed to kill off insects hatching in water, revealed that the poison permeated the plankton, which the fish ate, and birds living on the fish died. By the time DDT reached the top of this comparatively short and simple food chain, the birds, the concentration of DDT had multiplied 100,000 times. Scientists soon found residues of persistent pesticides increasing in other creatures high on the food chain, including humans, and it was causing reproductive failures in some. There was also a great increase in cases of insecticidal poisoning among applicators and other farm workers. In 1961 the Montana Livestock Sanitary Board reported that toxic agents were found in women, and that they could be hazardous for those pregnant or nursing. In March 1969 the Food and Drug Administration (FDA) impounded 28,000 pounds of Lake Michigan coho salmon en route to commercial markets because of excessive DDT concentration.

Commercially oriented operators are not customarily friendly to the appeals of idealistic environmentalists, but when they began losing their crops despite increased spraying, there was a reaction. The persistent pesticides have been used less in recent years, and are being replaced by the organo-phosphates, which are by-products of the poison-gas research conducted prior to World War II. While these compounds are highly toxic, they decompose rapidly, leaving no residue. Among the more common ones are malthion, parthion, demotonl, and tetraethyl phyrophosphate (TEPP). Scientists have also learned that if a poison is not applied for some time, the number of nonresistant insects will again have a chance to build up, and can be suppressed without fostering a generational takeover of a resistant population through careful timing. And the *Wall Street Journal* headlined a 1972 front-page report, "Farmers Cut Spraying to Encourage Enemies of Crop-Eating Pests."

It had also become so expensive to develop a new pesticide that some companies reduced or discontinued research and development. Between 1967 and 1970, development costs rose from around $3.5 million to $5.5 million for a single insecticide, and by 1972 they were estimated at up to $10 million. The lead time necessary also increased during the period, from five years to six and a half years, and the average number of compounds screened for a single insecticide rose from 5,500 to 7,500. Companies remaining in the field, however, now have a chance at a larger share of the market and are beginning to concentrate on more species-specific chemicals.

Biological Controls

When the limitations of chemical pesticides were confirmed, what is perhaps the most ancient approach to pest control underwent a revival, for records show that ancient Asians understood that natural predators could be introduced to control pests. The first accounts of parasitic biology were published in the seventeenth century, and in 1800 Erasmus Darwin (Charles' father) recommended using syrphid flies to control aphids. The first intercontinental shipment of beneficial predators took place in 1872 when a mite was shipped from the United States to France to control *phylloxera*, a plant louse.

The first major American effort in biological control was in 1885. The cottony cushion had been ravaging the California citrus orchards since 1872. The pest, feeding on the sap of orange trees, was a problem wherever it was found, except Australia, and entomologists deduced that Australia was its native habitat. A Department of Agriculture employee, Albert Koebele, was sent to California, and a local congressman arranged for him to attend an Australian fair as an aide (the department at the time banned official foreign travel). Koebele returned with *Vedalia* ladybird beetles for release, and in only two years the scale was suppressed.

The ladybird beetle, also known as ladybug, is usually small, round, reddish, and sometimes spotted with black; it has become ubiquitous from Alaska to Argentina, from Scandinavia to South Africa. The reddish-orange types eat up to fifty-six aphids daily, while darker types forage among scale insects, mealybugs, white flies, and spider mites. Yet, like many beneficials, when their prey are scarce, they may turn to honey dew, pollen, and even flower petals; and one variety likes garden beans. Some limit their diets to only a few kinds of insects, and others are so finicky that they eat their prey only at a particular stage of growth. Some live in trees, others prefer low vegetation, and some inhabit both. Some with migratory habits are difficult to establish locally, while others tarry.

It became clear during the 1920s that substantial business could be done raising ladybugs because some, especially those preying on orchard mealybugs, cannot overwinter. Throughout much of the country, they control many pests with no further effort on our part at all, until we destroy their natural habitats.

The California central valley was in trouble again in 1934 when the olive scale (*Parlatoria oleae*) invaded the area around Fresno. The olive scale feasts upon over two hundred other plants and trees besides olives, and it spread rapidly through the lush valley until, in the 1940s, it was probably the most destructive insect to invade the state in half a century. Entomologists introduced parasitic wasps, *Aphytis masculicornis* and *Coccophagiodes utilis*, which devoured 70 to 95 percent of the female hosts; later, other natural enemies moved in. In 1973 New York State University scientists discovered a parasitic worm with the potential for controlling the worm of the face fly, which causes nearly $100 million damage annually to livestock. The predator makes its way into the ovaries of the female face fly and fills them with thousands of its own larval worms, which rupture them.

In 1973 the Agricultural Research Service began building a new and larger insect-quarantine facility at Newark, Delaware, which will handle annually about a quarter of a million imported predatory insects. After a safety check approval, most of these insects will be distributed to other federal and state entomologists, and the rest will be kept at the laboratory for biological-control research.

Planted fish may also be used in insect control. The *Gambusia affinis*, for example, is a small fish that loves mosquito larvae.

Biological control has also been successfully applied to mammals, birds, and weeds. In Australia, the runaway rabbit populations were controlled when the disease myxomatosis was introduced. The rampant prickly pear, native to the Western Hemisphere, had damaged 59 million dryland acres in Queensland alone; it was controlled by the introduction of an Argentine moth. The Klamath weed, more often known as St. Johnswort, is toxic and causes livestock to lose weight and perhaps die, as it displaces range forage. Before 1946, the weed infested around 5 million acres of western rangelands and was so prevalent in parts of California that banks refused loans for the purchase of infested land. Chemical controls cost more than the land was worth. But several beetles were introduced, and one, the *Chrysolina quadrigemina*, was particularly effective against it. Control became effective in the mid-1950s and has lasted ever since.

Biological control may be effected, paradoxically, by the counter-seasonal release of additional pests. A cabbage worm predator eats only the larvae, not the metamorphosed butterflies, and seems to die out until after the new hatch of worms. By the time the parasite renews its population, the worm does plenty of damage. To eliminate this lag, entomologists raise the butterflies out of the normal season and time their release so that their eggs hatch before the predator dies out. Ensured of a continuous food supply, the beneficial predator maintains its population, ready to attack the next "normal" birth of worms immediately.

The general public as well as agriculturists must be oriented to scientific recommendations regarding the use of biological controls in place of chemicals. When the Long Island potato harvest was once threatened by aphids, a predator, the syrphid fly, was released to control them. The syrphids, however, mimic wasps and bees, and their sudden appearance in quantity caused a public-relations backlash in surrounding suburbs. "Somehow an inanimate chemical seems less threatening to many people than a live insect—even a helpful insect," writes entomologist Morton Grosser.

People have fortunately become more aware of the potential menace of chemicals, but there is always the danger of overreaction; after all, everything is constructed of chemical compounds, including man.

The Microbial Approach

Another pest-control alternative to chemical pesticides is the use of pathogenic micro-organisms such as bacteria, viruses, rickettsia (bacteria-like parasites), protozoa, microscopic algae, fungi, and nematodes (the last of which can also be a pest). All insects are subject to diseases, some of which afflict only one or very few species while others strike at a broader spectrum. The predominant route by which a pathogen enters its victim is through the mouth, though many penetrate through skin wounds inflicted by fungi, nematodes, other predacious organisms, and physical injury. The most common micro-organisms on insect surfaces are bacteria.

If man does not intervene in the infectious environment, the checks and balances between the pathogen and host are influenced by food supply, breeding habits, physical conditions, and the virulence of the pathogen. Under normal conditions, when the population of the host rises greatly, the disease breaks out and checks population growth. Chemical insecticides, by disrupting the natural play of the balances, make pest populations less controllable. "With many pathogens, there has to be a period of buildup," points out T. A. Angus, a Canadian insect pathologist, and "intervention with chemicals in effect removes the host insect and so terminates that buildup. However, in some cases, the insecticide does not reduce the population very much more than the pathogen would have done if left to itself [and] it has been found that in the next generation of the host, pest survival is enhanced because of the absence of the pathogen."

In nature, the epidemic may break out after the pest has had time to do a great deal of damage, so the approach is to precipitate an epidemic by introducing the pathogen when a population spurt is incipient. The idea of controlling insect pests with microbes was born in Europe a century ago, and around 1900 entomologists recommended using a fungus to control the chinch bug in the American central states. An early attempt brought what Howard T. Dulmage, a microbiologist with the Agricultural Research Service, calls only "limited and erratic success" because of lack of knowledge both of the pathogens and the microclimates into which they were introduced. Another reason for the limited success of early efforts was that there was no commercial activity in research and development comparable to that for chemicals.

There have been three periods of microbial endeavor. Prior to 1940, rather blind attempts were made at colonizing pathogens. But, around 1940, an induced milky disease epidemic controlled the Japanese beetle in the eastern United States. This disease, so far as is known, infects only certain closely related beetles of the family *Scarabaeidae*. From this point, the microbial insecticides' performance was measured against the capacity of chemicals to control pests, and the latter appeared much more effective. About 1970, however, microbials were reconsidered in an ecological context, and interest in them revived.

Many microbes associated with insects have been identified, and some have been proved pathogenic to their hosts. In 1968 *Agricultural Research*, a Department of Agriculture publication, reported, "If man can employ but a fraction of the several thousand diseases that attack insects in the wild, he will have as great a choice of biological weapons as there are conventional insecticides today." By that time, the department had collected and catalogued some 250 viruses attacking insects—many more than were known only two decades earlier—and nearly all of these are species-specific, which is important ecologically. Arthur M. Heimpel, an insect pathologist, concludes that "the insect viruses are the safest of all the microbial agents proposed for insect control and

are infinitely safer for other life forms than chemical agents."
Bacteria are less species-specific, but they are still potentially useful and not, so far as is known, likely to be dangerous. *Bacillus
thuringiensis*, which was isolated in 1914, is now known to be
pathogenic to 130 to 140 insects, and its use has been extremely
successful in some cases. In 1972 several specialists told the New
York Academy of Sciences that bacterial control is as effective as
the best chemical insecticides now in use. One paper stated:

> The bacteria exhibit little change in virulence toward
> their insect hosts, and the insects develop no apparent resist-
> ance to the micro-organisms as they do to chemicals. Of para-
> mount importance is that these bacterial insecticides do not
> affect the biocoeneisis [formation of biological communities],
> they pose no hazard to man and animals; and they do not
> pollute the environment.

Scientists believe they are also verging on important breakthroughs with protozoa. Fungi are considered less dependable, but
scientists at the Boyce Thompson Institute for Plant Research in
New York have identified one that is effective against mosquito
larvae. More than 1,200 microbes have now been examined as possibilities for microbial insecticides, and by 1973 encouraging reports were multiplying; scientists have identified certain viruses
affecting the corn borer and bollworm. In June 1973 the Environmental Protection Agency cleared the way for the first commercial
viral application by approving one manufactured by the International Minerals and Chemical Corporation for use against the
cotton and tobacco bollworms.

Yet the application of pathogens—a sort of germ warfare
against pests—is slowed by concern over their possible dangers to
man, other animals, and the environment in general. According
to Richard Hoffmaster, an entomologist at the Delmarva experiment station, farmers could probably release a virus to attack the
cabbage looper, which got its name from the looping trail it
makes as it devours its way across the bottom of the cabbage leaf.
When loopers are unchecked, there may as many as a quarter of a
million to a single acre. The Hoffmaster team has caught infected
loopers, ground them up, and used the mixture to infect healthy
loopers. About ten or twenty infected loopers are released over

each acre. It is hoped that this will eliminate about 90 percent of the loopers, which have no other major natural enemies. Health authorities fear the spread of the virus, but Hoffmaster argues that the virus could be controlled by other spraying. As one scientist put it, "Ever since DDT, the Environmental Protection Agency is more cautious than ever. It tries to rule out every possibility of something going wrong."

Advocates of microbial control believe that consumers must be educated to its value and environmental safety. They point out that if you have eaten cabbage lately, you have probably eaten viruses dropped by cabbage loopers. Some fungi produce toxins that cause stomach cancer in humans, but scientists say they have identified a fungus that attacks only aphids and therefore should not be considered potentially carcinogenous.

The possibility that pest insects might develop immunity is continuously weighed, and some suggestive evidence exists that some might be able to. In 1972, the Canadian agriculturist R.P. Jaques told the New York Academy of Sciences:

> . . . present knowledge indicates that it is highly improbable that insects will develop resistance to microbial insecticides. The statement is made that if resistance was going to occur it would have occurred long ago because the viruses, and to a lesser extent, the bacteria are naturally occurring. Thus the host insects have been exposed to them for many many years. Also laboratory tests have not indicated sufficient development of resistance to suggest that a wild population could become resistant.

The responsibility is, says Heimpel, "to make sure that we are not going to do any more damage with biological controls than with chemical pesticides, and hopefully less or none at all."

Another constraint against wider use of microbials is their cost. The delays of regulatory bodies in approving commercial release increases manufacturing expenses, and research and development costs are already high. Some authorities believe their main use will be for high-value crops, such as lettuce, broccoli, and cabbage. The microbial insecticides already developed and approved for release are applied, like the chemicals, as dusts or sprays, through nozzles or by aerial drops.

Birth and Death Control

The possibility of blocking reproduction of pests, particularly those that mate only once, has long fascinated entomologists. A notable breakthrough was made during the 1960s with the screwworm fly (also known as the flying piranha because the larvae fiercely attack flesh). Screwworm flies cross the border from Mexico into the United States, where they have no natural enemies, and the female lays her eggs in wounds on cattle, hogs, sheep, and horses. Each female is capable of depositing nearly 3,000 eggs during her three-week life span and discharges them at intervals of four to six minutes. There are 10 to 400 eggs in each deposit. During the first week, the eggs hatch into larvae resembling wood screws, and as they absorb nutrition from their host, they emit an odor that attracts more flies to the wounded animal. If untreated, the copious deposits of larvae all but consume whole animals within ten to fourteen days, and the larvae flee, burrowing into the soil where they metamorphose into flies in seven to ten days. In 1935, screwworm flies infested a total of 1.2 million cattle in Texas alone, of which 180,000 head died. By the middle of the century, they were causing an estimated annual loss of over $100 million.

Entomologists discovered that the female is monogamous and so experimented with the release of sterilized but virile males as population-control agents. Males were sterilized with radioactive Cobalt 60 and released in 1955 and 1956 on Curaçao. The experiment was successful and, a year later, mass production of sterile males began in Florida. Their release resulted in eradication of the screwworm flies in the state by 1961. The program was expanded until the pest was virtually eradicated from the United States. In past years, the Department of Agriculture has airdropped 200 million sterile males weekly along the American-Mexican border. Despite its success, however, the program was cut back, and in 1972 screwworm flies again invaded the Southwest after spending a winter under favorable conditions in Mexico. A Mexican-American effort was mobilized to move the buffer zone farther south, since the flies apparently migrate from Central America. Edward F. Knipling, director of the Entomology Research Division of the Department of Agriculture, underscores the necessity of maintaining programs, since once a pest population "gets out of hand, it is hard to regain control."

In an interview a few years ago, Knipling recalled, "The sterility technique started out as a concept, which at times seemed vague and remote. But it now appears as a significant tool in the control of insects." Yet a couple of years later, Knipling wrote, "the development of the sterility approach . . . will depend to a great extent on the advances that are made in the mass production of large numbers of insects at reasonable cost." Another problem in raising enough sterile males is the possibility of diseases killing them off during confinement.

Knipling, who was a leader in the development of DDT as a pesticide, expanded his division's experimental work in this form of biological control, and promising work has been done with the Mediterranean fruit fly, the codling moth, the pink bollworm moth in California, the boll weevil, the tsetse fly, and the Heliothis moth. The division's work has also shown that it is possible to release partially sterile males that breed sterile offspring. This second generation of sterilized flies can do the work that would otherwise require another release of artificially sterilized flies.

The genetic approach is used by the World Health Organization (WHO) for mosquito-control experiments. In an isolated Burmese village, an entire population of the *Culex fatigans* was wiped out after the introduction of sexually aggressive but genetically incompatible males that caused resident females to lay nonviable eggs.

By anesthetizing female Indian meal moths with carbon dioxide and mating them to males reared under continuous light stress, experimenters found that the egg laying and hatching plummeted by 93 percent. They have also found that sublethal doses of gamma rays from Cobalt 60 shortened the average life span of rice weevils and lesser grain borers and they ate less than untreated insects. Feeding damage by the rice weevil was reduced by 97 percent and by the grain borer by 90 percent. Sublethal doses are less expensive than lethal doses; and neither dosage contaminated stored grain.

In 1969 a city councilman in Portland, Oregon, suggested that starlings be controlled through bird seed laced with an oral contraceptive. Although the proposal was rejected, in 1966 ecologist Robert A. McCabe viewed "the entire area of birth control for lower animals" as a coming step in pest management. A "pill" has prevented reproduction of pigeons under experimental conditions over a six-month period, and a female sex hormone has been found that causes pregnant coyotes to reabsorb their embryos, or prevent implantation of the fertilized ovum if the timing is right. Mestranol, a synthetic of natural female hormones, blocks rat ovaries from functioning and also sterilizes the male. If ingested during early pregnancy, it halts embryonic growth, and if it is taken late in pregnancy, female pups and most male pups are born sterile. In 1968 a Harvard scientist, Karel Slăma, reported that hormones introduced into male linden bugs caused sterilization but not impotence, and when they mated, they passed on the sterilant to the females like a venereal disease; the females became barren.

Growth Regulators

Compounds that affect maturation in insects have also been used experimentally in controlling pests. Insects pass through three stages during their lifetimes: larva, pupa, and adult. During all stages, a hormone called ecdysone stimulates growth and development, and scientists have found that an excess of ecdysone accelerates maturation, bringing on premature, stunted adulthood and early death. Another hormone, called the juvenile hormone, controls the timing of the metamorphosis from youth to hibernating pupa, but if it persists, it deranges or halts development into a more mature stage.

Scientists have synthesized ecdysone and the juvenile hormone—compounds that, as one put it, "actually mimic the compounds which naturally occur in insects." When this approach was gaining momentum a few years ago, it was usually called hormonal control, but more recently, it has been known as insect growth regulation.

Compounds that mimic ecdysone may be used to induce sterility and early death in pests. Synthetic juvenile hormone, on the other hand, can be used to prevent the insect from reaching the reproductive stage of its life. It is especially effective against species of which the adult is the destroyer, and in cases in which the larva is the destroyer, juvenile hormone prevents the buildup of another generation.

Experiments and field tests have not yet disclosed any toxicity in growth regulators, even to the target species, and most of them degrade rapidly. Because the hormones are essential to the body chemistry of the insect—that is, they are not poisons—scientists doubt that insects will develop immunity to the synthetic compounds.

The Chemicals of Body Language: The Pheromones

Scientists have learned that insects and other animals, possibly including humans, communicate through the release of chemicals called *pheromones* (from the Greek words *pherein,* "to carry," and *horman,* "to excite or stimulate"). The most obvious one is the sex attractant, but pheromones exist also for feeding, recruiting, training, alarming, expelling, and "burying."

The sex pheromone, an odor secreted to lure a mate, interests pest specialists most. By 1972, synthetic sex attractants were available for some thirty major farm-insect pests, including the cabbage looper, the Oriental fruit moth, the Indian meal moth, the pink bollworm, and the gypsy moth. They are mainly the female pheromones and are usually placed in a container, which may entrap the males with glue.

Many insects, especially flies, tend to lay their eggs where they detect the odors of chemicals. From this discovery, an approach was developed for chemically signaling egg laying on barren matter, where the offspring would starve. A possible application of pheromones to vertebrates may come from the knowledge that when a strange male rat comes too near a pregnant female, his odor causes the female to reabsorb her fetus. Some traps use ultraviolet rays either to sterilize pests or destroy their mating ability. Aluminum foil has been used to reflect light on the undersides of leaves, which inhibits reproduction among those pests that prefer to forage and lay eggs in the shade.

Certain ways of interplanting are an effective biological control, too. Garlic, for example, repels mildew and aphids; geraniums growing among grapes deter Japanese beetles, and parsley wards off others. Indeed, some flowers, such as marigolds, are toxic to several pests, and the prolific aphids are repelled by tansy, rue, coriander, anise, and other herbs.

Repellent plants can also be used as a "fence" against pests that travel along the ground. Barley fields in Oregon have been protected from jackrabbits by planting a sixteen-foot strip of rye around them. (The rabbits do not like rye and therefore do not penetrate deeply enough through it to discover the cornucopia of barley behind it.) A variation of the trap-crop approach is the planting of a few rows of cotton plants especially treated with insecticides to attract and kill the weevils. The trap crop is then destroyed, and the farmer plants his harvest crop. Sterile male weevils are released in case some female weevils escape.

Plant geneticists would like to breed resistant crops, but this is an intricate task. Scientists might develop a plant resisting one type of leaf blight, but ten strains of the blight could exist in the environs. Since some insects do not like to lay eggs in prickly places, and birds do not like the sensation of being stabbed, plants may be made resistant by breeding in sharper hair follicles. In 1973 scientists reported that three new wheats that are twice as hairy as a widely grown variety are completely resistant to the cereal leaf beetle, a serious midwestern pest. Also in 1973, scientists, in a major breakthrough, bred into the major forage crop, alfalfa, resistance against anthracnose, which damages more than 4 million acres every year.

As R. M. Bacon states in the 1972 *Old Farmer's Almanac*:

> Since we gave up commercial insecticides, helpful insects have returned. These include the ladybug beetle, praying mantis, and lacewing fly. No need to import them from mail-order houses; their numbers are increasing naturally.

And as insects returned, so did beneficial birds. The extent to which birds control insects is a matter of dispute. An Audubon Society officer, Roland C. Clement, wrote in a handbook for the Brooklyn Botanical Gardens:

> On the one hand, enthusiastic bird lovers have repeatedly stated that insects would rule the earth if birds were eliminated. On the other, somewhat more objective observers,

who discover that birds normally eat only 5 to 20 percent of the insect fauna, pronounce them incapable of controlling insect numbers.

In 1926, however, W. L. McAtee, a federal investigator, analyzed American literature on the question and found 109 cases of demonstrable control of insects by birds and another eighty-eight cases of localized suppression. We also know that half of the food of some 1,400 American species consists of insects.

Integrated Pest Control

Of the golden age of chemicals, Ray F. Smith, head of entomological studies at the University of California at Berkeley says, "We lost good entomology during the period when 'the new,' 'the good,' and 'the great' insecticides overwhelmed us and took possession of economic entomology."

Paul DeBach, a biological-control specialist at the University of California at Davis, states:

> . . . the role of natural enemies in the agro-ecosystems is the main base upon which we have to achieve adequate pest control, whether we're using integrated approaches or whether we're relying mainly on insecticides. By far the greatest amount of control in any agro-ecosystem is due to natural enemies. The main pest problems we're concerned with involve the few percent, the 5 to 10 percent, of insects that are key pests because they lack adequate natural enemies.

Morton Grosser, an executive with Zoecon, a company developing synthetic insect-growth regulators, contends:

> The ideal pesticide is one that invariably proves fatal to the target animal, but harmless to everything else. It should be a substance to which insects cannot ever develop resistance or immunity, and it should be completely degradable, easy to apply, and cheap. The pesticide industry has yet to produce a single product that meets all these criteria.

Organic farming enthusiasts reject all synthetic chemicals, but nearly all other agriculturists would agree with Emil Mrak who chaired the Commission on Pesticides and Good Health which recommended eliminating DDT spraying: "You shouldn't wipe out food production to save the environment. You cannot live on the environment." What is wrong with chemicals, says Canadian insect pathologist Thomas A. Angus, is "not that they have a bad name. They're not good enough." Louis A. Falcon, an entomologist at Berkeley, suggests that a "whole new era [of control] may be opening," one in which we will "no longer think that the only good insect is a dead insect." Some disagreement exists, however; Knipling suggests that if a pest arrived as an alien, "the first goal is to eliminate it."

The pest problem is greater than ever, spurring investigation into such areas as species-specific chemicals, more selective application of insecticides, biological controls, and alteration of micro-environments. Because of the multiplicity of methods being developed, pest management increasingly requires interdisciplinary teams whose specialists collaborate in biological, chemical, and cultural control, in agricultural economics, and perhaps in systems analysis. In research circles, the integrated approach has taken on the fervor of a movement that has been described as a blend of "idealism, evangelism, pursuit of fashion, fund-raising, and even empire-building."

Economic Injury Level: A Recast Concept

The influence of the traditional conservationists was comparatively limited; politicians, farmers, and other businessmen called them impractical "do-gooders" and "bleeding hearts." It was not until pesticidal abuse thinned wallets and jeopardized credit ratings that they re-evaluated the brief of the environmentalists, that plant protection should be through a manipulation of natural balances with a minimum of ecological cost. The questions, then, are: At what level does a pest become financially damaging? What price should the farmer pay to preserve environmental equilibrium—in a sense, what is the ecological optimum?

Today, the emphasis is on economic entomology based on cost-benefit analysis. If a pest population injures a harvest only slightly, it may be more economic to leave it alone than to pay for suppression. If pests verge on a population explosion, or one has occurred, measures must be taken. Carl Huffaker, director of the International Biological Control Center in California, counsels that pest-control ecologists should "replace the pesticide salesman as a principle source of advice and should work, not for commercial companies like a pesticide manufacturer, but for the grower, whom they charge a fee. Their advice would then include not treating as well as treating." Unfortunately, however, economic threshold densities have not yet been established for most species of pests, and they are urgently needed for this approach.

Has the integrated approach worked out? After budworms ruined cotton crops in the Rio Grande Valley, spraying was handled with such precision that it left beneficial predators alive to control the remaining pests. "The revival of the old era when pest control was to a great extent ecologically oriented is now firmly established," says Ray Smith. We now know that pesticidal abuse "imposes an additional real cost on food production."

5

Energy and Power–Solar, Mechanical, and Chemical

Power and Implements

If the first agricultural revolution was the domestication of plants, the second one was ushered in by the invention of the plow. The earliest cultivators probably plowed with their hands, but the idea of using a pole as a hoe may have come quickly, and the concept of a plow hewn from a crooked branch or the stub of a branch left on a small trunk must have followed soon thereafter. The plow became more useful when man invented the yoke to harness it to animal power; we know from Egyptian art that draft livestock were used over four thousand years ago.

The early furrowing implements were heavy and awkward. Few improvements were made until 1793 when, in the United States, Thomas Jefferson invented a scientifically designed mold-board—the curved plate of the plow—which resisted the soil much less as it turned it over. Four years later, Charles Newbold of New Jersey obtained the first patent for an iron plow, iron except for the beam and handles. But the attempt to introduce an iron implement did not enthuse farmers, who thought the metal would poison the soil and encourage weeds. Over the next couple of decades, farm journals reoriented farmers' attitudes, and when Jethro Wood patented a much improved iron plow in 1814, farmers were more receptive. Unfortunately, the cast-iron plow could not move easily through the prairie sod of the Midwest, and the heavy, sticky soils clung to the moldboard instead of turning over.

In 1837 an Illinois blacksmith, John Lane, resolved the problem by fashioning strips of saw steel over wooden moldboards; since he neglected to patent the idea, blacksmiths all over the country were soon making them. Blacksmith John Deere of Illinois used steel for making a relatively lightweight, one-piece share and moldboard, which he merchandised aggressively, and by 1846, in partnership with sawmill owner Leonard Andrus, Deere was manufacturing about a thousand plows a year. Little more than a decade later, after he had moved to Moline, Illinois, where the company bearing his name still headquarters, he was turning out ten thousand annually. Demand for steel for plows surged; the steel plow had replaced most cast-iron plows on the prairies.

The farmer still walked behind his animal-drawn plows until about 1874 when the Gilpin Sulky plow was advertised as "the plow that took the farmer off his feet." It had a metal seat at the end of a wooden shank, mounted on metal wheels. Other improvements included a plow that one horse, rather than two, could pull; and new grain drills for seeding, including a rotary-drop corn planter said to seed "with great accuracy," which gradually replaced broadcasting, or scattering the seed by hand. The reaper was really a combined product of many minds in many countries, and American farmers began adopting it after 1847.

"Riding herd" was laborious, and the steam engine was the first response to demands for mechanization to replace animal power. As early as 1849, portable engines had been built for use with threshing machines; by 1870, several steam plows had been designed, and soon steam-traction engines were in production. The early steam tractors had some drawbacks, however; they were more useful in threshing than in plowing and other work, they were too big for any but the largest farms, their heavy weight compacted the soil, sparks from their smokestacks often set fires, and sometimes they exploded. Meanwhile, European farmers were looking over the new internal combustion engines. By 1920, many of them were using the Lang Bulldog, a 12-horse-power tractor whose adaptation to agriculture followed the pattern of its predecessor, the steam engine. First it was made portable by mounting it on wheels, then a drive was added to make it self-propelled.

In the United States, John Froelich of Iowa probably built the first successful gasoline tractor; two University of Wisconsin students, C. W. Hart and C. H. Parr, managed the first factory that manufactured it exclusively, around the turn of the century. The displacement of animals by tractors was gradual on American farms, and tractors did not outnumber horses until World War II created a demand for more farm products.

The typical early tractor was small, with outsize rear wheels, a narrow canopy-type hood with sides exposed, and a contoured metal seat that looked like a perch. By the early 1970s, farm tractors had an average horsepower of 48, compared with about 25 a little more than a decade earlier, and only 9 horsepower in 1950. In 1972 the most powerful models were 175-horsepower—60-horsepower was tops ten years earlier. Deere claims its most powerful model boosts the operator's combining capability by up to 25 percent.

The law of diminishing returns is likely to slow down or even halt the trend to more horsepower, but other mechanical refinements of the tractor have been added. The larger machines, which may stand 12 feet high and have rear wheels 6 feet in diameter, now offer enclosed cabs, curved and tinted windshields, power steering, four-wheel drive, a sophisticated instrument panel, and a citizens' band radio for field coordination. Some even have stereo tape decks, air conditioners, and heaters. These behemoths, with the power to pull a disc plow and planter simultaneously over twelve rows, sold from $10,000 and up in 1972, and explain why the average Indiana farm, which was 400 acres in 1973, typically had $90,000 invested in equipment; the average wheat farm in Kansas had 975 acres and $40,000 worth of equipment; and the average Delta farm had 300 acres and equipment averaging $60,000. Ten years before, the average American farmer had about a $3,500 tractor investment.

However important the internal-combustion tractor, the most vital single farming invention between 1830 and 1860 was the mechanical reaper. When a crop is ripe, time is critical: the laden plants are vulnerable to weather, pests, and thievery. The early settlers used the sickle and scythe for harvesting, but by the time of the American Revolution, they had replaced them with the cradle, a scythe with a light framework that gathers the stems while it lays the grain down evenly. Binders cut and bound as they were drawn, and a stationary machine threshed and cleaned. In 1833 Obed Hussey invented a practical mechanical reaper; about the same time, Cyrus H. McCormick of Virginia obtained a patent on another version. But a heavy labor requirement remained—the binding of cut grain; finally, all these functions were combined in one machine. Complete mechanization came when machinery united harvesting, threshing, cleaning, and delivering grain ready for storage. This is why, on the great wheat spreads, farmers and ranchers talk not of "harvesting" but of "combining." These combines were built first for the small grains, but by the early 1950s corn combiners were successful, bringing an end to the romantic era of husking.

Today, even the smallest combines boost output per man-hour by more than a hundred times over manual harvesting, and the giant ones do so by a thousand times. In the United States, mechanization, rather than bio-chemistry, became the spearhead of the new agricultural revolution. Bio-chemistry led in Europe, where soil depletion was the main constraint.

The mechanized harvesting of vegetables and fruits is more recent and was more difficult; before some machines could be employed profitably, geneticists had to alter the plant. For example, snap bean harvesters cannot reach close to the ground, so a plant must bear all or most of its beans several inches up on the stalk. Tomato pickers bruised the soft fruits, so tougher-skinned tomatoes were necessary—some say at the expense of tougher flesh and less taste. Some machines do not cut or pick as meticulously as food growers desire; in the case of asparagus, manual harvesting is still superior for the longer spears favored in the fresh-produce markets. Yields are also higher when cut by hand, but high labor costs make mechanized harvesting more economical.

Another type of machine is a tuber thinner, used for potatoes or beets. One model rumbles over six rows at three miles per hour, covering about thirty acres a day; it costs $15 an acre compared with hand labor at $25. It operates by selecting the plant to be saved, electronically signalling a huge knife, which then removes all unwanted plants for the distance required for the chosen plant to grow optimally.

By 1970, nearly 60 percent of the American vegetable harvest was mechanized, a figure projected to reach nearly 75 percent by 1975. Crops include most potatoes, peas, and snap beans, about half of the tomatoes destined for processing, and a good deal of the lettuce, cucumbers, and onions. A peach harvester, which jostles branches and catches the fruit, does the job of about twenty hand pickers; another shake method is used for apples, and there is a machine that reaches thirty to forty feet into palms to cut bunches of dates. Labor costs, which rose about 50 percent faster than the cost of machinery, encouraged mechanization.

"Stoop labor" is still needed for many crops, though, and among the fruits, a huge market exists in the orange orchards. The orange is snapped from the tree by a fast turn of the wrist, and picking, as one disgruntled worker put it, "requires the combined agility of a monkey and the stamina of a horse." Inventions have included whirling, flexible fins, a conical spring that applied a gentle force on the stem, claws that snipped, a cone that stripped, and inhalers like vacuum cleaners. An air-blasting machine knocked down the oranges all right, but it defoliated the tree; a giant mechanical arm that shook refused to loosen its grip and shook the trees to death.

Mechanization has entered livestock production, such as controlling a hog "environment" complex with prefabricated farrowing stalls and drinking troughs, feed mixers and distributors, and temperature control. Computers are used to monitor the growth of the animals and the feed-supply situation, and they may change mixes and time distribution of feed accordingly. Machines now exist to modify the weather. The wind machine, which at first glance looks like a slenderized windmill, but on second glance like a propeller-driven airplane motor and cockpit atop an oil derrick, is one. By blowing away frost-laden air, it creates a vacuum into which warmer air moves. (One with individually adjustable legs for hillside use is called the "dog-leg contour" model.)

Agricultural implement manufacturers have learned that, unlike car makers who can produce for a mass market, they have to custom their machinery to the specific needs of individual—and individualistic—farmers. The more mechanically inclined farmers often adapt purchased implements in their own machine shops, and a Deere executive says that farmers often are the first to conceptualize their requirements; they anticipated the need for more tractor horsepower before the manufacturers did, for example.

But the trend toward larger machinery, particularly wider implements, has slowed. As one midwestern farmer put it, "I don't see how they can get any larger without knocking down a lot of fences and widening the bridges." On the other hand, the machinery is becoming sophisticated: a new Massey-Ferguson plow is said to use up to 30 percent less power and to be more efficient in heavy, wet soils; a tractor with a "variable density cushion" that adjusts to the weight and height of the operator, has increased soundproofing, and a four-poster guard for protection in case of overturn.

New models now on the drawing boards will feature, among other things, medically and environmentally sound improvements, such as vibration and noise control. Spurred by the Walsh-Healy Occupational Safety Act, and the frequent difficulty in hiring and keeping trained operators, manufacturers will make the machinery more comfortable to operate, less likely to induce deafness and other ailments, and less objectionable to bystanders.

American agriculture, it has been said, is "dominated by the plow," a euphemism for mechanization, and an estimated five million tractors move about a quarter of a trillion tons of soil annually. But working with plows, disc harrows, roto spaders, till-rowers, and the like, may eventually reduce or destroy the productivity of the soil. Many farmers have become more interested in modified tillage, or even the no-till approach which, where successful, prevents erosion, conserves moisture, controls weeds, and reduces costs. For example, farmers may plant seed in plant residues, or they may terrace so as to make fewer tractor trips around the field necessary. Six million acres were planted under no-till in 1971, compared with only 10,000 acres five years earlier, and there were 30,000 miles of new terracing.

Energy

Much is made of the fact that one American farmer produces enough food for forty-eight people. This achievement, however, is based largely on the use of fossil fuel. In fact, according to the multi-authored report "Food Production and the Energy Crisis," published in November 1973 by *Science* magazine, "The principal raw material of modern U.S. agriculture is fossil fuel." While the use of energy in the United States has doubled in the past twenty years, in some types of agriculture it has increased more than threefold.

The on-farm use of fuels for tractors, heating, drying, and electricity has accounted for about 1.6 percent of national energy consumption, and another 1.9 percent has been required for the manufacture of inputs—fertilizer, pesticides, machinery, and building materials. But the major requirements of the food establishment are after the crops and livestock leave the farm; transportation and processing claim 7 to 12 percent of all energy, bringing the share for food production and distribution to between 10.5 and 15.5 percent. Since food output must increase to meet export as well as domestic demand, this percentage is likely to increase.

Farmers are especially fearful of fuel shortages during seeding and harvesting, while handlers of perishables are especially concerned about fast, reliable transportation—the baking industry, for example, collectively operates the largest fleet of delivery trucks in the country. In December 1973, William E. Simon, head of the Federal Energy Office, stated, "Agriculture is receiving top priority [in fuel allocation]."

The *Science* analysis focused on the energy requirements for growing corn, whose fuel needs fall between the extremes of the highly demanding fruits and the less demanding small grains and hay. In 1970 about 2.9 million kilocalories of fuel energy were used to raise one acre of corn—the equivalent of 80 gallons of gasoline per acre. Multiplying 80 gallons by the 1.4 acres

needed to feed one person, we find that it takes the equivalent of
112 gallons of gasoline to produce enough food for one person
annually. With 330 million acres planted to food crops in 1970,
the equivalent of 26.4 billion gallons (about 828 barrels) of gasoline were used.

The high fuel consumption on the farm is due in good measure to the substituting of machinery for labor; man-hours required per corn acre declined from twenty-eight in 1945 to nine
in 1970—a decrease of over 60 percent. During this period, the
number of tractors increased from 2.4 million to nearly 4.5 million, the average horsepower of each tractor increased by 2.6
times, the kilocalories of energy consumed by machinery rose
133 percent, and fuel consumption for all machinery rose from
an estimated 15 gallons to about 22 gallons per acre.

But the largest energy input in 1970 was fertilizer, which accounted for over 1 million kilocalories, most of it—940,800 kilocalories—coming from nitrogen. Between 1945 and 1970, the
use of nitrogen, which needs a great deal of natural gas as a
feedstock, increased nearly sixteen times, potassium nearly fourteen times, and phosphorous about five times.

Though pesticides do not account for as much energy use as
fertilizer, 22,000 kilocalories were required to protect the 1970
corn crop, whereas they were scarcely applied in 1945. Because
the hybrids now being planted grow farther into the autumn,
when the weather prevents adequate natural drying, grain requires more artificial drying; energy used for drying increased
nearly 12 times between 1945 and 1970. Transportation and electricity requirements increased by 3.5 times, irrigation by 1.8
times, and the energy for seed nearly doubled.

Table 5.1 shows the energy inputs in kilocalories in corn production for the years 1945 and 1970.

Fossil fuels actually contribute only 11 percent of the total
energy input for corn; the rest comes mainly from solar radiation. During the crop season, over 2 billion kilocalories of energy
reach each corn acre, of which about 0.4 percent is converted
into grain, and 1.26 percent into the total plant. That 1.26 percent represents 26.6 million kilocalories, to which farmers, processors, and distributors add nearly 2.9 million kilocalories. But
the additional energy input between 1945 and 1970 made possible

TABLE 5.1. ENERGY INPUTS IN KILOCALORIES FOR CORN PRODUCTION

Input	1945	1970
Labor	12,500	4,900
Machinery	180,000	420,000
Gasoline	543,400	797,000
Fertilizer	74,600	1,055,900
Nitrogen	58,800	940,800
Phosphorous	10,600	47,100
Potassium	5,200	68,000
Seed	34,000	63,000
Irrigation	19,000	34,000
Insecticides	0	11,000
Herbicides	0	11,000
Drying	10,000	120,000
Electricity	32,000	310,000
Transportation	20,000	70,000
Total Input Energy	925,500	2,896,000
Total Output Energy in Corn Yield	3,427,200	8,164,800
Kilocalorie Return per Input of Kilocalorie	3.70	2.82

SOURCE: "Food Production and the Energy Crisis," *Science* (November 1973).

the tremendous rise in yield which, translated into energy, climbed from about 3.4 million kilocalories to nearly 8.2 million kilocalories.

It should be noted, however, that sometime between 1945 and 1970, the law of diminishing returns became operative; the kilocaloric return per kilocaloric input dropped from 3.7 to 2.8.

As the energy crisis emerged, there was talk of shortening the workweek—in effect, cutting down or slowing up operations—to save fuel. Such a measure on food production would affect our lives more than in the case of other consumer items.

During the overly optimistic period following the green revolution, it was hoped that diets in underdeveloped countries could be upgraded significantly through intensive agriculture. Yet, to feed the average American diet to a world population of 4 billion for one year would require the energy equivalent of 488 billion gallons (over 15 billion barrels) of petroleum, a figure that would exhaust known reserves in 29 years. But if people were to subsist on corn alone, the reserves would support 10 billion people for nearly 450 years.

Alternative approaches to saving fuel have been advanced. Reversion to hand application of pesticides has been suggested, though the labor cost of hand spraying was, in 1973, four times that of tractor application. Higher-precision machinery and machinery that uses fuel more efficiently may save fuel—more fuel than could be saved by reversion to horses and mules, which consume much energy in feed. A return to animal and green manures is a possible alternative to artificial fertilization. In one year, one dairy cow or two fattening calves produce the 112 pounds of nitrogen that are needed for an acre of corn, and manure has several other ecological and economic advantages over chemical fertilizer. The costs of manuring are hauling and spreading, but agriculturists have computed that the savings in energy would be 1.1 million kilocalories per acre. The 1973 livestock manure output was estimated to be 1.7 billion tons a year; 50 percent of that manure would have fertilized 75 percent of acreage planted to corn in 1970.

In 1973 the energy crisis began accelerating changes that were already underway in American agriculture for environmental, economic, and dietary reasons. Much of the genetic engineering now conducted can, if successful, decrease fuel needs. Breeding may reduce the need for pesticides and irrigation, and breeding for high protein content may increase the ratio of meat produced per unit of feed.

What the energy crisis has finally brought home, though, is the fact that scientific agriculture is not as efficient as it seems; it rates low when its yields are measured against exploitation of industrial calories—gasoline or diesel oil for machinery, power for producing chemical fertilizers and pesticides and manufacturing equipment, electricity for irrigation works, and gas for storage elevators and processing. "The modern farmer," according to Dubos, "spends more industrial calories than he recovers in the form of food." And, as has been pointed out, he uses but a tiny fraction of the main available energy source, solar radiation, and has abandoned the use of windmills and waterwheels.

Artificial Oases

For twenty centuries, cultivators have sought to go beyond manipulating natural inputs in the field by creating much more fully controlled environments under glass. Greenhouses have been used for commercial food production for the past hundred years. Greenhouse history traces back to the Roman Emperor Tiberius Caesar, but until recently the greenhouse was used to maintain a warm enough temperature for the year-round growth of mostly ornamental plants. Its role in producing food crops has been limited to a few specialty vegetables and fruits.

New techniques and technology, artificial cooling, carbon-dioxide enrichment, artificial soil, liquid fertilizers, automated irrigation and new building materials now make possible more approaches to growing under glass, and a much wider variety of crops have been economically grown than had previously been thought feasible. In 1973 the United States had about 1,000 acres under glass or plastic structures, France had 2,700, Turkey 5,000, the Soviet Union about 5,300, and Japan about 25,000.

Hydroponics excited some experimenters a few years ago, but early efforts did not fulfill the visions, and more recently plants have been set in sand or gravel, into which water enriched with nutrients is released regularly. This is actually called *trickleculture*, though commercial operators still call it hydroponics.

The Environmental Research Laboratory at the University of Arizona has pioneered cropping under cover in arid regions. It joined with the University of Sonora in Mexico to build a prototype project on the desert coast of the Gulf of California at Puerto Peñasco. The initial goal was to de-salt water inexpensively and make the coastal desert agriculturally productive. They soon discovered that a flow of desalinated water would cost too much for open-field agriculture, so they began investigating methods for growing crops with as little loss of water as possible. This work led to a new type of greenhouse—an enclosure in which not only temperature but also water and humidity could be meticulously modulated. The staff settled on an enclosure of polyethylene inflated with air, the use of local sand, and a mixture of nutrients, with irrigation water applied only sufficiently to moisten the root zones. The controlled humidity of this closed system reduced plant transpiration, and the enclosure kept out insects and diseases quite well. Eighteen vegetables were successfully grown.

Word of this success reached Sheik Shaikh Zayed of Abu Dhabi, whose 50,000 subjects could buy vegetables only seasonally and in limited quantities. Most of the produce was imported because the country receives only two to three inches of annual rainfall and has strong, frequent winds; the few vegetables produced domestically come mainly from one oasis. Now desert farmers raise cabbages, cucumbers, eggplant, lettuce, okra, peppers, radishes, tomatoes, and turnips; and for the most part yields are higher than those on good American fields or at the oasis farm. In fact, the greenhouses produced five times more cabbage and okra, two to three times more tomatoes and lettuce, eight times more cucumbers, and twelve times more eggplant than a good American farm, and the ratio was even higher over the oasis cultivation. All told, the Abu Dhabi enclosures on five acres could produce a ton of vegetables a day, and in 1972 the tomato harvest was enough for 29,000 persons at the American consumption level. Some crops were exported. However, these enclosed controlled environments do not seem feasible for economic grain production.

The controlled-environment approach enjoys a certain vogue in parts of the United States, notably the Southwest. A California company expanded its facility at Tucson, Arizona, from 1.2 to 10 acres of greenhouses, the largest of which is 264 by 541 feet in size; and an Arizona firm sold 4 million pounds of tomatoes grown "hydroponically" in 1972—not much when compared to the 2.4 billion pounds consumed, but a good size enterprise nevertheless. It was also claimed that these tomatoes were more flavorful because they were vine-ripened before picking. And, if not thoroughly organic in culture, they at least were not sprayed with pesticides. One company built greenhouses by spraying foam plastic over inflated balloons, which they then deflated; the units collapsed, and so did the company. One laborious operation has been achieving pollination through the use of hand-held electric vibrators. While a new pollen blower carried on the back, saves time, one investigator reports that honeybees work almost as well inside plastic structures as outdoors, and is introducing honeybees experimentally on melons.

In the forseeable future, enclosed environments will probably be limited largely to arid regions and higher-priced crops. But when yields are significantly higher than in field agriculture and the price of land rises, as it has in the United States, this approach may be profitable in other areas. Air pollution may encourage the use of enclosed environments, though in 1973, California scientists discovered that pollution had damaged some plants inside oxygenated greenhouses.

Greenhouses also hold promise for the subpolar regions, such as Alaska, where the long photoperiod is an advantage.

6

Intensive Agriculture, the Biosphere, and Earthwatch

The environment is the aggregate of surrounding objects, conditions, and influences; the biosphere is that part of the earth's soil, waters, and atmosphere wherein organisms can subsist; and ecology is the branch of biology treating the relations between organisms and their environment. In nature, all environments work toward an equilibrium, which ecologists call the *climax*, or mature state. All constituents of an environment are interdependent, each reacting and influencing the behavior of the others and forming a series of dynamic loops. Each loop constitutes a micro-ecosystem that interrelates with other micro-ecosystems, and each is naturally self-replenishing, meaning that though it undergoes transformations, nothing is ever really lost. In a mature condition, the biosphere constantly recycles natural wastes and ideally becomes more or less self-sustaining. When equilibria are upset, those species that cannot adapt to the changes become extinct.

Man is capable of establishing himself in a wider niche than other creatures, and as he developed new skills, he gradually made more massive changes in his environment. Without doubt, man's mismanagement of agriculture, industry, and settlement, and his abuses of land, water, and air, have led to ecological calamities.

In early civilizations, no intervention was greater than agriculture—clearing, plowing, seeding, watering, fertilizing, assaulting pests, harvesting, and husbanding. Cultivation and settlement came to be glorified as "conquering the land," but some of the more polemical ecologists suggest that the earth was better off before man's interventions and would be better off if man vanished.

Yet nature is not perfect in maintaining environmental balance either. Before the interventions of man, volcanoes destroyed fertile soils and polluted the air, and ice sheets suppressed much of life over the Northern Hemisphere; their retreat apparently changed the climate over much of northern Africa, where green fields became scorched and barren. Nor do natural mechanisms always sustain optimum populations: Lemmings, muskrats, rabbits, deer, and many other animals suffer population crashes not only from famines but also through epidemics, hormonal imbalances, or mass suicides, often preceded by periods of aberrant behavior because of environmental stresses. As biologist René Dubos says, "The crashes constitute, at best, clumsy ways of re-establishing an equilibrium between population size and local resources. Admittedly, this is a solution, but I doubt, if you were a lemming or muskrat, you would think it a good thing."

In discussing the biosphere, it is important to remember that man, like an animal or plant or volcano, is a fact of nature; and Dubos presents a case for his intervention:

> . . . in a given area, there is usually more than one possible equilibrium state, and thus the *natural selection* is not necessarily the best or most interesting solution. . . . The symbiotic interplay between man and nature has often generated ecosystems more diversified and interesting than those occurring in the state of wilderness.

Within the global ecosystem is a multiplicity of agro-ecosystems created by the intervention of man; in many, the soil has remained fertile, supporting intensive farming. It is possible to cultivate according to the counsel of ecologist Barry Commoner, "Let us hope that we can overcome the myth of omnipotence, and learn that the proper use of science is not to conquer the world, but to live in it." Not all cropping is equally disruptive; it depends on the crop. The hay crops exhaust the soils least in growing; what remains after cutting may offer enough leaf and straw for restorative decomposition and matting for protective cover, and their deep root systems contribute to good soil structure, making it more porous and spongy. Rotation not only between planting and fallow but also among crops may also be helpful. The problem is that we do not employ the more environmentally sound cultivation practices to a great enough extent.

Prehistoric peoples made the transition from gathering to agriculture slowly, partly out of respect for the possibilities of natural backlashes. But success must have broken down this intuitive wariness, and many societies may have collapsed because cultivating practices failed to accommodate the demands of the environment. The Mesopotamian, Mayan, Maltese, Greek, and Roman civilizations declined because the soils were abused or neglected, possibly as outside pressures such as war and pestilence interfered with proper cultivation. In the instance of Mesopotamia (which actually had a sequence of societies as mutually hostile groups variously controlled the territory between the Euphrates and Tigris Rivers), the people failed to maintain their irrigation canals, allowing silt to build up and drainage to become clogged. This, in turn, caused "saline seep," or the salting up of the soils. While some accounts attribute the failure of the civilization to the destruction of the irrigation system by the invading Mongols in 1298, it appears that agriculture had already begun to deteriorate. What happened to the Mayan, and to the earlier Toltec and Olmec civilizations, cannot be documented, but authorities speculate that they vanished in the wake of an environmental holocaust.

In *The Soils That Support Us,* Charles E. Kellog concludes that social maladjustment can also result from a lack of understanding about the requisites of the biosphere, and suggests that the lawlessness and six-shooter justice in the Old West was a consequence of the failure of pioneering farmers to comprehend soils that were new to them. In New England the people were able to cultivate with their traditional implements or adopt Indian crops and practices, and so they adjusted to the soils; law-abiding life continued much as it had in the home country. But the tough root matting of the prairie sod made new implements necessary for growing enough food; and often the climate, with its unobstructed blizzards in winter and tornadoes in summer, made cropping more precarious than in the East—the Indians did not generally crop those lands. In the South, overplanting soil-depleting crops, notably tobacco, created problems.

Nowhere did the attempt to "subdue" the earth proceed more relentlessly than in America, and the Dust Bowl crisis of the 1930s forced a radical change in attitudes toward the land. The Great Plains, among the most fertile regions of the world, were originally shielded from capricious weather by a firm matting of roots and native grasses. But plowing, frequent periods of dryness, tornadoes, and hail gradually wore away the topsoil. During the early 1930s, prolonged drought parched the furrowed fields, and many farmers, under the stresses of weather and depression, planted no more.

Without cover of crops or natural sod, the soil pulverized, and in 1934, heavy winds began to sweep the dry powder off the plains and into the East. By 1936, the plains were barren, and thousands of destitute families were forced to migrate west. The crisis brought forth the most extensive conservation measures taken by the government up to that time: Trees were planted to block winds, straight furrows were replaced by short and angled (contoured) furrows, irrigation projects were conceived, and new watershed management practices were instituted. Government credit was made available to remaining farmers to halt foreclosures and abandonment of the land.

The soils regained their productivity. But we can never take rehabilitation for granted. Each change in our method of cultivation is a change in the way we intrude on the environment and demands a new equilibrium. Much of the Dust Bowl region suffered a long drought again in the 1960s, yet because of conservation practices, the devastation did not reach that of the 1930s. Nonetheless, in 1972, one county agricultural agent opined, "When this land was opened up for settlement, probably a lot of it never should have been plowed up. Never should have left cattle. A lot of people are going to cattle now." And in early 1974, as farmers vastly increased their plantings—the estimate was by

16 million acres—the Soil Conservation Service forecast that half of the "new" land going into crop production would be subject to "excessive soil erosion."

Land Use

The amount of land required to produce food supplies adequate to feed the population in America has decreased each year because the production potential of the land has increased. The quality of the land, however, and the amount of it available for agriculture, has begun to decline.

What we have called "land development" is often irrational exploitation. Urbanization is the chief cause of our dwindling land supply, and urbanized land, if damage is not irreversible, may be restored for agricultural use only at an exorbitant cost. Says Russell E. Train, now head of the Environmental Protection Agency, "The drained wetland, the flooded valley, the farmland that is subdivided or paved can never be restored in any practical sense." Indeed, air and water are more easily rehabilitated; soil is the least easily replenished natural resource.

The demand for water by agriculture, industry, and urbanization is also diminishing our supply of fertile soil. There is a vast flood-control project being constructed in Missouri, which will place over 200,000 acres in seven counties under water and displace 330 farm families, noted for their economic and social stability, as well as 550 nonfarm rural homes.

Much land use is based on the concept of "reclamation." Farmers have felt that land is for cultivation, whatever may be necessary to prepare it—deforestation, swamp drainage, prairie furrowing, or desert irrigation. In the middle of this century, the United States dredged, dammed, and filled a total of one-fourth of the marshes and bogs that we once had, and much of this reclaimed land is now cultivated. Yet the tidal marshes of our Atlantic and Gulf coasts are the richest spawning ground for fish in the country and comprise a major compartment of the biosphere. Literally billions of organisms, including 90 percent of the most important Atlantic commercial fish species, depend on the wetland food chain for their survival.

No thoughtful person can conclude that we are developing and conserving our lands prudently, nor are we set up to do so. According to Senator Henry M. Jackson of Washington, by 1970, land use was determined by some 60,000 separate jurisdictions, each with some measure of zoning authority. This naturally results in conflicts of essentially legitimate interests and a staggering waste of resources. The National Governors' Conference has proposed a state-by-state inventory of land not yet urbanized, for which prudent plans would be formulated, taking into consideration the needs of the environment, agriculture, industry, recreation, and urbanization, rather than simply letting the marketplace make all the decisions.

Water Use

Though damming, diverting, and transporting water is expensive, water itself has always been considered "cheap." This is not so, and it is especially untrue for agriculture. Irrigation experts today say that only rainwater is absolutely safe for crops—although even that might not be so if it contains certain pollutants. All other water, as it travels through the subsoil and over the surface of the earth, picks up the dissolved salts of various minerals. When it flows over cropland, it deposits the mineral salts in the topsoil if drainage is not sufficient to allow the salts to sink below the root zone.

Salinity has become a major problem on a great deal of land, and is becoming more of one. A sufficient amount of water will flush the salts through the root zone into the lower layers of the soil, but many farmers do not irrigate enough to achieve this effect, so the problem becomes one of both quantity and quality. Runoff from soil in which salinity has built up becomes ever more saline and returns more salt to the original supply sources. And water percolating upward as soil layers dry, saline seep, may be saltier than the oceans. By 1973, water-quality problems were serious in the lower Colorado, Rio Grande, Ohio, and Tennessee rivers, the rivers of the Southeast, the Great Lakes, and, to a lesser extent, the Mississippi, the Great Basin, and the rivers of California. And saline seep affects millions of acres over the

Great Plains. In the seventeen Western states, where irrigation is largely concentrated, about half of the watered lands have salinity problems, and recent estimates suggest that over a quarter of a million square miles of the northern Great Plains, extending into Canada, are in danger.

Thus, while irrigation water is sometimes returned to a stream, lake, or aquifer, this agricultural "recycling" does not necessarily provide for cleansing. The Colorado River has been to the Southwest what the Nile has been to Egypt and the Tigris and Euphrates to the vanished civilizations of Mesopotamia: a substitute for rains and a natural aqueduct for tapping. Yet it now presents an ecological horror story—so much so that some authorities suggest we have a "Mesopotamia West" in the making. All along its 1,450 miles, men impound and divert its waters, beginning in the mountains 20 miles from its source where the first dam siphons away 30 percent. Among the cluster of reservoirs are Lake Powell, backed up 180 miles behind Glenn Canyon Dam and holding the equivalent of two years full flow, Lake Mead holding about as much behind Hoover Dam, impoundment after impoundment for 400 miles through the Mojave desert, and finally, Morelos Dam which diverts what is left of the flow into Mexico.

By the time the water reaches Imperial Dam 30 miles above Morelos Dam, which provides water for the Imperial and Coachella Valleys of California and the Yuma area of Arizona, salinity has risen to 850 parts per million, cutting yields of lettuce and melons; in fact, few crops have not suffered as the salts clog their roots. But the water going to the Mexicali Valley of Baja California has reached as high as 3,000 to 4,500 million parts, largely because of the return seepage from the especially salty Arizona land, and the Mexicans claim the water is no longer usable for farming. (Sea water contains 35,000 parts of salt per million.) Under a 1914 treaty, the United States guaranteed the Mexicans 1.5 million acre feet of usable water a year, and Mexico threatened to claim reparations from the United States as the Mexicali farmers' protest mounted. So, in 1973, the United States agreed to build the largest desalination plant in the world to remove 90 percent of the salt as it treats 130 to 140 million gallons of brackish water daily.

Other evidence that planners did not pay attention to all the consequences comes from Lake Powell, now the longest man-made lake in America with 7 million acre feet of water. It is formed over porous sandstone, which one geologist, Bill Breed, likens to "building on a sponge"; the loss is estimated at 1.5 million acre feet annually—10 percent of the flow. Still more water is lost to evaporation. And sediment has been piling up much more quickly than had been estimated; by 1974, it was 75 feet deep at the head of the lake, indicating that the impoundment will be silted up in 75 to 100 years. It has also inundated one of the most beautiful canyons in the country. More dams have been proposed, including two in the Grand Canyon by two public utilities companies, though back in 1965 *Fortune* reported:

> The combined capacity of . . . existing dams on the Colorado is more than adequate to impound the river's peak flows, so Bridge and Marble [dams] are not needed. . . . Since water would evaporate from the lakes backed up behind the dams, construction of them would decrease, not increase, the available water supply.

A dam at Bridge Canyon would also back water deep into one of the nation's greatest natural wonders, Grand Canyon, of which Theodore Roosevelt, the founding father of reclamation, implored, "Leave it as it is. You cannot improve on it. The ages have been at work on it, and man can only mar it."

Another problem has been caused by the excessive "mining" of aquifers, which caused the water table to sink gradually. This occurred in the San Joaquin Valley over a quarter of a century ago, and by 1970, the land itself was sinking about a foot every year because water was being drained more quickly than it was being replenished. Canals built to carry in water to check further depletion and land damage were endangered by the sinking surface, and the quality of the water also declined.

Micro-climates

An undesirable side effect of irrigation is that it may create, in a previously arid zone, an oasis of humidity and plants that attract unwanted insects. In Israel, where arid lands have been made remarkably productive, farmers watering tomatoes with overhead sprinklers in one area found that they were harvesting yields one-half to one-third lower than plants receiving water flowing through furrows between rows of plants because the sprinkling raised the humidity and lowered the temperature, and the new micro-environment was hospitable to certain fungi.

Another ecological horror story comes from the largest man-made body of water in the world, Lake Kariba, which covers 1,700 square miles in Rhodesia and Zambia. Because it greatly extends the shoreline micro-environment, it is a congenial habitat for the notorious tsetse fly, which infects both cattle and man with sleeping sickness, and has so far defied control. (The planning, incidentally, did not include an environmental survey of the lake basin, which would have pointed up the fact that farmers in the area relied on livestock.)

Channelization, the practice of straightening meandering stream beds for flood prevention and improved drainage, has had both positive and negative impacts. In some cases it caused the flood problem simply to move downstream, increase in severity, and erode farmland there without achieving a counterbalancing gain in drainage. It also caused a lowering of aquifer levels, the degradation of water quality, and the destruction of trees and other shoreline vegetation, which, in turn, interferes with the hydrological cycle and consequently with the wildlife chain, including fisheries.

The floodplains on either bank of a stream channel are as much a part of the waterway as the channel itself. When the stream overflows, the flood plains receive the excess water, slow its flow, and allow it to spread out. They also serve as a basin for the precious topsoil washing down from the mountainous watersheds and as a huge storage tank facilitating the replenishment of aquifers. In 1910 Missouri farmers channelized the Blackwater River to drain floodplain swamps, so that they might be cultivated. But the water once absorbed by that floodplain now frequently floods a 46-mile stretch below the 18 miles of channelization, removing good farm soil because its rate of flow is increased. The state Conservation Department studied the impact on fish population and found that, where the river had not been straightened, there were 565 pounds of fish per acre, 449 pounds where slightly channelized, and 131 pounds where completely channelized. A study of the Tippah River in Mississippi showed that only 5 pounds of game fish per acre remained after channelization, whereas 240 pounds existed before. Increasingly, informed opinion is pressing federal agencies to end this "aqua-bulldozer" approach and to develop projects to protect and improve the natural development of floodplains.

Organisms

Since the clearing of natural vegetation for monoculture may offer lusher bounty than customary for a resident insect that was previously only a secondary pest or no pest at all, or encourage immigration of a pest, one would assume that the pest's predators would soon increase also. This is not necessarily the case, for two hypothesized reasons.

Kenneth Hagan, an insect nutritionist at the International Biological Control Center, believes that varying dietary factors are involved. Insect pests are generally lower on the food chain than the beneficials, meaning their food requirements are less complex—they need less diversity to survive. We are aware of the viability of the cockroach, probably the longest-surviving creature extant, and know that the beneficial, pollinating bee quickly perishes in many places where cockroaches find satisfactory nutrition. Monoculturing may become a complicating factor in that it may eliminate other food sources needed by beneficials, or in some other way destroy habitat support and protection; it creates for them dangers of an ecological desert. We can observe these phenomena in nature, too; when an adversity damages nests of some insects or higher animals, or lays bare their protective cover, driver or army ants may "march" upon the defenseless creatures, often destroying their colonies.

Changes in insect roles occur also in the fashion remarked by a western cattle breeder "I didn't mind the weed-eating grasshoppers, but unfortunately they thought my alfalfa was a weed." In other instances, the filling in of marshes—so-called reclamation —wipes out whole species of beneficial insects, fish, reptiles, and waterfowl. Even where there is no drainage and fill, pesticides

and other pollutants may kill these pest controllers or force them
to migrate.

Pollution of Agriculture

Not long ago, an extensive, brownish smog bank rolled eastward
from Los Angeles toward the San Bernardino Mountains, where
it hovered over a field of romaine lettuce. Before nightfall, the
field looked as if it had been swept by a blowtorch. Except for
the rapidity of the scorching, the episode was not unusual. Similar
episodes have been occurring over the past twenty years from
California to New Jersey. These clouds of pollution are particularly damaging to citrus fruits, and where they have not put
truck farmers out of business (notably in Illinois, New York, and
Pennsylvania), they have sharply reduced incomes.

Many gases, including sulfur dioxide, nitrogen dioxide, PAN
(peroxyacetyl nitrate), fluoride, and chlorine, are toxic to plants.
They may damage the outside of the plant, destroying the market
value of the crop; or they may retard photosynthesis, affect water
intake, and reduce yields. Certain fluorides mar leaves without
affecting yields, but excessive amounts in forage make it useless
as feed. Some pollution simply slows down plant growth in a
manner too subtle to observe, which might suit a house owner
with a lawn to mow, but not a grower of food crops. Ray Thompson, a plant pathologist at the University of California at River-
side, proved, by growing fruit in greenhouses in which the air
was filtered, that dirty air has cut grape poundage by 60 percent,
oranges by 50 percent, and lemons by 30 percent. In extreme
cases, air pollutants can denude an area, render fertile soils non-
productive, or make the land unusable for certain crops.

For many years, pollution damage to harvests went unrecognized. On the Delmarva Peninsula, plant pathologists studied a
potato blight known as "speckle leaf" for a long time without
making a successful diagnosis. The culprit proved to be no pathogen, but the internal combustion engine, and the offending pollutants were traced north as far as New York City.

A case study appearing in the *Wall Street Journal* described
the effect of pollution on a large truck farm in California. On

hot and sunny days, when the air stagnated and irrigation added to the humidity, plants would be severely damaged by a level of pollution far below that which would irritate humans.

Procedures for estimating the dollar value of the losses have not been successfully evolved, nor has there been much investigation into the damage to essential nutrients of a crop. In its 1970 annual report, the federal Council on Environmental Quality estimated yearly pollution damage to food production at half a billion dollars or higher. But in 1973 the Stanford Research Institute released a study claiming to use more sophisticated techniques of analysis that projected a lower, though still substantial, loss of $132 million annually, nearly two-thirds of which resulted from damage to food crops. The most severe damage was reported in the heavy industrialized areas of the Middle Atlantic, Eastern, and North-Central states. Harris M. Benedict, a plant physiologist and chief researcher for the Stanford project, said that earlier estimates had been computed from observations in fields randomly selected and emphasized that this study was the first based on a systematic analysis of crop yield, emission sources, and weather conditions in 551 of the country's 3,134 counties, which were selected because they had the highest pollution levels.

Because the Stanford report estimated comparatively little damage, and because it was sponsored by the Coordinating Research Council (a nonprofit organization funded by the American Petroleum Institute and the Motor Vehicle Manufacturers Association, as well as the Environmental Protection Agency), the study's analysis was closely scrutinized and criticized for not taking into account the less obvious losses. "It is not difficult to assess what the loss might be," said one critic, "if the crop is just not up to snuff." There are other effects to consider—for example, erosion subsequent to the death of crops and the costs for a grower to relocate.

At present, county farm agents are receiving instruction on how to determine direct pollution injury, and scientists are constructing mathematical models to project the total costs of damages. Methods of protecting crops, such as spraying with an antioxidant, have been tried, but they have so far been unsuccessful. This, of course, may approach the problem from the wrong end; the only solution may be the reduction of pollutants.

Pollution by Agriculture

The prominent British environmentalist Kenneth Malleanby said in 1971, "We will have the environment continuing to deteriorate if agriculture goes on developing as it has. We are learning to deal with urban pollution. But we haven't learned to deal with rural pollution. I think this is going to be a big question for the future." And the Council on Environmental Quality reported in 1972, "Land runoff from farms and even urban land, as opposed to discharges from cities and factories, has a much greater impact than we realized. In all types of river basins, the concentration of nutrients is increasing."

Silt is the greatest pollution problem caused by agriculture. Others are pesticides and fertilizers, and the heat produced by return flows of irrigation water and, increasingly, the excesses of excreta in large feedlots and chicken "factories."

Concern over agricultural pollution is not new, but early investigations had little impact. In 1888 J.W.Sanborn, the director of an agricultural experiment station in Missouri, conducted a series of long-term growing experiments to establish the effects of contemporary practices on crop yield and on the soil. Over fifty years later, the station published an alarming report based on its patient study of the effects of nitrate fertilizers. Essentially, what the study found was that while nitrate fertilizer sustains crop growth, it fails to restore the humus nitrogen lost from the virgin soil. "The organic matter content and the physical condition of the soil on the chemically treated plots have declined rapidly," the report said. "These altered conditions have prevented sufficient water from percolating into the soil and being stored for drought periods. Apparently, a condition has developed in the soil whereby the nutrients applied are not delivered to the plant when needed for optimum growth." It appeared that the soil did not hold most of the nitrogen not used by the crop, resulting in denitrification, or the reduction of nitrates to nitrites, ammonia, and free nitrogen.

In 1967, the ecologist Barry Commoner, in the prestigious Norman Bauer Memorial Symposium at the annual meeting of the American Association for the Advancement of Science, compared the potential danger of excessive use of nitrate fertilizers to that of radioactive fallout:

In effect, the Sanborn Field studies were a warning that in humus, depleted soil nitrate fertilizer tends to break out of the natural self-containment of the soil system and to penetrate the air and the water. . . . Therefore, we must look for some of the 6 million tons of nitrogen added to the U.S. soil during the last year not in the soil, or in the harvested crops, but in the nation's lakes and rivers, and in the rain and snow that falls on the land.

Thus, like fallout from nuclear testing, the massive use of inorganic fertilizer during the last twenty-five years has intruded on vital processes in the environment.

But few data were available at the time, and the only detailed national survey of nitrogen in rain and snow had been reported in 1958. There were striking regional concentrations, notably in the corn belt and the Southwest.

Many vegetables and forage crops now contain appreciably more nitrate than formerly. Although nitrate is normally innocuous, under certain conditions bacteria living in an animal's digestive tract can convert it into nitrite, a dangerous substance. If nitrite reaches the blood, it can destroy the capacity of hemoglobin to transport oxygen, leading to respiratory failures. This condition may also develop in humans, especially in infants, whose intestines are more likely to contain those types of bacteria that convert nitrates. The Missouri Agricultural Experiment Station has reported excessive nitrate content in some commercial baby foods, especially those based on beets and spinach. Some drinking water, especially from rural wells, contains nitrate. It is possible that nitrite is carcinogenic.

Inorganic nutrients leached from heavily fertilized land disrupt the balance of aquatic biology. A Wisconsin study in 1947 showed that the annual drainage of nitrogen from a square mile of farmland was equivalent to the amount of nitrogen represented by the sewage produced annually by 750 people. Agricultural runoff contributed dramatically in recent years to the pollution of Lake Erie. Commoner stated:

. . . the lake's nitrogen balance has been upset by a stress about equally derived from the city and the farm. Much of this material has accumulated, largely as organic matter, in the lake bottom. Instead of Lake Erie forming a waterway

for sending wastes to the sea, it has become a trap which is
gradually accumulating in its bottom waste material dumped
into it over the years—a kind of huge underwater cesspool!

In advocating limitations on the use of inorganic nitrogen fertilizer, Commoner conceded it could cause "a massive dislocation"
in the present system of farming.

Within two weeks, the National Plant Food Institute, one of
the fertilizer trade associations, forwarded the AAAS paper to
soil experts at nine major universities for reaction, and at the
time the economic consequences of reducing fertilizer application
were more apparent than the ecological consequences. But further
concern developed when health authorities in Decatur, Illinois, in
routine checking, discovered that the municipal water supply
had contained more than the 45 parts per million of nitrate than
recommended by the FDA. The water comes from Lake Decatur,
a reservoir on the Sangamon River, and tests showed excess nitrate
in both river and impoundment. Followup investigation by the
Washington University Center for the Biology of Natural Systems and other studies showed that a minimum of 60 percent of
Lake Decatur nitrate originated from artificial fertilizer nitrogen
used on adjacent farms in the river's watershed area. Sometime
later the Illinois Pollution Control Board made an unprecedented
proposal: state regulations to govern the use of fertilizer.

The urgency was underscored by reports of infant methemoglobinemia from excessive nitrate from France, Germany, Czechoslovakia, and Israel, and finally in Illinois. Abraham Gelperin, a
medical researcher at the University of Illinois, has reported that
in five counties the mortality rate for female infants born during
April, May, and June, when nitrate levels were high, as 5.5 per
1,000, compared to 2.5 per 1,000 when levels were low. Commoner suggests in *The Closing Circle*, "This may be the first evidence of the cost in human health of the intensive use of fertilizer nitrogen. . . . All this reflects the unexpected result of an important technological advance, which was permitted to intrude
significantly on the environment before we were aware that it
would not only improve agriculture, but also harm human
health."

The question of how much chemical fertilizer is safe remains.

In 1973, two University of Minnesota researchers, Robert Gast and Philip Goodrich, reported that if a buildup of inorganic fertilizers and animal waste occurs in the soil, "there may be a slow but irreversible movement of nitrates through the soil into the groundwater for years in the future," though they suggested that the problem is not universal. They remarked that the practice of "chopping," or trimming back crops to boost the growth rates, has "continuously removed more plant nutrients, especially nitrogen, than have been returned to the soil by fertilizers, plant residues, legume crops, rainwater, and animal wastes" and contended that increased application of fertilizers rich in nitrate is the only way to maintain harvest levels.

Of nearly four hundred federally inspected poultry plants in 1970, no more than one in ten had a treatment or even primary treatment system for waste water; in that year, poultry plants used over 27 billion gallons. Only one in four with private treatment facilities met the best practicable control-technology standards, while over half used municipal treatment facilities. The Federal Water Pollution Control Act requires that meat and poultry plants discharging effluent into a navigable body of water obtain a certificate attesting that the effluent meets water quality standards, and no discharge is allowable if it endangers the health or welfare of any person. (Jurisdictional disputes sometimes arise over the disposal of waste. The Department of Agriculture may require a smooth, nonporous floor, easily washed down, for plant cleanliness and removal of waste, while the Department of Labor, charged with enforcing the Occupational Safety and Health Act of 1970 (OSHA), could find the floor slippery and recommend a rough surface for sound footing. In order to bring about effective and uniform codes, the Council of State Governments in 1973 suggested a model law that would protect the environment from damage caused by unregulated animal feedlots.)

Since the expansion of livestock feedlots and poultry confinements, the disposal of animal wastes has become a problem. It has been remarked that feedlot operators get used to odors more quickly than other people, who quickly scent groundwater into which feedlot wastes seep under certain soil conditions. In fact, in those parts of the West where feedlots may service 100,000 head of cattle, some underground water has become unfit for animals as well as humans. Colorado scientist F. G. Viets suggests that these operations be moved into drier areas of the country.

The potentials of recycling have recently been drawing attention. For example, a cow utilizes only 40 to 60 percent of the energy available in the cell walls of forage and excretes the rest, which means that "wastes" still contain a good deal of nutrition. Barn wastes have been blended into dehydrated and pellet rations, and, with certain chemical treatments, these can be converted into more digestible food for ruminants. (Safety tests on these have been underway for the past couple of years.) And poultry operations do not generally salvage blood and grease, which could be made into protein supplements for feed and other by-products.

Manure was once a crop fertilizer, and a midwestern corn-and-hog farmer told me how, within his memory, people would ask him if he had any to spare. Later, he would offer manure to people if they would simply haul it away. And by the 1970s he had to pay for disposal. There are other wastes, including urine, bedding, unused portions of carcasses, and the carcasses of those animals that die before slaughter. In 1972 it was calculated that American livestock produced 2 billion tons of waste annually, of which 1.2 billion tons are solid animal waste, 400 million are liquid animal wastes, and 400 million are animal-associated.

But today chemical engineers are re-evaluating what has been characterized as "a monumental problem of disposal," and Arthur Humphrey, dean of the College of Engineering and Applied Science at the University of Pennsylvania notes that animal manure could have been profitably recycled into single-cell protein (SCP) in 1973. SCP comes from single-cell micro-organisms which, as they grow on agricultural wastes or fossil fuels, convert inorganic nitrogen to cellular protein; the microbial cells often contain more than 65 percent protein. The cost to produce SCP from manure has been estimated at $270 to $300 per ton, previously not economical, but in 1973 it compared to soy meal at $260 a ton.

The New Earthwatch

In July 1972 the United States shot into polar orbit the ERTS-1, or Earth Resources Technology satellite, a spacecraft that looks like a moth with an oversize body and undersize wings. It soars at an altitude of about 570 miles, completing an orbit every 103 minutes, and every day transmits up to 752 photos, each covering an area 115 miles square. All objects, animate and inanimate, emit, absorb, or reflect light in their own way, that may be visible or invisible, and can be picked up by remote-sensing devices. The patterns of emission, absorption, or reflection, called *spectral signatures*, can be recorded by the satellite for relay back to earth. Among spectral signatures of value to agricultural analysts are those indicating crop variety, stage of growth, and vigor; states of soil fertility and moisture, including snowcover; pest and disease infestations and their migratory directions; degrees and types of pollution in the air, ground, and water; and cases or threats of erosion. Agricultural surveillance was integrated into the Apollo and Skylab programs.

Several agricultural states are drawing upon the photos for land-utilization planning, according to Arch Park, chief of NASA Earth Resources Survey Program, and several foreign governments have requested surveys of soil types for farm planning. Analyzing photos of the Imperial Valley, agriculturists found that they could distinguish between fields that were fallow, freshly plowed, seeded—though here the distinction between newly planted and barren land was more difficult—and fields with maturing crops. From photos of 3,200 square miles in Arizona, they were able to differentiate among 29 types of vegetation. Also in California, the effectiveness of pest-control efforts, particularly against the citrus black fly and cotton boll weevil, are being monitored.

In examining photographs of especially lush vegetation in Florida, a scientist located an area surprisingly rich in ground-water. Photographs of Oklahoma revealed that a chemical defoliant had injured timber that planes had failed to spot, and a plague of spruce beetles occupying 200,000 acres was mapped in Alaska. Ocean dumping and the spread of films of surface pollutants were tracked, and underwater effluents piped into the Niagara River were sighted. Scientists have been able to keep under observation an area of California where, after a frostkill of trees, a record growth of grass and wild oats has become what has been described as "the greatest fire hazard of the century."

One of the major missions of the Skylab 1 astronauts included photographing the soil salinity of the Rio Grande Valley, a rampant tree blight northwest of the mouth of the Rio Grande, and the moisture cycle and a plague of locusts in the Sudan. They also attempted to spot feeding fish off Panama City and Pensacola, Florida. And Skylab took an inventory of land use and land conditions in Ecuador and the Philippines.

Much of what is being learned will be useful to a new UN program that was established in 1972 to safeguard the human environment. The program will comprise a global network of 110 stations to monitor conditions of the land, water, and atmosphere. One hundred stations will monitor regional trends, and the other ten, called baseline stations, will be located in some of the more isolated, clean parts of the earth, providing a standard for determining the severity of pollution elsewhere. After the General Assembly approved the program, Maurice F. Strong, a Canadian industrialist who will head the new Earthwatch Governing Council, said, "What has happened today may be a turning point . . . in the history of our planet."

But in the drive to safeguard the global environment generally, and, more specifically, to foster food agriculture and commercial fishing intelligently, analysts will be needed more than ever to take advantage of the new monitoring technologies. Robert N. Colwell, professor of forestry and associate director of the Space Sciences Laboratory at Berkeley, told the 1974 meeting of the American Association for the Advancement of Science:

> While computer-based systems may ultimately provide the most efficient method for gathering agricultural statistics of extensive areas, at the present time the human interpreter represents the most expedient way to perform an operational inventory in the United States. For many of the emerging nations of the world where both national agricultural statistics and computer systems may be non-existent, the data gathered by human interpreters can provide a valuable input to the management decisions for agricultural resources.

Part II / The Cornucopia of Agriculture

7

The Imperative of Nutrition

Globally, the dietary situation is critical. Specialized agencies of the United Nations report that over half of all peoples are chronically malnourished, and this estimate may be conservative. P. S. Venkatachalam, an M.D. specializing in clinical nutrition with the UN Protein Advisory Group (PAG) calls "specific famine" that state in which one does not starve to death from lack of enough food but suffers from deficits of essential nutrients. According to Sripati Chandrasekhar, a respected Indian demographer, perhaps 80 percent of Indian children suffer from "malnutritional dwarfism." In *The Hungry Future*, French scholars, René Dumont and Bernard Rosier, write that "the world is now in the grip of a colossal famine . . . the disease of slaves." Most of the victims of specific famine are among the poor, unskilled, and uneducated of the Third World, a large proportion of whom— over one-third in some areas—are also unemployed.

Higher incomes and education do not ensure high dietary standards. Many well-to-do Americans consume too much fat, sugar, and alcohol; others rely too heavily on "health" foods which may be poorly balanced. While about 15 million of our poor suffer from undernutrition or malnutrition, some 70 million Americans are overweight and have gotten that way by overloading themselves with unnutritious foods which can lead to obesity, heart disorder, or diabetes. According to Paul LaChance, a nutritional physiologist at Rutgers, studies show that half of all American families have at least one member "eating helter-skelter" and suffering from a vitamin deficiency. More than 98 percent of Americans have suffered dental decay, which is often related to dietary deficiency, and some 20 million Americans have lost more than half of their teeth. Most serious, perhaps, is mental retardation and malfunctioning of the nervous system, which experiments have related to the lack or imbalance of certain nutrients.

The National Nutrition Survey completed in 1970 showed that among 83,000 living in 10 states one-fourth of those subsisting below the poverty level were anemic. The diets of 17 percent were deficient in vitamin B_2, or riboflavin, 8 percent in vitamin A, and 7 percent in vitamin C. Similar deficiencies, though less extensive, existed among those in higher income brackets.

Adolescents ten to sixteen years old showed the highest prevalence of malnutrition, and persons over sixty in all income and ethnic blocs suffered general undernutrition. The Department of Agriculture, in a more recent survey, found that in all age groups, regardless of income level, the average of several essential nutrients—vitamin B_6, calcium, iron, and magnesium—was below what is recommended for good health. George M. Briggs, a nutritionist at Berkeley, suggests that borderline deficiencies in vitamin B_6 and folic acid, the trace elements potassium and zinc, and possibly selenium and magnesium may be spreading throughout the population. Such stresses as pregnancy, illness, medicinal drugs, psychological pressures, and the consequences of genetic abnormalities may cause persons with normally adequate diets to be deficient in some nutrients.

In testimony before the Senate Select Committee on Nutrition and Human Needs chaired by George McGovern, Jean Mayer, the Harvard nutritionist who headed a presidential study, recommended a crash program of nutritional education. That malnutrition is extensive among the affluent as well as poor Americans is not difficult to understand in light of limited nutritional knowledge taught high school and college students. Furthermore, nutrition is a subject that medical schools have overlooked in their curricula, so most physicians are poorly informed, except in such conditions as ulcers or diabetes where special diets become therapeutically involved. According to C. E. Butterworth, chairman of the American Medical Association's Council on Nutrition, only about a dozen of the nation's 120 medical schools have full departments of nutrition, and the average medical student may learn little or nothing about how to feed a normal human being to maintain good health.

Actually, much of what we know about nutrition was established by veterinarians, agriculturists, and bio-chemists, not by medical specialists. Theodore Van Itallie, who pioneered hospital-based nutrition research and is director of medicine at St. Luke's Hospital in New York, says that "nutrition has been plagued by mediocre research, [and] with a lot of animal feeding experiments that are not particularly relevant to human development." Since clinical nutrition lacks prestige, talented medical researchers prefer more glamorous fields.

In trying to establish new recommended dietary allowances for nutrients, the Food and Nutrition Board of the National Academy of Sciences and National Research Council reported that "there is often a paucity of human data, and knowledge is limited for many nutrients," and that there is a "scarcity of definitive studies" on which to base conclusions.

Commercial food promotion is hardly remedial—on the contrary, it has been at times actually misguided. Advertising, says Mayer, "too often represents a massive threat to nutrition education." The director of the Columbia University Institute of Human Nutrition, Myron Winick, says, "Our choices are not nutritional choices, but instead are governed by a constant barrage of advertising and the speed of supermarket turnover. The food industry doesn't compete on the basis of the nutritive quality of the product." For example, when whole wheat is milled into white flour, it loses more than half of each of its fourteen essential vitamins and minerals; but when white bread is "enriched," only four of them are added.

It has been said that America is a nation of "nutritional illiterates." To the extent that people concern themselves with eating standards, they largely emphasize weight control and flavor rather than the sound functioning of body and mind. Many meals, especially restaurant meals, lack the necessary variety of nutrients, and many are high in what Mayer calls "the deadly trinity of cholesterol, sugar, and sodium." Snacks, particularly those preferred by children and adolescents, may fill half of their calorie requirements while being deficient in essential protein. Certain recent changes in food habits have hardly been encouraging. Between 1955 and 1965, the average consumption of enriched white flour dropped 41 percent, fresh milk 19 percent, and fruits and vegetables 10 percent. Consumption of baked products rose 65 percent, soft drinks 76 percent, and potato chips and snacks 83 percent. The increase in our consumption of meat (at least until the 1973 surge in meat prices) somewhat counterbalances the degeneration of our diets. The final irony of all this is that a balanced diet is more likely to lead to an attractive physique and may also cater to taste and smell.

The rich, fatty diets, indulged in by so many Americans have been statistically correlated with heart attacks. Deaths resulting from complications of high blood pressure rose among the Germans and Japanese when their diets became higher in calories. In the area that now has the world's highest incidence of heart attacks, North Karelia, Finland, the average diet is high in saturated dairy fats and low in vegetables. Until a recent rise in incomes, the North Karelians sold their cream, drank skim milk, and were less apt to have heart attacks. (Doctors point out, incidentally, that chances of heart attack multiply when the cholesterol level rises even slightly and other risk factors—notably smoking and high blood pressure—combine. One risk factor doubles the chances of a seizure, two factors triple the chances, and all three increase them tenfold.)

One of the most significant longitudinal studies of the natural history of malnutrition has been underway in Lahore, Pakistan, since 1964. A specialist in children's diseases and professor of medicine who has headed the investigation, L. M. K. Wasti, observes that underweight children are likely to catch up to the norm if not subject to deterrent factors. But, he wrote, if stressed by malnutrition, undernutrition, or disease, "the child will be overwhelmed and slump back never to catch up." He characterizes such children as "adversity adapted" because they give up trying to be fully normal. Many of them die, and the survivors are sickly. Adults also exhibit this pattern. Aaron Altschul, a leading Department of Agriculture nutritionist, states, "Evidence shows that poorly fed people lose the ability and incentive to perform up to their potential." Arnold E. Schaefer, who headed a national nutrition study with a sample of 70,000 persons in 10 states, told the McGovern committee in 1971 that preliminary reports disclosed "a high prevalence of signs associated with inadequate nutrition, including growth retardation." His study disclosed that unacceptable levels of vitamins A and C and iron were common.

So disturbing were the findings that, when publication of the report was held up and Dr. Schaefer tried to avoid further public discussion, Senator Ernest F. Hollings of South Carolina accused the Nixon administration of threatening to send the nutritionist into involuntary retirement. The problem of malnutrition was put baldly by Hollings when he appeared before the McGovern committee:

> . . . many is the time that my friends have pointed a finger and said, "Look at the dumb Negro." The charge too often is accurate—he is dumb. But not because of the color of his skin. He is dumb because we have denied him food. Dumb in infancy, he has been blighted for life.

Nutrition

As a science, nutrition is quite new; until far into the last century, most people did not differentiate greatly between the health values of most foods. But the groundwork for the reorientation of popular attitudes was laid by some sound deductions, despite the absence of scientific understanding of how nutritional deficiencies caused medical problems.

When affluent classes of the past seemed to be overindulging at the table, rulers sought to restrain them through sumptuary laws. Economic and moral factors were probably involved in the passage of these laws, but it is very likely that excessive eating was considered unwholesome as well as wasteful. In the fourth century B.C., Greek authorities passed a measure limiting the number of dinner guests to thirty; the French government passed similar legislation sixteen centuries later, in 1294. In the early fourteenth century, Edward II of England issued this proclamation:

> By the outrageous and excessive multitude of meats and dishes, which the great men of the kingdom used in their castles, and by persons of inferior rank imitating their example, beyond what their stations required, and their circumstances could afford, many great evils had come upon the kingdom, the health of the King's subjects had been injured, their property consumed, and they had been reduced to poverty. . . . Great men of the kingdom should have only two courses of flesh meats served up to their table: each course consisting of only two kinds of flesh meat. . . . On fish days they should only have two courses of fish, each consisting of two kinds, with an intermeat of one kind of fish if they thought fit.

Violators were to be "severely punished." A French dictum of 1629 forbade putting more than six pieces of food on a platter, but for the next century the wealthy continued to revel dietarily, sometimes assembling morsels into pyramids as high as eighteen feet. Historically, sumptuary laws were about as effective as Prohibition.

Nineteenth-century reformers who suggested a more analytical approach to diet planning were generally considered eccentrics or cranks. In 1869, however, Yale University awarded Wilbur O. Atwater a Ph.D. for his dissertation on the chemical compositions of different varieties of corn, and later, as the first director of the Office of Experiment Stations in the Department of Agriculture, Atwater devoted much of his energy to nutrition research, encouraging others to do so, too. (The department dedicates to his memory an annual lecture given by a person of signal achievement in the field.) Until early in this century, American food-control laws and regulations aimed mainly at preventing adulteration and ensuring sanitation. It was not until 1921 that the journal of the American Public Health Association could editorialize, "the center of gravity of the [food] problem has shifted from sanitation to nutrition."

By 1912, pioneering nutritionists had proved that diets restricted to fats, proteins, carbohydrates, and inorganic salts are insufficient for good health. Yet modern medicine was slow to pick up the gauntlet. The 1965 *Today's Health Guide* (the latest one published), which is prepared periodically for family reference by the American Medical Association, scarcely mentions the major nutritional deficiency diseases. In 1965 a World Health Organization (WHO) committee stated:

> . . . the importance of the interaction of nutrition and infection . . . receives little emphasis in the training of physicians and public health workers. In general, neither health workers concerned with nutrition nor those engaged in the control of communicable disease [recognize] the value of coordinated measures.

Of Fetal and Brain Sparing

We now know that nutrition affects a woman's reproductive performance, her ability to bear the soundest possible offspring, and that, in the early months of life, it is a powerful environmental influence on genetic potential.

Early in this century, investigators assumed that the fetus, like a parasite, "robbed" its host of nutrients. They based the hypothesis on studies showing that babies born to poorly fed mothers weighed about the same as those born to other women; it was nature's way, they said, of helping the species survive. They called it *fetal sparing*. But in 1968 a nutritional bio-chemist at Johns Hopkins University, Bacon F. Chow, learned that malnourished female rats and mice bore offspring that were physically stunted, mentally retarded, and behaviorally aberrant. "As mature animals," he reported, "they learned standard mazes less rapidly than the offspring of adequately fed mothers, were more vulnerable to disease, gained less weight on the same food intake, and seemed generally ill-equipped to live." The complications multiplied ominously. Chow further found that females lacking protein bore offspring that utilized protein less efficiently than normal animals even when well fed after birth. This impairment also occurred if, during the nursing period, the mothers were poorly fed. The catalogue of abnormalities included stunted physiques, catatonic stances (a syndrome of muscular rigidity and mental stupor) that at times alternated with excitement and confusion as in schizophrenia, reduced learning capacity, production of fewer antibodies against disease and less successful stimulation of the antigens which produce them, and signs of less efficient uses of nutrients.

"Our work shows definitely," wrote Chow in a personal communication, "that for rats and mice, maternal diet can and does affect the growth and development of offspring."

The debunking of the theory of fetal sparing led scientists to re-examine the theory of *brain sparing*; that is, if diet is deficient during gestation or infancy, the body, in allocating available nutrients, favors the brain. In several species, including rats, mice, piglets, and dogs, experimenters found that diets deficient in protein fed to the progeny even of well-nourished mothers resulted in damage to the central nervous system of the young: piglets walked on tiptoe with a "hobble skirt" gate, puppies became irritable, rats had faulty visual perception, and mice had poor memories. Examinations of nerve and neurological cells in the spinal cord and medulla revealed physiological changes. Still more disturbing, some of these symptoms—including delayed psychomotor development and lower scores on IQ tests—appeared to be passed on to at least two future generations as though they were genetically transmitted.

The brain grows in three phases: by cell division alone, then by both cell division and cell enlargement, and finally by cell enlargement alone. In the human being, the critical cell-division period normally lasts up to six months after birth. Animal experiments show that malnourishment during these phases of brain development results in subnormal brain weight, protein content, and cell number.

Proper nutrition is as important to the mother as it is to the fetus. In an investigation at the University of Toronto, 90 out of 210 pregnant women who ate poorly during the first half of their pregnancies were placed on sound diets. The well-fed mothers showed better health for the remainder of their pregnancies, while the others suffered much higher incidences of anemia, toxemia (poisons in the blood often self-generated by pregnant women), threatened and actual miscarriages, premature births, and still births. The healthier women also labored about five hours less than those poorly nourished, and their infants were in better health throughout their first six months. Rats deprived of proper nourishment during cell division never make up the loss unless their diets are improved just before the phase ends, and piglets show brain changes, including fewer neurons in the gray matter.

Determining the consequences of malnutrition in the human brain has been difficult because experiments cannot be conducted humanely and verifying examinations cannot yet be performed on the living. A Cornell team examined the brains of nine Chilean infants who had died of malnutrition and found that all had subnormal numbers of brain cells; three had as much as 60 percent fewer than normal. Although cell loss is permanent physical damage, its relevance to intelligence and behavior has still to be learned. The formation of the fatty protective covering of nerve fibers, myelin, which the fetus begins to form in the seventh month, is also impaired by severe malnutrition. If the formation has been impaired, the child's brain is likely to function poorly.

After birth, the brain continues growing rapidly, doubling in size within six months, and doubling again by age four. Then growth slows down, and at about age twenty, the brain is only another 15 percent larger. During those first four years of growth, the infant's sensorimotor and conceptual development advances far more rapidly than it ever will again. The importance of this period has been emphasized by the director of the Institute of Human Development at Berkeley, Paul H. Mussen, who points out that reasoned learning, once thought to be a later stage of development, may begin from the first day of life. Large advances not only in motor skills but in language, cognition, experimenting, and even defining goals occur during the second year. Two investigators with the Soviet Academy of Medical Science, I. A. Alekseeva and S. I. Kaplanskaya-Raiskaya, investigating nutrition and mental performance in man within the framework of the Pavlovian conditioned-reflex school, found that children who were short of protein had disturbed cortical functioning related to the cerebrum, that their capacities to elaborate new conditioned reflexes declined, and that those already established then became depressed or were eliminated.

Conclusive evidence on malnutrition-induced injuries during

formative stages of human development was all but nonexistent until the late 1960s. Certain diseases, it was discovered, were caused not by genetic but by dietary factors. Nobel laureate Linus Pauling, for example, suggested that a "localized cerebral deficiency disease" or "cerebral scurvy," previously thought hereditary, actually was rooted in a chemical imbalance caused by dietary deficiency. Yet observations were contradictory. Pediatrician Paul Gyorgy observed that preschool Indonesian children on meager diets, although small of stature, nonetheless have well-proportioned bodies and "far from being lethargic or peevish, are without any other obviously truly pathological criteria of protein-calorie deficiency diseases."

To resolve questions such as these, the Hospital Infantil de Mexico conducted pioneering investigations in Tlaltizapan, a community whose quite uniform economic and social composition eliminated socioeconomic differences as possible influences. The studies confirmed correlations between malnutrition, infection, physical stunting, and mental retardation. A child dwarfed by malnutrition, for example, was more likely to score poorly in visual acuity, skin sensation, and integrating responses (body movement).

What Bacon Chow described as "a hitherto unrecognized phenomenon of food waste" in malnourished 9- and 10-year-old children was also discovered a few years ago in Taiwan, where poor families subsist mainly on low-protein sweet potatoes. Their children actually lose weight when put on a diet sufficient for normal weight gain among children whose families serve ample animal-protein foods; in fact, up to 30 to 40 percent more food is needed for these deprived youngsters to gain weight.

A Balanced Diet

Sound nutrition means getting all the nutrients our bodies need, the right quantity of each, and—often crucial—in proper proportion to each other. So far as is known, forty to fifty nutrients contribute to the building, maintenance, and repair of the body. The macro-nutrients—those nutrients we need in large amounts

—are protein, carbohydrates, and fats; micro-nutrients—those of which we need relatively little—are vitamins and minerals (some of the latter are technically classified as "trace elements" because only minute quantities are needed). When the body lacks the quantities of food energy it needs, it is said to be undernourished; when it lacks the balances needed, it is malnourished.

Those short of macro-nutrients are likely to feel hungry, experiencing pangs. Proteins normally build our bodies, but if we take in too few calories, the body draws on protein for energy —in severe cases, on its own muscle. This is the process of starvation as it is popularly understood. On the other hand, those suffering from a shortage of one or more micro-nutrients may not feel hungry at all, though the peril to their health may be greater.

Specific dietary requirements are not the same for everyone; they vary according to age, type of work, weight, to some extent climate, and perhaps sex—pregnancy obviously alters dietary needs of women. A physically active man in a temperate zone needs 3,500 calories daily for effective work, personal growth, and extended longevity. These calories, the source of energy, should be balanced by 71 grams of proteins, 25 of which should be "complete"—that is, containing the eight essential amino acids in proper proportions.

With the goal of improving the national diet, the federal government recently sought recommendations from the National Academy of Sciences and the National Research Council and, with their guidance, formulated the Recommended Daily Allowances (RDA). By setting maximum and minimum amounts for essential nutrients, the RDA meet the requirements of over 95 percent of the normal, healthy population. Previously, the Food and Drug Administration had operated around a generally lower standard called the Minimum Daily Requirement, which set levels only high enough to prevent disease and not necessarily high enough to ensure robust health.

Table 7.1 shows the RDA and permissible composition ranges for dietary supplements of vitamins and minerals.

The RDA of protein is generally 0.424 grams per pound of human weight (including overweight). Growing children and pregnant or nursing women are advised to add about 10 and 20

TABLE 7.1. U.S. Government Recommended Daily Allowances and Permissible Composition Ranges for Dietary Supplements of Vitamins and Minerals

Vitamins	Unit of Measurement	Infants and Children Under 4 Years of Age — Recommended Daily Allowance		Adults and Children 4 or More Years of Age — Recommended Daily Allowance		Pregnant or Lactating Women — Recommended Daily Allowance	
		Lower Limit	Upper Limit	Lower Limit	Upper Limit	Lower Limit	Upper Limit
Vitamin A	Int'l Units	1,250	30	2,500	—	5,000	8,000
Vitamin D1	Int'l Units	200	0.2	400	5,000	400	400
Vitamin E	Int'l Units	5.0	15	15	—	2,500	60
Vitamin C	Milligrams	20	60	45	30	60	120
Folacin[2]	Milligrams	0.1	0.3	90	0.4	0.4	0.8
Thiamin	Milligrams	0.35	1.05	0.75	2.25	1.5	3.0
Riboflavin	Milligrams	0.4	1.2	0.8	2.6	1.7	3.4
Niacin	Milligrams	4.5	13.5	10	30	20	40
Vitamin B_6	Milligrams	0.35	1.05	1.0	3.0	2.0	4.0
Vitamin B_{12}	Micrograms	1.5	4.5	3	9	6	12
Minerals							
Calcium	Grams	0.125	1.2	0.125	1.5	0.125	2.0
Phosphorus[3]	Grams	0.125	1.2	0.125	1.5	—	—
Iodine	Micrograms	35	105	75	225	150	300
Iron	Milligrams	5.0	15	9.0	27	18	60
Magnesium	Milligrams	40	300	100	600	100	800

SOURCE: Food and Drug Administration.

[1] Optional for adults and children 4 or more years of age.

[2] Optional for liquid products.

[3] Optional for pregnant or lactating women.

grams respectively to their normal allowance. A protein deficit, it should be pointed out, is not necessarily reflected by a loss of weight, and many obese persons suffer from a loss of bodily protein reserves.

The main energy sources are carbohydrates—sugars and starches—and fats. The brain requires only carbohydrates for energy, but the body can use carbohydrates and fats interchangeably. The most concentrated source of food energy is fat, which is also high in vitamins A, D, E, and K. In the body, deposits of fat provide insulation and other protection, and fat is the major source of energy for muscles. Some fat is also needed for the absorption of the fat-soluble vitamins, A, D, E, and K.

The body converts fat into fatty acids, which are needed for normal growth, and which also prevent certain infant skin disorders. Although the precise mechanisms by which fatty acids fulfill specific bio-chemical functions are yet to be determined, their indispensability was demonstrated in 1929 by George O. Burr and M. M. Burr, who experimented with rats at the University of Minnesota. If the animals did not have at least one of three fatty acids, they failed to grow, their tails withered, their skin became scaly, their hair fell out, their kidneys degenerated, blood appeared in the urine, and eventually they died. Some studies have also indicated that fatty acids are associated with lower cholesterol concentration and therefore may be a prophylactic against atherosclerosis.

Fats are characterized as saturated or unsaturated, depending on their chemical structure. Saturated fats, such as those in meat and butter, are the ones mainly eaten by the typical American. They are usually solid at room temperature. Once in the blood, they transport more cholesterol—a fatty alcohol in animal and dairy fats and egg yolks—than the unsaturated fats, and therefore may cause higher cholesterol deposits, which can clog the arteries and lead to atherosclerotic heart disease. Unsaturated fats, such as those in vegetables, are typically liquid at room temperature. Fats in our diets, say the National Academy of Sciences, the American Medical Association, and the American Heart Association, should provide 35 percent of our calories, rather than the average 40 to 45 percent they do now; and saturated and unsaturated fats should be eaten in equal quantities. Fats improve the taste of foods and gratify our appetites, since they take longer to digest. It is difficult not to eat quite a bit of fat, because about half the amount we eat is "hidden" in many foods. Extremely low-fat diets, incidentally, should be avoided unless medically prescribed.

Protein and Kwashiorkor

Protein is composed of amino acids. Twenty-two amino acids have been identified, but adult humans need only eight. The essential ones are isoleucine, leucine, lysine, methionine, phenylalanine, threonine, tryptophan, and valine. During childhood, the body also needs histidine.

If all essential amino acids are not regularly and concurrently within our bodies, those that are present cannot fully combine to build a complete body protein. If one or more are in short supply, the body does not get total utilization of all the others. For example, if lysine is present only at 50 percent of the requisite level, the body can use only 50 percent of all the amino acids, even if the others are present in adequate supply. The rest are excreted as waste.

We sometimes call complete protein *animal protein* because meats are sources of complete protein, notwithstanding the fact that some vegetables (notably soybeans, broadbeans, and lentils) also provide complete protein. Among foods that offer complete protein are red meat, poultry, fish, eggs, milk, cheese, and some vegetables.

Three-fourths of our body substances and many internal functions, including the production of hormones and enzymes, depend upon protein. When children fail to receive enough complete protein, they develop a condition known as *kwashiorkor*. An apparent variation of this ailment, known as *marasmus*, occurs in adults, although some experts say this is mainly caused by caloric deficit.

Freely translated from Ghanian, kwashiorkor means "the sickness the child gets when another baby is born" or "deposed child." It strikes most often among children aged one to four, after a new infant monopolizes the mother's milk.

Kwashiorkor progressively ravages the appearance, and visible symptoms include hair changes, diffuse pigmentation, a moon face, and ulceration and bleeding lesions, especially on skin exposed to sunlight. The skin may show red patches, or what is called "flashy paint" by blacks. Some types of hair become reddish, and black hair becomes grayish white, straw-colored, or brown. It also becomes brittle and sparse, and is easily pulled out. While the muscles waste, an edema causes the abdomen to distend and the legs to puff out with its effusion of fluid into tissue spaces and body cavities. The liver enlarges and its structure changes, and apparently the blood plasma does not carry vitamin A well, resulting often in avitaminosis—the vitamin A deficiency condition. Psychomotor activity is disrupted. At first the child is likely to be irritable, and then apathetic, perhaps whimpering. As atrophy progresses, the face of the child transmogrifies into the shriveled countenance of an old person.

Studies in the United States, Jamaica, and South America have shown that six-year-olds with kwashiorkor have the mental and physiological development of children only half their age, and the electrical activity of their brains is abnormal. Altschul has stated:

> Children who survive a protein-deprived childhood cannot learn as well in their formative years as their well-fed counterparts. . . . Evidence is accumulating that their mental capacity, because of retarded brain growth, is permanently impaired.

The Vitamins

Vitamins are a discovery of the twentieth century, though the existence of unknown but essential nutrients was suspected in the late nineteenth century. J. B. A. Dumas, who investigated the effects of infant diets during the 1870–71 siege of Paris, was apparently the first scientist to question the adequacy of a diet made up only of protein, carbohydrates, and salts. In 1880 Estonian bio-chemist Nikolai Lunin fed mice pure food concentrates of all the nutrients then known, and, except for those fed on milk alone, they died within a few weeks. In 1906 Frederick Gowland

Hopkins, an English bio-chemist and Nobel laureate, called the unknown nutrients "accessory food factors," and in 1911 Casimir Funk, a Polish chemist working in London, named the substances *vitamines.*

One reason why nutritional deficiency was not quickly accepted as a cause of diseases was, ironically, Louis Pasteur's and Robert Koch's discovery that bacteria cause diseases. But in 1918 a bio-chemist, Elmer V. McCollum, wrote, "Milk and the leaves of plants are to be regarded as protective foods and should never be omitted from the diet." By 1922, the existence of vitamins A, B, C, D, and E had been proved, and in 1926 researchers discovered that the B vitamin took at least two forms. Later they found it was a complex family; the most recent vitamin discovered, in 1948, is B_{12}.

The vitamins act as organic catalysts affecting many bodily functions, some essential to good health and others essential to life itself. As the body consumes more calories, it needs proportionately more vitamins, since they are necessary in the utilization of calories. Some vitamins are soluble in fat and others in water, a distinction that is important to good food habits. The body can store A, D, E, and K, which are fat-soluble, but it cannot reserve B and C, which are water-soluble. Excesses of water-soluble vitamins are discharged and must be replenished when needed again. As late as the 1940s it was thought that excesses of any vitamin were excreted, but recent evidence has shown that excesses of some, notably A and D, are retained and can be injurious.

Because deficiencies in vitamins cause disorders, the idea that more of a good thing is better grew and then climaxed in mega-doses of vitamin capsules—megavitamin therapy—and more controversy. Psychiatrists Humphry Osmond and A. Hoffer began treating schizophrenics with niacin in 1952, and later concluded that mental illness can result from a low concentration in the brain of any of several vitamins. Orthomolecular psychiatry, the treatment of mental illness with huge amounts of vitamins, is opposed by the American Psychiatric Association and the National Institute of Mental Health. Some authorities say that the approach is not nutritional but pharmacological. In any event, in 1973 the Food and Drug Administration classified vitamin pills with more than 150 percent of the recommended daily allowance as drugs, and powerful doses of vitamins A and D now require a prescription.

Vitamin A and the Eyes

Vitamin A is essential to good vision and contributes to healthy skin and other epithelial tissue, such as membrane around the eyes, lining of blood vessels, and covering in the respiratory tract. A mild case of vitamin A deficiency is likely to bring on night blindness or snow blindness, or to aggravate color blindness, while a more serious deficiency may cause *keratomalacia*, which affects the cornea, or *xerophthalmia*, which results in a drying of the membrane and other parts of the eye. Both these conditions, without early treatment, can result in partial or total blindness. Of children suffering from both keratomalacia and protein-calorie malnutrition, up to 30 percent may die, 25 percent may lose their sight totally, and most of the remainder will suffer permanently impaired vision.

The critical factor in protein–vitamin A deficiency is balance. A child that grows slowly because of protein deficiency and also lacks vitamin A may nevertheless have healthy eyes, for, although both nutrients are inadequate, they remain in balance to one another. But if the protein deficiency is remedied with no increase in A, the disproportion may precipitate xerophthalmia. Skim-milk distribution programs in Brazil and Indonesia, which bolstered protein consumption, have been followed by epidemics of both keratomalacia and xerophthalmia because A, in which the diets were also deficient, was not correspondingly increased.

A deficiency may also cause a dermatosis symptomatized by a dryness and roughening of the skin and by itching.

Among poor people, the lack of vitamin A has been one of the three most serious dietary deficiencies (protein and iron are the others), and probably the main cause of impaired and lost vision. High incidences of eye affliction have been observed during famine. In India in 1970, health authorities estimated that nearly 5 million were blind from avitaminosis and that 12,000 to 14,000 children have been losing their vision annually. Even the 1970 American Nutritional Survey showed that, in New York City, nearly a third of the children under the age of twelve were deficient in vitamin A. The incidence was almost three times as great among children of lower-income families.

Yet the vitamin is readily available at low cost. A deep-yellow or orange color indicates its presence, which means it is found in carrots, sweet potatoes, apricots, peaches, cantaloupe, butter, and Cheddar cheese. Dark-green vegetables, including spinach, mustard greens, and Swiss chard also provide it, and so do fresh milk and fish-liver oils. A substance called *carotene*, which is called a precursor or provitamin because the body converts it into vitamin A, is contained in some red and yellow fruits.

Vital as it is, vitamin A in large doses is dangerous. The recommended daily allowance for adults is 4,500 to 5,000 international units, except for pregnant and lactating women, who are advised to take 6,000 and 8,000 respectively. Overconsumption in adults can cause headaches and decalcification of the bone resulting in aching joints; in children it can cause excessive fluid in the brain resulting in symptoms that mimic the symptoms of a tumor. The 1973 FDA restrictions define vitamin A capsules above 10,000 units as a prescription drug.

The Vitamin B Complex

Several important nutrients are included in the vitamin B complex. There is an RDA for six of them, which are folacin, thiamin, riboflavin, niacin, B_6, and B_{12}. Others also contribute to wholesome nutrition, but enough of these are generally consumed when the diet provides the RDA of the others.

Before the complexities of the B compounds were understood, B was associated with pellagra, a neurological affliction symptomatized by impairment or loss of intellectual capacity and disintegration of the personality. *Pellagra* translates as "rough skin," which is another symptom. The Spaniard Gaspar Casal first described pellagra in 1735, when he observed it among peasants subsisting mostly on corn. The disease was endemic among many Americans into this century, and especially among poor southerners, both white and black, who got along mainly on corn. It was so rampant along the Mississippi during World War I that it became known as "Pellagra River." The member of the B complex that prevents it is niacin, or nicotinic acid.

Many doctors thought that pellagra was infectious until Dr. Joseph Goldberger, assigned to investigate it by the U.S. Bureau of Public Health, discovered in 1915 that it was not transferable, and that it was prevalent only among those who relied on cornmeal rather than meat, milk, or eggs. Some primitive people discovered that they could avoid pellagra by soaking corn in lime water before grinding. Actually, most foods contain niacin, but it is particularly plentiful in meat (including liver and fish), whole-meal cereals, and pulses. Unlike the other water-soluble vitamins, the body can store niacin to some degree in the liver. The body can also convert the amino acid tryptophan into niacin.

Thiamin is also known as B_1, aneurin, and aneurine. A deficiency of thiamin, combined with an excess of carbohydrates, causes a disease of the peripheral nerves known as *beriberi*. Among adults, beriberi has two syndromes that are quite different in appearance. The "dry" form, characterized by neuritis, a nerve inflammation, is a wasting away of the limbs in which the leg muscles in particular atrophy and become paralyzed. The "wet" form is characterized by edema, swellings of the limbs and abdomen as fluid accumulates in tissue spaces or body cavities, and eventually by heart failure. If a nursing mother lacks thiamin, her infant may share the deficit, which may cause it to relapse from an apparently good condition into a syndrome of screaming, stretching of the body, hardening of the stomach, labored breathing, thready pulse, and a facial paleness or bluishness. These attacks, lasting from a half to a full hour, recur with increasing severity. Acute beriberi occurs with a sudden onset of nausea and vomiting, an enlargement of the heart, and an accelerated pulse. In rudimentary beriberi, there are mild symptoms of weakness in the legs, some swelling, abdominal pain, and heart palpitations, which may persist for years or abruptly transform into a condition critical to life.

Beriberi has been under observation for centuries. Chinese writings of the third, seventh, and eighth centuries refer to it as *Kak-ke*. The first European description was published in 1642 by a Dutch physician, Jacobus Bontius, who was with the East India Company in Batavia. Dutch medical journals began publishing reports on its incidence in the navy in 1859, and there were hundreds of cases a year among Japanese seamen, who called it *kakké*. The deathrate was over 8 per 1,000. In the late nineteenth century, beriberi was also frequent among Japanese soldiers, police, shop boys, and students, especially in the larger towns. In the 1880s a Japanese medical officer, whose proposals for changes in the naval diet were rejected, finally proved his point by supplying vessels for the same long voyage with different food stocks, one with a standard diet high in rice carbohydrates and the other with more meat, fish, vegetables, and condensed milk, and less rice. The latter ship returned after a voyage of 287 days with no deaths and only 10 cases of beriberi, all of which occurred in men who had refused to eat all of the new ration— especially the milk and meat. The other ship had 160 beriberi cases and 25 deaths.

But the lesson did not get through to the Europeans, who remained preoccupied with the discovery of the bacterial origin of diseases. Those who focused any attention at all on food in relation to beriberi assumed that rice must contain some toxin.

The key discovery was made by accident in 1897 by Christian Eijkman, who headed a new research laboratory of bacteriology and pathology in Batavia, and had once served on a commission hunting for the cause of beriberi in the East Indies. He kept some poultry in the laboratory and fed them mainly white rice left over from a military hospital. The poultry soon developed *polyneuritis gallarium*, which resembles beriberi in man. For some unknown reason, the fowl were switched to cheap brown (unrefined) rice (one account claims a budget-obsessed administrator ordered it), and the polyneuritis disappeared. Eijkman first erroneously deduced that white rice contained a toxin counteracted by the outer coating, but an associate, Gerrit Grijns, found that birds eating various native beans as well as white rice also stayed healthy.

So confusing did the literature become that Edward B. Vedder of the U.S. Army Medical Corps, who studied the problem in the Philippines from 1904 to 1913, said that it was difficult "to sift the wheat from the chaff, or the rice from the rice polishings." Vedder correctly deduced that the husk contains a substance preventing beriberi, but he did not isolate it.

During this period, two British physicians, H. Fraser and A. T. Stanton, through feeding experiments with two camps of road workers, disproved the hypothesis that white rice contained toxic substances and concluded that something in the brown husk, which had been removed in refining, prevented the illness. A young scholar subsequently associated with Vedder, R. R. Williams, finally isolated the anti-beriberi vitamin, and spent twenty-six years determining its chemical structure and developing its synthesis. We now know that thiamin is also particularly important in the metabolism of carbohydrates.

Thiamin is in all plants and animals, but the richest sources are seeds, peas, beans and other pulses, soybeans, peanuts, and yeast. In animal foods, thiamin is more concentrated in liver than in muscle. Today, enriched bread is a major protection against beriberi.

Thiamin deficiency may occur among the more affluent for a number of reasons. In the Far East, white rice is considered a socially superior food to brown. And thiamin is soluble in water and destroyed by high temperatures, so when vegetables are boiled in a lot of water and the water is discarded, the vitamin is lost. Soda and certain other chemicals used in food processing also destroy thiamin.

A deficiency of vitamin B_2, or riboflavin, causes cracking of the mucous membranes of the lips and mouth, an inflamed tongue, changes in skin around the base of the nose, and bloodshot eyes. In the past this syndrome was sometimes mistaken for venereal disease because of the similarity of some of the observable symptoms and because they usually occurred among the lower classes, thought by elitists to be promiscuous. A shortage of riboflavin also impairs the metabolism of other nutrients, and is associated with tumors. Richard S. Rivlin, a Columbia University professor of medicine, describes its effect as "complicated" in that "in some ways it inhibits tumor growth and in other ways enhances it." It is difficult to gauge the amount needed for good health.

Riboflavin is available in milk, milk products, liver, fish, poultry, eggs, and whole-grain breads and cereals.

Still less is known about the need for vitamin B_3, or pantothenate; it is known to be necessary for the growth of pigeons, and it is a factor in chick pellagra. Abram Hoffer, a Canadian psychiatrist and the president of the American Schizophrenia Association, reports that massive doses of vitamin B_3, along with niacin and vitamin C, have been used successfully in treating schizophrenia in its early stages. The nutrient is in all animal and plant tissues, especially liver, kidney, yeast, wheat, bran, and peas.

Vitamin B_6 was discovered in 1936. It is not a single substance but a collection of substances, of which at least one is essential to the functioning of more than thirty enzymes. A deficiency of B_6 caused convulsive seizures in human infants. Evidence of a deficiency disorder is not conclusive for adults, but when an inhibitory analogue of the vitamin is added to a diet deficient in other respects, adults develop a syndrome characterized by dermatitis, a lip inflammation, a tongue inflammation, and mental depression. It also appears that an insufficient amount of B_6 in the diets of pregnant women leads to unsound metabolism. In fact, the vitamin plays an important role in all protein metabolism and in the synthesis of hemoglobin and serotonin—a compound occurring in the brain, intestines, and blood platelets.

B_6 is found widely in animal and plant foods, especially ham, fish, liver, milk, eggs, whole-grain cereals, corn, and lima beans. The body does not store much of it and can handle a great deal before a toxic level is reached. B_6 is vulnerable to heat.

Pantothenic acid, discovered in 1938, functions as a part of the enzymes involved in the metabolism of fats and carbohydrates, and is essential for the synthesis of steroids, including cholesterol, adrenalin, and sex hormones. A deficiency of this substance in adult men has produced such subjective neurological symptoms as numbness, tingling or burning sensations in the feet, and an impaired sense of balance. Liver, kidney, eggs, cereals, and yeast are good sources, and milk and vegetables contain moderate amounts; fruits and muscle meat are poorer sources.

Folacin is another member of the B complex. It is also known as folic acid and pteroylmonoglutamic acid and was discovered in 1944. It is involved in a number of metabolic processes, including the synthesis of methionine and the formation of components of DNA. It appears that a deficiency quickly affects the maturation of the red and white blood cells, and may contribute to pernicious anemia.

Folacin deficiency is associated with megobolastic anemia among women taking contraceptive pills, and it is related to pernicious anemia. If women become pregnant after discontinuing the pill, the earlier nutritional deficiency may lead to the risk of complications which some authorities believe can be prevented with supplements of this vitamin.

Folacin is found in many animal and vegetable foods, particularly glandular meat, green leafy vegetables (including grass), and yeast. Milk, muscle meat, and cereals are lower in it. Storage, processing, and cooking cause a considerable loss of folic acid.

The most recently discovered vitamin is B_{12}, or cyanocobalamin. It was discovered in 1948, and is essential for the normal functioning of all cells, though only 141 *billionths* of an ounce is needed per day. Its discovery resulted from an intensive search for a control of pernicious anemia; it was found that a high dose —a millionth of a gram daily—relieves all symptoms in man. It also helps treat some other types of anemia, although not always to the extent that folic acid does. Physicians found that a shortage of B_{12} caused stunting among the children of a British vegetarian sect and sore tongues, stiff backs, and nervous disorders among the adults.

Although the precise functions of B_{12} are yet to be determined, some evidence suggests that it is involved with folic acid in the synthesis of DNA components and the formation of methionine. It is absorbed from the intestinal tract, but only if a certain substance called the *intrinsic factor*, produced by the gastric mucous membrane, is present. Absorption may also be disrupted by certain parasites, such as a fish tapeworm found in people who eat seafood raw.

Many foods contain B_{12}, especially animal products. Liver, milk, eggs, and fish and shellfish are particularly high in it. Plants have virtually none.

Vitamin C

Man is one of the few species whose bodies cannot synthesize or store vitamin C, or ascorbic acid. We should eat it daily, but in no event less often than once a week.

The deficiency disease most commonly associated with it is *scurvy*, the symptoms of which are swollen and bleeding gums, dark-bluish discoloring of the skin, exhaustion, and depression.

It is also involved in the healing of wounds and resistance to infection, and is necessary for the functioning of some glands and for the formation of collagen, the cementing substance of the cell walls, which is required for healthy gums. Infants, children, and pregnant and lactating mothers need it in large quantities.

In 1970 Linus Pauling, a Nobel laureate, in his book, *Vitamin C and the Common Cold*, advocated large doses of vitamin C to prevent or cure colds and flu. Some nutritionists are skeptical. Excessive intake of vitamin C can clog the urinary tract and acidify the urine, and it can harm some persons with kidney stones. Diabetics may have trouble testing themselves for the correct insulin injection if the vitamin C level in the blood is high. Consumers' Union cautioned that high dosages might cause a dietary imbalance resulting in other disorders, but Pauling continued to assert that we need ten times more than the amount specified by the FDA Food and Nutrition Board. In 1973 Man-Li S. Yew of the University of Texas at Austin tested dosages on guinea pigs, and suggested that Pauling's recommendation might be conservative. He found that small amounts of C did help the animals' growth, sound healing, or resistance to surgical stress, but that there was a larger, optimum amount. In an article in the *Proceedings of the National Academy of Sciences*, he recommended that children take in 1,500 milligrams of C daily—about fifteen times the RDA.

Scurvy has traditionally been known as the sailor's disease. A British expedition to the Pacific in 1740 lost 626 of 961 men, mostly to scurvy, and at least 10,000 died of it during the Gold Rush, stimulating the founding of the citrus orchards in California. Because the military persisted in the belief that scurvy was a sea ailment, no precautions were taken during the American Civil War, and nearly 31,000 cases and at least 338 deaths were reported. It was rampant during the siege of Paris of the Franco-Prussian War; during the siege of Port Arthur of the Russo-Japanese War, half of the beseiged soldiers had it; and thousands of men came down with it during World War I.

Yet preventive measures had long been known. Jacques Cartier, a Frenchman exploring Canada in 1535 and 1536, learned that the Indians cured scurvy with juices of tree leaves and their dregs. He did not identify the tree, but the leaves and twigs of several trees, including pine, some other evergreens, and willow, have C. In 1720 an Austrian army surgeon observed that fresh vegetables cured scurvy and that dried vegetables did not.

Vitamin C is water-soluble. It is in high supply in many fruits, including citrus, cantaloupe, mango, papaya, strawberries, and guava, as well as in such vegetables as tomatoes, raw greens, cabbage, green pepper, potatoes, and broccoli.

Vitamin D

Of all the vitamins, only D is available at no cost, and yet the major disease that it prevents, *rickets,* still occurs. There are some eleven provitamins in or on the skin, which are converted into vitamin D when exposed to sunlight or ultraviolet rays. D is necessary to the use of calcium and phosphorous, and thereby contributes crucially to skeletal growth and to the health of bones and teeth. A deficit in children causes rickets, which is a softening and possible deforming of the bones. The disease is most severe among children also deficient in calcium. Adults, especially pregnant women, may also experience a softening of the bones, debility, and pain.

The incidence of rickets is high throughout the world, especially in areas where little sun strikes the streets. Children in slums are more likely to have rickets than the general urban or entire rural population. In a study in New York City in 1921, two-thirds of the children showed symptoms, and the rate approached 100 percent among children of poor Italian immigrants and blacks. It was particularly common among European children during industrialization. In certain cultures, excessive clothing may be responsible—the Mohammedan rule of purdah, for example, forbids women to expose even their full faces out-of-doors, and where darker skins are considered low class, it may be customary to cover a child fully to ensure paler skin. When missionaries persuaded them to abandon their nudity, the Polynesians developed soft bones and other deformities. (It should be noted, though, that excessive exposure to sunlight is also harmful, and some experts believe that sunlight between 10 A.M. and 2 P.M. may induce skin cancer.) According to a survey conducted by the

Academy of Pediatrics shortly before 1970, the incidence of rickets in the United States remained surprisingly frequent.

Another reason for the prevalence of rickets is that vitamin D is not widely present in foods. Long before its discovery in 1922, the Scots in the eighteenth century observed that cod liver oil prevented it, and since early in this century, it has been used therapeutically. The two important forms of vitamin D are known as D_2 and D_3, the first found in plants and yeasts after ultraviolet irradiation, and the second in fish-liver oil and in animal products after irradiation. Egg yolk, cream, and butter contain some, and milk is usually fortified with it.

Massive doses of vitamin D can be toxic, softening tissues throughout the body and depositing calcium in the arteries. Overdoses of D_2 demineralize the bones, leading to trauma and then multiple fractures. In children, excessive D causes loss of appetite, nausea, vomiting, abdominal pain, colic, sometimes diarrhea but more frequently constipation, weight loss, dehydration, apathy, and possibly headaches, fever, cramps, convulsion, and visual disturbances. The clinical picture may mimic tuberculosis, meningitis, or encephalitis.

Vitamin E

Aside from vitamin C, the nutrient causing the most excitement and controversy has been vitamin E, or alpha-tocopherole (the Greek word for "oil of fertility"). Not much is known about it, though it was discovered in 1923. Yet it has been recommended as a treatment or preventive for heart disease, sterility, miscarriage, senility, rheumatic fever, hypertension, acne, and muscle disorders; since its virtues were extolled in 1964, drugstore sales have exceeded those of vitamin C. In 1973 it was estimated that up to 50 million Americans were taking vitamin E in capsule form. A deficiency of vitamin E causes sterility in male rats, and it therefore became reputed as a fertility and virility vitamin; but the National Research Council in 1973 reported that investigations on its effects on humans had failed to prove that it is helpful in megadoses and advised against them.

Investigations of extravagant claims have been inconclusive if not disappointing, but the exceptions have been intriguing. In

1973 a Swedish physician, Knut Haeger, reported substantial improvement in over one thousand elderly male patients with an arteriosclerosis-connected vessel disorder after many years of large doses of E. In premature babies, E prevents anemia and has shown promise in treating an eye condition that can cause blindness in extreme cases. According to Canadian cardiologist Wilfrid Shute, it might be useful in treating damaged hearts, and some authorities say it is useful for some digestion problems. University of Cincinnati scientists have used vitamin E successfully in treating animals suffering from a muscular deterioration similar to muscular dystrophy in humans, and other animal studies suggest that it prevents lung-cell damage caused by two common air pollutants, nitrogen dioxide and ozone. It is certain that E prevents the oxidation of polyunsaturated fats needed by the body cells.

Most of us obtain enough vitamin E without particular attention, since it is present in leafy vegetables and vegetable oils, meats, eggs, wheat germ, wheat sprouts, whole grains, and nuts. Most infants require 10 international units and adults 30, and there is little evidence that overdoses are toxic. It is fat-soluble.

Vitamin K and Other Compounds

Vitamin K is a fat-soluble vitamin discovered in 1935. It contributes to the clotting of blood in wounds and hemorrhages. Although no RDA is stipulated because the level needed is unknown, doctors often give infants 1 milligram daily as a prophylactic against hemorrhaging. K is present mainly in green leafy vegetables, liver, soy oil, egg yoke, cabbage, and cauliflower.

Other Substances

At least three compounds play roles similar to vitamins, but generally scientists do not classify them as such.

Choline contributes to nerve functioning, fat metabolism, and tissue building, and is the precursor of acetylcholine, which helps transport nerve impulses. Rats suffer retarded growth, bleeding kidneys, fatty livers, paralysis of the hind legs, and poor reproduction and lactation when they are deficient in choline. Dogs develop fatty and cirrhotic livers, and chicks grow poorly and develop perosis. Choline is not present in fruits, but it is present in meats, egg yolks, whole grains, legumes, and milk; consequently, few humans or animals lack it.

Inositol is believed associated with fat transport and is a constituent of compounds found in the heart and brain. Much more of inositol is required than of most vitamins. Unlike some vitamins, it does not function as a co-enzyme, but is part of a structural unit in the body. A deficiency slows growth and causes dermatitis and loss of hair in mice, and fatty livers and poor eyes in rats. Inositol is contained in liver, milk, fruits, vegetables, and cereal grains.

Para-aminobenzoic acid (PABA) is important as a nutrient of the micro-organisms residing in the intestinal tract, and is associated with the intestinal synthesis of various B vitamins. It is also indirectly in the synthesis of certain amino acids. It occurs in many plants and animals, and it is especially abundant in yeast.

The Minerals

Although the relationship of some of the minerals to sound health has long been understood, we have recently been learning about the contributions of others. In 1973 the RDA listed five major minerals—iron, calcium, iodine, magnesium, and phosphorus (the last optional for pregnant or lactating women). While some of the others, usually referred to as trace elements, are vital, the quantities needed are small, and believed normally provided by reasonably good food habits.

Iron

Iron is a constituent of hemoglobin, the substance in the blood that carries oxygen, and several enzymes. A shortage of iron reduces the number of red blood cells or cuts the amount of hemoglobin carried by the cells. Hemoglobin carries about three-fourths of the iron we take in, and the rest is stored in the liver, spleen, and bone marrow, which release it when it is needed to maintain the requisite level in the blood. Because blood tests may still indicate adequate hemoglobin while the reserves of iron are nearly depleted, an examiner may overlook incipient deficiencies.

Anemia is a deficiency of hemoglobin, and it is the most widespread nutritional deficiency disease in the United States today. (There are nine major types of anemia, and iron-deficiency anemia is distinct from pernicious anemia, which is caused by a lack of folic acid and vitamin B_{12}.) Anemia usually progresses slowly. Early symptoms of fatigue and weakness are followed by shortness of breath; heart palpitations during exertion; soreness at the corners of the mouth; numbness in the hands and feet; swelling of the feet and ankles; and thin, rigid, easily broken fingernails.

The main victims of anemia are pregnant and nursing women, for whom the RDA is double that for other adults, and young children, especially those from six months to two years, who need nearly as much as a normal adult. Women fitted with intrauterine devices may menstruate twice as copiously as previously and therefore require larger amounts of iron. An estimated 40 percent of the women in some African countries suffer from this type of anemia, and in India a survey revealed that about 14 percent of adults of both sexes have it. As anemia worsens, membranes around the eyes and mouth become pale. The "laziness" ascribed to many poor people, especially in the tropics, may often really be the lethargy of anemia.

Sexual differences exist in iron requirements. A woman during her reproductive years needs a great deal more iron than a man, to replace losses through menstruation and to nourish pregnancies and suckling infants. The blood in pregnant women must increase in volume by one-fourth, and the iron requirement increases proportionately. Among poor women, anemia is a major contributor to maternal mortality; the anemia mortality rate in Latin America, for example, is sixteen times that in the United States.

The iron content is particularly high in liver and kidney, but other meats, dairy products, vegetables, and fruits also contain some. An iron supplement of 35 milligrams—twice what the average woman needs daily—costs about a penny at American discount drugstores.

Calcium and Phosphorus

Calcium, probably the best known among the minerals because of its popular association with teeth and bones, also supports nerve functions. The body requires more calcium than any other mineral except phosphorus, for these two minerals are the major constituents of bones and teeth. The chronic deficit of calcium among so many of the poor is symptomatized even among the young by missing teeth. In India, where people get less calcium than in any other country, periodontal disease is a major adolescent affliction. In a study of poor people in Chicago, 22 percent had lost permanent teeth and another 25 percent had cavities necessitating extractions; altogether, 95 percent suffered from tooth decay. Generally, low-income Americans need about fourteen times as many extractions because of tooth decay than do the more affluent, and, according to a 1967 Survey of Needs for Dental Care, they need dentures twenty times more often. Indeed, dental caries have been described as the chief nutritional disease of North Americans. In experiments with dogs, twelve months of calcium deficiency resulted in the degeneration of the supporting structures of teeth and tooth loss.

Again, proportions may be involved. Decay may be caused by an excess of phosphorus compared to calcium, of sugar to protein, and by bacterial activities, which in turn may be more injurious because of low resistance due to other dietary deficiencies. Intake of calcium and iron must also be balanced, for an excess of one obstructs the absorption of the other; the loss of iron is more likely because more people consume too much calcium.

We can obtain calcium from milk, cheese, and green leafy vegetables. Phosphorus comes from these same sources, as well as from meats and cereals. A daily diet including at least two glasses of milk or two servings of cheese provides adequate calcium. The main source of calcium for most people is milk or milk products, but it is also in bones of fish and poultry, which some groups include in their diets.

Iodine

Iodine is one of the nutrients most frequently absent in poor peoples' diets, yet is among the easiest and least expensive to obtain. It is important to the functioning of the thyroid gland, which secretes a hormone that regulates body metabolism and growth. Without iodine, the thyroid enlarges in the front and on the sides of the neck, becoming what is called a *goiter*. In 1960 WHO estimated that, throughout the world, nearly a billion people, or about one out of every fourteen, had goiter. Among the most vulnerable are preschool children, among whom the incidence is as high as one in five in some areas; girls between the ages of twelve and eighteen; and boys between nine and thirteen (suggesting an interaction with pubertal stresses). It occurs in all regions, among all races, and within all socio-economic groups.

Treatment was not widely given until early in this century, a lag which could have been avoided. Nine years after Bernard Courtois discovered iodine in 1811, a Swiss physician, Jean François Coindet, recommended its use for goiter. But doctors administered overdoses, and the side effects made its use so disreputable that when a French chemist statistically correlated dietary iodine intake with low goiter incidence, his contemporaries rejected the finding.

The association of goiter with iodine deficiency was finally accepted when a young medical researcher, David Marine, studying causes of high deathrates among young livestock, analyzed their thyroids, and documented the link. Later, he conducted a study involving nearly 5,000 Akron schoolgirls (an investigation of then unprecedented scope for a nutritional ailment) that demonstrated both the preventive and therapeutic effects of iodine.

The soil in which plants grow determines their iodine content, but some plants, such as spinach, absorb more than others. Generally, vegetables—especially those with green leaves—and legumes have more iodine than cereals and fruits. Meat and milk fall in between. Seaweeds and some other seafoods are rich in iodine, which they get from seawater, and people living along seacoasts apparently absorb some iodine from the atmosphere.

Only fifty years ago, the incidence of goiter was high in the United States, but we and some other nations have largely eradicated it by requiring salt to be iodized. It is a reliable approach to fortification, since virtually everyone uses salt, and it adds only infinitesimally to the price.

Magnesium

Magnesium is extremely important; it activates many enzymes and is a constituent of all soft tissues and bone. Deficiencies rarely develop among persons with good eating habits because it is provided by many foods, including sea plants.

The Trace Elements

Minute quantities of some other minerals are also needed, including chromium, cobalt, copper, iodide, manganese, molybdenum, selenium, and zinc. Generally these occur in lean and organ meats, green leafy vegetables, and whole grains.

It was only recently recognized that a shortage of chromium impairs the body's utilization of glucose (sugar). A chromium supplement has restored normal carbohydrate use for some diabetics, middle-aged and elderly people, and malnourished children.

The body also requires a balance of elements known as electrolytes, notably sodium, chloride, and potassium. Foods rich in potassium include several meats, eggs, orange juice, bananas, peanuts, and baked potatoes. Because these elements are readily available in common foods, most of us eat enough of them, although sodium, which is contained in table salt, should not be taken excessively.

Fluoride is necessary for the bones and teeth, and helps prevent tooth decay. Although milk, cheese, and fish are good sources, most people do not customarily eat enough of these to prevent decay, which is why there has been a movement to introduce fluoride into drinking water.

Zinc contributes to fetal development and, in experiments depriving animals of it, deformities similar to those caused by thalidomide have occurred. Children lacking zinc have failed to complete sexual maturation, and persons low in it experience more slowly healing wounds. As in the case of iron, an excess of calcium may cause a zinc deficiency. In 1973 scientists reported also that undersized, rundown children, who spurn food because "everything tastes like sawdust," may not be psychosomatic, as previously thought, but that zinc deficiency suppresses their taste and smell. For when a group was fed a diet with liver, kidneys, and other zinc-rich organs, their appetites improved markedly. The investigators suggest that lack of copper and nickel may also suppress the appetite.

Water

Not to be overlooked in any sound diet is water, though many of us do not customarily think of it as a nutrient. But we can survive longer without food than without water, and nutritionists recommend one to two quarts of fluid daily.

The Synergistic Threat

It was once held that a malnourished host offers an inhospitable environment for pathogens. Now it is known that a malnourished body is not only a hospitable environment but actually a more favorable one. And, while malnutrition encourages disease, disease in turn may decrease the body's ability to utilize nutrients. These effects were described in 1964 by Nevin Scrimshaw, head of nutrition and food sciences at the Massachusetts Institute of Technology (MIT), at a symposium sponsored by the National Academy of Sciences and the National Research Council:

> The major mechanisms involved in a body's resistance to infection have been shown to be affected by a variety of nutritional deficiencies when these are sufficiently severe. . . . A close examination of the situation reveals that indeed it is the synergism of malnutrition and infection that is responsible for both the retarded growth and development and the high rate of morbidity and mortality. . . . The nutritional state of the malnourished pre-school children is made worse by the frequent infections to which they are exposed, and

fatal clinical nutritional deficiencies are often precipitated. On the other hand, measles, respiratory infections, and intestinal parasites are all the more serious in malnourished children.

We may speculate that this holds true for adults also, but because of the lack of historical data on nutritional deficiencies, this is difficult to document. Nevertheless, if we assume that the poor are more likely to have lower eating standards, then some comparisons of disease rates will support the synergism theory. During the 1960s, the national tuberculosis rate was 24.2 new cases per 100,000 persons annually. For New York City, it was 47.7 cases, nearly double the national rate, and the city-wide figure camouflaged vast differences. In middle-income Flushing, the rate was 20 cases, which was below the national average; in Central Harlem, where the average income is low, the rate was 226, nearly ten times the national level. The tuberculosis rate for Watts was four times higher than that of Los Angeles County, and in 1966 the only diphtheria and brucellosis cases in the country, many of the polio cases, 45 percent of all typhoid cases, and 25 percent of all mumps cases occurred in Watts.

Food Habits

If the upper classes have disdained those who tilled the land, and scholars have until recently slighted the study of soils, they have always paid homage to the fruits of the tillers and to the culinary arts. The poor have eaten to sustain life, but the better-off have eaten increasingly for pleasure.

A historical review of eating habits suggests that the early peoples must have tried just about everything chewable at one time or another, and paid some unpleasant penalties for their experiments, but scholarly, folkloric, and religious responses to eating experiences were sometimes soundly based despite the shortcomings of early empirical methods. People living under primitive but stable conditions have often displayed an intuitive awareness of the need for certain nutrients. "Backward" Africans in some areas accurately associated kwashiorkor with both famine and the arrival of a new baby, and Brazilian slaves developed a well-placed taste for animal organs and entrails discarded by their owners. Some authorities believe that a "protein hunger" may, in fact, be the motive for cannibalism.

Although many of us grew up with notions of cave dwellers gnawing on great joints of prehistoric beasts, orgiastic feasts in ancient Rome, groaning tables in the great halls of European manors, and peasantry joyously partaking of an animal roasted on a spit, most people, from Mesopotamia through the Renaissance, subsisted almost entirely on cereal grains. In the early days of every great civilization, nearly everyone ate grains, more frequently in the form of porridge than of bread. As cultures flourished, the poor usually continued to eat cereals, except perhaps during festivals, while the diets of the upper classes improved. Naturally, culinary histories tell us more about the food habits of the privileged than of the common people.

Perhaps prehistoric man relied more on meat than his immediate successors, because the frozen ground of the long Ice Age was hostile to vegetation. People probably survived on the mammoth, the most edible parts of which were the tender muscles, liver, and brain, and on the rhinocerous. All races, at least in time of need, have also been cannibalistic.

Grain and flour go back at least 20,000 years, but bread probably was not discovered until around 6000 B.C., when Swiss lake dwellers learned how to mix flour and water into a dough, which they poured onto heated stones to bake. By 5000 B.C., man no longer was mainly an eater of red meats.

Food Habits and Health

During the Golden Age of Greece, thinkers puzzled over the apparent link between good health and foods, especially herbs and spices. At first they assumed that foods warded off or caused one or another malady—that is, they considered foods medicines, not nutrients. They observed that "overdoses" of some foods seemed related to such reactions as fits and other nervous disorders, whereas others seemed to calm the mind, and Hippocrates recognized "proper diet" as one of his four cardinal principles of treatment. Their inability to verify hypotheses and their reliance on deduction led these early nutritional counselors into startling contradictions over the centuries, and several foods have been variously held to be beneficial and poisonous.

Three beneficial categories evolved—medicinal, aphrodisiacal, and divine. Among the foods considered medicinal have been the acorn, butter, cabbage, carrot, celery, cucumber, eggplant, garlic, Irish moss, milk of asses and mares, mushroom, olive, onion, orange, pomegranate roots, radish, rice stalks and leaves, sugar cane, and honey. But of these, the cucumber, eggplant, garlic, mushroom, and onion have also been considered harmful, as have been peas, potatoes, and tomatoes. Even Hippocrates was ambivalent toward garlic and the onion, which he thought were generally good for the body but injurious to the eyes. Avocado, carrot, celery, eggplant, grenadilla, pomegranate, potato, soybean, tomato, duck eggs, eels, and oysters were at one time or another viewed as aphrodisiacal. The French folk belief in the powers of oysters was so strong that during World War II there was a joke going around about the lady who sent her lover to the bistro to revitalize himself by eating a half dozen oysters after each performance. When, finally, his response to her weakened, she accused him of indulging in another liaison. Of the aphrodisiacs, at least four—the eggplant, mushroom, potato, and tomato—have also been considered pathogenic.

Of the foods once considered divine—cabbage, corn, garlic, honey, mushroom, olive, orange, rice, and soybean—apparently only garlic and the mushroom have been believed poisonous. Rye has been considered dangerous, and Malaysians believed that fish leave worms. Some groups have considered certain meats, especially pork, unfit for eating.

Food habits have often been institutionalized within societies through taboos or religion, frequently for what was believed to be the sake of good health. The Old Testament distinguished between "clean" and "unclean" animals, the former being animals that chew their cud and have cloven hooves. (A notable example of the latter is the pig, which has cloven hoofs but does not chew its cud.) Slaughter of acceptable animals was ritualized by the Hebrews, perhaps to ensure the delivery of meat that was fresh since they were customarily killed in the presence of the people who would eat the meat. The Torah also forbade the eating of most winged insects, reptiles, creeping animals, birds of prey, and fish with neither fins nor scales. Both the Torah and Islamic teachings prohibit the eating of long-dead animals, blood, and pigs. In ancient China, cow's milk was considered unfit for humans. In India, the Hindu caste system determined the diet, and most Hindus, especially the Brahmin, are vegetarians. The Code of Manu, a sacred Hindu writing dating to A.D. 300, counsels against eating meat, drinking liquor, and taking life; thus the cow is sacred, as are milk and ghee, a clarified buttery liquid. Most pious Hindus also refuse eggs, and some castes will not eat blood-colored items, such as tomatoes and lentils. What does this leave in plentiful supply then? Rice.

Buddhism also prohibits the taking of life and the injuring of living creatures. Buddhists have held the cow sacred since about 1000 B.C.; before that time, people slaughtered cows. This religious stricture probably was formulated because forage land was limited and what cattle could be raised were needed badly for pulling plows and carts and for their dung, which was (and still is) used for manure or dried for fuel and building blocks.

Some taboos against certain foods were not as arbitrary or ill-placed as they might appear. The potato is a good example; its leaves are toxic, and if its tuber is exposed to sunlight while growing, it may become bitter and sometimes toxic too. Recent findings suggest that a blighted potato, if eaten, can cause such defects as spina bifida and anecephaly in the newborn. Because so many toadstools are poisonous, it is easy to understand why episodes of mistaken identity led to taboos against mushrooms. Improperly cooked pork has been a source of trichinosis (*Tricheinella spiralis*) which is symptomatized by fever, vomiting, diarrhea, and debility. Some ancient societies proscribed milk because it was subject to contamination in transit, and some Indian villagers today will not accept it unless they watch it being drawn.

Even the notion that certain foods contribute to sexual performance and enjoyment may not be far-fetched—not because they are aphrodisiacal, but because they supply nutrients that might elsewhere have been in short supply, affecting libido and performance. The well nourished are more likely to be erotically fulfilled than the undernourished.

Irrational Group Prejudices

Ethnic, religious, and class prejudices often influence food habits for the worse. The primitives in all probability noted the foods that animals thrived on and adopted these foods themselves; conversely, when they observed a food that made animals ill, they avoided it. But, in time, man's attitude toward his beasts of burden changed from the early husbander's respect to the "civilized" man's scorn. In ancient times, the Scythians disdained the Gauls for eating oats, which they considered cattle feed, and centuries later the English scorned the Scots for the same reason. Yet the oat is higher in protein than most other grains—indeed, as Schaefer points out, animal breeders today pay more serious attention to the nutritional needs of their stock than many people do to their own diets. During the sixteenth century, the English working class scorned the potato simply because potatoes were eaten by the Irish, and in this country, less-than-broadminded Protestants abhorred fish simply because fish was eaten by Catholics on fast days.

Though Europeans have been known to starve rather than eat corn, some of the dishes they have preferred seem less than rational choices. The peacock, for example, has tough flesh without a particularly good flavor, but it was a festive bird from imperial Rome to the mid-sixteenth century. Often it simply boils down to the fact that there is no accounting for people's tastes—or distastes.

At other times, rulers have had to set examples to improve the people's diets. Charlemagne, for instance, deplored the disfavor into which fruits and vegetables had fallen and successfully encouraged their consumption. Food fashions, like most fashions, are generally set by the rich, and when people get the means to eat what is fashionable, they will. People generally eat more meat —primarily beef—as their incomes rise; this trend set in some time ago in the United States and Western Europe and recently spread to Eastern Europe, Mexico, the more quickly advancing Latin American countries, parts of Africa, and some groups in India. But if people are not nutritionally educated, the "upgrading" of eating standards may be dietarily unsound. Asians, for example, switch from unpolished to the socially-preferred polished rice without sufficient income to buy other foods to compensate for the nutrients lost in the polishing; Americans have taken to white bread and heavily processed snacks, which, without additives, are lower in nutrients than the breads and baked goods of less affluent times.

American Food Habits

The average American eats about 1,000 pounds of food a year. In 1972, nearly one-third of a typical family's food budget was spent for meat. The average American diet is 21 percent meat and fish and 25 percent grains and potatoes, or staples—at least until the food-price inflation since 1973.

Though regional specialties, such as fish chowder and hominy grits, have developed in America, American cuisine is similar to that of Western Europe. American eating habits, however, were changed considerably with the introduction of "convenience" foods, and television has catalyzed the transition. Europeans traditionally shop every day—or even twice a day—so that they do not need to store as much. Consequently, they do not eat frozen foods to any extent, they use fewer processed foods of all types, and usually buy their bread fresh.

In 1930 Americans did not have frozen orange juice, frozen vegetables, or margarine. They generally ate chicken only on the weekend and ate pork nearly as often as beef; the average person ate some 120 pounds of meat a year. In 1972 we ate nearly 300 pounds, and most of the increase was in beef consumption. We eat fewer dairy products, however, except for cheese which has become more popular, and fewer fresh vegetables, except for lettuce, tomatoes, cucumbers, and celery. We eat the same amount of fruits and cereals, but our consumption of processed fruits and vegetables and salad and cooking oils has risen.

The acceptance of new food technologies follows a pattern. The introductory stage is usually marked by limited sales and little, if any, growth. Then a takeoff occurs and continues until the product reaches a "maturity," when sales growth levels off, which is the "saturation" stage. When sales decline, the product has arrived at "old age." A mature item may experience a stable sales level for years. Prices reflect these stages. Poultry pies, after their introduction in around 1950, sold as high as 40 cents. Improved production techniques halved the price, which remained stable until inflation drove it up again.

Processing

Processing, to a considerable degree, means preserving foods, although modern food technology mixes, adulterates, and often changes them. The most familiar preservation methods are refrigeration, freezing, canning, evaporation, and drying. The first three methods depend on relatively new technology, while evaporation and drying, as well as pickling and smoking without sealing, are ancient processes. Dry freezing, which reduces the weight of foods, has recently been introduced commercially, and irradiation, which can reduce bacterial levels and disinfect grain and flour of insects, may also be used soon.

Approximately 3,000 chemicals are used in food processing, 1,000 of which are direct food additives while 2,000 come into indirect contact with food through packing materials. The demand for convenience foods with long shelf lives and low cost, and the need for shipping foods long distances, have encouraged the use of chemicals.

An additive is any substance, or mixture of substances, joined to basic foods during processing to change their appearance, taste, texture, preservability, and/or nutritive content. Salt, vitamins, minerals, and spices are therefore additives. Antitoxins prevent oils and other fats from turning rancid, and emulsifiers keep ingredients such as the oil in peanut butter from separating. Thickeners and stabilizers alter textures in such foods as ice cream, and coloring and bleaching agents, such as those used to make butter and margarine yellow, serve as "cosmetics." Growth inhibitors prevent mold or bacteria infection from forming.

The increased use of additives has caused a good deal of popular concern over their possible side effects. The FDA maintains a list of additives that are "generally recognized as safe." The GRAS list once included around 600 additives, but some, such as the cyclamates, were removed with the accumulation of evidence of potential injuriousness. The Pure Food and Drug Act, passed in 1906, and the 1958 Food Additive Amendment (which includes the Delaney Clause, that no substance may be added to food that "is found after tests which are appropriate to induce cancer in man or animals"), enable the government to legislate against harmful additives, although the FDA has been charged by consumer groups with inefficient and unenthusiastic investigations of additives.

Food fortification—that is, nutritional enrichment—was introduced in the 1940s to restore nutrients lost in processing of food, and to add desirable nutrients. The B vitamins were added to bread and cereals to compensate for losses, while D was added to milk, which never had it. When margarine began replacing butter, A was added to it, and iodine has been added to table salt for decades. Since 1970, the FDA has been interested in tripling the amount of iron in bread because of the high incidence of anemia among adolescent girls.

Among poultry products, whole chickens have always been the single largest-selling item, but chicken and turkey sold in parts or processed into other dishes are enjoying more and more favor among consumers. Of 7.8 billion pounds of chicken meat handled by federally inspected slaughtering plants in 1972, nearly one-third, or 2.3 billion pounds, were cut up, while just under 22 percent were cut up in 1967. Chicken is now available fresh or frozen, raw or pre-cooked, in slices, pies, patties, rolled loaves, and whole dinners. Ground chicken meat has been tested as a competitor to hamburger, since it can be seasoned and used in chili, meatloaf, and stew.

The impact of convenience foods has actually been more dramatic in the turkey industry, probably because whole turkeys have never been the popular regular fare that chickens have been. In 1972 processors cut up about 300 million pounds of turkey into parts and further processed 639 million pounds. The amount of turkey that underwent processing beyond being cut into parts was nearly double that of five years before. Turkey is now available in products similar to those made from chicken; one company also produces turkey salami and pastrami, which are flavored to taste like their namesakes.

Many convenience chicken items come from old birds rather than young broilers. Before World War II, "spent chickens"—

chickens from egg-laying flocks—were marketed to an accepting public, but when the broiler industry suddenly expanded after 1950, the cost of these chickens was lowered and consumers demanded younger fowl. Chicken producers recycled the spent chickens into convenience foods. Still another source of meat for prepared dishes are the less desirable parts, such as the neck and back.

Chicken prices dropped, but processors do not necessarily maintain protein levels as might be expected. In June 1973 *Consumer Reports* stated, "Our tasters were mildly heartened to find that some of these convenience foods were almost as good as a freshly cooked dinner," and they found the items "fairly" free of contamination, but their investigators were less than enthusiastic about nutritional content and were sharply critical of the cost of the nutrients:

> Nutrient values were, for the most part, satisfactory, although not sufficient to support an adult's needs as a main meal day after day. But people who indulge themselves in buying this kind of convenience product shouldn't blind themselves to the fact that it is very expensive.

Protein in frozen fried-chicken dinners averaged $10 per pound, although the costs per pound of the dinner ranged from 57 to 86 cents. One dinner costing an astronomical $33.35 per pound of protein and $1.09 per pound of food was marketed as a children's dish. (A year earlier, incidentally, *Consumer Reports* stated that the hot dog provided less protein than generally believed and much less than it had in the 1930s, and at a cost much higher than hamburger.)

Processing has been responsible for nutrient loss in many foods. In an experiment reported to the National Academy of Sciences, two-thirds of a group of rats that were fed on commercial white bread for ninety days died and the remainder grew up stunted. Industry spokesmen retorted that rats and humans are different, and that most Americans do not exist on a single food. Later, a congressional hearing disclosed that popular breakfast cereals were also low in nutritional value.

8

Important American Crops

Plants have always been our main food source, and however important "harvests" from the sea or products from unconventional sources may become, they are likely to remain so. Yet, while their seeds, fruits, leaves, stalks, and roots provide nutrients, most plants are deficient in some things too, notably in the essential amino acids for our protein. But plants provide the feed for our best sources of complete protein, the red-meat animals, poultry, and fish. Throughout history, however, these have been widely available only to the more affluent. A survey of the important foods and feeds illustrates not only the diversity of what we eat, but also the complexities and possible directions of future development in agriculture.

A region may produce so much of our national harvest that it is called a *crop belt* (the best known of these has been the corn belt), and the dominance of a crop economically in an area means there is a *crop economy*, such as a wheat economy. Changes in demand, availability of transportation and storage facilities, costs of production and equipment, and environmental intrusions have caused geographic shifts in some belts, and more changes are likely to occur during the next few years.

The wheat belt, for example, shifted late in the last century, moving north and west from Illinois and Iowa as the Northwest was penetrated by railroads, elevators were built, carload-lot handling became possible, and implements were improved for dryland cultivation. The spreads produced bumper crops and by 1890 were called "bonanza" wheat farms. Today, Illinois and Iowa produce comparatively little wheat. The wheat belt now centers in Kansas, which produces 22.5 percent of the national harvest, stretches northwest over Nebraska, the Dakotas, Montana, parts of Idaho, and into Washington, and also southwest over Oklahoma and into Texas. The big-six states—Kansas, North Dakota, Oklahoma, Texas, Montana, and Washington, in order of output for 1973—harvest over half the total crop, but other states may be important for specific wheats, such as Colorado for winter wheat and Minnesota for spring wheat.

The corn belt lends itself to more cohesive geographic centralization, since the five leading producers—Iowa, Illinois, Nebraska, Indiana, and Minnesota, in order of output for 1973—harvest, stretches northwest over Nebraska, the Dakotas, Monwestern. The corn belt is often considered the ten midwestern producers, but an examination of harvest data shows that it really stretches into parts of a few other states. It might be said to center in Iowa, which produces about a fifth of the national harvest, and to stretch east across Illinois, Indiana, Ohio, and into Pennsylvania, north over Minnesota and Wisconsin, south and southeast into Kentucky and North Carolina, south into Missouri, southwest into Kansas, and west over Nebraska.

The next major grain in terms of bushels harvested, sorghum, is concentrated in a smaller belt. It reaches from Texas, which produces over 43 percent of the national harvest, through Kansas and Nebraska; these three together produce over 83 percent of the national output.

Traditionally, the rice belt was considered Arkansas, Louisiana, and Texas, perhaps with parts of Mississippi; but California became increasingly significant, and in 1973 rose from fourth to second place.

What finally has confused these handy designations of crop belts is the soybean. Its growing centers are Illinois and Iowa, the leading corn producers, and the soybean belt fans eastward into Indiana, southward into Missouri and Arkansas, and northward into Minnesota. Agriculturists are increasingly speaking of the corn-soybean belt, which is also the center of hog raising. The leading six soybean producers harvest 73 percent of the national output. Nevertheless, as often with other crops, important, localized plantings may be cropped elsewhere. For instance, when Mississippi cotton farmers were in price trouble a few years ago, they switched to the more profitable soybean, which, according to a state political leader, Frank Barber, "saved many delta farmers."

Other crops may be important to local economies, and plantings may dominate the countryside—lettuce in California and Arizona; orange orchards in California and Florida; tomatoes and grapes in California; potatoes in Maine, on Long Island, and in Idaho; peanuts in Georgia. Grazing cattle and feedlots appear prominent in much of the West and Midwest, as do dairy farms in Wisconsin.

The Department of Agriculture divides the continental United States into ten "farm production regions," as shown in the following list:

Region	*States*
Northeast	New England states, New York, New Jersey, Pennsylvania, Maryland, Delaware
Appalachia	Virginia, West Virginia, North Carolina, Tennessee, Kentucky
Southeast	South Carolina, Georgia, Alabama, Florida
Delta	Arkansas, Louisiana, Mississippi
Corn belt	Iowa, Missouri, Illinois, Indiana, Ohio
Great Lakes	Minnesota, Wisconsin, Michigan
Northern plains	North Dakota, South Dakota, Nebraska, Kansas
Mountain	Montana, Idaho, Wyoming, Colorado, Utah, Nevada, Arizona, New Mexico
Pacific	Washington, Oregon, California

Although a biological or species classification of meat sources does not cause any confusion, attempting to group food plants botanically dissembles their appearances in food and culinary uses. A vegetable, according to the dictionary, is "any herbaceous plant whose fruit, seeds, roots, tubers, bulbs, stems, leaves, or flower parts are used for food." The trouble with this definition is that it covers wheat, soybeans, potatoes, carrots, lettuce, oranges, cherries, walnuts, and a host of other foods. Fruit is defined botanically as "the edible part of a plant developed from a flower" or "the developed ovary of a seed plant with its contents and accessory parts, as the pea pod, nut, tomato, pineapple, etc.," though by popular and commercial definitions a fruit is a fleshy, succulent container of seeds which is usually sweet when ripe. Variations in characteristics within families of fruits and vegetables are manifold. The peanut, for example, is eaten as a nut and matures underground like the potato, to which it is unrelated; the peanut, in fact, is akin to the soybean, which is not a bean at all but an oilseed that grows above ground. Legumes such as alfalfa are vegetables, but the term customarily refers to plants producing food directly for human beings and not to the hay crop.

For practical reasons, I shall discuss the major food-and-feed staples and other important cash crops, and then go on to cover vegetables, fruits, and nuts grouped according to the appearance of that portion we normally eat.

Staples and Other Major Cash Crops

"For 15,000 years," wrote H. E. Jacob in *6,000 Years of Bread*, "the epic of grain has been one with the epic of man." Because of their low cost, cereal grains are the major source of food energy for 97 percent of the people of the world; they make up more than 82 percent of world food output and 73 percent of actual food consumption. A few grains are also staples for livestock. In some societies, however, non-grain crops are equally important, notably potatoes and cassava. And the soybean, long vital as a food to the Chinese, has emerged in recent years as challenger to corn as the most important feed crop in the world, while new food technology is making it much more important on the meal table. Staple foods are rich in calories, the stuff of energy, and they are filling; unfortunately, most of them are low in protein and other nutrients essential to human beings. The soybean, on the other hand, is high in good-quality protein.

Worldwide, 53.7 percent of the population eat mainly rice, and 35.5 percent rely largely on wheat products. The average American consumes 150 pounds of wheat annually, about the same quantity of potatoes, 56 pounds of corn, and nearly 8 pounds of rice. Corn is the most valuable American crop in dollar value, though mainly for feed. (Much corn is fed on the farm where grown and does not enter the grain market, but corn was the leading American agricultural export until 1973, when soybeans, which had only shortly before displaced wheat in second place, became the leading agricultural foreign-exchange earner.)

Wheat (genus *Triticum*)

Wheat enjoys a market in virtually every country, particularly among the more affluent, who traditionally associate it with higher status. Americans, Canadians, Europeans, and Australians eat wheat more than any other single foodstuff; the Japanese, whose incomes are rising, recently began eating more wheat and less rice. Wheat consumers are so accustomed to buying its multifarious products that they tend to think not of the grain at all but of the forms into which it is processed.

Only three species of wheat are commercially important: common wheat (*Triticum aestivum*), club (*T. compactum*), and durum (*T. Durum*). Together they make up about 90 percent of all wheat harvested. Within these species, wheat is also classified by texture, color, and growing habits. If it is planted in the autumn for harvest early the next year, it is known as winter wheat; if sown in the spring for summer harvesting, it is called spring wheat. The Economic Research Service of the Department of Agriculture lists six main classes—hard red winter, hard red spring, soft red winter, soft red spring, durum, and white. These also break down into varieties, of which American farmers grow about 230—more than any other nation.

The processing qualities of wheat vary. Hard wheats bake and leaven well, and are known in the trade as "bread wheats"; white wheats grown in the West, such as durum, are used almost exclusively for pastas and are known as "noodle wheats." Soft wheats are milled into flour for crackers, cookies, cakes, and pastries.

In the late 1960s, when grain surpluses re-accumulated and prices fell, stockmen and poultry producers began using more wheat for feed. Earlier in the decade, only about 3 percent of the harvest was fed to animals, but by 1970 the figure had risen to 15 percent. (This diversion was not without precedent; during World War II, the government sought to reduce wheat surpluses by encouraging their use for feed to increase the rationed outputs of meat and also milk and eggs.)

The protein content of wheat, averaging 12 percent, is higher than that of most grains; wheat also provides some of the vitamin B complex, E, and iron. Though wheat may lose part or all of some nutrients in milling, its products supply Americans with about 16 percent of their calories, 15 percent of their protein, and 20 percent of their iron.

Wheat is one of the crops most resistant to drought, although yields drop in drier weather. According to the eminent Russian geneticist Nikolai Vavilov, the oldest varieties of wheat grew on the high Abyssinian (Ethiopian) tablelands near the source of the Nile, and farmers first cultivated it around 7000 B.C. After the Egyptians learned how to make leavened bread, they favored wheat over all other grains. Its cultivation spread, but because it was hard to grow on poor soil, wheat products were generally luxuries until the eighteenth century. Columbus carried wheat seed to the New World, but it was not until the 1870s, when a Turkish variety was introduced on the Great Plains, that attempts to raise it in America were successful.

The English reap the highest yields—nearly 60 bushels per acre; the United States ranks seventh. In America the cost of irrigation necessary to achieve more productivity in some areas has not been economical so far, but dryland yields have also been rising steadily. In 1971, American average yield rose to a peak of 33.8 bushels, compared with 25 in 1962, 17 in the 1940s, and 13 to 14 during the 1920s. The Soviet Union is usually the largest wheat producer, but Russian farmers harvest only about 12 bushels per acre, not much above yields on traditional farms in India.

Wheat is grown in forty-two states, but the yield per acre bears little relationship to the amounts produced. Kansas, our largest producer, harvests about a fifth of the national output; because farmers there rely on dryland or rain-fed farming and moisture is limited, their yield (34 bushels per acre) is modest compared with nearly 50 bushels in Washington, which has higher precipitation, and two states where wheatlands are irrigated, Arizona (68) and Nevada (58).

Corn (*Zea Mays*)

Although corn is less widely eaten than wheat and rice, it was a mainstay among the Indians of the Americas and some Africans, and the Chinese prefer it to wheat as a staple second to rice. It was corn, adopted from the Indians, that kept the early American settlers from starving, and in the first substantial account of Indian agriculture, a Virginia colonist named Thomas Hariot wrote admiringly, "It is a graine of marvellous great increase; of a thousand, fifteene hundred, and some two thousand fold." At first, settlers probably grew a long, slender-stalked, usually yellow northern variety that matured early and resisted spoilage because of its hardness. Later they planted a white variety of Mexican origin that matured late and yielder better than the northern variety. As early as 1812, farmers had hybridized the two varieties, combining their better traits.

Corn is peculiarly dependent on human hands for survival and is said to be the only food crop so radically altered since its ancient cultivation—at least as early as 3500 B.C.—that its origins remain obscure. Wild maize grew at least 7,000 years ago. The domesticated plant did not improve much until about 2300 B.C., when it apparently crossed with wild corn. About 1500 B.C., the number of varieties suddenly increased, and several ancient American civilzations sprang up on the cornerstone of corn cultivation. When Columbus arrived, the Indians had already developed between 200 and 300 varieties—essentially all that exist today. "Theirs was the most remarkable achievement in plant breeding in all of man's existence," says George Beadle, a Nobel laureate and former University of Chicago president. Corn germ plasm was particularly exploited by the Mexican Indians, who have grown the grain at elevations of 4,300 to 7,300 feet and have raised plants rising from 3 to 20 feet with cobs from 3 to 16 inches long. Some varieties of Mexican corn mature in three months while others take as long as eight months.

Americans have achieved two spectacular advances in corn breeding, one an enormous commercial success and the other a nutritional success yet to become commercially viable. The first of these advances was the development of modern hybrid seed corn. In the nineteenth century farmers assumed that they could raise their best harvests by selecting the best ears for seed, but these inbred plants became weak, and some strains died; even the healthiest survivors of these selected plants yielded only half as much. Following up the experiences of these farmers, William James Beal, a botanist at the University of Michigan, achieved the first controlled crosses of corn varieties in 1878, and later two scientists working independently, E. M. East at the Connecticut Agricultural Experiment Station and George H. Shull of the Carnegie Institution, learned that by crossing inbred strains they could restore the original vigor and yields. These successes led Donald F. Jones, who headed the Connecticut station, to mate two different single crosses, creating a double-crossed breed. Compared to the national average yield of 42 bushels per acre, and the inbred yields which had dropped below 40, the new double crosses yielded 100 to 120 bushels per acre. Jones' studies were published between 1918 and 1922, and by 1923 every experimental station in the corn belt was attempting the approach.

Henry A. Wallace, Sr., Secretary of Agriculture under the Harding and Coolidge Administrations, accurately forecast that the new corns would have an impact on the lives of everyone in the corn belt. "The revolution has not come yet," he wrote, "but I am certain that it will come within 10 to 15 years. The problem now is to find the very best inbred strains of corn." Mating two unrelated hybrids proved difficult, and it took another eleven years and a good deal of money to create an acceptable hybrid corn seed.

Persuading farmers is never an easy task, and they were especially resistant to the hybrids as they staggered out of the Great Depression. One company obtained the names of the best farmers from county extension agents and persuaded some to plant a bushel of its hybrid corn seed. When the farmers harvested higher yields from it, the company tempted them further with a 15 percent commission on sales of its seeds to their neighbors. By 1935, the demand for hybrid seed exceeded supplies, stimulating a rapid expansion of the seed business, and, after some years, farmers planted the hybrids almost exclusively. The new corn had far-reaching effects, eventually influencing domestic and foreign agricultural policies.

The other great advance was the discovery of a high-lysine gene, making more nutritious varieties of corn possible. Although corn is a good source of starch, its protein level is lower than that of other cereals, and it contains only small amounts of other nutrients. The sweet yellow corn commonly eaten in the United States averages about 2 to 3 percent protein; because it lacks vitamin B_3, many poor people for whom it is a staple develop the deficiency disease pellagra. White corn is less nutritious than yellow.

Yields of corn have continued to rise, from an average of 64.3 bushels per acre in 1962 to a high of 97.1 bushels in 1972. The huge American production figures for corn refer to what the Department of Agriculture terms "corn for grain"—a record total of over 5.6 billion bushels in 1973, mainly for feed, though it has other uses, not the least of which is for bourbon. During 1973, its price fluctuated between $1.32 and $3.33 a bushel, and in early 1974 reached a record $3.30. Output of sweet corn is but a fraction of the "corn for grain," and is reported as a vegetable on a poundage basis; it wholesales by the crate.

Rice (*Oryza sativa*)

Rice is so critically important in Asia that more folklore has been built around it than any other crop. Ancient Japanese society had a rice etiquette, not so much as a matter of manners as a means of preventing waste; held only their emperor more sacred than rice; and extolled a rice god, Inari. The Chinese traditional salutation is not "How do you do?" but "Have you eaten your rice today?" They also sprinkled rice in front of brides in the belief that the fecundity of the grain is transferable; the Western custom of tossing rice over newlyweds probably derives from this ancient ritual.

China, India, and Java each claim to be the native habitat of rice. Its cultivation probably spread from Asia about 3500 B.C. Rice reached America when the captain of a trading ship called at Charleston, South Carolina, in 1865 and sold a bag of seed to a local merchant.

Rice grows in a wider range of climates than any other grain. It is cultivated from the equatorial belt to as far north as Czechoslovakia and from sea level to as high as 10,000 feet in the Himalayas. It is commonly thought of as a quasi-aquatic crop since it grows in areas with 200 inches of annual rainfall and in flooded paddies, but it also grows where precipitation is as low as 20 inches a year. The plants grown traditionally in the tropics have hollow stems that allow oxygen into the roots. These plants grow five to six feet tall, adapting to quiet, deep water, which is an advantage in flood areas. They flourish reliably without fertilizer in poor soils, where they block weeds and require little management, but these varieties yield poorly and grow badly if closely spaced.

Rice became popular because it yields more abundantly and reliably than other staples. A ton of rice can keep ten persons alive for a year, though it would be a more realistic ration for a family of five. But like most other staples, rice, high in calories, is not very nutritious and is vulnerable to nutrient loss in modern processing. The highly polished white rice is less nutritious than brown rice retaining some of its husk. Protein levels range from 6 to 15 percent, and they are of somewhat better quality than most other staples because lysine is less limited. Recently scientists have succeeded in breeding into some varieties not only 25 percent more protein but also more distribution of it throughout the kernel, so the amino acids are more resistant to loss in processing. The problems, however, are ones of maintaining high yields and the taste and texture of the traditionally preferred types.

Americans eat only 8.5 pounds of rice per person per year—

the typical Thai consumes a pound a day—but this represents a 60 percent average increase over 1966. Asians produce and consume about 90 percent of the world's output, and only about 2 percent of all rice grown goes into international trade. Though the United States produces less than 1.5 percent of the world harvest, American shipments make up about a fifth of all exports. American farmers raise three classes of rice—long-, medium-, and short-grain, in that order of quantity. In 1973 farmers harvested 9.3 billion pounds, 9 percent above the 1971 record. Yields averaged 4,277 pounds per acre, down from 4,700 pounds the year before.

Yet in 1973 American rice stocks, like those of other staples, were at their lowest level in a decade, and world supplies became the tightest on record. The price rose to over $10 per hundredweight, an all-time high, up from an average of $6.73 for the previous crop year.

American wild rices are really aquatic grasses and are only distantly related to the common varieties. They are higher in protein and vitamin content, but difficult and expensive to harvest, and sold as a specialty. Minnesota is the main producer of wild rice.

Other Grains

More American acreage is planted to three grains other than rice—sorghum, oats, and barley, in that order—though none is planted nearly as extensively as corn, wheat, and soybeans.

Sorghum grain (genus *Sorghum*) is the fourth most important feed-and-food crop in the world; while we use it mainly for feed, it is a staple for 10 percent of the world population—the third most important food crop globally. The rising costs of water-control schemes are likely to make sorghum more important in the future, for though it responds well to irrigation, it can withstand hotter climates than corn because of its unusually spreading root system and its peculiar ability to "hibernate" when moisture is unavailable. It also survives on soils too infertile for other crops; today, along the southern fringes of the Sahara and in some other areas, it is the final crop planted when conditions deteriorate. The sorghum plant can also be used for ground cover and green manures, and the grain can be used for industrial alcohol of the type commonly made from corn.

Most sorghums are from 8 to 20 percent protein, but typically are around 11 percent. In 1973 Purdue agriculturists, after analyzing 9,000 varieties of sorghum from all over the world, discovered two Ethiopian strains—sorghum probably originated in Africa—that have far better protein than any of the commonly cultivated varieties. Newly weaned rats fed on one strain gained weight three times more rapidly, and rats fed on the other twice as rapidly, as those fed on common sorghum. These strains, high in lysine, are not cultivated extensively, possibly because they are light in color and attract birds, which spurn some of the dark-colored common varieties.

In the United States, sorghum is grown throughout the Great Plains and in the Southwest. About half of the national output goes for feed, a small amount for syrup and molasses (from crushed stems of the sugar sorghum), and the rest for forage and silage (forage preserved in silos).

Although many of us remember growing up with oatmeal porridge—traditionally the most popular breakfast cereal—oats (genus *Avena*) are used mainly for feed; less than 5 percent are used as human food. Oats are high in nutritional value—hence the expression "feeling one's oats"—but they have nevertheless endured a good deal of scorn, and people who have eaten them have been disdained for not eating "better" than their livestock. Samuel Johnson called oats "food for men in Scotland, horses in England," and a Scot is said to have rejoined, "England is noted for the excellence of her horses; Scotland for the excellence of her men." Geneticists have found wild species of oats with far more protein than those under cultivation—as high as 30 percent—and if these protein genes can be combined with the better growing attributes of cultivated varieties, it is possible that oats will become more important for both food and feed.

Barley (genus *Hordeum*) is the fifth most cultivated American grain, but worldwide may rival wheat as the most cultivated. First cultivated in Asia Minor about 7000 B.C., it became the dominant cereal in Europe during the Bronze Age; today it is raised mostly for feed and for malt, an. ingredient in beer, though it may also be made into leavened bread. Pearl barley,.

which is what we use in soups and stews, is only around 8 percent protein, but it has some vitamins and minerals. North Dakota produces nearly a fourth of our national harvest.

Rye (*Secale cereala*) has suffered the extremes of public fickleness. Because it was once the most commonly eaten grain in North Central Europe, it acquired the reputation of being fare for poor tables. As incomes rose, people switched to the more prestigious wheat bread, and rye became mainly a feed or forage crop. But rye is now the second most important European grain, and in the United States rye bread has regained prestige because it is more nutritious than wheat loaves made of heavily milled unenriched white flour. Rye is also a source of whisky, gin, and beer; and its stalks are used for mattress stuffing, thatching, paper, and hats. The plant has an adaptability to environments normally detrimental to many other crops. It is better adapted to cold zones than other grains, and grows as far north as the Arctic Circle and at altitudes as high as 14,000 feet. It also grows on comparatively poor land. The top producing states are the Dakotas and Minnesota, especially South Dakota which crops over a fourth of the national output.

The Soybean *(Glycine soja)*

From 1932 to 1972, American production of the soybean increased nearly a hundred fold, and the value of the crop increased almost five hundred fold; it had earned a reputation as the world's most efficient and least costly source of protein, and it also provides several vitamins and minerals. It has become so significant commercially that the Chicago Board of Trade, once mainly a grain exchange, now assigns three of the eight pits on its trading floor to soybean commodities—one each for raw beans, meal, and oil. Acreages planted to soybeans have been expanding in thirty states, from fewer than 2 million acres fifty years ago to over 56 million acres in 1973, and the corn belt might now be more appropriately called the corn-soybean belt.

Few consumers have ever seen a soybean, much less bought a bag of them. Hardly any supermarkets sell them, and in urban areas a buyer might find them only in a Chinese market or a health-food store. But we all buy items with soybean products in them—margarine, mayonnaise, salad dressing, cooking oil, Worcestershire sauce, pet food, and, of course, soy sauce. Soy milk, a by-product, may be used in sour cream and ice cream, and it is also fed to babies who are allergic to cow's milk. The Chinese and Japanese drink soy oil as "milk," and the Japanese drink bowls of bean-paste soups as Americans drink coffee. Soybeans can also be roasted whole to resemble nuts. A few cents' worth of soybeans can serve four to six people, but they are usually not eaten in their natural form because they take long to prepare and are not very palatable served alone. Dried soybeans must be soaked overnight and may take four to seven hours to cook. They are mealy in texture and their taste, sometimes bland and other times strong, requires seasoning, but they may mix well with other foods.

Yet some marketing experts maintain that the soybean is still the "Cinderella crop," pining for a merchandising knight to convert it into regular shopping-basket fare. Probably not more than half of the world harvest goes for direct human consumption; only 3 percent of the American soy protein output goes for food, 65 percent for animal feed, and the rest for industrial products. "As a food," the research director of Archer Daniels Midland Company, F. E. Horan, told the first World Soy Protein Conference in Germany in 1973, "the soybean is passing from the island of the small 'cottage' industries . . . in the expanding markets of the industrialized world. . . . The soybean is . . . undoubtedly the fastest growing segment of American agriculture." In 1970, seventeen firms produced soy protein for food, and several new companies have since entered the competition.

The soybean is the most important legume—a plant used for food, feed, or soil improvement—in China, Japan, Korea, and Malaysia; it was probably cultivated in Asia by 3500 B.C. Over a thousand varieties are known, seventeen of which are commercially important in the United States. The plant has bushy foliage, rough brownish hairs on its stems, leaves, and pods, and grows from one and one-half to six feet high; the typical American plant is hip-high. The pods hold two to four round, fat seeds—which may be black, brown, green, or yellow—that are somewhat larger than a pea. Because soybeans need less rainfall than corn and can be planted nearly a month later in some midwestern areas, a corn farmer hit by poor weather can either skip seeding corn or plow up an injured crop and switch to soybeans. Many farmers did this in mid-May of 1972, and in 1973, when Mississippi flooding delayed cotton planting until it was too late, there was still time for some farmers to go to soybeans instead; some did it again in 1974 after their corn was rained out.

The sudden breakthrough of the American soybean was long in coming. It was introduced into the United States in 1804 mainly as a rotation crop. George Washington Carver discovered its high protein content and several of its other attributes, and the soybean subsequently interested farmers in midwestern livestock areas as a feed crop. During the 1930s depression, Henry Ford, Sr., attempted to help the American farmer by developing industrial uses that included horn buttons and gearshift knobs for his Model As and early V-8s. Ford also believed that food should be the least expensive commodity in the world, and by 1949 his chemists had developed simulated foods from protein fibers, opening the way for the development of meat substitutes from soybeans that are high in good-quality protein.

Today soy flour, concentrates, and isolates have protein levels of 56 percent, 72 percent, and 96 percent respectively. The cost of processing the flour has been well under one-fourth that of processing dry milk and less than one-tenth that of processing most other complete proteins. Soy flour can be mixed with wheat flour for baking or used in gravies, sauces, baby formulas, ice cream, dietetic foods, and convenience mixes. In 1972 the demand for soy meal outstripped demand for soy oil, initially the most-sought-after soy product, and soy meal has become so important in trade that the meal of all other oilseeds and that of fish is now measured in terms of "soy meal equivalent."

Soy concentrates, made from soy flakes or flour, are used as extenders in such items as hamburger, ravioli, soup, breakfast cereals, baked goods, and baby foods, while isolated soy proteins, produced by further isolation of protein from soy flakes, are used as binding agents in sausages, canned meats, and dairy-type products like whipped toppings, coffee creamers, frozen deserts, and cheeselike spreads.

The most recent breakthrough, and one that established soy

products as an acceptable American food in their own right, is the textured soy protein. Unlike earlier soy proteins, which had a powdery consistency, textured soy protein products have an identifiable texture and structural integrity and through two processes can be made into food analogs that mimic in texture and flavor hamburgers, bacon strips, ham, chicken, beef chunks, seafood, pasta, chow mein, coconut chips and other nutmeats, and hors d'oeuvre dips; even a boneless T-bone is in prospect. One process is spinning the isolated soy protein into fibers, which are processed by combining with fats, flavors, and coloring. The other is an extrusion-type processing of soy flour, which has a definite shape and chewable texture and may be in tiny bits or bite-size chunks. Textured soy protein products may be dry and rehydratable, or wet, either canned or frozen in granules, bits, chunks, slices, or loaves and usable as purchased. Food processed from the textured soy proteins has no bones, skin, or excess fat, and there is no shrinkage or waste; flavor, texture, and shape can be built in as desired, and supplemental nutrients can be added. These products have a long shelf life and are convenient to use.

In 1971 the Department of Agriculture authorized the use of textured vegetable protein in school feeding programs, and when the price of red meats soared, "beanburgers" gained widening acceptance. In 1973 the amount of soy protein sold as meat substitutes rose to about 100 million pounds—double the amount of the year before—and some food specialists project that by 1980, as much as 20 percent of the "meat" we eat will be imitation.

(The peanut industry has been watchful of soybean food technology, and researchers have developed a high-protein peanut flour that does not taste like peanuts, though some people think it would be better if it did. In 1973 J. H. Mitchell, Jr., of Clemson University, claimed the biggest breakthrough for this oilseed since the invention of peanut butter eighty years before—the peanut flake. It is white, bland, pre-cooked, rapidly rehydratable, and has been used as a major ingredient in poultry dishes, ham rolls, lunch meats, and spreads. Protein levels of up to 63 percent were claimed. But the flakes are considered too expensive for livestock feed, and Mitchell doubts that they will displace the soybean.)

One process for producing meat analogs, according to Arthur R. Odell, special projects director at General Mills, converts nutritious but unappetizing (if not inedible) high-protein oil-seed meals into mouth-watering forms ten times more efficiently than some food animals. His company's process is claimed to have a conversion efficiency of 70 percent, while a steer's conversion efficiency is only 7 percent.

The change relative to artificial food is important because of the contribution that "textured vegetable proteins" can make in this era of high meat prices, particularly those processed from soybeans, and they are also convenience foods. In a 1974 interview, the FDA chief, Alexander M. Schmidt, pointed out that about 50 percent of American meals already were previously prepared outside the home, and predicted that by 1980, the proportion would reach two-thirds. "We do know that some chemical and pharmaceutical companies are making large investments in artificial hams, artificial cheeses, and similar new types of food," he said.

If the soy has become "superbean," as *Time* magazine suggested in 1973, it is not because of its superior yields. They have increased only about 35 percent during the past quarter of a century—hardly comparable to corn yields, which have increased 130 percent in the past 20 years. One of the reasons for this is that the soybean does not respond to heavy fertilizing, though scientists believe that they are on the verge of a genetic breakthrough in this area. On the other hand, when soybeans are planted to land on which corn grew the year before, they need very little fertilizer at all—a definite advantage when fertilizer prices rose and supplies became short in late 1973 and early 1974. In fact, because of their unusual ability to fix nitrogen from the air, with the assistance of certain bacteria in the soil, soybeans need less fertilizer for optimal growth than any other common food crop, and they return nitrogen to the soil—a saving for a farmer rotating with corn, which obtains its nitrogen from the earth.

Seed companies have genetically engineered the soybean for various rainfall and growing seasons, enabling many southern farmers, who have a longer growing season, to double-crop with grain. Farmers in other areas are clamoring for new varieties adapted to their environments.

The United States now produces about three-fourths of the world soybean output. American farmers harvested a record of nearly 1.6 billion bushels in 1973, up 23 percent from the previous high the year before. The average yield was 27.8 bushels per acre, equal to the 1972 record; the highest yields were 35 to 36 bushels, and the lowest was 15 bushels. The two largest producers after the United States are China with 12 percent and Brazil with 8 percent, the latter of which, however, is now the second leading exporter.

In the United States during 1973, soybean futures prices fluctuated from a little over $3 a bushel to over $12, but toward the year's end they hovered around $6. With the fallback and a strengthening in the price of corn and cotton, commodities analysts reported that they would be more profitable to plant, and a Department of Agriculture survey of grower intentions in January 1974 indicated that for the first time since 1958, soybean acreage probably would not increase over the prior year, and could be reduced 3 to 4 percent, unless weather or other factors caused farmers to change their minds.

Hay

Most people do not realize that more American acreage is planted to hay than to any other crop. In 1970 farmers planted over 62 million acres to hay (7 million more than was planted to corn), and total output reached a record 134.6 million tons. Nearly 70 percent of harvested hay was alfalfa; the rest was mainly clover, timothy, and wild hay (which includes prairie, marsh, and salt grasses). The American hay crop in 1971 was worth around $3.3 billion, making it the third most valuable crop, after corn and soybeans. But only about a fifth of the harvest is sold; most of it is fed to livestock on the same farm on which it is grown.

Hay itself is low in protein, but it becomes a major indirect source of our protein because the animals we eat are able to synthesize complete protein from it. Recently, many people have adopted alfalfa as a health food, but it is no nutritional substitute for meats, fruits, or vegetables. Alfalfa does contain vitamins A and K, but ordinary green vegetables have more. However, a bland white edible protein concentrate can be produced from fresh green alfalfa juice and used as a food additive, and the juice yields a dry green protein product used for poultry feed.

Alfalfa was introduced into America by Wendelin Grimm, a German who brought a 20-pound bag of seed to Minnesota in 1857. His first harvests were nearly wiped out by winterkills, but he collected seed from surviving plants until he finally produced harvests tolerant of Minnesota weather.

Vegetables

Americans eat many vegetables frequently, if not necessarily as regularly as potatoes; and some vegetables, notably beans, are staples for other people. Tomatoes are the most valuable non-staple crop; in 1973, we grew nearly 120 trillion pounds (60 million tons)—about 600 pounds per person. They are also the most important imported vegetable, coming mostly from Mexico—750 million pounds (350,000 tons) in 1973. Probably the most popular fresh vegetable is lettuce. The Department of Agriculture reports regularly on twenty-two vegetables, of which eleven are considered important as processed crops—asparagus, green lima beans, snap beans, beets, cabbage for kraut, cucumbers for pickles, sweet corn, green peas, spinach, and tomatoes, and several others are important as specialty items.

The Potato *(Solanum tuberosum)*

Of the tubers—the fleshy, thickening outgrowths of roots and blossom stems that turn into the soil—the potato is a staple of many people. The white or Irish potato is as close to being an everyday item as any other food, and commercial demand for it is usually inelastic; most people, irrespective of incomes, eat about as many potatoes as they desire. Besides its low cost, the potato owes it popularity to its taste, which is unaggressive, and its texture, which lends itself to many ways of cooking.

Since 1970, potatoes have been undergoing a merchandising revolution based on the introduction of processed products. This accounts for an increase of average consumption from 102 pounds in 1952 to 119 pounds in the 1970s. In 1962, one-fourth of the American output was processed; today, roughly one-half is. The most important processing method is freezing, but potatoes are also dehydrated, canned, and fried as chips and shoestrings.

Unfortunately, protein content is only 2.1 percent—nearly the lowest for any staple—and it is low in other nutrients. Some people avoid potatoes because they are fattening; certain cooking methods, especially those not calling for the addition of fats, can minimize this effect. Europeans at first viewed potatoes suspiciously, perhaps because the leaves and stems, which some tried, are mildly toxic; the tuber itself can be toxic if exposed to the sun during growth. The Spaniards, however, were poor and hungry when the Conquistadors brought the potato back from South America, and when they saw how quickly it grew they adopted it. Spanish men also thought it restored masculinity. Soon potato consumption spread throughout Europe, except in France where psychological barriers persisted, and in England where potatoes were scorned because they were the staple of the disliked Irish. Early in the eighteenth century, the Irish brought potatoes to North America.

The increase in potato yields is another success story. In the United States, average yield was 5,000 to 6,000 pounds per acre, until the mid-1960s when yields surpassed an average of 20,000 pounds per acre and, in 1972, attained a peak of 23,600 pounds. In 1971 American output reached a record 31.9 billion pounds; the 1973 output was 29.7 billion pounds. During the recent food-price inflation, potatoes have been much affected, rising to over $9 per hundredweight, compared to around $3 in 1972 and much lower in years earlier; yet per capita consumption remained stable into early 1974.

The Tomato *(Lycopersicum esculentum)*

Tomato tonnage accounts for about half of the table vegetables processed in the United States and ranks fifth, after lettuce, cabbage, carrots, and celery, in the fresh market. The Department of Agriculture reports a total of some 20 billion pounds for ten "important" processed crops—asparagus, green lima beans, snap beans, beets, cabbage for kraut, cucumbers for pickles, sweet corn; green peas, spinach, and tomatoes. The tomato, native to

the American tropics and botanically a fruit but generally called
a vegetable, did not reach this ascendancy easily, and has experienced a reputation more checkered than any other food. At one
time, people called it the *pomme d'amour*, "apple of love," a
euphemism for aphrodisiac; during the sixteenth century, the
Italians adopted it as a staple. But other Europeans of the period,
who grew both red and yellow varieties as ornamentals, warned
that tomatoes were poisonous, and for some decades after they
were transplanted to the United States in 1781, they were still
considered dangerous. Thomas Jefferson is the first American recorded to have grown them, but as late as 1900 many Americans
avoided eating them raw and usually used them in purees. Since
1895, plant breeders have created many new types, emphasizing
resistance, vigor, and, more recently, textures that withstand the
rigors of mechanical harvesting. Today, a coalition of health-food
enthusiasts and environmentalists argue that these new varieties
neither taste nor feel as good as those requiring manual picking.

American tomatoes are divided into three main types. The
small, compact plants, called *determinates*, have stems only 12 to
18 inches long and stop bearing once they attain full size. Slightly
larger plants, called *semi-determinates*, produce until their stems
reach 18 to 24 inches. And the third type, the *indeterminates*, are
widely ranging vines that grow and bear indefinitely. Some varieties are excellent for special purposes; the oval Roma, for example, is used extensively for tomato paste. Sizes vary from the little
cherry tomato to the Ponderosa, which may be up to six inches in
diameter and weigh a pound and a half.

Americans consume large quantities of tomato juice, ketchup,
puree, paste, and sauce, in addition to fresh and canned tomatoes.
In the early 1970s an estimated 1 percent of the winter food
budget of the average American family was spent on tomatoes
and in 1973 Americans ate an average of 433 tomatoes per person. Despite its low protein level, the tomato is higly nutritious.
A medium-sized tomato gives an adult half of his daily requirement of vitamin C; it is high in vitamin A, the B complex, calcium, and iron; and it has but 35 calories.

American demand for tomatoes has been so high that 1973
production was unable to meet it, but some American growers
would like to restrain foreign competition nonetheless. In the
early 1970s, when the Department of Agriculture imposed restric-

tions on the size of tomatoes marketed, Mexican farmers, who export smaller types to the United States, felt that they were discriminated against in favor of Florida growers, who had lobbied for the action. Ensuing protests hinted at the possibility of "tomato border shootouts," if not a "tomato war."

The Leaf Vegetables

The leaves of many vegetables can be eaten, but they are usually less popular than other parts of the plant. The leaves of some plants are toxic, but often, as in the case of the turnip, they are much more nutritious than the favored part. A number of vegetables, however, are cultivated solely for their heads.

The most frequently eaten leaf, and perhaps the most frequently eaten of all vegetables, is lettuce (*Lactua sativa*). Of the many types, the most common fall into three categories—head lettuce, loose-leaf lettuce, and butterhead lettuce. The widely consumed iceberg, also known as crisphead, is a head lettuce. Other types, sometimes considered delicacies, are romaine or cos, escarole, and Kentucky Bibb or limestone, which has a delectable tiny head that can cost up to $20 a pound. In 1972 the average American ate 22.2 pounds of lettuce, up from 19.8 pounds a decade earlier. In that year the United States produced 4.8 billion pounds at a total value of $277 million—over one-fifth the value of all fresh market vegetables and second only to tomatoes.

Several other leaf vegetables are of importance commercially or in our eating habits, though a few do not appear particularly "leafy." There are the cabbage and its relatives—brussels sprouts, broccoli, cauliflower, and kale—and chard, chicory, endive, and spinach. Parsley, sometimes treated as a herb, is used widely for garnishings and flavoring; and some varieties of dandelion, once thought a depression food and not commercially important, are regaining popularity, as well they should for their high levels of several vitamins and minerals.

Pulses

Pulse is the common name for *Leguminosae,* a large plant family with 550 genera and 13,000 species, which typically have seed-bearing pods. (Soybean and peanut plants also have seed-bearing pods but these are commercially classified as oilseeds.) The major pulses are beans, peas, chickpeas, and lentils.

The Department of Agriculture differentiates between "dry edible beans," which are eaten as seeds, like the navy or pea bean, and are characterized by their mealy texture and nutlike taste; and the snap, green, or string beans, which are long, edible pods containing tiny seeds. The dry edible bean is important because it is approximately 8 percent protein, and it is fairly rich in several other nutrients. Snap beans have less protein but are good sources of several vitamins and minerals.

For the peoples of temperate zones, the pea is possibly the most popular of all summer vegetables. It is fairly high in protein, and has a good deal of several other nutrients.

Other Tubers

Several tubers (other than the white potato) are important culinarily, and some, notably garden beets, carrots, onions, and sweet potatoes, are produced in large quantities. The sweet potato is no relative of the white potato; it is popular in the American South, where it is often known simply as a "potato," and it is a staple for some tropical and subtropical peoples. The yam is often confused with the sweet potato—indeed, it is called a sweet potato in parts of the American South—and is similarly starchy and sweetish. Overseas, the yam is usually a secondary crop, but it is an important food in West Africa and some other high-rainfall areas, and some South Sea Islands have a variety whose tuber grows phenomenally to 8 feet in length and 80 pounds in weight. Both the sweet potato and the yam are low in protein, but they are good sources of a few other nutrients. Radishes, turnips, parsnips, and garlic are common but less extensively cultivated tubers.

Another tuber that is an important staple is the cassava or manioc. While most Americans know it only as a specialty item, tapioca, and it does not enter commercial trade to a great extent, 3.3 percent of the world population rely on it, making it the sixth most important staple globally; in some impoverished tropical areas, it is the mainstay for most people. But it is only .6 percent protein, the lowest level for any staple, and contains virtually no other nutrients. Because of the difficult world food situation, geneticists are trying to breed more nutritious varieties at research institutes in Africa and Latin America.

Oilseeds

Another oilseed that is important domestically and globally is the peanut. It is about 30 percent protein, and it is cheaper than any other popular high-protein food except dried beans. In 1972 peanut protein cost from $1.66 to $2.27 per pound, while all-meat hot dogs were $7.00 per protein pound and hamburger was $4.00. The major processed product is peanut butter, of which *Consumers Report* recently said:

> Do you feel a twinge of guilt when you slap together peanut butter sandwiches and milk for your kids' lunches? Do you feel as though you should be taking more time to fix them something more nourishing? Even though they love peanut butter? Well, don't. . . .

A child between eight and ten years old can obtain 40 percent of his daily protein needs from two peanut butter sandwiches, each spread with about two level tablespoons, and by adding an eight-ounce cup of milk, he receives 83 percent of his requirement. The combination also provides about one-third of the needed calories.

The peanut is grown on every continent (except Antarctica) and in nearly every warm area of the world. It is a staple in several African areas, and is a major crop in India (the leading producer), China, and several other Asian countries. Carver pioneered commercial plantings in the United States and discovered how to make more than three hundred products from peanuts.

The average American eats about 7.5 pounds of peanuts a year; about half of this is in the form of peanut butter while the rest is eaten roasted and salted, mixed with candy, and as "ballpark peanuts"—that is, bought in the shell. Peanut oil is also used in margarine, in canning meats, and for cooking and salads. Roasting does not affect the protein level significantly, but does reduce the vitamin and mineral content.

Sixteen states raise peanuts, but Georgia alone raises almost one-third of the national output—nearly 3.5 billion pounds in 1973—making it the state's largest cash crop. Even with the renewed food shortages, American peanuts remained in surplus, the reason being, according to the Department of Agriculture, that peanut prices were kept unnecessarily high through a federal price-support program. In 1973 the secretary of agriculture called for an end to these subsidies. One reason for the move was that the price of peanuts was approaching the support price of $328.50 per ton (16.42 cents a pound). But previous agricultural legislation still sets a minimum national acreage allotment for peanuts and provided for a high support price at prices prevailing until 1973. Earlier in the decade peanuts were around $140 a ton, and subsidies were costing the taxpayer around $70 million a year. After the legislation was passed, farmers doubled their yields, so that from 1966 to 1971, national output rose five and a half times faster than national consumption. The government bought the surplus at the high support price, which, incidentally, also made peanutland far more valuable than most neighboring farmland. The move to place peanut farmers in the free market, however, did not set well with the chairman of the Senate Agriculture Committee, Herman Talmadge (D.-Georgia), who represents the number-one peanut state. "A cut in the support program would be disastrous to all rural residents who depend upon the economic activity generated by peanuts," he said. Nevertheless, the secretary placed restrictions on the 1974 program, one of which eliminates transfer by lease, sale, or owner privilege for acreage allotments, no support for peanuts containing aflatoxin, and an increase in inspection and other charges.

The olive has always been an important crop around the Mediterranean, but Americans consider it a specialty. It grows on small, picturesquely gnarled trees, which grow slowly but may attain great longevity, and survive under minimal care in many arid lands. The Conquistadors brought the first olive trees to the Americas, and trees were planted in Georgia and South Carolina in the 1780s. In the same century, the Franciscans brought olive trees to California, which today dominates American production. Despite their popularity and diverse uses, olives do not provide many nutrients, except vitamin A and some protein and calcium.

The coconut is a major crop in some countries, but Americans grow its palm mainly as an ornamental. Its "meat" is used for confections, and its fatty milk or oil for cooking.

Other oilseeds of agricultural importance are cottonseed, sunflower seed, and flaxseed; they are generally crushed for oil, meal, and cakes. The world produces over 22 million tons of glanded cottonseed annually, of which over 5 million is in the United States—the equivalent of some 10.6 billion pounds of nearly 70 percent protein flour. The barrier to cottonseed crushings as a product for food is the toxicity of gossypol, the main substance in the pigments in a collection of glands in the seed. Though much progress has been made in removing the gossypol, experts say that more needs to be learned about the basic chemistry of cottonseed in order to invest in more effective removal methods. Geneticists created a new variety of glandless cottonseed for the high plains of western Texas, but it has yet to become commercially competitive with the soybean.

Sunflower seed, which is important in some parts of the world including the Soviet Union, and flaxseed are becoming more important in the United States. Kansas farmers, overcoming their prejudice toward the plant as a weed (even though it is the state flower), have planted it more seriously since 1970, and flaxseed plantings are increasing because of higher prices.

Specialty Crops

Some specialty crops are important to various local economies and may be rewarding financially to individual farmers. Mushrooms, for example, which were becoming much more popular in the United States until the 1974 botulism scare, are grown mainly in Pennsylvania, where about 550 growers produce 57 percent of the national crop. Consumption increased by a third during the second half of the 1960s, and the dollar value jumped from $53 million at the beginning of the decade to $90 million in 1971 and nearly $110 million in 1973. Other valuable crops grown on a smaller scale are the artichoke, asparagus, celery, cucumber, eggplant, squashes, onions, peppers, and herbs.

Sugar Crops

The two primary sources of sugar are sugar cane and sugar beets; other sources are the wild date palm and the palmyra or borassus palm (common sugar sources in India), the sugar palm, which grows wild as well as under cultivation in Malaysia and Indonesia, and the black maple and sugar maple of the United States. The average American eats about 102 pounds of sugar each year, as compared to 9 pounds in 1823. In most underdeveloped lands, per capita annual consumption is less than 10 pounds.

Sugar cane provides more than half of the world sugar supply, and yields most highly in the humid tropics with plenty of sunshine, though it grows in the subtropics as far north as Louisiana. Sugar cane is a member of the grass family, rising to 20 feet, with leaves somewhat like those of corn. Its pithy stalk is up to three inches in diameter and segmented by nodes like bamboo. On modern plantations it is cut by giant machines; in poorer countries, most cutting is still by hand. After harvesting, new stalks ratoon—that is, sprout from the point at which the stalk was sliced—and these shoots are ready for another harvest in about a year. Up to fifteen annual harvests are possible from a single planting, but yield gradually declines with each ratooning, and replanting much earlier is customary.

Ancient Asians probably first found the stalk pleasant to chew, if a little dry, and eventually learned to crush it to obtain a sweet juice. The earliest cultivators were the subcontinental Indians, who refined crystals from the juice as early as 1000 B.C.; refining advanced over the centuries. Until the sixteenth century, sugar was expensive and was sold by spice merchants as a medicinal and luxury item. Columbus introduced cane into Hispaniola in 1509 on his second voyage to the Western Hemisphere, and within three decades it was the most popular crop. As is spread throughout the West Indies, they became known as the "Sugar Islands" and were the main supplier of Europe. In 1751 the Jesuits transplanted cane to Louisiana, which is today one of the leading sugar-producing states. The other big producers are Hawaii, Puerto Rico, and Florida, where plantings were extended during the 1960s into the marshy, fertile soils of the Everglades.

In countries too temperate for cane, the sugar beet is the most important source of sugar. It is related to the garden beet and is white with roots 12 to 15 inches long. Over half the sugar produced in the United States, and nearly all sugar produced in the Soviet Union, comes from beets. Beet sugar is indistinguishable from that of cane, and much of it is also used for molasses—a good feed as well as a cooking ingredient—and industrial alcohol.

Although the sugar beet was known in pre-Christian times, it was not until about two centuries ago that a German chemist proved that plants did not need tropical heat to produce sugar and that beets could be a commercial source of sugar. Under his procedure, 6.2 percent of the root could be made into sugar, but today, with better varieties and improved processing, 15 to 20 percent of the root is converted into sugar. The leaves make good fodder, and the pulp that remains after sugar has been extracted is also usable as a feed. The residue from the extracted juice can be used as fertilizer.

To maintain orderly world prices in sugar, traffic in which is known as "the sweet trade," international agreements have fixed prices and export-import quotas, and some nations, including the United States, have imposed domestic production controls. Quotas have also been used as an instrument of diplomacy. For example, after the difficulties with Fidel Castro, the United States, traditionally its major buyer of sugar, cut Cuba out of the American market. The Soviet Union, though itself the leading sugar producer, helped out its ally with increased purchases. Both the American and Russian actions were examples of "sugar diplomacy."

In the United States, the 1934 Sugar Act established an arrangement of quotas on domestic output and imports, and some domestic producers have long relied on this government support of the market. In late 1973 the Department of Agriculture floated a trial balloon in recommending the release of sugar from production controls, and because during the year the International Sugar Agreement appeared collapsed, the government could also move to decrease domestic sugar prices by enlarging the import quota. But within six months, world demand had suddenly outstripped production, and even though price quotes reached the highest levels since World War II, some beet farmers were switching to still more profitable crops. In June 1974, reacting to irked consumers and industrial users, such as the soft-drink manufacturers, the House of Representatives voted against renewing the Sugar Act.

The United States, which consumes over 23 billion pounds of sugar a year, produces around 13 billion pounds. In 1972 world production rose to 148.4 billion pounds.

The sugar maple was a favorite tree of the Indians, who converted its amber or brown sap into syrup and sugar by methods essentially the same as those we use today. Most commercial syrup is now a mixture of maple and cane sugar, since pure maple syrup costs more than most people are willing to pay. New York and Vermont vie as the leading producers, and together account for about two-thirds of the national syrup output, which was nearly 1.1 million gallons in 1972.

Honey, while not strictly speaking a sugar, was the principal sweetener in the world until the eighteenth century. It is enjoying a resurgent popularity in the United States because of the health-food movement, and beekeeping remains an important specialized vocation in areas where growers use bees to pollinate orchards. In 1973 American beekeepers produced 238 million pounds of honey—up 11 percent from the year before—from 4.1 million colonies, which did not represent an increase; the yield rose from an average of 52.6 pounds per colony to 58.1 pounds.

Fruits and Nuts

Most of our fruits originated in China and southwestern Asia, not far from where the Garden of Eden is thought to have been. Today they are cultivated most intensively in the advanced countries of the temperate zones. Plant breeders have genetically altered many species, and approaches to cultivation have changed. Traditionally, fruit growers raised nearly all their fruit in small orchards, vineyards, berry patches, and backyards, and, except for what they reserved for their families, sold it mostly to local markets. But cultivation has shifted to the areas most suited for growing of specific types, the size of operations has increased, and markets are frequently much more distant. In the United States the leading fruit-producing states are California and Florida, and orchards are important in many localities in other states. Another major development has been the genetic engineering of dwarf trees, some of which are only one-fourth the height of traditional trees. While dwarfs usually yield less per tree, the ease of harvesting them is a major economic advantage.

In reporting fruit production, the Department of Agriculture maintains two broad categories—*citrus fruits*, which are a botanical group that grow on evergreen trees, and non-citrus or *deciduous fruits*, which are a mixed bag botanically but will grow on trees that shed their leaves. Deciduous fruits may be grouped into the *pomes*, whose fleshy portion are greatly swollen receptacles containing small seeds and covered by thin skin; the *drupes*, which are vernacularly known as stone fruits because they bear but one sizable seed enclosed by a hard covering; the *berries*, which are agglomerations of druplets; and, as in the case of vegetables, a number that defy categorization.

Citrus Fruits

Americans eat two to three times as many citrus fruits as any other people, and citrus constitute the largest section—in terms both of money and weight—of the American fruit market. Oranges are the single most important American fruit crop. The grapefruit is the second leading citrus fruit in the United States, and Americans grow 90 percent of the world output. The lemon is the third major American citrus crop; other American citrus fruits—limequats, limes, tangors, tangelos, tangerines, and temples —are grown as specialty crops.

The citrus probably originated as a bitter fruit on the Malay Archipelago over 20 million years ago. The strong currents of the Indian Ocean may have swept the seeds to India, Africa, and finally the Mediterranean Basin; and seafarers carried both seeds and trees to more distant points. Columbus carried seeds to the Caribbean, and Ponce de Leon and Hernando de Sota are believed to have planted citrus in Florida in the sixteenth century. It was not until Florida became an American possession that orange groves began proliferating, and the first trees were planted in California about 1800.

American cultivators grow over 25 varieties of oranges. The Valencia makes up about half the harvest, and the Hamlin and Navel a good part of the remainder. Output fluctuates; in the 1972–73 marketing year, a record 223.8 million boxes of oranges were produced, about three-fourths coming from Florida and most of the remainder from California. Over 70 percent of the output was processed, mainly into frozen concentrate. Grapefruit output totaled 65.2 million boxes, about two-thirds of which were grown in Florida.

Deciduous Fruits

The most popular fruit in the world, though it ranks third to oranges and grapes in the United States, is the apple, a pome. It keeps well, and until this century was virtually the only fruit available in winter in temperate zones. Despite the saying, it is less deserving than some other fruits of the reputation for keeping the doctor away, for it has little protein and only modest amounts of a few other nutrients. The majority of today's varieties probably descended from varieties native to southwestern Asia, but the earliest ancestor may have been the wild crab apple, which probably originated in northeastern Asia. The English brought apples to America; early itinerant trappers and peddlers carried them westward. The pioneer orchardist John Chapman, known in legend as Johnny Appleseed, contributed appreciably to the founding of the American apple industry in the nineteenth century. By 1877, 1,500 varieties were identified in the United States and by 1969, over 7,000. Only a dozen of these, however, are important crops. The American and world leader is the Red Delicious.

We produced over 6 billion pounds of apples in 1973, nearly a third of which came from the state of Washington. France is the world's leading producer, growing nearly as many apples for apple cider alone in some years as Americans harvest altogether. In dessert and cooking apples, the United States is the top producer.

The second most popular fruit in the world is another pome, the pear. The United States and China are the leading producers; in 1973, American output was over 1.4 billion pounds. Pears are a comparatively good source of calcium and vitamin A and have smaller amounts of several other nutrients.

Peaches, a drupe, are the third most important deciduous fruit in the world, and fourth most important in the United States. There are thousands of varieties, but only a handful are commercially valuable. The two main gastronomic categories are the tender, juicy peaches that are delicious when freshly picked; and the larger, firmer, darker ones that are more suitable for canning. We generally eat freestone peaches fresh and clingstone peaches canned. In 1970, total American output was nearly 3 billion pounds, but it has since dropped (it was about 2.6 billion pounds in 1973). The nectarine is essentially the same fruit as a peach, except that it is smaller and firmer. California produces virtually all clingstones and nectarines and about 60 percent of all varieties. Other important American drupes are the apricot, plum, and cherry; the persimmon and pomegranate are grown as specialties.

The most renowned berry is the grape, and more grapes are produced than fruits of all deciduous trees. Worldwide, 70 to 80 percent of the grape output is used for wines, brandies, and liqueurs.

The vinifera grape (*V. vinifera*), which is common in Europe, may have originated around the Black and Caspian seas; it was transplanted to America where the phylloxera louse destroyed it. But North America had many native species of grape, and colonists hybridized the native *V. labrusca* with vinifera to obtain resistant vines. The phylloxera established itself in Europe over a century ago, so European growers cultivate their local grapes now on resistant American rootstock.

The American wine industry has grown phenomenally in the last few years, and some connoisseurs consider its best vintages competitive with, if not superior to, some leading continental wines. In the United States in the 1960s only around a fifth of American grapes were grown for wine, but between 1970 and 1973, growers in California, which produces three-fourths of American wines, planted nearly 100,000 more acres of wine grapes. Other states have been joining the boom, and the United States now ranks sixth in wine production. By mid-1974, though, inflated prices threatened vintners' prosperity.

One of the most versatile grapes grown in the United States is the Thompson seedless, the sweet green berry familiar in supermarkets in late summer. It is used mostly for wine and is grown on over half of California's grape acreage. In 1973 American growers produced over 7.7 billion pounds of grapes, down from the 1971 record of nearly 8 billion pounds. Despite the enormous growth of the wine industry, nearly 60 percent of California grapes go for raisins, as compared to about 20 percent for wine and 12 percent for the table.

The other commercially important berries are the cranberry and the strawberry, the latter of which, however, is not a true fruit but a rosaceous herb. The blackberry, blueberry, currant, huckleberry, June berry, and raspberry enjoy specialty markets.

Among the individualists are the melons which we eat as fruit, though the Department of Agriculture reports them as vegetables. The most important melons are the cantaloupe, watermelon, and honeydew.

The pineapple and banana are popular in America but neither of them is grown commercially in the mainland states. The pineapple, a wild plant native to the American tropics from Mexico to Brazil, did not achieve global popularity until appropriate shipping methods were developed. The Portuguese apparently were responsible for transplanting it in much of the tropical world and it was growing in most tropical regions by the seventeenth century, where it became second only to the banana in popularity. It grew in importance as an exportable cash crop, and modern plantations for its cultivation emerged. Nearly half the world output and more than half of all canned pineapple comes from Hawaii.

In the "banana republics," dictators or juntas may come and go, but the banana seems to rule forever. Bananas are now raised throughout most of the humid tropics and subtropics, and have been the mainstay of some economies. Bananas generally make up no more than 1 percent of the American diet, and our supplies come mostly from Costa Rica and Ecuador, the latter of which produces about a fourth of those traded internationally. The chief variety in world trade is the Gros Michel, but there are many other kinds.

Other fruits of some importance in the United States are dates and figs, grown in the Southwest, and the avocado, which grows in the tropics and in California and Florida.

Nuts

Nuts, with the occasional exception of the acorns, have not generally been an important source of nutrition. Yet they are better sources of protein than most fruits and vegetables, and they have other nutritional value. Their chief attribute is their ability to keep for long periods. In Europe, walnuts and almonds were blanched, pulverized, and soaked in water to provide a "milk" that was a staple of many households at least until the end of the eighteenth century. The Department of Agriculture classifies walnuts, pecans, almonds, and filberts as being of major commercial importance, in that order, and it also reports on the specialty macadamia.

Nut output has been rising; the almond industry, which is concentrated in California, is one of America's recent success stories. Production has risen tenfold since the 1930s, and both domestic and world demand is still rising. In 1973 the United States harvested 260 million pounds of almonds, and the almond tree has become the most valuable nut tree in the country, the second most valuable of all tree crops, and the ninth most valuable of the hundreds of crops grown in California, the leading agricultural state. In 1972 sales reached $85 million, and they rose in 1973.

Workers used to bang almonds out of trees with poles, catch them in canvas sheets, and sort them into burlap bags; now, hydraulic knocking-and-pickup machines rumble among the trees, and bulk trucks carry the nuts away. Once almonds were sold only in the shell, and then mostly during the Christmas season, but now they are sold blanched, sliced, diced, split, and roasted. The world's largest almond plant is in Sacramento, where the nuts are processed into a thousand different grades. The major customers are confectioners, who buy about 44 percent of the crop.

The United States harvests nearly half of the world supply of walnuts, mainly in California, Oregon, and Washington. The pistachio nut, of which the United States has been the major importer, may soon become an important domestic product. Traditional pistachio nuts have a reputation for needing a sledge hammer to open, and Middle East growers run them under a stone wheel. But an investigator at a California agricultural station reportedly found a strain, the Kerman, whose nuts mature uniformly and crack open simultaneously, which are advantages for mechanizing and processing. Now a third of these trees are growing in a California nursery and may be the foundation of another nut industry in America.

9

Of Mammal, Fowl, and Fish

Red meat has been glorified over the centuries—in chronicles, etchings, and cookbooks—but it has never been common fare. Difficulties include hunting animals in the wild, tending them after they are domesticated, the need for animal power on farms when pasture was limited, and earning enough to pay high market prices. Americans, who have been able to afford more red meat than most peoples, rely mostly on cattle, hogs, and sheep; but we also eat some rabbit, goat, horsemeat, and game. Our poultry consumption is limited mainly to chickens and turkeys, although ducks and geese are sold, and some game birds, notably pheasant, are raised commercially. Linked to livestock, of course, are dairy products—milk, cream, butter, and cheese—and eggs. We eat comparatively few fish, but the inflation of red-meat prices will probably change this. Meats, dairy products and eggs are good sources of balanced protein—so much so that "animal protein" is often a term used synonymously with "complete protein"—and several other nutrients.

Early in this decade, before the world food shortage inflated prices, nearly a third of the typical American family's food budget was spent for red meat; average consumption reached a peak of nearly 192 pounds per person in 1971, an increase of about 30 pounds over 1960 consumption. With higher prices, the average began dropping, to just below 190 pounds in 1972 and about 176 pounds in 1973—the lowest since 1967. The United States is the world's leading meat producer, accounting for a fifth of all output (including poultry but excluding fish).

Beef has been by far the most popular meat; its consumption in the United States increased by over a fourth during the 1960s, is nearly double what it was as recently as 1950, and as incomes of many families have risen in other countries, demand for beef has risen abroad. Americans eat about half as much pork as beef, and consumption has not risen much since 1960. We eat much less lamb and mutton, whose consumption has been declining. Of all meats, chicken is the third most popular, and has doubled from 1950 to 1971. The following table shows American consumption of the principal meats:

TABLE 9.1. AMERICAN PER CAPITA MEAT CONSUMPTION
(pounds per year)

Type	1950	1960	1965	1970	1971	1972	1973
Total Red Meat	144.6	160.9	167.1	186.3	191.8	188.9	175.9
Beef	63.4	85.0	99.5	113.7	113.0	116.0	109.8
Pork	69.2	64.9	58.7	66.4	73.0	67.4	61.5
Veal	8.0	6.1	5.2	2.9	2.7	2.2	1.8
Lamb and Mutton	4.0	4.8	3.7	3.3	3.1	3.3	2.8
Total Poultry	25.1	34.6	41.3	50.0	50.5	52.4	51.2
Chicken	20.6	28.0	33.4	41.5	41.4	43.0	41.8
Turkey	4.1	6.0	7.4	8.2	8.5	8.9	9.1
Other	.3	.6	.5	.3	.6	.4	.3
Fish	13.8	13.2	13.9	14.8	14.4	15.2	15.1
Total All Meat	163.5	208.7	222.3	254.0	256.7	256.3	242.2

SOURCE: U.S. Department of Agriculture.

In 1945 egg consumption averaged was 403 per person annually, but it fell after the war, leveling off at between 315 and 335 during the 1960s. It began dropping in 1972 because of concern over cholesterol content, and by 1974 had fallen to 292 eggs per person, the lowest since 1936. Though eggs are rich in vitamin A and calcium, and egg yolk is high in protein, with some iron and the B complex, the yolk of one large egg has between 250 and 275 milligrams of cholesterol. The egg, in fact, is the highest cholesterol source in the human diet; experiments show that healthy people eating two to four yolks a day have cholesterol levels 10 to 50 percent higher than they do when on cholesterol-free diets. Some health groups recommend a daily maximum of 300 milligrams of cholesterol if atherosclerosis, a common cause of heart disease, is to be avoided. Other factors contributing to the drop in egg consumption were the weakening of the American tradition of having eggs for breakfast, a growing preference for convenience breakfast foods, and the rise in egg prices.

Egg producers, feeling a crisis point had been reached by 1974, established a promotional war chest of $3 million. One of their tactics was to characterize the egg as "sexy" on the grounds that cholesterol is a building block of sex hormones. Nonetheless, Americans still consumed an estimated 63 billion eggs in 1973, down from around 70 billion in 1970 and 1971; and we are still eating nearly twice as many eggs as recommended by health specialists. Furthermore, producers' 1973 receipts were nearly $3 billion, up from $1.8 billion in 1972.

Milk and cream consumption has decreased from an average of about 161 quarts per person in 1960 to 129 quarts in 1972, while ice cream consumption has held to around 16 quarts (18 pounds) annually. The average person consumes 5 pounds of butter a year, down from 7.5 pounds in 1960, but we were eating about 5.5 pounds more cheese per year in the early 1970s than we were in 1960—a total of 13.8 pounds in 1973.

Husbandry

We know little about the earliest efforts to domesticate animals, but some ancient societies domesticated all that we raise today and antelope, gazelles, hyenas, and dormice as well. Until recently, scholars believed that husbandry, like agriculture, began around the Zagros Mountains of Iran and Iraq; using new methods for the precise dating of old bones, however, they suggest that south-eastern Europeans may have husbanded as early. Goats, probably the first animals to be husbanded, were domesticated around 8050 B.C. They were followed by sheep, dogs, pigs, cattle, asses, and finally the more difficult horses, as table 9.2 shows:

TABLE 9.2. PROBABLE DATES AND AREAS OF FIRST ANIMAL DOMESTICATION

Animal	Date	Area
Goat Sheep }	8050 B.C.	Near East
Dog	7300 B.C.	England
Pigs Cattle Ass (onager) }	7000 B.C.	Greece
Horse	4350 B.C.	Ukraine

SOURCE: Reiner Protsch and Rainer Berger, "Earliest Radiocarbon Dates for Domesticated Animals," *Science*, No. 4070 (January 1973), p. 179.

The origins of domesticated poultry are murkier, but some ancient societies raised more species than we do today.

Larger animals were needed to pull plows and carts, and the gradual loss of grazing land to cropping led later to limited husbanding for food. In the first century A.D., Romans considered killing an ox as serious as murdering a citizen, but they subsequently began eating more beef, which led to overgrazing and shortages of animal power. Beef disappeared from European tables until the introduction of hay crops and turnips, which enabled farmers to keep more cattle over winter and offer freshly killed carcasses the year around.

Full-time butchers and retailers did not exist in either Homeric Greece or, for some centuries, in Rome. The earliest butcher shops served the poor for the most part, largely because butchers' standards were low and the few regulating laws were not well enforced. Even salted meat was not necessarily properly cured, despite its higher price. Erasmus tells how people held their noses when they passed a butcher shop, and as late as 1863 an official English report warned that over a fifth of the meat sold in markets came from diseased cattle. But throughout the Middle Ages, even the rural poor kept a few chickens, and while towns were still small enough, people obtained fresh meat from the neighboring countryside. As the cities grew, the rich continued to find ways of supplying their tables, but lack of refrigeration restricted meat supplies for the poor.

Livestock in America

Most American livestock, like many of our food crops, has been imported. The Spanish missionaries introduced cattle into Texas during the 1690s, and by the 1780s settlers' stocks had been improved by importing superior breeds from England. Shorthorns were introduced in 1738, and longhorns and Herefords after 1800.

The building of a beef industry was slow and difficult. Smallholders let their animals and fowl run loose, perhaps corralling or cooping them at night and during the winter. Before the West was developed, the most important beef-raising region was the South, particularly the Carolinas and Georgia; but farmers moving westward in the early nineteenth century drove their herds ahead of them. Stock was driven to northeastern markets on the hoof, so the meat could not have been very tender; in the forty- to fifty-day trek from Ohio and Illinois to New York, the animals lost as many as 150 pounds.

The scarcity of beef in the North inflated prices and led to the celebrated cattle drives across the western plains to the railheads in Kansas. The famous Texas longhorns were first sold in New York in 1854. Their meat was somewhat tough because their Spanish ancestors had been bred to tolerate the Andalusian heat and drought; but they adapted well to the arid Texas rangeland, resisted diseases, and were capable of the thousand-mile or longer drive to the railheads. Between 1870 and 1885, a large business was done in fattening cattle on the northern plains before driving them to the great Chicago slaughter yards.

Husbanding in America was initially based on a policy of free grazing land, but the Homestead Act of 1862, which led to the fragmenting of much rangeland into crop farms, had unintended consequences. Stockmen often allowed their herds to overgraze land, since they did not know when it might become unavailable because of homesteading. But in the 1880s a livestock depression followed a severe winter that killed as much as 75 percent of some herds. Stockmen began buying or leasing land; they fenced it, sank wells or dammed streams, and provided feed and shelter. The period of the open range ended.

Ranch grazing remains important, but since the 1950s feedlot technology and practices have modified it, and animals are confined and fattened on special diets. The time of confinement varies among types of stock. An assembly-line approach to confinement has been highly successful with poultry raising, and "chicken factories" have virtually displaced the barnyard. Not many years ago, chicken was one of the more expensive foods, but the revolutionary changes in raising, processing, and marketing brought the price of chicken down during the last two decades—in fact, withstanding inflation until 1972.

The confinement approach to husbanding, genetic alterations, and dietary supplements reduced production costs from one-fourth to one-half from 1950 to 1965, and the number of weeks needed to raise a broiler dropped from 13 to 8.5 during that period. The labor required to produce 1,000 birds fell from 100 man-hours to about 25, and the amount of feed needed to raise one pound of broiler meat declined from 3.4 to two pounds.

In 1950 the typical American family preferred to buy poultry fresh from the butcher; later, sales of processed poultry zoomed, and by 1972 more than a third of all frozen dinners contained chicken, another fourth contained turkey, and about two-thirds of all meat pies contained chicken and turkey. One reason for the popularity of these new products was that the advent of television and television advertising coincided with the introduction of these convenience entrees. Not everyone is enthused over the new chickens—some have argued that they lack the tastiness of the barnyard variety—but it is hard to argue about the lower prices; and with world meat shortages it becomes harder still to argue about the efficient production method. Marketing specialists have called the American broiler industry the world's most advanced system of producing food in quantity and nutritional quality.

The success of chicken factories led to a conviction that similar approaches could be worked out for the red-meat animals, but, while changes have been appreciable, they have not been as far-reaching. In the mid-1940s, only one-third of American cattle were given special feed, but by 1950 the figure had jumped to half, and by 1960 to over three-fourths. Calves are usually raised on ranges, transferred to feedlots for fattening, and shipped to markets when they weigh about 1,100 pounds. In the better feedlots, they receive at least two hot meals containing supplements a day, while a nutritionist monitors and regulates the feeding program and a computer controls the mixes of each truckload of feed. The slaughterhouse or packer dresses each carcass down to about 485 pounds of beef, and the rest goes into by-products (especially hides, of which the wholesale price rose from $7 or $8 to as high as $25 between 1971 and 1973) and waste. Though final butchering may still be handled by retail outlets, regional beef plants are also packaging individual cuts, and some authorities believe that centralized meat processing will predominate by the end of this decade.

Output of red meat expanded greatly from 1951 to 1971 because of greater use of artificial breeding, crossbreeding, and sire testing, which was due in part to the expanded use of feedlots; the beef industry is becoming economically integrated from insemination to slaughter.

Recent years have seen a change in the distribution of large-scale beef production. In the late 1950s, growth was rapid in the West; during the late 1960s, it was rapid in the Southwest and Plains states. Marketing was once centered in Chicago, Omaha, Kansas City, and Saint Paul, but the meat-packing industry has decentralized. It is now located in the main producing areas, such as the Texas Panhandle; on February 1, 1971, the Chicago stockyards of Carl Sandburg's time were closed.

During 1973, ranchers and feedlot operators handled about 122 million cattle, an increase of about 4 million (3.5 percent) over the previous year, a record, and the sharpest annual gain in a decade. The United States accounts for a fourth of world beef output, and, though it is the number-two beef importer, it brings in less than 5 percent of what it consumes.

The expenses incurred by a modern stockman, in order of size, are the cost of the animal, corn, silage (stored forage), protein supplement, interest, labor, transportation and marketing, power, equipment, veterinary medicine, and depreciation. These prices rose steadily quarter by quarter in 1972 and 1973, as table 9.3 shows, and slowed the growth of the farmer's profit margin as the retail price of beef rose.

TABLE 9.3. QUARTERLY COST OF RAISING A FEEDER STEER

	Year	
Quarter	1972	1973
1st	$369	$475
2nd	384	575
3rd	401	580
4th	420	—

SOURCE: *Livestock and Meat Situation* (Washington, D.C.: U.S. Department of Agriculture, December 1973), p. 22.

The hog farmer watched the Omaha price of feed corn rise from $1.50 in January 1973 to $2.71 in August, a hike of about 60 percent. Almost as important, the price of high-protein hog feed also rose by about 60 percent. Additionally, his capital costs and interest rates rose, discouraging the expansion of facilities.

For these reasons, the increase in herds that was expected to reduce consumer prices in 1973 failed to materialize; instead, herds declined somewhat.

Because beef production is slow, supply does not react to demand as quickly as it can for other livestock. The average lifespan of a steak, from conception to counter, is about thirty-two months; it is known as a cattle production cycle, or simply as cattle cycle (the hog cycle is only about eight months). For cattle, gestation lasts nine months; maturation, during which both mother and calf graze, takes eighteen months; and the animal then passes five months in the feedlot. Consumer demand must communicate itself through the marketing system to the cattleman, who decides if it is worth his while to increase the size of his herd and raise more calves for the feedlots. This decision may involve holding back more calves for future breeding, which occurred in 1973 even though demand for beef mounted.

By spring 1974, the cost-price situation had deteriorated. The price paid for choice beef to the feedlot operators had dropped from 60 cents a pound to 41 cents a pound, while feed costs had doubled from the year before, mainly because of the price of corn, the main feed ingredient, and operators were losing over $100— somtimes much more—on each steer sold to processors. Holding back animals from slaughter is no solution, since the additional weight gained in the meantime is mostly fat, and packers pay less per pound then. In March, young cattle put in field lots, called "placements," were down 20 percent from the year before, and while the price of beef paid by retailers fell in the spring, fewer cattle on feed portended tighter supplies of beef and higher prices some months later.

The growing consumption of meat among the affluent is putting greater pressure on farmland. It takes about 7 pounds of grain protein to produce one pound of protein in meat, which means it takes approximately a ton of grain annually to supply meat for the typical American. But the typical third world citizen who eats grain directly as a staple, consumes annually 400 pounds of grain. Put another way, it takes about two acres of arable land to support the average American with the meats to which he has become accustomed—yet the world has less than one acre of arable land per person.

In 1972 the Department of Agriculture concluded that the ranges were being grazed as intensively as was considered desirable, and that fulfilling future demand for beef would require improved raising techniques. Both grass and water are limited, and the rapid expansion of the 1950s and '60s is not likely to be duplicated. A further complicating factor in the recent effort to stabilize beef prices was the banning of diethylstilbestrol (DES), a hormone added to cattle feed that promotes growth and lowers raising costs. Studies showed that residues might remain in the meat and possibly present a cancer danger. Though the ban was lifted, subject to certain conditions, the uncertainties about a reimposition left most manufacturers reluctant to renew DES manufacture, thus limiting supplies.

Among alternatives to DES that were examined was the selling of meat of bulls, which produce a good balance of their own growth hormone, rather than of steers which do not because they

are castrated. Bulls also gain weight faster—up to 20 percent—
than steers. Montana rancher A.B.Cobb, who has specialized in
raising bulls, believes this beef tastes as good if not better, though
it is darker. But bulls are more aggressive than steers and are
therefore more difficult to raise.

The "big three" among American beef herds have been the
Hereford, the Angus, and the Shorthorn or Durham, English
breeds which displaced the Longhorn of the Old West because
they are fleshier. Both output and quality of beef can be improved
by systematic crossbreeding. Stockmen traditionally bred cattle
for appearance, but they are becoming more interested in breeding for such traits as reproductive performance, weaning weight,
post-weaning growth, feed-conversion efficiency, and carcass merit.
In 1960 only one stockman in ten experimented with genetic
improvement; today, three in ten are conducting genetic experiments.

In recent years, increasing interest has been shown in crossing
herds with foreign or "exotic" breeds. The Black Angus, for example, which is tasty but grows rather slowly, has been crossed with
the Swiss Simmental, which grows faster but does not taste as
good. At weaning, the Simmental calf is heavier than those of
common breeds; the cows are easy calvers, attentive mothers, and
are good-tempered. Much is known about them, for their records
go back a thousand years—longer, some say, than any other
breed's. One Iowa farmer found that 98 percent of animals crossbred with Simmentals yielded choice and prime meat—nearly
twice as many as in an ordinary herd—and their carcasses were 10
percent heavier than uncrossed cows of the same age. Geneticists
also believe that crosses will be ready for market in eighteen
instead of 24 months, which would mean that feedlot operators
could handle about one-fourth more cattle annually with their
present facilities.

The Italian Chianina, perhaps the oldest living breed of cattle,
is also being experimentally crossbred with American cattle.
Gaining weight at the rate of 100 pounds monthly, as compared
to 75 pounds for the ordinary bull, reaching maturity in three-
fourths the time, it grows quite large and, some say, is the most
efficient meat producer of all cattle.

Among other breeds being crossbred with American cattle are

the Anjou, Brown Swiss, Charolais, Gelbvieh, Limousin, Maine, and South Devon, some of which have been grown in the United States as specialty purebreds.

In 1969, the experiment station at Clay Center, Nebraska, in collaboration with experiment stations in several other states, began what has been characterized as a multi-phase "cattle-swapping" program. One preliminary finding of the experiment suggests that more importance should be paid to selecting and breeding cattle for the environment in which they will be raised. In 1961 scientists at research stations at Miles City, Montana, and Brooksville, Florida, exchanged Hereford cows originating on or near the two stations. At the Montana site, they found that bull calves of Florida origin were 18 pounds lighter at weaning than those of Montana origin, while Montana bull calves weaned 45 pounds lighter in Florida than the local calves.

In addition to crossbreeding, prize cows are being treated with drugs to increase the frequency of ovulation from once a year, embryos of prize cows are being transplanted to ordinary cows for gestation, and other drugs are being used to synchronize heat in a herd so that all cows can be artificially inseminated at the same time to save labor.

A more futuristic approach to increasing the efficiency of husbanding involves techniques that would assure calves of the desired sex. Female calves, for example, are more valuable to dairy farmers than bulls, but bull calves are more valuable to beef producers because they are about 40 pounds heavier than cows at weaning, and they are about 10 percent more efficient in feed utilization. Scientists have developed two techniques of altering sperm so that animals predominantly of one sex or the other may be conceived, but in view of past disappointments in this area of experimentation, breeders have adopted a stance, as characterized by one, of "interested skepticism."

Reproductive inefficiency is one of the most costly difficulties in producing beef. The most efficient cows have their first calf at about age two and can be rebred successfully within about three months of each calf; but many cows do not reach puberty in two years and do not go into heat again after calving for long periods. The number of calves weaned every year total about 80 percent of the number of cows inseminated, and even this ratio is dependent on many repeat matings; 40 percent of all initial matings do not result in conception, and 16 percent must be repeated a third time. Scientists are experimenting with nutritional, hormonal, and genetic methods to reduce the age of puberty, shorten the post-calving or anestrus period during which cows do not go into heat, increase the percentage of conceptions on first mating, control the sex of offspring, and induce twinning.

Investigation is also being made of new feed sources, some of which are yielding ecological benefits. The American animal industry generates about 2 billion tons of waste a year. One year's cattle manure, however, contains more than 10 million tons of high-grade protein; and passing manure through a sieve to separate fibrous material, hair, and sand, and filtering or centrifuging what passes through, produces a cake of nutritious material called the feed portion. It weighs about 43 percent as much as dry whole manure and is about equal to soybean meal in protein content and amino-acid balance. Another ecologically sound replacement for part of the diet is newsprint flavored with molasses.

Unconventional feeds, such as feedlot and cannery wastes, are likely to be used, if proved safe, but most of the feed needed for expanded herds of the future must come from improved conventional sources. Since the 1930s, plant breeders at Tifton, Georgia, have crossed some 5,000 hybrids with one of the South's worst weeds, common Bermuda grass, to create a good forage plant, and the region could become one of the world's greatest grasslands.

Hogs are likely to become more important in the American and world meat economies because they are comparatively cheap to raise. They are omnivorous, efficient foragers if let loose and marvelous converters of feed in enclosures; they have shown more promise in "assembly-line" production than the other large red-meat animals. In 1966 a Department of Agriculture brochure advised, "You can raise hogs on your place for less money per pound of pork than it takes to buy pork for your family." They require little shelter—just a house, some shade, and water. The largest expense is feed, but the small operator may be able to use surplus garden produce and table scraps. In addition, a hog's gestation period is only 112 to 115 days, and a piglet weighing 35 pounds at eight weeks reaches a butcher weight of 200 pounds in about four months. The total cycle lasts less than eight months, only one-third the length of the cattle cycle.

"Everything in a pig is good," wrote Grimond de la Reyniere, the French gastronome. "What ingratitude has permitted his name to become a term of opprobrium?" The reason that the hog suffers a tarnished image is, in part, the very reason that it is potentially the most valuable food animal in the world—it is a scavenger. It was important to the medieval peasants and to American colonizers and pioneers.

Technically, a pig is a sexually immature hog, and its meat is generally known as pork. The hind leg severed from the carcass at about the second joint of the vertebrate is the lavender flesh known as ham; and strips from the back, sides, breast, and flank sections of a cured and smoked pig are called bacon. Its snout, ears, cheek, other head meats, feet, sweetbread, uterus, testicles, and matrix are all edible and have been considered delicacies.

People once valued hogs mostly as a source of lard, but the demand for lard declined with the availability of cheaper vegetable oils, and packers began asking for less fat and more lean meat on the carcasses. The Danes and Poles, among others, were producing leaner pork before American farmers; and in 1934 the United States imported the Danish Landrace hog for crossbreeding experiments. "Twenty-five years ago," an Iowan farmer told me, "the typical hog being fattened for market had its belly dragging on the ground. You don't see that anymore."

The search for the "streamlined" hog continues to meet with difficulties, for many of the lean crossbreeds develop hypersensitivity, called the "pork stress syndrome." The Landrace, an aristocrat of the hog world, becomes upset en route to and while waiting at the slaughterhouse, and its meat drops in quality and changes color. The Landrace was a milestone when it was developed around the turn of the century, for it had eighteen instead of fourteen ribs. Yet a leading world authority on pigs and reputedly the father of the Danish bacon pig, Hjalmer Clausen, suggests that the decline in the variety is now so marked that perhaps it needs to be crossbred with another variety.

In 1973 there were about 61.5 million hogs in the United States, nearly a fourth of them in Iowa alone. The United States ranks third in world pork output, after China, which raises about a fourth of all hogs, and the European Economic Community. There were an estimated 680.6 million hogs in the world in 1973, a slight drop from the previous year, attributed largely to declines in the United States and the Soviet Union.

Lamb, the meat of young sheep, and mutton, the meat of older sheep, run a poor third in popularity among American meats. Yet in the Middle East and northern Africa, where vegetation is too sparse for cattle and people do not eat pork for religious reasons, sheep are the most important livestock. They can be fed largely salvage-type feed, and their pasture is likely to be less expensive than for other stock. Sheep convert their feed more efficiently without a full fleece, and in the United States wool is an important income source for sheepmen. Lambing occurs twice a year, and gestation lasts only 140 to 150 days. Healthy rams are virile and can be bred to about 50 ewes in 50 or fewer days.

Some authorities believe that sheep are more vulnerable than other livestock to parasites of the skin, such as mites, lice, and ticks; and of the organs, such as flukes, tapeworms, roundworms, and several species of protozoa. One of the more inspiring successes in pest control in the United States, the suppression of sheep scabies, was achieved in 1970, following a decade-long program of inspection and pesticide treatment.

The world total of sheep increased by 1.6 percent in 1973, to over 1 billion head, of which 170 million were raised in Australia and 139 million in the Soviet Union. But the United States maintained only around 15 million head of sheep. Nearly half of the 1973 herd were raised in western states, of which Texas was the leading producer.

During the depression, Mayor Fiorello La Guardia recommended horsemeat to New Yorkers as a beef substitute, but the idea did not catch on. When red-meat prices rose steeply last year in the United States, there was a revival of interest in horsemeat, which costs one-fourth to one-half less than beef. But it was no more eagerly accepted than during the Depression. Horsemeat is produced in the United States mainly for export, particularly to France, where it is eaten regularly.

A small animal that could contribute more to meat supplies is the rabbit, whose reproductive efficiency is well known. It requires little space and lends itself to small operations—even backyards. But demand for rabbit meat is not great, and availability is limited.

With beef shortages and high prices, cattle rustling is back, and in 1973 livestock thefts were the most serious crime problem in rural areas. Modern rustlers often operate with helicopters, motorcycles, and radio-equipped and sometimes refrigerated panel trucks; some are so efficient that they complete their theft and get away within five minutes. In some areas, law-enforcement officers predicted a 75 percent increase in rustling; in Iowa in 1972 cattle and hog thefts were estimated at $3 million. In one Alabama case, rustlers hijacked a truckload of 150 calves, none of which was recovered. The hijacked beef is sold through a black market to restaurants and other users. The governor of Utah described the situation as verging on an emergency, and the state offered rewards of up to $1,000 for rustling information on grounds that "the financial stability of the livestock industry in some areas is definitely threatened." In Idaho, policemen were being sent to "cattle-theft schools" to familiarize them with means to prevent rustling.

Poultry

The chicken has become the most important food bird in the world, and probably will become even more important. It rose to popularity because it is nutritious, less expensive than red meat, and lends itself to many different preparations. (Larousse's *Gastronomique* lists 258 recipes and is not a complete compilation. Unfortunately, the typical American restaurant prepares chicken poorly, which is why dinner-speaking tours are known as the "rubber-chicken circuit.")

Among species raised in the United States are the Rhode Island Reds, noted for their stamina, Plymouth Rocks, noted for their full breasts, Austrian Cross White, and King Cornish hens, which are miniatures. Of approximately 3.5 billion chicks hatched in 1970, poultrymen raised nearly 2.8 billion broilers, or about a dozen per person. In 1973 broilers totaled a record of over 9 billion pounds. The total output slipped somewhat in 1973.

American broiler production is concentrated largely in the South, especially in Georgia, Arkansas, and Tennessee.

The turkey is larger than the broiler, but it is less economical to buy because of its heavier bones; and it is usually a little tougher and drier. About 132.3 million turkeys were raised in the United States in 1973, a rise of 2 percent over the 1972 record, but only a fraction of the number of chickens. As late as the 1920s, American farmers raised turkeys on a small scale, and annual consumption was around 8.6 pounds per person from 1964 to 1973. Recent genetic growing and processing developments (such as the creation of a "self-basting" bird) will probably make the turkey more popular. Some turkey eggs are sold to processors of frozen eggs.

The famous Long Island duckling industry began back in 1873, when a Yankee clipper captain arrived with a small flock of tall white Peking ducks from China and gave seven of them to a farmer. The birds took to the sandy marshlands, and the ducklings became special fare in the restaurants of New York City and in dining rooms of ocean liners. In 1972 American poultrymen raised 48 million ducks, half of which came from Long Island. Ducks are slaughtered at the age of seven weeks, when they weigh an average of 6 to 7 pounds, of which 4.5 pounds are marketable. But no part of a duck is wasted; the feet are frozen into 30-pound blocks and exported to Hong Kong for duck soup, broiling, or candying, and the heads and viscera are shredded and ground, then frozen also into 30-pound blocks which bring 3.5 cents a pound as mink food. Duck feathers, which are ten times more abundant than chicken feathers, are sold for stuffing pillows, quilts, sleeping bags, and upholstered furniture.

In 1973, the gross American poultry income, including eggs, totalled $6.8 billion, up from $3.8 billion in 1968.

Dairying

Until the 1973 inflation drastically affected feed prices, the development of American dairying, particularly with respect to the productivity of milk cows, was a dramatic story. Between 1920 and 1945, the average dairy cow produced about 4,100 to 4,600 pounds of milk, or some 1,850 to 2,100 quarts (milk weight varies, but 2.2 pounds to the quart is a common rule of thumb). Then the per-cow output began rising at an annual average of 3 percent, until in 1972 it reached a high of 10,271 pounds, or about 4,670 quarts. Similarly, the average cow yielded 172 pounds of butter fat in 1937, 199 pounds in 1947, and 235 pounds in 1957. Because of the increasing yields, total milk output remained high in spite of an appreciable decrease in the number of dairy cows, from 17.5 million to 1960 to 12.0 million in 1970 and 11.4 million in 1973.

From 1955 to 1972, per capita milk consumption decreased every year, but in 1973 it rose from 561 to 563 pounds, or from 255 to 256 quarts. Total consumption of milk and other dairy products rose by 1 percent, from 115.9 billion pounds to 117.3 billion pounds. Production, however, fell to 116.5 billion pounds, due largely to a reduction of milk output per cow for the first time in thirty years. One reason for the increase in consumption was high meat prices, but the demand on milk began inflating its price, too. A quart of milk rose 42 percent in Chicago, and some stores charge as much as 50 cents a quart.

While farmers received nearly a third more for their milk in 1973, their costs rose also. Feed accounts for about half of a dairyman's outlay and the cost for a dairy feed ration increased by about 46 percent. But the high return for cows sold for slaughter became attractive, and dairymen decreased their herds by selling them.

Since husbanding began, man has kept cows, goats, ewes, camels, donkeys, asses, mares, and reindeer for their milk and milk products, and some of the animals were the main protein source for nomadic peoples. But because milk spoiled quickly, production was at best a cottage industry (even then it was produced largely for cheese) until Louis Pasteur discovered that boiling milk removed the bacteria that caused spoilage. Dried and condensed milk were developed in the nineteenth century, making cheap milk available for the first time to the urban poor.

In the United States, an increasingly urbanized population spurred the development of a specialized dairy business, and it grew rapidly from the middle of the last century. Between 1870 and 1890, the number of dairy cows doubled; though the number of cows per person actually decreased, technological advances made possible a per capita rise in the output of dairy products. The first American silo, permitting improved year-round feeding of cows, was built in 1873. Two years later, railroads used the first refrigerator cars for dairy products and other perishables. In 1882 the centrifugal separator for skimming cream from milk was invented in Sweden, and a few years later it was imported into the United States. At about this time, the thermometer was introduced in the making of butter and cheese, and in 1890, Stephen M. Babcock, the chief chemist at the University of Wisconsin experiment station, devised a simple, accurate test for measuring the fat content of milk that is still used today.

American agricultural colleges began encouraging dairy management around 1910, but during the next fifty years, dairymen went bankrupt at an annual rate of 30 percent, and the number of dairy farms continues to decline. Many remaining dairy farms are large, but there is a limit to the economics of size because cows require personalized attention if they are to produce most generously.

For many years, cows were kept in narrow stalls, where they were nurtured on scientific formulas. Being temperamental, however, cows often did not brook the confinement. Now dairymen turn them out to pasture or free them in exercise lots, and bring them individually into a "milking parlor" for extraction. In an article in *Harper's,* Pennsylvania dairy farmer Joan O'Harvey wrote that "when it comes to milking . . . neither bells, bruises, nor moral suasion will induce a cow to let down her milk. She will part with just as much, or as little, as she pleases. . . . She does like to be comfortable."

If some of the traditional practices in caring for the animals have been brought back, traditional marketing symbols —notably the glass bottle and the milkman—have all but disappeared. Milk is now sold mostly in plastic or paper containers and purchased in supermarkets or other outlets. In the mid-1930s, as much as three-fourths of all fluid milk was delivered to the doorstep, usually from nearby dairies, but by the mid-1950s milkmen were delivering little more than half our milk; the latest figures show less than a fifth delivered.

Milk-processing plants have declined, from around 8,500 some years ago to just over 2,000 in 1971. But the drop is counterbalanced by an extension of delivery service. In the mid-1940s, plants rarely distributed their dairy products beyond a 30- to 40-mile radius, but today a radius of 100 miles is common and 200 miles not unusual. This is not to say that a few major competitors dominate many markets—in the fourteen largest markets in one study, the four major rivals captured less than a quarter of all milk sales. Nonetheless, supermarkets have been buying or building their own milk-processing plants, and their share of commercially processed milk sales advanced from 3 percent in 1964 to nearly 9 percent in 1972.

Fluid milk makes up by far the largest share of milk and milk-product sales—about 45 percent in recent years—followed by butter and American cheese at about 16 and 14 percent respectively. Domestically produced cheeses of all types make up about 20 percent of all milk and milk-product sales. Other important dairy products are frozen, evaporated, and condensed whole milk, creamed cottage cheese, and dry whole milk. Butter consumption has dropped markedly since 1950, from 27.8 billion pounds a year to 18.9 billion pounds in 1973. Per capita consumption dropped from 5.8 pounds in 1965 to 4.1 pounds in 1972, doubtlessly due to rising food prices and the availability of the much less expensive margarine. Consumption of canned milk, fluid whole milk, and fluid cream also declined, but consumption of low-fat fluid milk, cheese, ice milk, cottage cheese, and ice cream increased (size of increases in that order).

Cheese is now more important than butter to American dairymen, who sold a record 23 billion pounds, or around 13 pounds per person, in 1973. The United States is now the leading producer, with about one-fourth of the world total, followed by France at about 10 percent. The Italians rank first in cheese consumption, and Americans are in tenth place, though our consumption has increased by about 50 percent since 1950. Contributing to this rise has been the recent surge in pizza eating and heightened demand for fast-service cheeseburgers, snacks, spreads, specialties, and meat substitutes. Higher-income families eat more than twice as much cheese as the poor. Of the more than 400 varieties described by the Department of Agriculture, the most popular is Cheddar—Cheddar, in fact, made up 80 percent of American output in 1971.

Cheese is an ancient dairy product. One of its chief advantages is that it does not necessarily require rapid or refrigerated transportation. The Pilgrims carried it on the *Mayflower*, and it became a staple in the colonies. As recently as a century ago, most cheese was made on farms and varied a great deal in quality, even when made by the same farmer. The first cheese factory was established in Oneida County, New York, around the middle of the last century, but the production center shifted to Wisconsin, which is still the leading state.

Fisheries

The waters of the world offer no fewer than 350 kinds of edible fish, as well as several mammals and aquatic plants. Of our main food sources, only fish is still gathered mainly in the wild, but man hatches fish for "planting" in wild waters, and since ancient times he has cultured food fish under controlled conditions, often as an adjunct to land cultivation

Scientists at the Woods Hole Oceanographic Institution believe that the seas may contain twice the total protein needed for 10 billion persons and, speaking practically of the needs of a doubling population, Paul M. Fye, director at Woods Hole, says:

> Simple arithmetic can demonstrate that the oceans can furnish sufficient animal protein to sustain such a population, if the difficult problems of harvesting, storage, and distribution of sea food in a timely manner can be solved.

Complete-protein levels in fish range from about 18 to 25 percent, depending on species, and some nutritionists consider fish a better source than red meats because fats in fish are unsaturated. The amounts of other nutrients vary considerably among species, but most commonly eaten fish have a good deal of the vitamin B complex, calcium, and iodine, plus a little iron; some are also high in vitamin A. Yet only a fraction of 1 percent of man's total food comes from fish; this includes, however, 3 percent of his total protein and 10 percent of his complete protein.

Fish lend themselves to many types of preservation, and to an extent can be kept alive in tanks until sold. Early fishing ships may have carried their catch in water tanks; and people have dried, smoked, salted, pickled, and iced fish, and preserved them in honey. Historically, though, most fish have been eaten near where they were caught. Around 1500, English explorers discovered the great cod shoals off Newfoundland, and other Europeans and the colonists exploited them.

Worldwide, the most frequently caught fish in the last decade were anchovies, marine herrings, menhadens, pilchards, and sardines (a generic term applied to several species), followed by cods, hakes, and haddocks. Tuna, salmon, and sardines are major food fish in America because they can be canned or frozen; but typical fish markets, especially those near coastal areas or serviced by fast, economic transportation, feature, among salt-water species, striped bass, sea bass, bluefish, cod, flounder, haddock, mackerel, pompano, porgies, snapper, shad, smelts, sole, swordfish, shrimp, lobster, crab, and such shellfish as clams, oysters, mussels, and scallops. Among the fresh-water fish sold are trout and catfish (which are being increasingly "farmed"), pike, pickerel, whitefish, and the giant prawn.

Modern fishing fleets of most countries are of four main types —near-water trawlers that operate closely to shores; middle-water trawlers that mainly ply the deep waters above the continental shelf; distant-water trawlers with greater capacity; and factory trawlers and stern freezers, often called "base ships" or "mother ships" because they may have facilities for freezing, canning, and storing up to 50,000 cases of fish, and often carry "catcher" boats for the pickup of nets. A typical Soviet mother ship is over 500 feet long, is operated by a crew of 640, carries 12 catcher boats, and stores 50,000 cases. One Soviet factory ship that is used for whaling is 715 feet long—the largest in the world—can handle 65 whales per day, and carry 18,000 tons of frozen meat. Aircraft, especially helicopters, are sometimes used for spotting shoals, and small submarines lay and pull in nets. A modern fishing vessel can bring in an average hourly catch nearly a third greater than a decade ago, even where the waters have fewer fish.

Until this decade, there was hope that sea fishing would relieve the world protein shortage, as the world catch increased greatly, from around 40 billion pounds in 1948 to over 80 billion pounds in 1960, to a high of 134.5 billion pounds in 1970. "The great sea fisheries are inexhaustible," wrote Thomas Huxley, the great British scientist of the last century, and the rising catches seemed to bear him out. Then came the 1972 slippage to 123 billion pounds, and 1973 was another poor year.

The competition for fish has become so great that some countries are demanding or claiming jurisdiction much beyond the three-mile limit set by international law. In 1952 Chile, Ecuador, and Peru issued the Declaration of Santiago, claiming 200 miles of offshore waters; Mexico has claimed "patrimonial" jurisdiction over 200 miles; and Canada announced a desire to control its continental shelf, part of which extends more than 200 miles into the Atlantic. The Truman proclamation of 1945 asserted sole United States rights to the riches of its continental shelf, which extends from only a few to more than 200 miles offshore. Throughout 1973, sophisticated fishing vessels of many countries, but notably the Soviet Union, Poland, and East Germany, were severely depleting the fisheries of the North American continental shelf, though the Truman proclamation presumably could have been invoked. The Emergency Committee to Save America's Resources, which also has the editorial support of a number of sportswriters, is agitating for a 200-mile limit. In 1973 legislation was introduced into Congress to stop "foreign exploitation of U.S. fisheries" and to provide for "scientific management of fishing resources"; and the UN called a 1974 Law of the Sea Conference, to meet in Caracas, Venezuela, in an effort to resolve the fisheries questions.

The 1972 world-catch slippage was not due entirely to depleted stocks; a number of control measures had been instituted by governments—area and species quotas, the closing of some areas, protection of spawning grounds, and restrictions on gear. Yet the demand for fish was rising, and higher prices led some governments to restrict the processing of food fish into fishmeal for livestock feed.

Fisheries were also reduced by pollution and other environmental intrusions. In the 1960s, the most dramatic disclosure of contamination of fish up to that time came from the Great Lakes and its tributaries, where coho salmon were condemned because of dangerous levels of DDT residue. In 1970 a further scare came when excessive mercury, believed caused by industrial charges, was found in white bass, perch, sheepshead, and walleyes in Lake St. Clair, Illinois. There was also a scare over high mercury levels in swordfish, though later the Smithsonian Institution found high levels of mercury in fish preserved for thousands of years, perhaps exonerating modern pollutants. Petroleum discharges into the Hudson River, one stretch of which is a major striped bass spawning ground, give the fish a repulsive flavor, though they do not necessarily render the fish unhealthy. Thermal pollution, caused especially by nuclear power plants, also disrupts fisheries, particularly spawning waters. Hot-water discharge from a proposed operation in the Haverstraw Bay area of the Hudson River threatens millions (perhaps as many as 20 million) of striped bass. The Atomic Energy Commission has predicted the killing of 30 to 50 percent of the annual hatch unless the builder, Con Edison, equips the installation with a closed-cycle cooling system. In the Northwest, salmon, which spawn up the Columbia River as far as 800 miles inland, are endangered by both dams and pollution; in 1970 a dam-caused phenomenon called nitrogen supersaturation killed many salmon and steelhead trout that overcame obstructions, and the pollution at three new dams on a tributary killed 70 percent of the salmon hatch.

Nevertheless, evidence suggests that the oceans could yield more than they have if we fish prudently and explore for new fisheries more effectively. Massive fish kills have been observed where fisheries were not known to exist or were not exploited. In the Arabian Sea in 1957, a Soviet merchant ship observed an estimated 40 billion pounds of dead fish—the equivalent of that year's total world catch—spread over an area of some 100,000 square miles.

It is time for fishing nations to stop snatching the choicest or most fashionable fish from one another and to start investigating the abodes and migratory habits of large shoals. One such project, called Eastropack (an acronym for "eastern tropical Pacific"), is studying more than 7 million miles of water from the coasts of South and Central America to about 3,000 miles offshore, an area yielding about 10 percent of the world catch.

Aquaculture

The limitations of wild fisheries and rising protein demands have increased interest in aquaculture. Also known as *mariculture* and *sea farming*, it is believed to have started in about 2100 B.C. in China, where rice paddies were used for "corraling" and perhaps planting some fish. The most successful aquacultural nation today is still probably China, where 40 percent of all fish protein comes from cultured fish, mainly the rapidly growing carp. The Egyptians and Romans practiced aquaculture, and people continued to build artificial ponds in many countries after dissolution of the Empire.

In the United States, state fish and game agencies have long restocked sports fisheries, especially trout and bass, and the approach has been applied to some commercial fisheries by caring for the eggs after induced spawning in hatcheries and systematically releasing the young fish into wild waters or artificial lakes. Unfortunately, cultivated fish may be unable to compete with naturally spawned fish for food or to protect themselves as well against predators (anglers believe they are also easier to catch). According to I. R. Idler of a Nova Scotian fisheries research laboratory, hatchery fish cannot maintain the speed of wild fish, and a hatchery salmon released into the bay at Halifax "would not last beyond the length of the drainage pipe." The Russians, he says, have experimented with placing captured naturally spawned fish temporarily with hatchery fish "to train them for survival."

The Lake Michigan food fishery was revived after the lamprey eel, entering the Great Lakes after the Saint Lawrence Seaway was opened, killed off what remained of a once-great trout population already depleted through overfishing. The alewives, on which the trout had fed, subsequently became so numerous that they suffered mass die-offs, causing widespread stench. Marine biologists poisoned the eel, found that planted coho salmon gorged themselves on the alewives, and established a marvelous new fishery which now also includes lake and brown trout. (But some fisherman say that the government has since cut back its eel-control program, and the predator is returning.)

The introduction of new food species is, nonetheless, not without dangers. A complicated case study comes from the Chagres River in Panama, where the chicla, a basslike fish native to the Amazon, was introduced. Feeding voraciously on an abundant supply of smaller fish, the chicla grew in number and size and by

1973 had spread throughout the waterway and into Lake Gatun. In one area, they eliminated six of eight previously common fish and greatly reduced a seventh, destroying the food supply of migrating giant tarpon and many birds. The chicla are probably there to stay, but only if they can find enough food, and at this writing a new equilibrium has not been established.

American commercial aquaculture has focused largely on such specialty items as shellfish, shrimp, lobster, and frogs. Some of the pilot projects have been encouraging, but many have yet to live up to expectations. Most shrimp do not reproduce in captivity, and shrimp grown by a fresh-water operation in Hawaii that is considered successful are nevertheless smaller than other varieties and more susceptible to disease. A company that tried to raise pompano in Florida abandoned the effort when the fish would not reproduce out of its natural habitat. Scientists have bred the giant Florida fresh-water shrimp, *Carsinus macrobrachium*, which grows from 6 to 24 inches long and has meat of lobsterlike texture and delicate flavor, and commercial-scale rearing is now being attempted.

At the Massachusetts Hatchery and Research Station at Oak Bluffs, John T. Hughes, who has reputedly spent more time studying lobsters than anyone in the world, raised the survival rate of young lobsters from 0.1 to 40 percent by protecting them in special tanks and feeding them a rich diet during the early hazardous weeks. At a new aqualab at Bodega Bay, California, researchers have achieved a 90 percent survival rate of lobster larva and, by feeding them a brine shrimp diet, grew lobsters to market size in one year, less than half the normal time.

Trout, a gamefish, has been raised commercially for some years and sold as a delicacy. About 20 million pounds of trout, 90 percent of which are raised in Idaho, are sold each year. Trout farming is spreading to other states, and a Montana operation now processes half a million pounds a year into filets, smoked-trout cheese dip, trout chunkies, and a dozen specialty products. The enterprise encourages ranchers with the necessary water to cultivate trout by selling 2-inch fingerlings for about 5 cents each, and buying them back when they have grown to 11 inches. Rainbow trout may double in size annually for the first three years after planting in artificial lakes in Montana. Their stomachs often contain wheat blown from the surrounding fields as well as insects and aquatic feed, and their flavor is excellent.

Only one fish is commercially cultivated on a major scale on American farmland. In 1960, a few pioneering specialists produced about 200,000 pounds of catfish in 200 acres of ponds. At about this time, someone thought it would be a good idea to retain a consultant, so an FAO expert, Shao-wen Ling, who was much respected for his successes in aquacultural projects in Asia, was invited to a southern research station. The move inspired a zealous UN publicist to issue a news release announcing "reverse foreign technical aid," but in the interest of the possible sensitivities of the hosts, that line of public relations was quietly stopped. In some areas, catfish have become big business. In 1970 farmers harvested about 78 million pounds of catfish from 58,000 acres at a sales value of $27 million; by 1974, according to Porter Briggs, editor of the *Catfish Farmer and World Aquaculture News*, 100 to 120 million pounds of catfish were being raised annually in the United States. Catfish farming was the fastest growing food-producing enterprise, worth $6 million a year, though ten years before there had been virtually no commercial catfish output. The major producing states are Mississippi and Arkansas, but the catfish-farming boom has spread as far north as Illinois and west to California; livestock feed producers now offer feed mixes with varying degrees of protein for fish.

In southern rice-growing areas, many farmers started raising catfish by using flooded paddies; some, finding catfish more profitable than rice, went into catfish farming full time. In fact, in the early 1970s, catfish brought twice the return of rice; it may be more profitable than any crop in some warm areas. In some cases, existing ponds were cleared of undesired fish; in others, ponds were built by damming up a gully on land not suitable for cultivation. Man-made ponds are now the most frequent rearing waters, and they may range from a single acre to more than 25 acres. Catfish farmers have the options of fertilizing and adding feed to their ponds, and some of them report obtaining two pounds of fish for every three pounds of supplemental feed. Harvesting may be accomplished by hook and line, by net, or by drainage, the last of which is the most efficient. Most catfish go to processors, but some are shipped live to restaurants; they are, incidentally, remarkably hardy, often surviving for some time out of water.

How soon catfish may compete with chicken, pork, or other fish is hard to predict. In the first place, catfish is not cheap; it retailed at $1.10 to $1.30 a pound in 1972, and fillets were up to $2.00. Many people have never tried catfish—a recent government survey showed that nearly 70 percent of easterners had never eaten it. Among nonsoutherners, the fish are unpopular because they are scavengers, but southerners have eaten them for years, usually coated with cornmeal and fried in deep fat. Nonetheless, by 1971 catfish were reaching such metropolitan areas as Chicago, Kansas City, Peoria, and Los Angeles. These cultivated fish, incidentally, tend to have less pollution residue than those in the wild because of the economic necessity of keeping their ponds clean and free of pesticides. (In some rice-growing areas of the world, food fish can no longer be raised in the paddies because of spray residue.)

Catfish have a high feed-conversion ratio—around 1 pound of fish meat from 1.5 pounds of feed compared to up to 9 for red meat—and adapt readily to commercial operations. Farmers apply their customary jargon to catfish raising; they speak of "acres of fish" like acres of grain, "harvesting" them like a crop, and "dressing" them like livestock. No processing plants existed in the South before 1967; quick and efficient methods of harvesting, skinning, and dressing had yet to be developed. In 1968 six farmers and a businessman in Yazoo, Mississippi, claimed that they had invented "the only catfish skinning machine in the universe," and by 1972 the South had at least fifteen processing plants.

Like other types of farming, catfish operations require large capital outlays, and the "crop" is vulnerable to hurricanes and flooding (during the 1973 floods in the Mississippi Valley, thousands of catfish escaped, to the delight of local fishermen).

The catfish success has encouraged further cultivation of other species, despite earlier disappointments; new technology and higher investment have come into play since 1970. Some experts now say that an enclosed tank and silo system, which can produce a consistent product by controlling climatic conditions, water temperatures, and waste products, are the most productive and efficient for large-scale aquaculture. Domsea Farms in the state of Washington incubates and hatches salmon eggs and raises the fish in tanks and shallow channels, called *raceways*, until they molt. Then they are pumped into four large seapens, where they are raised, not to maturity, but to a length of about 12 to 14 inches. This growing operation is based on work done there by Jon Lindberg in 1972, when he succeeded in halving the period of maturing by raising pond temperature; the fish raised today also receive a feed of ground shrimp shells and other nutrients that bring on "pinkness" prematurely. Another approach being used for trout in Idaho by the Marine Protein Corporation involves a 20,000-gallon vertical rearing unit, a silo with continuous water circulation and aeration, which is said to produce 40,000 pounds of trout yearly. The company is also working with salmon and striped bass. Several other large corporations have invested millions of dollars in research and development, but it remains to be seen if they can do better than the farm-pond aquaculturist.

Genetic engineering is also progressing. At the University of Washington, a professor of fisheries, Lauren R. Donaldson, culminated forty years of research in 1973 by developing a trout that laid 27,636 eggs—a world record; when he began, his trout laid only between 450 and 500 eggs. In 1966 Congress passed the Sea Grant Act to foster improved practices in replacing and supplementing wild stocks, and though funding so far has been restricted, the legislation is expected to encourage much more aquacultural work in the future.

Aquatic Plants

The seaweeds and other marine algae, both wild and cultured, are high in some nutrients; some species have ten times as many trace elements as land plants. Most seaweeds flourish along ocean shores in a belt of water about a mile wide (the outer limit of the belt is determined by how deep light can penetrate). They absorb nutrients from the surrounding water, and under favorable conditions some kelp grow a foot a day. Ancient Asians referred to "sea vegetables" and "sea gardens," and Oriental people are still the main eaters of aquatic plants, of which they use over a hundred species. The Irish have harvested a seaweed called *carrageen*, "Irish moss," for over six hundred years, and in Massachusetts the gathering of carrageen is recognized as an industry. Marine plants may be mixed with salads, other vegetables, and stews; stuffed with rice; and processed as bases for soups, drinks, baby foods, and even ice cream. The Japanese often eat shredded seaweed like a breakfast cereal, and the Irish traditionally made it into a pudding with milk and sugar. One species of seaweed is the building material of the bird's nest that is made into the famous Chinese soup. Today, marine plants are used also for feed, fertilizers, and industrial products.

Seaweed is among the most prolific of plants; there are at least 17,000 species, from single-celled plankton to giant kelp with fronds (leaflike expansions not differentiated from the stems) that grow longer than the height of redwood trees. Because marine plants grow quickly—a culture of algae may double bulk daily—they may be entrées on future space menus; the National Geographic Society calculates that on a 516-day trip to Mars, an astronaut would need more than half a ton of food, a quantity that might well be supplied by an algae culture.

Seaweed may have more important food uses in the future, for recent experiments have shown that it influences the growth of plants and livestock in unusual ways. During the 1950s, scientists at Clemson University in South Carolina tested seaweed as a soil additive for crops. Some other research centers scoffed, but the group made such startling discoveries that the National Science Foundation recently offered grants of nearly $400,000 to support further work. One type of seaweed was found to alter plant metabolism by changing the rate at which the plant takes in carbon dioxide, and it caused interruptions in the growth of tomato seedlings during five cold months when frost would otherwise have killed them. Two stockmen found that their animals converted their regular feed more efficiently when fed a Norwegian kelp additive.

Other encouraging work is being done in Nova Scotia, where in 1970 scientists experimentally doubled the growing speed of carrageen and are also trying to encourage the reproduction of its microscopic seeds. Understanding of the mode of reproduction of this plant is quite recent, and cultivating it is difficult because there are sexual and asexual types which cannot reproduce, and it is virtually impossible to tell the types apart.

The most frequently eaten fresh-water aquatic leaf plant is watercress, which is grown all over the world. It is a specialty crop, and there are only about thirty American producers, but they are spread over the country. Though its sprigs grow out of the water, no one has invented a mechanical harvester, and some of the hand laborers employed at a major Florida watercress farm have worked at it for a quarter of a century.

Part III / The Farm–Rhetoric and Realities

History records the battlefields on which we lost our lives, but it disdains to tell us of the cultivated fields by which we live; it can tell us the names of kings' bastards, but it cannot tell us the origin of wheat, such is human folly.

—J. HENRI FABRE

10

Evolution of Farming

American folklore and political rhetoric idealize the "family farm" and romanticize the intrepid and resourceful pioneer yeoman. On the other hand, urbanized Americans, like most urbanized peoples, have traditionally demeaned the farmer as a hayseed, bumpkin, hick, or rube; they do not seem to recognize that their life, based on manufacturing and service industries, is only possible when farmers produce enough of a surplus to support the necessary labor forces. City people take food supplies for granted, protesting when an item is missing, in unsatisfactory condition, or priced too high. Until the recent upheavals in food supplies and prices, few outside of agribusiness, agricultural research, and rural politics sustained an interest in farms.

It is time for an examination of realities.

As popularly conceived, the family farm scarcely exists anymore, but commercial farming under family ownership has not been displaced by giant corporations. It has, however, become much more demanding.

Food production, processing, and merchandizing together constitute the largest industry in the country today. In 1972 agro-industry generated about $370.6 billion cash flow—about one-fourth of the gross national product (GNP)—and retail grocering generated another $95 billion. The combined total was nearly one-third of the GNP.

Agriculture is such a large and complex industry today that when the Science Advisory Committee, a group of more than two hundred specialists, published *The World Food Problem* in 1967, they set forth not one but three definitions.

They defined agriculture narrowly as the cultivation of crops and the tending of livestock (including fish when they are raised for profit in farm ponds). More technically, agriculture is "the utilization of biological processes on farms to produce food and other products useful to man." And a broader definition, which also applies to agro-industry or agribusiness, embraces the farm and all enterprises that receive and transfer the output of the farm, including storage, distribution, marketing, and processing. Under this definition, agriculture may be divided into three components—farming; agri-support, or the web of industries, sciences, and services that relate to the farm; and agri-climate, or the totality of the economic, political, and cultural factors affecting the other components. Canadian agricultural economist W. David Hopper gives us a metaphoric summary:

> The development of farming is akin to the construction of a three-legged stool. The legs of discovering technical potentials, of creating economic incentives, and of establishing operational practicabilities give the stool stability and make it useful. . . . Each must be fashioned and their legs made equal, for they must establish and support the heavy task of making progress feasible.

The History of Farm Development

The organization of agriculture proceeded gradually until the last century, when science accelerated the rate of technological breakthroughs, setting off a series of agricultural revolutions. But progress has always been uneven.

Organized farming began in Jarmo, Mesopotamia, between 9000 and 8000 B.C. Excavations of Hassuna, which is also in Mesopotamia, have unearthed stone hoes, storage jars, and grain bins dating to about 5750 B.C. In southwestern Turkey, when people probably were in a transition from gathering to community farming, they made simple metal tools.

The inception of market gardening occurred along the shores of the Caspian Sea in about 6000 B.C., probably a millennium earlier than anywhere else. From there, gardeners fanned out over what became known as the Fertile Crescent which stretches from the Nile in the west to the Indus River in the east. These gardeners grew most of the food plants we know today, except for those native to the Americas, and they developed irrigation systems.

By 2000 B.C., Chinese farmers in the Yellow River Valley were growing cereals and husbanding cattle. By 1940 B.C., they also tended pigs, sheep, goat, water buffalo, and ducks. The early Greeks did not make much progress, largely because of poor soils and partly because of the abundance of fish. On other European coastlands of the Mediterranean, the people concentrated on olives and oil production, and grapes and wine production; the Egyptians became great grain cultivators. The first civilized inhabitants of central Italy, the Etruscans, raised both olives and grapes, and the early Romans, despite their contempt for these people, willingly adopted Etruscan agricultural practices.

During the following centuries, European land was owned by great lords, the church, and a small number of peasants who toiled in common cultivation; most people labored in the fields of the estates. A community-planning approach governed farming practices, with specified times for plowing, sowing, and reaping. In some areas, landowners divided their arable land into three great fields, which they then subdivided into strips and assigned to serfs. One field was planted to wheat or rye; another to barley, oats, vetches, beans, or peas; and the third was left fallow. There was a commons for grazing livestock until the harvest, after which animals were loosed into the fields to forage. Comparatively few crops were raised, and no one could introduce new crops without the agreement of the community, which customarily rejected such proposals. Farmers used such crude tools as hoes, spades, and mattocks (soil looseners that looked somewhat like a pick), and planted by hand, cut with scythes, tossed bundles of grain with reaping hooks, and threshed with flails (a staff or handle from which a bar swung freely). Large, cumbersome wooden plows with iron or wooden-toothed harrows were usually drawn by oxen.

In the eighth century serfs raised onions, pigs, calves, chickens and eggs, and game, and in the south of Spain around 900, the Saracens were market gardening. From the tenth to fifteenth centuries, the best farming was being done in the Po Valley and on the rich plains of Lombardy in Italy.

By the early early fifteenth century, a change was taking place. The market gardens on the outskirts of Amsterdam were famous for their salad ingredients, and early in the seventeenth century, the English adopted market gardening from Flanders, along with Dutch methods of husbanding cattle and sheep. The French moved ahead gradually, giving little thought to orchards and gardens until the sixteenth century, when popular interest awakened and a number of books on them appeared. A lot of nonsense was perpetrated during that period—one writer counseled that the word *Raphael* written on a plowshare would render the soil fertile, and many relied on the signs of the Zodiac to guide them in grafting and pruning.

Agricultural innovation became fashionable among some royalty and great landowners, and the range of cultivated plants expanded astronomically. In the seventeenth century, Louis XIV's gardener, Jean de la Quintinie, distinguished between the more and less desirable food plants and learned how to develop early and late crops. Another French agriculturist of the time, Olivier de Serres, operated an experimental farm that became a model for market gardeners throughout the Continent and used selective breeding to produce varieties maturing earlier and later in the season. In 1721, for the first time since the reign of Tiberius, cucumber was grown under glass. Louis XV imported plants from all over the world and founded royal nurseries in nearly every province. King George II maintained a model farm at Windsor Castle, and the Duke of Mantua knighted his gardener. In 1761 the French established their first veterinary school in Lyon. By then the French agricultural revolution was in full swing, and a new variety, implement, or husbanding technique appeared every year. There were prizes and grants to stimulate invention, and influential people organized societies to sponsor food production. In the early eighteenth century, agricultural reformers in Britain promoted more highly yielding varieties, superior livestock breeding, and more efficient transportation; and Jethro Tull, a lawyer by education and gentleman farmer by desire, invented a seed drill and reintroduced the hoe, or cultivator.

Diets improved for a period in France and Britain, but war, revolution, and irrational management brought back hunger, and land-use practices changed significantly. Common fields gave way to enclosures, individual control, and private initiative, and many smallholders and farm laborers had to look for work elsewhere. Later in the eighteenth century, farmers converted larger holdings of fertile croplands into sheep pasturage in response to the demand of the growing textile industry for wool. Lower food harvests inflated prices, and the remaining smallholders, who were unable to afford either the larger acreages needed for sheep or the higher food prices, were squeezed out.

War on the Continent in 1792 stalled the recovery of French agriculture, but farms were restored during the half decade of peace from 1800 to 1805 when vegetables, grapes, tobacco, and cattle were raised. Napoleon, although he personally was more interested in industry, understood the importance of agriculture, and he appointed A. A. Parmentier to a high post with a mandate to plant potatoes all over the country. In 1843 the first agricultural experiment station was established at Rothamsted, near London.

Recent discoveries in the Western Hemisphere suggest that the Indians may have organized their agriculture nearly as early as any people. Though they had no draft animals, wheeled vehicles, or metal implements when the Europeans came, they had mastered the cultivation of some twenty species of crops and had developed some types of processing as well. In Mexico, they grew corn, white potatoes, and peanuts as staples; they also cultivated kidney and lima beans, tomatoes, sweet potatoes, squash, pumpkins, avocados, and chili peppers. The American Indians adopted most of their crops from Mexico, and today over half of the American crops, measured in dollar value, come from plants domesticated by the Indians.

Columbus's most valuable contribution to European society was corn; Europeans had never before seen this grain, which matured in but three months and required neither plow nor oxen. On his second trip to the New World in 1493, Columbus carried wheat, barley, grapes, sugar cane, and horses, completing one of the greatest exchanges between peoples and continents ever to take place. In 1585, the potato was also introduced into Europe.

The first settlers arriving in America used agricultural methods that had been only slightly improved over the previous two thousand years, and after their grains failed, they adopted crops and technology from the Indians. Later, the settlers succeeded in cropping European grains, and introduced the plow, draft animals, and carts. They combined cropping with husbanding, used manure for fertilizing, and improved seeds. The Indians probably obtained 10 to 20 bushels of corn per acre, but between 1600 and 1800, the settlers were reaping an average of 25 bushels. New land was opened according to an established routine: first they sowed corn as their staple, making it into cornbread or hominy; then they added squash, pumpkins, turnips, and other vegetables. They also raised tobacco (although it depleted the soil) and peanuts as cash crops. The first hogs were imported in 1652, and they adapted well to the frontier; they foraged for peanuts and forest acorn, scavenged on kitchen waste, and ate feed corn. Swine were preferred because they grew quickly, and pork kept well. Later, sheep were imported for mutton and wool.

Although agriculture still centered on large estates in England, the early New England and mid-Atlantic farmers worked family farms. They diversified their crops, aiming at self-sufficiency, first for their families and gradually for their communities, but subsistence farming continued for some time. Below Pennsylvania, however, tobacco, cotton, and rice were cultivated as cash crops on plantations emulating the English system. Later, in the Southwest, the Spanish hacienda was the model.

In the Dutch colony in New York, the earliest settlers preferred trading furs to raising crops, so in 1623 the Dutch East India Company offered land along the Hudson River to any ship's officer who carried fifty settlers over at his expense to cultivate it. Soon they harvested grains and tobacco, and later added garden vegetables, apples, and peaches. They built the first American flour mill in 1626 and erected windmills for grinding and pumping. They must have been fairly successful for there is no record of hunger in the New Netherlands.

The Swedes first settled along the Delaware in 1638 where, after two decades of competing with the Dutch for the fur trade, they lost out and turned to raising fruit, tobacco, and milk cows and goats. They favored rye among the grains, though they also grew corn, wheat, barley, beans, cabbage, and parsnips; they made wine from native grapes and beer.

In 1664, about 230 Quaker families emigrated to New Jersey where their experience was like that of that of the first American settlers; until they harvested their first crops, they lived in caves and wigwams and obtained corn from the Indians. The New Jersey soils were fertile, and the hillsides offered good pasturage. To the south, German immigrants known as the Pennsylvania Dutch soon achieved agricultural self-sufficiency.

Several major food products were introduced during the next century. In 1695 South Carolinians commercialized rice cultivation with seed from Madagascar. In the 1690s Spanish missionaries imported livestock to America, particularly to Texas, helping to found the livestock industry in the West; as farmers moved inland early in the eighteenth century, they drove herds ahead of them. Jesuits brought sugar cane from Santo Domingo to Louisiana in 1742, and toward the end of the century, the Bahia or navel orange was successfully transplanted from Brazil. In 1798 John Chapman, who subsequently entered American legend as Johnny Appleseed, planted the first apple seeds in the Ohio Valley. By the early 1800s, progressive farmers had developed superior varieties of wheat, and in 1864 Russian immigrants brought durum or red wheat to the arid prairies of the Dakota Territory.

Before the Revolution, agricultural development took place mostly along the coastlands, the standard approach during the age of colonization to the problem of providing food for merchant fleets. But resettling creates its own momentum, and an attempt by the British king in 1763 to prohibit migration west of the Alleghenies became a direct agricultural cause of the American uprising.

The first modern agricultural revolution began in Europe, taking off quickly especially in England. But it bypassed America for more than a century, while the pioneer farmers generally blended the know-how of the period of their migration with that of the Indians. Nonetheless, in the intellectual ferment preceding the Revolution, increasing attention was paid to agriculture. Thomas Jefferson was a vigorous advocate of families living close to nature and providing food—an idea originated by the eighteenth-century French philosopher Jean Jacques Rousseau— and several of the Founding Fathers were serious farmers. George Washington, for example, observed that his tobacco crops exhausted the soil, and conceived the practice of rotating wheat, corn, and flax.

Scientific organizations such as the American Philosophical Society, founded in 1743, the American Academy of Arts and Sciences founded in 1780, and the first strictly agricultural society founded a year later, encouraged investigation of European farm experiences, experimentation, and education. The Philadelphia Society, founded in 1785, was the first to publish its findings, and soon others were publishing journals. The first journal dedicated to farming exclusively was *The Agricultural Museum,* begun in Georgetown in 1810, but the earliest publication to achieve prominence and relative permanence, the *American Farmer,* appeared in Baltimore in 1819. It's publisher, John Stuart Skinner, became known as the founder of American agricultural journalism. Members of these groups generally were not dependent on farming for their livelihoods, and their direct influence on farmers of the time was limited.

Westward expansion demanded new technologies. The European plow did not break the prairie sod, but the steel plow produced in quantity by John Deere from the early 1840s made farming in the Great Plains productive. Farmers built windmills to power their pumps, and barbed wire was invented for more secure fencing against animal poachers. As farmers began producing surpluses, they became concerned with access to markets and that required new methods of transporting food to the growing populations of factory workers in the cities.

Modern Agriculture in America

As noted, agricultural output began to accelerate earlier in Europe than in America, but the patterns of growth are similar.

Whereas the French takeoff occurred in 1750, the American spurt did not occur until about 1850, but the American rate of growth —around 2.7 percent yearly—was more substantial than in France. After 1900, the growth rate retreated to about 0.75 percent, and farmers went through bad times after World War I. Agriculture stagnated as overproduction depressed prices and then the economic collapse reduced purchasing power. The Great Depression and the prolonged drought over the Great Plains obscured scientific advances until favorable weather returned and World War II stimulated rapid and extensive adoption of improvements in mechanization, pesticides, fertilizing, genetics, livestock nutrition, and conservation practices (such as the planting of cover crops and windbreaks to rehabilitate the Great Plains). Most significant were the rises in yields per acre, which soared to an annual average rate of 5 percent. Yet these unprecedented increases took place in an era when labor, machinery, and other inputs were scarce, and little more acreage was planted.

The trend in the number of farms as American agriculture has evolved indicates its restructuring. The number of farmers and farms rose until 1935. In 1870 there were over 2.6 million farms; and ten years later, there were 4 million. Late-nineteenth-century homesteading pushed the total to over 5.7 million, until it peaked at nearly 6.9 million. Between 1935 and 1940, the number dropped sharply to 6 million, and from then on about a million farms disappeared every decade. But the rate of disappearance has begun decelerating, from an annual decrease of 106,000 in the 1960s to around 45,000 in 1970 and 1971 and 38,000 in 1973, when there were about 2.8 million. The Department of Agriculture projects 2.1 million for 1985.

Farm Size

Since 1935, the average size of farms has substantially increased, and although the number of farms has decreased, the total land available for cultivation from the nation's 2.3 billion acres has been expanded. Table 10.2 shows how American farms averaged 150 to 160 acres from the homesteading days into the 1930s, until consolidations brought the average size to nearly 400 acres in 1973. Except when the government has restricted production by paying farmers to set aside acreage, total output has generally

TABLE 10.1. TOTAL NUMBER OF FARMS AND LAND IN FARMS

(selected years)

Year	Number of Farms (in millions)	Total Land in Farms (billions of acres)	Total Land Harvested Preceding Year (millions of acres)
1850	1.5	.294	—
1860	2.0	.407	—
1870	2.7	.408	—
1880	4.0	.536	166
1890	4.6	.623	220
1900	5.7	.839	283
1910	6.4	.879	311
1920	6.4	.956	349
1930	6.3	.987	359
1935	6.8	1.1	296
1940	6.1	1.1	321
1945	5.9	1.1	352
1950	5.4	1.2	344
1960	3.9	1.2	324
1970	3.0	1.1	293
1973	2.8	1.1	318
1985 (projected)	2.1	—	350

SOURCE: U.S. Department of Agriculture

risen, and since yields have steadily increased, the loss of harvests from idled acreage was often counterbalanced. In 1875 farmsteads had 475 million acres total; in 1973 the total was about 1.1 billion acres, somewhat more than four years earlier, at the time of the last agricultural census. In 1969, which might be considered a fairly "normal" year, 333 million acres were planted to crops; 51 million acres idled or were in cover vegetation; 88 million were in cropland pasture; 452 million were in grassland; 112 million were in woodland; and 28 million were in farmsteads, roads, and other uses. In 1973 harvested cropland was estimated at 318 million acres, with 264 million more acres considered

TABLE 10.2. GROWTH IN THE AVERAGE ACREAGE PER FARM
(selected years)

Year	Average Acreage per Farm	Total Acreage Increase per Farm	Average Increase per Year	
			Acres	Percent
1875	150	—	—	—
1935	160	10	0.17	0.11
1945	195	35	3.5	2.2
1960	297	102	6.8	3.6
1965	340	43	8.6	3.0
1970	373	33	6.6	1.9
1971	377	4	4.0	1.1
1972	381	4	4.0	1.1
1973	383	2	2.0	0.5
1974 (estimate)	385	2	2.0	0.5

SOURCE: U.S. Department of Agriculture

suitable—though some acreage would compete with forestry. The government projects that in 1985, American farmers will harvest 350 million acres.

Yet the proportion of Americans gainfully engaged in agriculture has steadily declined. In 1790, 90 percent earned all or most of their livelihoods from farming, compared with fewer than 5 percent in 1970. While the acutal number of farmers did not decline until the interwar period, table 10.3 shows a progressive decrease in the proportion of farmers to the rest of the population.

In examining acreages, we find that, in this decade, the smallest farms are disappearing while the largest are increasing, but only slightly. The trend is not now toward ever-bigger operations among the largest-scale farms, but toward gradually expanding operations of the moderately large ones. During the second half of the 1960s, farms under 220 acres declined in both number and as a percentage of the total, and at the same time, these smaller farms disappeared at a more rapid rate than the total decline of all farms. Meanwhile, in some regions the percentage of farms 220 to 500 acres climbed, and in all regions those of 500 to 1,000 acres also increased. But the largest farms, those of 1,000 or more acres, increased only slightly in number in most regions. Only

TABLE 10.3. U.S. AND FARM POPULATION

(selected dates)

Year	Total Population[1]	Farm Population[1]	Percent of Total
1790	4,000,000	3,600,000	90
1860	31,000,000	17,980,000	58
1890	63,000,000	27,090,000	43
1910	92,000,000	28,520,000	31
1920	106,000,000	28,620,000	27
1940	132,000,000	23,760,000	18
1950	151,000,000	16,610,000	11
1960	180,007,000	16,635,000	8.7
1965	193,709,000	12,363,000	6.4
1970	204,335,000	9,712,000	4.8
1971	206,557,000	9,425,000	4.6
1972	208,439,000	9,610,000	4.6

[1] Figures rounded.

SOURCE: U.S. Department of Agriculture publications.

where farming traditionally is most extensive, such as over the Northern Plains and in the Northwest, did the number of very large farms increase significantly. The main reason for the rapid disappearance of the smallest operations is the high capital investment required for technology, especially machinery. Even a smaller-scale farm is now a business in which a purchase price of $6,000 has replaced the simple purchasing of a mule for $60. Mechanized harvesting is not generally economical for a corn, wheat, or peanut farm of 50 acres, though it is for one several times that size. On the other hand, corporate off-farm supervision has not been up to the kind of decision making that is necessary to run very large farms, with the exception of poultry, feedlots, and a few vegetables and fruits.

Acreage figures, however, are inconclusive and can be misleading. The basic question is, How successful is the farm as a business operation? This question involves the diversity of crops to which the land is suited, the value of the produce, the cost of inputs, the degree of intensification, and net profit. Americans tend to believe "the bigger, the better," but the law of diminishing returns also applies to land use.

The recent trend to largeness is not new in American agricultural history, and an example from the past may still be instructive. Late in the last century, a new process for fine-grade flour created a great demand for hard spring wheat. The Red River Valley of northern Minnesota and North Dakota is well suited to the grain, and farmers planted much greater acreages. Overproduction resulted and prices dropped, ruining the large holders. Then came a drought, and by the end of the century, most of these large, single-crop farms had been subdivided and diversified.

Another approach to size comparison is dollar value of sales. The Department of Agriculture has three categories—those grossing $10,000 and over, those selling less, and "residential farms." Farms in the first two categories each constitute about 38 percent of the total number of farms, but those whose gross annual sales total $10,000 or more receive almost 90 percent of all farm cash receipts and are therefore the backbone of the American agricultural economy. It is also significant that the number of farms in this bracket increased by a third during the 1960s, while those with sales under $10,000 declined by 42 percent. Only about 8 percent of farms market over $100,000 worth of products each year.

TABLE 10.4. PERCENTAGE DISTRIBUTION OF FARMS BY GROSS RECEIPTS

(selected years)

Cash Receipts	1960	1970	1972
Up to $2,500	46.6	39.6	36.2
$2,500–$5,000	15.6	14.2	14.6
$5,000–$10,000	16.7	13.7	12.5
$10,000–$20,000	12.5	12.9	12.3
$20,000–$40,000	5.7	11.6	14.1
$40,000 and over	2.9	8.0	10.3

TABLE 10.5. PERCENTAGE DISTRIBUTION OF FARMS BY NET INCOME
(selected years)

Cash Receipts	1960	1970	1972
Up to $2,500	13.5	7.1	5.5
$2,500–$5,000	10.3	4.7	4.1
$5,000–$10,000	18.5	8.3	6.5
$10,000–$20,000	22.7	15.1	12.1
$20,000–$40,000	16.7	23.9	24.5
$40,000 and over	18.3	40.9	47.3

Technological Growth

By contributing to the general enlargement of farms and the rises in commercial sales, and enabling fewer farmers to feed more people, mechanization has had enormous social significance. When farms were first being mechanized around 1850, the average farmer produced enough food for 4.68 persons—fewer people than in the average family of the time. In 1910, when mechanical and animal power were used together, he provided for 8 persons. By 1951, the number had doubled to 16, and within another year it rose to 18; the new agricultural revolution was in full swing. In 1961 a farmer supplied enough food for 28 people, and a decade later for almost 48.

The successful application of new technologies boosted productivity in several ways: output per man-hour rose to 3.3 times that of the 1930s, crops yielded more per acre, and more livestock were handled. During that period, custom arrangements for machinery—and for operators when required—replaced large capital outlays, but capital investment nonetheless rose appreciably. A study of Missouri farms between 1965 and 1970 showed that total farm capital investment climbed nearly 50 percent, the average rising from over $163,000 to nearly $240,000. Productivity during this period went up by 15 percent, and production value by 13 percent.

With mechanization, farm labor needs began dropping. In 1961, the farm labor force totaled 6.9 million; in 1970, it was

TABLE 10.6. AVERAGE NUMBER OF PEOPLE FED PER FARMER

(selected dates and major contributing factors)

Year	Number Fed	Historical Stage of Farming
1850	4.68	Traditional farming with human and animal power on the eve of mechanization
1910	8	Mechanical and animal power used together
1951	16	Mechanical power largely displaced that of animals
1953	18	Agricultural revolution in full swing, and takeoff beginning; chemical pesticides and fertilizers increasingly applied, and machinery becoming more powerful
1961	28	Momentum of agricultural revolution maintained
1971	48	Force of agricultural revolution levels, and productivity increases at a slower rate

4.5 million; in 1971, 4.4 million, and in 1972 it fell another 50,000. Nearly all of the reduction since 1970 has been in hired workers; family workers decreased but slightly. By 1980, farm employment is expected to drop to about 2.5 million.

One aspect of manual labor still needed—mainly on produce farms—is the migrant work force, traditionally poorly paid and poorly housed. Unionizing efforts to obtain collective bargaining rights were not successful until 1966, when Cesar Chavez formed the United Farm Workers of America; their main weapons were the strike and the boycott, especially against lettuce and grapes. In 1973, the International Brotherhood of Teamsters moved in energetically and began getting the new contracts; UFWA membership dropped from about 50,000 to about 10,000. In the meantime, however, the UFWA had become affiliated with the AFL-CIO. That organization contributed a war chest, and its president, George Meany, charged, "This is a battle to protect the Farm Workers Union from a collusive campaign by the growers and the Teamsters to destroy this newest affiliate of the AFL-CIO."

What effect, if any, this struggle will have on produce output, particularly in California, is unclear at this writing.

Today, many American farmers no longer earn as much from their spreads as they do from other sources. If agriculture does not promise the desired income, a farmer may shift partially or wholly to other work, sell his farm, or leave his land idle. A good deal of this shifting had been anticipated a short time ago, but part-time farming has recently showed considerable stability; many farmers work a 40-hour week at jobs nearby, yet manage their farms during early mornings and evenings and by taking leave of their jobs during planting and harvesting. They can also hire extra hands during those seasons.

These farms produce 90 to 95 percent of our corn. In 1966 there were nearly 700,000 persons in the corn belt farming for income, but less than 10 percent of these—about 60,000—were full-time farmers. Another 200,000 appeared to be highly motivated part-time farmers. According to government studies, successful farmers in these two groups will probably continue to farm. There are, however, about 400,000 farmers in this area who do not earn at all well. These people generally lack assets, skills or motivation to keep working the soil; they are often in debt, ineligible for tax breaks or subsidies, and are usually over forty-five years old. They are more likely to give up their farms. An exodus of this low-income group may very well affect the proportion of farms over 1,000 acres in this region in the coming years.

Frequently overlooked in the polemicizing over the family farm is the racial aspect. While the majority of subsistence and low-income farmers are white, a high proportion of them are black, and they, too, are being forced off the land. In 1910 an estimated 15 million acres had been accumulated by black farmers, mostly in the South, but today they own no more than 5 million acres. The number of black-owned farms has declined rapidly since 1950, from 560,000 to fewer than 98,000 in 1970. Typically, black farmers have received few if any direct subsidies. The total black farm population, according to the National Sharecroppers' Fund, decreased by nearly two-thirds, from 3,158,000 to 938,000, when the mid-century mechanization eliminated many rural jobs and set off another migration to the North.

Farm Incomes and Parity

The food producers of mid-century America have been poorly recompensed compared with many skilled and even semiskilled workers, despite the capabilities, including managerial, required of them. During the last decade, the situation gradually improved, but it was not until the greatly increased overseas demand beginning in 1972 that farmers' incomes improved substantially, and they wonder if the improvement will last. It is said to be characteristic of farmers to be phlegmatic when times are good and anguished after adversities. In 1973, they were phlegmatic.

The following table shows how gross farm income has been rising, and while expenses also rose, they did so at a slower rate through 1973. The average net income per farm—a more meaningful figure—reached an all-time high of $9,193 in 1973. That year, the per capita disposable income from all sources for farm people reached a record $3,913, which was 93 percent of the $4,200 earned per person by nonfarm people, up appreciably from the 82.7 percent of 1972, 76 percent of 1971, 68 percent average of 1961 to 1968, and 55 percent of 1960.

Since 1933, agricultural programs have aimed at achieving a just "parity" between farm and nonfarm incomes. The ideal percentage of the income earned by nonfarm workers with commensurate responsibilities was originally based on the percentage earned by farmers from 1910 to 1914, which was considered a good period for American farmers.

FARMER'S INCOME

Year	Gross Income	Realized Net Income	Expenses	Net Income Per Farm	% Increase
	(Billions of Dollars)				
1960	38.3	11.4	26.8	$2,773	
1965	45.3	12.0	33.4	4,190	47.5
1970	58.4	14.5	44.0	5,757	37.4
1971	60.4	13.0	47.4	5,233	−9.1
1972	69.5	17.6	51.9	6,856	31.0
1973	91.2	24.4	66.8	9,193	33.0

SOURCE: *Farm Income Situation, and Agricultural Statistics 1968,* February 1974, U.S. Department of Agriculture.

Between 1952 and 1972, the rise in net farm incomes was a modest 3 percent, while hourly wages of the national industrial labor force during the same period increased 240 percent; service industry workers' incomes increased by a phenomenal 390 percent, and government employees' by 330 percent, and for stock market investors, dividends rose by 200 percent. Because of these inequities, nearly 2,000 farmers were quitting the land weekly in 1970, and others obtained part- or full-time work off the farm in order to continue farming. Farmers "moonlighted" as store clerks or gasoline station attendants. Others set up adjunct business operations, such as providing room and board to tourists, developing campsites, selling fish bait, stocking ponds with boats for rent, or charging for hunting trespass rights. In 1972, the personal income of the farm population totaled $34 billion, of which little more than half, $18.1 billion, was from farm sources and $15.9 billion from nonfarm sources; income from farm sources was up 19 percent from 1971, while that from nonfarm sources rose 14 percent.

Like most averages, income figures disguise inequities in distribution. About 36 percent of our farms account for only 2 percent of the total farm marketings, and their sales average under $2,500 per farm. Many of these are part-time farms or farm residences of retired or semiretired people; farmers in this group who still work average about $20,000 a year in off-farm income, or nearly eight times what they could earn from agriculture. But other farms in this category are subsistence or marginal farms, whose operators are underemployed—that is, they do not regularly put in a full day's work because there is not that much to do—and live at poverty levels. Nonetheless, the capitalization of these small farms is not inconsequential—over a million of them (10 percent of all farms) have $3.5 billion worth of machinery.

The steadily rising cost of operating a farm must be taken into account in determining parity. During the past twenty years it has gone up by 50 percent, and it spiraled in 1973. Early in the year, the cost of farm operations averaged 14 percent higher than they were in the first half of 1972. Feed was 42 percent higher, seed 16 percent, and machinery 8 percent. A further pressure on the farmer has been the cost of holding the land. Municipalities, eagerly trying to increase tax revenues, have often raised either value assessments, tax rates, or both.

How, then, were farmers able to stay in business in 1972? The answer is productivity.

Quantifying efficiency is sticky business, and one or more indices may be used, depending on what we are trying to find out. In a country short of food and unable to import any, total output may be the main criterion. During World War II, for example, Americans owning any soil were urged to plant "victory gardens," irrespective of their relative efficiency; during the recent world food shortage, an "inflation garden" movement sprung up. Under ideal conditions, it is more instructive to consider what the farm produces per unit of input. Broadly speaking, inputs include all those factors contributed by man and nature to cultivation. Efficiency may be expressed in terms of land units—acreage is a valuable criterion where fertile soils are limited or water units where irrigation is expensive. Investing in irrigation, for example, may produce many more bushels of grain per acre, but the high cost of water control may make irrigation unprofitable if the prevailing price of grains is low. In the simplest terms, efficiency is measured by the return realized on each dollar invested in inputs —that is, the dollar value of wheat harvested per so many dollars worth of land, water, seed, fertilizer, pesticides, machinery, labor, management, interest, and other services. The productivity index has not risen steadily over the years. From 1940 to 1950, it rose by 18 percent; from 1950 to 1960, 26 percent; but from 1960 to 1970, only 3 percent. While the index scored records twice during the 1960s, the rate of increase slowed markedly for the decade as a whole because the impact of new technologies began leveling off. While the output per man-hour in manufacturing increased 1.7 times from 1950 to 1970, it increased 3.3 times in farming. One government farm-income specialist concluded in 1971, "Farmers are the only ones in the country who get stuck for being too efficient." Prices were then depressed largely as a result of a new corn glut, and he predicted "a lot more farm sales."

The 1973 income rise changed this situation dramatically, but such a rate of increase is unlikely to be sustained since favorable weather will eventually return to stricken areas abroad. Demand, both at home and abroad, normally increases when populations and incomes increase; population growth rates have been declining in this decade, and the income factor will probably be more crucial.

The dollar value of agricultural products was indeed high in 1972, but these records should not obscure the fact a price hike, and not an increase in production volume, made the difference. Total cash receipts for farm products were nearly $60.7 billion, up $7.5 billion from 1971. Livestock brought in $35.6 billion, crops $25.1 billion, and government payments just under $4 billion. During the first half of 1973, cash receipts were nearly 30 percent higher, despite slightly lower volume (1 percent) than in that period a year earlier. For all of 1973, farm products earned about $91.2 billion.

The "Corporate Farm"

While changes were occurring in acreage holdings and capital investment, a national debate began over whether the economically feared "corporate farm" was displacing the sentimentally favored "family farm." "Corporate" and "family" are polemical code words, which confuse the public about the nature of the transformations in American agriculture. In 1966 a Chase Manhattan Bank newsletter tried to clarify misconceptions among businessmen about who the farmer really is:

> Official pronouncements in the past have often generated the impression that our farm policies promote yeomanry, reward the pioneer spirit, and preserve the family way of life. But such pronouncements are grossly misleading—as shown by the sharp decline in the number of farms, the emergence of large corporate farms, and the payment of 60% of our agricultural subsidies to less than 15% of our farmers . . . . Giant strides in technology have transformed agriculture into one of the nation's most efficient industries.

There is no universally accepted definition of what a "family farm" is. Sociologically, it is one operated by a family unit, in which decisions are made by the head of the household or by the family members. But what kind of farm results when a son becomes head of a family while operating a farm jointly with his father, or if two or more brothers-in-law control the operation? If a single operator adds acreage, buys expensive machinery, and incorporates with partners who may or may not be family members, and may or may not be active in management of the farm, does he have a "corporate farm"? What if he adds active partners or enters a cooperative but does not incorporate?

Actually, farms can be consolidated without changing the legal basis of ownership—which may be proprietorship, partnership, cooperative, or a corporation—and a family operation requiring no hired labor can also be incorporated. "The new managerial concept, not the legal form, is the heart of the matter," says Don Paarlberg, chief economist at the Department of Agriculture. Two Purdue agricultural economists, Noah Hadley and Paul Robbins, suggest defining the contemporary American family farm as one on which a single person or family unit makes the decisions and uses relatively little hired help. According to the Department of Agriculture's description, the "family-size farm" employs no more than eighteen months of labor per year and, on the average, does not need more than family labor. *Only 5 percent of American farms are large enough to employ more labor than that, and the average amount of family labor on a farm has been relatively unchanged for a decade.*

Still another definition of the traditional family farm system terms it "dispersed" production and marketing, meaning the farmer has multiple outlets from which to purchase and to which to sell, which is contradistinct to "concentrated" farming, meaning the farmer is dependent on one or very few such outlets. The outlet in concentrated organizations is generally a food systems conglomerate embracing virtually everything from farming to processing to marketing. Harold F. Breimyer of the University of Missouri-Columbia and Wallace Barr of Ohio State University write in *Who Will Control Agriculture?*, "By using the general term of dispersed farming, we avoid being bound to a particular system of the past or present."

What is commonly called the corporate farm, then, is a large-scale operation, probably but not necessarily owned by a giant company with sufficient financial power to be a factor in the marketplace, that recruits a manager or management team responsible to a board of directors. Corporate farming is based on the concept that the principles of scientific management can be widely applied to farming (particularly because of the mounting capital investment needed) and that any capable professional administrator can manage a farm. Until very recently, this concept went unquestioned—except by old-fashioned farmers. In 1967 a front-page report in the *Wall Street Journal* summarized the prevailing attitudes:

> It wasn't nostalgia for the soil that prompted executives of the Kansas City-based "conglomerate" company this year to begin swapping CBK's sundry manufacturing and distribution facilities (e.g., women's apparel, films, asphalt, printing) for corn and soybean acreage. They are simply searching for bigger profits and they expect to find them in farming.

In California, where more than a third of the nation's vegetables and much of its fruits and nuts are produced, the Tenneco corporation, a well-established conglomerate, seemed about to become a dominant agricultural force. An officer of the corporation told the 1971 Tenneco stockholders' meeting that the "goal in agriculture is integrating from the seedling to the supermarket." The company owned and rented land, manufactured a major line of farm implements, produced fuel and pesticides, packaged groceries, and retailed through its own gas-station stores.

By 1972, large corporations produced some 40 percent of California tree fruits and nuts, and 90 percent of its melons. From 1960 to 1970, the state lost 22 percent of its farms, and most Central Valley farmers (or their wives) with fewer than 100 acres took jobs off the farm. According to a Fresno County farm adviser, "Small farmers have nearly run out of ways to cut production costs," and a Bank of America officer said that the small farmer lived in a jungle where "it's simply going to be survival of the fittest." Some concerned leaders began asking if such giant corporations, with their generous lines of credit, would soon be able to dictate price, quality, and variety of many foods.

Efficiency was not the only area in which corporate farms were thought to have the advantage. During the 1960s, the code phrase "economics of scale" implied the larger the size, the wider the profit margin; and corporations naturally owned the largest farms.

But things did not work out quite the way they were expected to. CBK went bankrupt. So did Black Watch Farms, Gates Rubber, Agronomics, Multiponics, Great Western Land, and other large corporate farm operators. Tenneco, feared by so

many California farmers, began divesting itself of purely cultivating operations. The conglomerates had made a discovery: not
every professional administrator is a good farmer; additional apti-
tudes are necessary.

The Competent Farmer

To be successful, a farmer must be a marketing specialist, purchasing agent, budget director, mechanical engineer, and general
ecologist. He might also need to be a proficient manpower manager, computer client, and systems analyst. In short, he must be a
businessman applying knowledge of biology, botany, soil science,
hydrology, meteorology, psychology, mechanics, and financing. It
is particularly important that he be oriented toward the marketplace, since he is no longer simply the supplier of his family's
food but a purchaser of goods and services, for which he must earn
cash to pay. Like the manufacturer, the farmer must evaluate
costs, prices, labor, and transportation. A farm is a business,
whether it is a vegetable field, a fruit orchard, a grain spread, or
a feedlot, just as a food store is a business whether it is a mom-
and-pop grocery or a supermarket chain.

The modern commercial farmer is even more susceptible to
the vagaries of the marketplace in certain respects than other
businessmen; for, though all producers must project supply and
demand, the manufacturer can slow down or speed up his production line when demand does not conform to his expectation.
Once a farmer has seeded, he lacks this flexibility—unless he
can afford to make the expensive decision not to harvest. In
addition, the manufacturer literally builds walls against the
weather; the farmer, for the most part, must accommodate it.
And most industries, because they do not require anything from
the land but surface on which to build, can be relocated if economic conditions are more favorable elsewhere. These are the
reasons why Jack Whittington, an executive with Dulaney-United
Foods (which raises crops only when it cannot buy them reasonably), says, "We don't want to be farmers."

What sets the farmer apart from other businessmen, however,
is his need to understand nature. The farmer must analyze soil

fertility, new seeds, moisture supply, water quality, pest out-
breaks, and weather prospects. He must understand the patterns
of crop and livestock growth and must, it seems, possess a certain
environmental intuition—a "country wisdom" guiding him in
the use of the land.

The American experience with super-size farms, incidentally, is
not so different from that of the Soviet Union; the huge collective
or state farm, like the American corporation-owned farm, is run
by a "professional" manager or management team, which reports
to a higher governing authority (in one case a government agency
and in the other a board of directors). By the early 1970s, smaller
plots in the USSR were producing about half of all potatoes and
other vegetables, and farmers owned about 40 percent of all cows.
This is not to say that the essentials of collective farming or other
approaches are unworkable—in Israel, the communal approach
has worked well, and in France, where family farms predominate,
they operate efficiently for some crops but not for others.

A statistical breakdown of types of American farms provides
some insights into questions of size and organization. For the
purposes of the 1969 census of agriculture, a commercial farm was
one with sales of $25,000 or more; in 1969, there were 1,733,683
such farms. Of these, only 21,513 or 1.2 percent were corporations, and of these, only 1,800 had more than ten shareholders—
little more than 8 percent; actually, about two-thirds remained
family enterprises, generally with no change in entrepreneurship,
incorporated for tax, inheritance, or other reasons. Incorporated
farms were, however, larger in both acreage and dollar volume
of sales than average farms. Some 8,000 sold over $100,000 worth
of commodities a year; but even of these, 7,000 had ten or fewer
shareholders and were largely family-owned.

In all sales classes, sole proprietorships remain the dominant
type of farm. Of all farms with sales of over $100,000, they com-
prise nearly 60 percent. Partnerships make up another 25 percent
of these, and corporations 16 percent. Among farms selling from
$40,000 to $100,000, corporations operated 2.5 percent; of those
$20,000 to $40,000, 0.9 percent; and of those $2,500 to $20,000,
more than a million were sole proprietorships, compared with
6,000 that were incorporated.

The amount of food produced, of course, does not necessarily equate with profitability, and though extremely large farms may gross more revenues than more modest-sized operations, studies have shown that they have not always been highly profitable in terms of net margins. In 1971 the Department of Agriculture found that the rates of foreclosure and delinquency in loan repayments were greater on large loans to bigger units than on smaller advances to families.

Nevertheless, the issue of entrepreneurial control in farming remains a nagging one. "The hallmark of the agricultural revolution may not prove to be the mechanical devices, chemicals, or hybrid seeds and animals," suggests Marshall Harris, an agricultural economist at the University of Iowa. "The new business form may accommodate the needs of agriculture as successfully as the corporate structure has met the needs of industry." The change will come as a consequence of rapid changes in technology, marketing, and processing. Harris's 1974 study published by the Department of Agriculture, "Entrepreneurial Control in Farming," sees "substantial elements of entreprenurial control in farming . . . being shifted from the farm to off-farm firms and government agencies" through six influences—production contracts leading to vertical integration, farmer cooperatives and collective bargaining on a regional or national scale, ownership changes under farm leases, agricultural credit institutions, investor corporations, and government programs. But they all do not have the same impact—a family incorporating, for example, may have no impact at all—and each may affect some types of farming more than others. On the other hand, a bank refusing credit to a dryland farmer, who wishes to develop irrigation facilities, may, in effect, make the decision that the farmer must stay in dryland cultivation.

In April 1974, the Agribusiness Accountability Project, a public-interest research group, issued a report, "Who's Minding the Co-op?," charging that the giant agricultural cooperatives are subverting the interests of farmer members. "The average farmer is being pushed aside," it said, "as co-ops invite food firms and conglomerates to form partnerships with the cooperatives . . . and even invite corporations to join cooperatives."

The Ideal Modern Farm

If larger is not necessarily better—and may be worse—then what is the optimum size for a farm? Basically, it is the maximum acreage that a farmer and his machinery can plant, cultivate, and harvest with the greatest efficiency for the most satisfactory profit. The optimum is relative, particularly to the type of crop, but also to the form of the land, perhaps to the intensity of cultivation, and to individual differences in competence. In Indiana the typical grain and livestock farm is most efficient if it is 500 to 600 acres and is managed by two persons. A dryland wheat ranch on the Great Plains, which must be cropped with expensive machinery, should be much larger—perhaps 5,000 to 10,000 acres. In cattle ranching, the criterion is not acreage but the size of the herd—since costs are related to keeping the animal rather than cultivating an acre of land. In 1972 the optimum herd was generally 300 head, but land requirements varied greatly—150 acres were needed in irrigated areas while 36,000 were required in southwestern desert areas. Mechanizing repetitive milking may not be as fully efficient as it should be, because individual cows often choose how much milk to give or withhold in response to how they feel they are being treated—and they seem to prefer having an understanding family farmer around

Optimum size has not remained the same, mainly because of mechanization. Since the early 1960s, farmers have shifted from four- to six-row planters and cultivators for corn, soybeans, and potatoes; and small-grain farmers are also using wider tillage machines and seeding drills. The 1972 optimum size for a one-man-crop farm was likely to be twice as large as that fifteen years earlier. In 1950 an Iowa farmer, helped by one or two sons, could earn a living from 180 acres; in 1973, 500 acres were likely to be unprofitable. Yet virtually all midwestern corn, wheat, and livestock farms are still family operations, and some gross over $100,000.

Today, farms are usually best managed by two men. Don Paarlberg says:

> For the majority of farms in the U.S., most efficiencies of size have been gained with a suitably equipped two-man

operation. This is true for wheat farms, dairy farms, and diversified feed grain-livestock farms.

The real measure of efficiency is output per unit of input. And for the most of agriculture, something approaching optimum efficiency is attainable within the capability of a well-equipped two-man operation.

In 1974 the Department of Agriculture released a report stating, "A one-man farm, with the right machines and enough land to use them effectively, is just as efficient in terms of unit costs, as any enterprise employing more labor. In fact, it's even more efficient on occasion." This is not to say that these farms are small; they have, when of optimum size, increased in acreage and capital investment during the last decade. For example, average cash grain farms in the corn belt now have double their former acreage, and one-man farms contributed to this increase. The optimum size also varies according to type of farm; a Kansas wheat-grain sorghum farm averages 1,950 acres with a $255,000 value, an Indiana corn-soybean farm averages 800 acres with a value of $610,000, and a California vegetable operation averages 200 acres with a value of $485,000. (Value includes land plus other capital.)

Prices, the Farmer, and the Consumer

Food prices based on the government's "food basket" of a typical American family household of 3.2 persons, rose 2.5 percent in 1971, over 4 percent in 1972, and then leaped by 17.2 percent in 1973, the sharpest one-year rise in twenty-five years. A number of reasons were put forth for excluding farm commodities from controls under the New Economic Policy, including the difficulties of enforcement and the possible emergence of a black market. But the principal reason was the lack of income parity for farmers and the likelihood that more farms would be abandoned.

There was also the official belief that Americans generally enjoyed a bargain in food prices. The Department of Agriculture pointed out that one hour's work at average factory wages earned enough to buy 8.7 pounds of frying chicken in 1971 and only 4.7 pounds in the 1950s, 6.1 half gallons of milk in 1971 and 11.0 in the 1950s, 3.4 pounds of beef in 1971 and 2.7 in the 1950s, 3.8 dozen oranges in 1971 and 3.2 in the 1950s, 41.2 pounds of potatoes in 1971 and 34.8 in the 1950s. In short, wages rose more rapidly than food prices.

Despite rising costs in 1973, this trend appeared at first to be continuing. In March, Clayton Yeutter, an assistant secretary of agriculture, predicted total food expenditures going up 7.5 percent for the year, while disposable personal income would rise by 9.5 percent. "And," he added, "the share of disposable income consumers pay out for food, a record low of 15.7 percent in 1972, is expected to drop even further this year to about 15.5 percent."

Thus the dilemma: How can the farmer enjoy satisfactory income while the consumer enjoys a high eating standard at reasonable cost?

Perhaps no American has followed the changes in American farms more closely than James G. Patton, who for years served as the head of the National Farmers Union (NFU). Up until the early 1960s, the NFU was considered the most liberal (or radical) farmer organization. In the late 1960s, amid anguish over the "vanishing" family farms, Patton said this in an interview:

> What we called the small farmer of my day is gone, not because of the corporate farm, but because of the increasing sophistication of agricultural production, the need for capital, and because the return to the small fellow is better in the cities in an industrial job. But the number of family-operated farms, the percentage, is actually on the increase, and for the last 10 years the large corporate farms have been on the decrease. Percentage-wise, the big decrease has been among the small, underemployed, subsistence type of farmer. The government price support programs have been of no advantage to him.
>
> [The farmer of the future] will be quite a bit bigger; he's been getting bigger right along. He's going to have a much higher capital investment. I think the family farmer, where members of the family have the investment in management, is going to survive for a long time.

11

The Politics of Agriculture

As individuals, farmers have not generally involved themselves in political organization. During the nineteenth and early twentieth centuries, when industry groups were merging into trade associations and factory workers were organizing unions to lobby, cultivators did not operate as cohesively because of dispersion, diversity of interest, lack of communication, and typically independent attitudes. Nevertheless, when under excessive strain or in the grip of a new idea, farmers have formed organizations and even third parties, the best known of which have been the Populist party, Nonpartisan League, Farmers' Alliance, Holiday Association, the Grange, the American Farm Bureau Federation, the National Farmers Union, and the National Farmers Organization.

The transition from subsistence to commercial farming was not easy for farmers, except those who had concentrated on cash crops like cotton and tobacco. A national cash economy evolved in the last third of the nineteenth century, but agriculture lagged and farmers suffered. In the late 1860s, rural tensions were mounting. The Civil War brought inflation, which culminated in the Panic of 1873, and "middlemen" were chronic irritants—farmers felt they controlled prices and fixed transportation rates, thereby reducing their potential incomes.

The first national farmer organization, the Patrons of Husbandry, was founded in 1867, initially as a social fraternity with secret rituals and degrees. It was popularly known as the Grange. By 1872, the year before the panic, its membership had grown to 1.5 million and it had written a declaration of purposes— to buy less and produce more, to make farms more self-sustaining, to diversify cropping, to buy and sell together "for our mutual protection and advancement," and to eliminate the "surplus of middlemen." Its main targets were the railroads, the grain-elevator operators, and the dealers, and it demanded that dealers be forced to pay a decent price for grain and public carriers charge lower rates. The organization became politicized, and the Grangers won control of several Mississippi Valley state legislatures one after another of which enacted laws fixing ceilings on freight rates and elevator fees. The middlemen fought back, challenging the constitutionality of these acts, but in 1876 the Supreme Court upheld the Grangers. Overproduction, drought, debt, and foreclosures, however, continued.

Conditions improved after 1900, and were quite good for farmers from 1910 to 1914. During those and the war years, farm prosperity was based largely on foreign demand. But the United States terminated its credits to the Allies in 1920, and, as a consequence, Europeans expanded their agriculture. As the postwar slump brought hardships back to the farms, the farmers' political strength increased, and a bipartisan approach to agriculture was evolved. In 1921 Iowa Senator W.S. Kenyon brought a dozen colleagues and several government officials together in the offices of the American Farm Bureau Federation for the founding meeting of what has since been called the "farm bloc." Senator Arthur Kapper of Kansas wrote:

> From the very beginning this movement was non-partisan and a recognition of the economic crisis; an endeavor to outline a plan for an economic re-adjustment rather than a scheme to gain partisan advantage.

American farm groups believed that difficulties of decreased demand could be resolved without involving government through the creation of large-scale commodity co-ops, or groups of farmers formally joined together to market a particular product. This view represented a reversal of the farmers' traditional anti-monopolistic attitude and a new willingness to adopt the practices of big business. But the co-op approach did not work out; there were too many farmers who were too accustomed to behaving independently and output expanded considerably while demand did not. Farm prices dropped to just over half of what they had been in wartime, while nonfarm prices dropped only by a fourth. This was the first time that farm prices and other prices did not react similarly.

The farm bloc has always been comprised of both Democrats and Republicans, most of whom have come from the Midwest and the South, where farmers once constituted sizable constituencies. One-third of the country lived on farms, and farmers constituted electoral pluralities in some states during the interwar period and crucial vote margins in others. In 1924, 251 of the 435 U.S. Representatives came from districts in which 20 percent or more of the population lived on farms. This number has steadily declined, dwindling to 165 by 1954, 53 by 1964, and 31 by 1970. "I doubt if farmers, by themselves, could even elect a county attorney in most places," said W. R. Poage, chairman of the House Agriculture Committee, recently.

But we still speak of a farm bloc, and its spokesmen in both chambers of Congress are influential. Leading Democrats and Republicans from states economically dependent on agriculture are more often than not of a single mind on central farm issues. The imperative of an ensured food supply influences congress-persons, and even many representatives from cities are chary of going against the advice of legislators with agricultural experience. Furthermore, each dollar of farmer income generates three to four dollars of related business, and all these affected persons constitute what politicians call a "pocketbook vote."

During the 1920s and '30s, other farm groups came into being, and, where the Grange remained strong, they have often been at odds with it. The largest organization is the American Farm Bureau Federation, founded in 1920. It is usually conservative, and since World War II it has advocated the progressive removal of production controls and the reduction of price supports, the latter of which it supported during the depression. The Bureau has been powerful in the Midwest and parts of the South. It probably has reflected the views of more prosperous farmers, and at one time it had enough influence to block legislation. The National Farmers Union (NFU), which has been strong in the plains area and some mountain and Great Lakes states, claims to be the spokesman for the "family farmer." It has favored high supports and rigid controls, accused the Bureau of working on behalf of processors, and has allied itself with liberal Democrats and sometimes the labor unions. The Grange has traditionally favored a dual-price support, which means high support in the United States for a certain portion of farm products, while the rest is sold on the free market at the world price. Its strength has been in the Northeast, Pennsylvania, Ohio, and the Northwest.

The agricultural revolution of the 1950s brought forth a more militant group, the National Farmers Organization (NFO), which aims at improving the negotiation positions of farmers by arranging for the sale of commodities while members hold back production until an acceptable price has been agreed upon. It now has branches in all mainland states, and warns that unless farmers receive fair prices and profits, "corporate interests will take over agricultural production."

But only when farmers have been sufficiently aroused have they themselves been the source of policies; more often they have had difficulty understanding alternatives presented to them. "As matters now stand," Dale Hathaway, a national authority on farm policy at Michigan State University, said in 1970, "a great deal of attention is given to a few recognized spokesmen for farm organizations and to public officials. As one would naturally expect, the primary attention of such persons is to convince farmers that the positions that they are taking on a specific issue are right."

It is said to be characteristic of farmers to be phlegmatic when times are good and vociferous after adversities. The farm vote, therefore, has historically been erratic. When their earnings are adequate, farmers usually favor the party in power, but many may not bother to vote. When their incomes are squeezed, they usually vote for the party out of office, and, in effect, constitute a new group of voters. The farm revolt was crucial to Truman's 1948 upset, when he carried much of the traditionally Republican Midwest; such was the situation again in 1958, when disenchantment with the Eisenhower-Benson farm policies and pronouncements led to the defeat of many farm-state incumbent Senators and Representatives. In 1960 Kennedy was still able to exploit this discontent.

Agriculture and the Government

Farmers joke that the army could never carry out a coup d'etat because the Department of Agriculture legions would never allow it. The fact is, state as well as federal government enters virtually every phase of food production and distribution. Public inspectors certify seeds for varietal purity, fertilizers for nutrients, pesticides for conformity to laws on poisons, and crops and meats for quality and for absence of chemical residues. The government is also involved in the handling and pricing of foodstuffs by producers, brokers, jobbers, wholesalers, and retailers. Federal grants support scientific researchers; and agricultural economists collect, evaluate, and publish data and projections to aid the government in its subsidy and control programs and the farmer in making production and marketing decisions. There are laws controlling the disposal of farm wastes, occupational safety standards, the nutritional content of marketed food, and the safety of additives. The government has also fostered agriculture directly by building railroads, highways, and canals, which have broadened the market for farmers' products and contributed enormously to the transformation from a small-farm economy to agribusiness.

In 1796 George Washington recommended the establishment of a National Board of Agriculture and John Quincy Adams directed diplomatic consuls and naval officers to ship back promising seed and livestock from abroad. In 1839 Congress appropriated the hardly munificent sum of $1,000 from Patent Office fees for distributing seed, conducting research, and collecting farm statistics. One commissioner of patents, Henry L. Ellsworth established an agricultural division within his office, and in 1854, this forerunner of today's mammoth Department of Agriculture employed three specialists—a botanist, an entomologist, and a chemist.

Legislation establishing the Department of Agriculture was signed by Lincoln in 1862. It was one of three key measures enacted that year to serve the interests of the family farmer (the other two were the Homestead and Land-Grant College Acts). Congress directed the department "to acquire and to diffuse among the people of the United States useful information on subjects connected with agriculture in the most general and comprehensive sense of that word, and to procure, propagate, and distribute among the people new and valuable seeds and plants," and its secretary was finally raised to cabinet status in 1889. In 1875 in Connecticut the first agricultural research station was established.

The department collaborates with state agencies and land-grant colleges, and its agricultural attachés report cropping intelligence from around the world. Contact between government and farmers is made directly through the system of county extension agents, an approach developed in 1903 by Seaman Knapp, then a seventy-year-old employee of the Bureau of Plant Industry and a one-time farmer and university president. He was convinced that only practical demonstrations conducted by farmers would convince other farmers of the workability of an innovation. For some time, the appointment of agents remained scattered and the financing makeshift, but agitation for federal aid increased and a first bill authorizing funding was introduced into Congress in 1908. In 1914, the Smith-Lever Act was finally passed, providing for "cooperative extension work," and by 1960, cooperative demonstration was being conducted on thousands of farms in a dozen states, served by nearly four hundred traveling agents.

Areas of Intervention

Land Distribution

At the bicentennial celebration of the Pilgrims' arrival, Daniel Webster said:

Their situation demanded the parcelling out and vision of the lands; and it may be said fairly that this necessary act

fixed the future frame and form of their government. . . .
The consequence. . . . has been a great subdivision of the
soil and a great equality; the true basis, most certainly, of
popular government.

The need to provide farmland for settlers and to control specu-
lation was perceived early in our history. The Ordinance of 1785
defined basic principles for the survey and disposal of the public
domain, and the ordinance was amended or rewritten every few
years. From 1797 onward, Congress was petitioned regularly to
give away land to settlers who intended to crop it, and by the
beginning of the second quarter of the nineteenth century, the
idea garnered the support of many eastern reformers as well as
those who wanted to move westward.

The South was opposed and, naturally, so were land speculators. But in 1849 the Free Soil party was born, and in 1860 the
Republican party adopted a free-homestead plank. Yet, had it not
been for secession, Congress would not have passed the Homestead Act, for a favorable majority prevailed in 1862 only because
the southern legislators had withdrawn.

The Homestead Act provided 160 acres to any head of a family who was over twenty one, and was either a citizen or had
filed naturalization papers. It was aimed at settling the West. At
the time, however, 160 acres were too many for irrigated farming
and too few for dry cultivation or grazing, and the measure was
not coordinated with other land legislation. As a result, the act
was actually of more importance as a symbol than as a practical
measure.

Soil Conservation

Interest in soil conservation began late in the last century, but
for a long time practical measures were generally left up to the
individual farmers. By the 1920s the need for immediate profits
to pay for land, machinery, livestock, and seed had led to such
land abuse that farm leaders worried not only about diminishing
fertility but the physical loss of the soil itself. In 1928 the Department of Agriculture issued an incisive and widely discussed cir-
cular, "Soil Erosion—a National Menace," in which it was re-

ported that not less than 126 billion pounds of plant nutrients were being lost annually, mainly from cultivated and abandoned fields and overgrazed lands.

This was the situation when the great drought of 1934–36 struck. In response, New Deal legislation included erosion-control projects in its re-employment program, restricted the marketing of "soil-depleting" crops, and subsequently organized the Soil Conservation Service, whose goal was to help farmers understand the causes of waning productivity and apply corrective measures. The program provided for payment of part of the farmer's conservation costs and aided local conservation districts.

Today, about 3,000 conservation districts, supervised by some 18,000 district officials, cover virtually all privately owned land and provide services to about 2.2 million farmers voluntarily carrying out conservation practices. Among the district's functions are evaluation of data on soil and water, provision of technical services, and sponsorship of conservation projects. There are also large-scale programs, such as the federal Great Plains Conservation Program, which involves ten states. The latest national inventory of conservation needs, published in 1971, showed that nearly two-thirds of our agricultural and other rural lands require restoration to varying degrees, and that nearly 9,000 upstream watersheds need preservation or development. Among other serious problems are the silting of streams, lakes, and reservoirs, much of which is caused by highway construction and commercial siting, and flooding caused by rechanneling of streambeds. Erosion was found to have damaged 55 percent of the land inspected. Conservation measures were found adequate on little more than a third of the cropland and on somewhat less of the pastures and ranges. Only 7 percent of our land retains what is called Class I capability.

Water Rights and Irrigation

Water rights have always been difficult to determine. Under Mohammedan law, which governs much of the earth's more arid regions, water is a free right like air. But the right to water is more complicated in most of the world, and there are some 250 laws involving its distribution throughout the world. They deal with the question of who can acquire water and how, and define suppliers' rights and obligations, the role of users' associations, the functions of agencies granting authorizations, methods of payments, and the duration of rights. But water management, says Stuart Mulford, project manager of the model desalination plant in San Diego, "is often dictated as much by custom as by any other reason."

As the West became more fully settled, Congress began legislating water use. The Desert Land Act of 1877 allowed individuals to buy 640 acres of public desert land at $1.25 an acre, providing they agreed to irrigate within three years. It was followed by the Carey Act of 1894, which granted each state a million acres of federally owned land within the state to be sold for settlement and cultivation; the state was obligated to use the funds received to reclaim other lands belonging to it. But by 1902 fewer than 9 million western acres were under systematic irrigation, and costs of irrigation works were rising. That year, Congress passed the National Reclamation or Newland Act, which provided that the government would plan and build irrigation works, and users would pay for them over a period of years. Under this legislation, nearly 30 million acres—over two-thirds of them in western states—were irrigated in the next fifty years.

But the supply and quality of water is likely to be a constant issue. At a Western Governors' Conference in 1967, the California chief executive announced his hope of persuading the host governor of Montana to part with some of his state's water; the governor of Montana was silent and California has yet to get any of that water. The United States and Mexico signed a water treaty in 1944 that assured the Mexicans of 1.5 million acre feet of usable water annually for an area of 75,000 acres, but as Americans farmed more land, the drainage from their irrigating carried so much salt back into the river that its salinity had doubled by 1961. Settling the subsequent dispute in 1973, the United States agreed to build a desalting plant on the Colorado by 1978; it will be the largest one in the world and will serve as a global pilot project.

Education and Research

Agricultural education was sparse until the mid-nineteenth century, when Iowa, Maryland, Michigan, Pennsylvania, and some other states founded agricultural colleges. In 1841 the president of Norwich University in Vermont, Alden Partridge, proposed that Congress appropriate funds from the proceeds of the sales of public lands to endow schools with courses in the natural sciences and agricultural economics as well as in engineering, manufacturing, and commerce. A decade later, the Illinois state legislature petitioned Congress to fund these activities, and a Vermont congressman, Justin S. Morrill, took up the cause. President Buchanan vetoed his bill, but Congress passed it again in 1862; Lincoln signed it, and it is popularly known as the Morrill Land-Grant Act. (Although Lincoln deserves as much recognition for his role in stimulating agricultural development as he does for the Emancipation Proclamation, much of the farm-support legislation that came into being under his leadership had undergone a decade or more of what one chronicler described as "formative discussion," and had either failed to pass or was vetoed.)

But the legislation did not alter the facts that there was relatively little technology to teach. In 1871 a convention of several land-grant colleges urgently requested Congress and the state legislatures to set up research and experiment stations, and in 1875 Connecticut became the first state to support one. By 1887, 14 states supported experiment stations, and in 13 other states, colleges funded similar work. Finally, in 1887 Congress passed the Hatch Act, providing for an annual grant to each state for the support of an agricultural experiment station; by the 1890s, the stations were disseminating scientific information and fostering laboratory research.

In 1887 the Association of American Agricultural Colleges and Experiment Stations was formed—it is now called the Association of Land-Grant Colleges and Universities. The "Second Morrill Act" of 1890, the Adams Act of 1906, and the Purnell Act of 1925 increased federal appropriations for the state schools. What has been called "the greatest university extension program that the world has ever seen" was included in the Good Roads Act, passed under the Wilson administration, which provided for the stationing of an agricultural agent in every county.

But agricultural vocation teaching was still not reaching rural youth, and new information was reaching few farmers. The Smith-Lever Act of 1914 (supplemented by the Capper-Ketcham

Act of 1928) modernized the entire extension program by making the college a directing and clearing center for the extension effort, involving county agents and boys' and girls' clubs. To bring agricultural training to secondary schools, Congress passed the Smith-Hughes Act of 1917 (supplemented by the George-Deen Act of 1936), which provides federal funds for the states on a matching basis to aid vocational-agricultural—commonly called "vo-ag"—programs.

The 1968 Vocational Educational Act expanded the curricula of vocational-agricultural schools by providing funds for training rural youth in off-farm, farm-related occupations. In 1969 though, only a fourth of the American high schools offered any "vo-ag" courses, a situation which neither kept rural youth interested in farming nor prepared them to handle agribusiness.

The Credit Issue

American farmers have traditionally disliked borrowing, and lending institutions have been disinclined to take agricultural risks. In the past, farming was not an expensive business to start; as recently as the mid-1930s, a man could buy a piece of land, a plow, and a draft mule or horse team for a total investment of under a thousand dollars. Today, even a subsistence farm would cost more. In 1970, farms with sales over $20,000 had average production assets worth nearly a quarter of a million dollars each. There were some 600,000 of these farms, and they produced 75 percent of our food. The required investment was over $200,000, more than double the amount needed only a decade before, when only 340,000 farms were in that sales category. It is projected that by 1980, the financial requirement may double again. Naturally, this capital will have to be obtained mostly on credit.

Until World War II, money was generally scarce, prices were low, and risks were high. If the small-scale farmer did get a loan, interest was exorbitant. After the Civil War, many eastern farmers began to shift from subsistence to commercial farming, but the transition was slow because access to credit at reasonable rates of interest remained limited. Theodore Roosevelt, who was influenced by Populism, appointed a Country Life Commission to study approaches to rural credit in other countries, especially Germany, where the rural credit system was comparatively advanced. William Howard Taft and Woodrow Wilson promoted further studies, and both political parties had planks favoring rural credit in their 1912 platforms. In 1916 Wilson recommended the passage of the Federal Farm Loan Act, which authorized the establishment of federally insured, privately owned, and cooperative farm mortgage banks.

This was a beginning, but a good deal more legislation was necessary. In 1916, an assistant Secretary of Agriculture Carl Carl Vrooman wrote:

> For half a century the department has used its utmost endeavors to show the farmer how to fight the chinch-bug and the army-worm, the cattle tick and the Hessian fly, and other insect pests, but had not even so much as attempted to show him how to protect himself from the yearly toll levied upon the fruits of his toil by such human pests as the usurer, commercial pirates posing as legitimate middlemen, and other business parasites of the agricultural world.
>
> The farmer who makes two blades of grass grow where only one grew before may be a good agronomist, but if he cannot sell his second blades at a profit, he is a poor farmer.

Wilson understood this and appointed an economist as secretary of agriculture. During Wilson's administration, Congress passed the Rural Credits Bill providing for a system of land banks offering more funds for loans, longer terms, and lower interest than commercial sources. By 1928, the farmers' situation had so improved that a German economist found that in agricultural economics, a study scarcely existing before 1900, "America has outstripped all other countries in this field."

Throughout the beginning of the period of heavy mechanization, farmers continued to refrain from buying new implements until what they had was beyond repair or hopelessly obsolete, and credit still was not easy to come by. After 1950, the situation began to change; lenders felt that the risks had declined, and a new generation of farmers began to cost-account debt servicing as simply another input. In recent times, farmers have been good risks; the repayment periods averaged less than two years, and three-fourths of the total outstanding debt was repaid or renewed annually—a sign of the financial viability of the new agriculture.

Today, the system of financing is complex, but funds are available; increasing credit is now generated by private sources, such as commercial banks, life insurance companies, and suppliers. When farmers cannot obtain credit from commercial sources at reasonable interest, they can apply to the federal Farm Credit System, a financing enterprise of thirty seven banks that extends into the smallest farm community and is supervised by the government but owned by farmers. The system comprises twelve Federal Land Banks, which make long-term loans, chiefly for land and buildings; twelve Federal Intermediate Credit Banks, which make loans up to seven years mainly for seed, feed, livestock, and equipment; and thirteen Banks for Cooperatives, which lend to farm cooperatives. The Farm Credit System raises funds for its loans by selling bonds and notes in the money and capital markets. (In 1972, the Farm Credit System sold $15.3 billion in bonds and notes, making it the biggest borrower after the U.S. Treasury.) In 1972, more farmers used more money than at any time in over a generation—more than $20 billion, according to E. A. Jaenke, head of the Farm Credit Administration. This amount represents 30 percent increase over 1971 and a 50 percent increase over 1968. The increases are the result of new farm-credit legislation passed in 1971 that allows the banks to finance up to 85 percent of the current market value of the farm; Until then, they had been permitted to finance up to 50 percent. Still another government-supported source of credit is the Farmers Home Administration, which lends for seed, fertilizer, livestock, feed, tractor fuel, and other equipment. In fiscal 1972 the FHA loaned $350 million.

Some of the Farm Credit System members believe that their banks have more expertise than commercial banks in the area of agricultural loans, but some commercial bank officers consider the Farm Credit System operations a problem of growing government competition.

In the past, farmland was not considered worth a high price, but much of it has escalated in value because of its potential for suburbanization, industrial parks, highways, airports, and recreation, and, since 1973, as cropland. Bankers have never been reluctant to grant mortgages on marketable land; they have never, however, been eager to accept farm machinery as collateral because repossessed implements, unlike cars, have little marketability in poor times—a situation that may be changing as demand for implements exceeded manufacturers' ability to supply them in 1973. During the last decade, machinery manufacturers doubled the number of loans for equipment purchases from 102,-000 to 215,000, and the average loan rose by nearly 70 percent, from around $2,600 to over $4,400. The total value of the loans went from just over a quarter of a billion to nearly a full billion during that period. Manufacturers also advance loans to dealers, who rent out machines. Although the amount of business conducted this way remained relatively small as late as 1970, it has increased 3.5 times since 1967, and all six major companies had such programs.

Middlemen are another source of credit for farmers. Roy Scola, head of a firm in the San Francisco Produce Market, describes this type of arrangement:

> You'll have a man come in and say that he needs $5,000 or more on his berries. So you take a mortgage on the crop.
>
> But, really, you are taking a mortgage on his person. If the crop fails, we know that he's out unless he puts in another crop. So we'll lend more money to help pull him out. We know it's a risk of the business.

Why does a wholesaler like Scola lend? "We lend," he says, "because the banks won't."

The availability and use of credit vary with the times. During the boom of the late 1960s, competition for funds was keen; but during the recession of 1970, many lenders were soliciting prospects. "If the farmer is a good credit risk," says an Iowa county extension agent, "he can get the money—although interest rates may be said to be too high."

The changed world food situation and inflation brought new financial pressures on farmers in 1973; while their produce earned much more, the costs of fertilizer, feed, machinery, pesticides, and land rose rapidly. The total farm debt was estimated at $80 billion, 10 percent over the year before, and it was estimated that it would be double that by the end of the decade.

Overproduction, Parity, and Subsidies

When the Russians contracted for a fourth of our wheat harvest in 1972, columnist Art Buchwald reported a new Communist conspiracy. The key, he said, lay in Khrushchev's threat that the Soviet Union would "bury" the United States. The Russians will do it, wrote Buchwald, by buying enough American wheat to create a world grain shortage, and the rising prices would stimulate America to go on a farming binge. " 'When the entire American economy is devoted to growing wheat,' " said the plotting Khrushchev, " 'we tell United States that we have too much wheat and we cancel order; United States is stuck with billions of tons of wheat and capitalistic system is buried under its own grain.' "

Buchwald's tale hits at the bane of the American farm economy —ensuring adequate food supplies without jeopardizing profits through overproduction. In the ideal world, farmers would produce enough to meet demand at prices returning a satisfactory income. But some overproduction must be planned as a buffer against adversity. At the same time, if this leads to a cheap food policy, with low returns for the farmer's work and investment, it is unfair. It could cause more farmers to quit agriculture, and the remaining ones might lower their output until demand outpaces supplies.

The history of cushioning farmers against national and international economic dislocations begins with the Wilson administration. Up to that time, people concerned with agricultural policy usually thought in terms of tariffs, monetary and banking practices, and the sale and improvement of public lands. When President Taft proposed measures "to give us more farms and more farmers," he added that they were "not to subsidize the American farmer. Fortunately for this country, he does not need it, nor would he accept it." Reform legislation did not focus on prices, which had been good since 1910, until they collapsed after World War I. The hard times of the early 1920s affected farmers more than other groups. Food prices plummeted and, as an implement manufacturer lamented, "You can't sell a plow to a busted customer."

By 1924, the Bureau of Agricultural Economics had developed

the basis for the most controversial farm legislation of the decade, the McNary-Haugen Bill, which aimed at supporting domestic farm prices at their pre-war purchasing levels while exporting surpluses. Introduced three times, passed twice, and twice vetoed, the approach was opposed by many agricultural economists, who still believed that the best way to deal with surpluses was through cooperative marketing. The co-op approach was finally attempted in 1929 through the Agricultural Marketing Act, which created the Federal Farm Board. This was the first time the government assumed any responsibility for farm prices. The Great Depression aborted any impact that the board might have had. By 1932, farm prices had fallen by over half, overseas agricultural expansion reduced export demand, surpluses mounted, and farmers' net incomes were under a third of those of 1929. When the unsuccessful Farm Board disbanded, it called for restrictions on output, and the notion of helping farmers balance supply with demand through a domestic allotment plan gained an increasing following.

The New Deal in Agriculture

Truly massive federal involvement in agriculture did not occur until Franklin D. Roosevelt became President. In 1933, one in four Americans lived on a farm, prices were so low that farmers had neither the means nor the incentive to adopt new technologies, and the next year the two-year drought began.

The first ninety days of the Roosevelt administration produced the Agricultural Adjustment Act (AAA), aimed at attaining "such balance between the production and consumption of agricultural commodities, and such marketing conditions therefore as will reestablish prices to farmers at a level that will give agricultural commodities a purchasing power with respect to articles that farmers buy, equivalent to the purchasing power of agricultural commodities in the base period [1910–14]." Among the tools the act provided for were acreage reduction, marketing agreements, price controls, processing licenses, and processing taxes. This act touched off much dispute. Although the Supreme Court declared the original AAA unconstitutional in 1936, within two years Congress had re-enacted most of its programs and added some others. It set the pattern of controls for the next forty years. The orientation of the Court was also redirected by new Roosevelt appointees.

The New Deal programs officially recognized agriculture as a basic and essential national industry, and operated on a broad-spectrum basis. They curbed production, improved roads between farms and markets, promoted rural electrification and telephone systems, encouraged resettlement and conservation, purchased submarginal land, and granted loans to halt foreclosures. There were also direct government purchases, nonrecourse loans, set-aside programs, and what was called the ever-normal granary, which meant the maintaining of reserves in case of food harvest failure. The Commodity Credit Corporation (CCC) was established by the second AAA in 1938 to manage surpluses and distribution programs. The Agricultural Marketing Act of 1937 sought to raise incomes for producers of perishables—milk, fruit, and vegetables—by obligating processors to pay minimum prices in local marketing areas and by setting quotas. The second AAA also provided price supports and production controls for non-perishable commodities. Because the government became the owner of surpluses, distribution programs, such as donations to the hungry and school meals to raise nutritional standards, were also conceived. In 1938 Secretary of Agriculture Henry A. Wallace studied a proposal for a food-stamp plan, which subsequently became a mainstay against hunger. Roosevelt established the Rural Electrification Administration (REA) in 1935, which provided farmers' cooperatives with 2 percent loans for power development, and later became involved in community projects such as schools and hospitals.

Post-World War II farm programs have generally fallen into two categories: one type includes technical advice, cheap credit, soil conservation, water assistance, and pest control, which affect the market indirectly; the other directly bolsters farmers' incomes through price supports, surplus disposal, and production controls.

The central issue for the farmer is income parity, a return comparable to that of persons making equivalent economic contributions. Politically, the principle is not controversial, but means of achieving it are. Price supports have caused the major difficulties. In order to maintain prices at the level fixed by Congress since the New Deal, the government takes excess supplies off the market at a given price. Over the years, corn, wheat, rice, soybeans, peanuts, dry edible beans, flaxseed, and dairy products, as well as cotton, tobacco, wool, and crude pine gum, have been eligible for support, and efforts to change the approach were defeated until 1973.

The Truman Administration and the Brannan Plan

Farmers remembered the depression of the early 1920s and anticipated a price break after World War II. Congress provided for 90 percent parity for the first two postwar years, but the anticipated slump did not occur, and prices held at about 110 percent parity until 1948.

The mood of uncertainty persisted, however, and in 1948 Congress voted to continue the wartime level of support for basic crops for another two years. Potatoes, milk and milk products, hogs, chickens, and eggs were to be supported at 90 percent parity; certain other commodities, at 60 percent. However, Congress also decided to replace the fixed high-level supports for basic crops with flexible supports as of 1950. (Flexible supports were more in line with the 1938 AAA.)

The range of flexibility varied from 60 to 90 percent of parity, depending on the size of the supply. (Prices were to be supported at 90 percent parity only if the supply reached 130 percent of normal.) In a 1956 study for the Twentieth Century Fund, *Can We Solve the Farm Problem?*, Murray Benedict described the intentions and probable effects of the bill:

> The plan thus contained what was, in essence, a provision for price floors designed to prevent price declines of disastrous proportions. It was not a guarantee of highly satisfactory prices. If the crop was short, say as low as 70 percent of normal, the price in the market would in all probability be above the support price. Hence the level would be of little consequence. It was in times of large supply that such a plan presumably would have an important influence.
>
> The principal intended effect of the act was to substitute a flexible price-support arrangement for the 90 percent of parity supports provided in the wartime legislation but now about to lapse. It was a plan for a partial return to a freer

market and a partial retreat from the government's commitment to support farm prices at high levels.

Another provocative feature of the bill was a revision of the
method of computing parity, which was done mainly because
costs had not increased uniformly for different crops.

A bitter fight broke out in Congress between proponents of
this comparatively moderate approach and the fixed-parity fac-
tion. The debate persisted up to the last day before Congress was
to adjourn for the national nominating conventions, when a compromise was finally reached: high supports to be continued on
basic crops and relaxed on some others. "The action taken was an
election-year compromise," Benedict states, "which meant passing
up one of the best opportunities of the postwar years for orderly
and gradual return to a freer and more flexible marketing
arrangement."

Meanwhile, the anticipated drop in demand had finally set in,
and in 1949 a large surplus of wheat began to accumulate. The
stage was now set for one of the hottest agricultural policy debates
ever. On April 7, 1949, the Senate and House committees on agriculture convened in an extraordinary joint session to hear the
new secretary of agriculture, Charles F. Brannan, present his
long-awaited views on farm policy.

What became known as the Brannan Plan never was enacted—
until parts of it became law under the Agriculture and Consumer
Protection Act of 1973—but it served as a lightning rod for the
political oratory of its opponents into the 1960 presidential election campaign. Brannan proposed the highest level of support in
history and the extension of income protection to farmers producing certain perishables. The guarantees would be computed,
however, according to a formula of "income support" rather than
price support, and benefits extended to commercial farms were
to be based only on that part of their production which could be
handled by an efficient "family farm." Also, farmers would forfeit
benefits if they failed to abide by approved conservation practices
and specified production and marketing controls. Leo Christenson, who devoted a book to the Brannan Plan, recalls the controversy:

> In addition to producing a first-class row in Congress, a bit-
> ter feud between the Secretary of Agriculture and the leader

of the biggest farm organization [Farm Bureau], and a major split in the so-called "farm bloc" . . . the Brannan Plan provoked a lusty national debate on agricultural policy. . . .

Although the enemies of the Brannan Plan managed to convert the Plan into an epithet, and won a smashing victory over it, many thoughtful students of agriculture have retained a continuing interest in it. They have insisted that one of its central ideas—protecting the farmer from the hazards of the free market by a system of compensatory payments instead of price supports—merits far more serious congressional attention than it has ever received.

Of the major farm organizations, only the Farmers Union had supported the Brannan Plan. The others generally felt the direct subsidies to maintain an income standard would make farmers dependent on congressional whim for their earnings.

The Democrats (who had lost control of Congress in the 1946 elections, but regained it in 1948) refused to go along with Brannan. Albert Gore, Democrat of Tennessee, then a representative, introduced a substitute bill in 1949 extending the wartime levels of price supports for the basic crops for a year, but authorizing a decrease to 80 percent for crops in surplus in 1951 as a sanction. It also redefined parity. Nearly all House Republicans voted in favor of the substitute bill, while the Democrats opposed it two to one. When the measure reached the Senate, the sides divided evenly; Vice-President Allen W. Barkley, a Democrat, broke the tie by voting in favor of it.

Eisenhower's Frustration

Workable solutions to large surpluses and low prices eluded President Eisenhower, and the politicking involved in farm plans was distasteful to him. Early in his first campaign he was in conflict between what his intuition told him was right—an equitable return for the farmer—and his advocacy of a free market, which was the national Republican position. At the National Plowing Contest in Minnesota, he was reported to have agreed that farmers should receive "full parity", but in his memoirs he recalled only promising to uphold the agricultural act of the time until its expiration at the end of 1954. The existing act provided for 90 percent parity and allowed farmers who planted the number of acres specified by the government to borrow from the government for the full support price, with his crops as collateral. If the market exceeded that level, the farmer paid back the government and sold his crop on the market. Otherwise he kept the money and the government took possession of the crop.

Eisenhower felt that the mounting surpluses showed that past support machinery, much of which was devised to meet the needs of World War II and the Korean War, was outmoded, and chafed at the storage costs which were then running at half a million dollars a day. He was also disturbed by the inequitable distribution of subsidies—a problem that still defies solution.

The Republican platform favored a program "aimed at full parity prices," and the new administration proposed supports to ensure between 75 and 90 percent parity as a gradual move toward a freer if not a free market, a parity formula that would take into account the high costs of technology which did not exist in the 1910–14 base period.

As his secretary of agriculture, Eisenhower appointed Ezra Taft Benson, a respected Mormon elder of extremely conservative bent. Benson would have preferred to eliminate supports, but, since he could not succeed in that, he lowered them. He became the most controversial member of the cabinet throughout his eight years as secretary and a lightning rod for Democratic attacks. In 1954 Congress passed an agricultural act authorizing between 82.5 to 90 percent parity for the next year, and then a reversion to 75 to 90 percent.* The legislation also authorized the disposal of surpluses through noncommercial channels.

But the surpluses mounted, and every bushel of wheat disposed of was replaced by one and a half bushels in the stockpile. Eisenhower fretted; the government could not store the food forever,

---

* That year, Secretary Benson dropped the level of price supports for all dairy products from 90 to 75 percent parity—and caused what was called the great cheese scandal. Earlier, the large cheese distributors of Wisconsin and neighboring states had contracted to sell 90 million pounds of their local Cheddar to the government at the high support price of 37 cents a pound; when the price-support level was decreased, it lowered the price on government-owned cheese to 34¼ cents. The distributors bought back most of it, making a profit of nearly $2.5 million—and the cheese had never physically left the warehouses. No government officials profited, the taxpayers got a $2.5 million laugh, and Benson never repeated the mistake.

it could not sell it within the United States without competing with farmers and probably driving the price down, and massive distribution overseas might disrupt the economies of friendly nations. The only alternative was to dispose of some surplus outside normal commercial channels, such as domestic welfare, school lunches, sales for soft currencies, and donations to poor countries. Eisenhower argued that the 1954 act was sound in principle, but by 1956, the situation had not improved much and it was clear that more needed to be done.

A "soil bank" was proposed to reduce planting in two ways. The first was by reducing acreage planted to wheat, corn, rice, and cotton, which were then in serious surplus. The farmer would receive certificates for uncultivated acres, and the value of these certificates would reflect the return for normal yields on these acres. He could redeem the certificate either in cash or kind. The second way in which planting would be reduced was a con- servation-reserve program. Farmers would be paid for using some of their land that needed conservation measures for forage, trees, and water storage for periods of from three to fifteen years. The government paid up to 80 percent of the expenses involved.

In 1956 congressional factions resumed their traditional battle lines, the liberals typically favoring high supports and the con- servatives favoring flexible supports—except those from farm states or districts. Eisenhower called the compromise bill they finally passed "a monstrosity" because, though it gave him his soil bank, it "made the great error of going back to the 90 per- cent of parity price supports for the six basic crops [wheat, corn rice, peanuts, cotton, and tobacco]." It also set 80 to 90 percent support levels for whole milk and butter fat. Eisenhower vetoed the bill, telling a national television audience that the soil bank would be rendered "almost useless" by the other provisions. In his memoirs, he wrote, "In effect, it was less a piece of farm legis- lation than a private relief bill for politicians in that election year."

The bill went back to Congress, where it was reconstructed to provide what Eisenhower especially wanted—the soil bank as a means of retiring land from production and so reduce sur- pluses. It authorized two types of programs: first, acreage reserve under which farmers could set aside land previously planted to basic commodities (wheat, corn, rice, peanuts, cotton, and tobacco) and receive compensatory payments from the government; and, second, a conservation reserve, authorizing contracts to be signed from 1956 to 1960 for converting any type of productive land to specified conservation practices for periods of from three to fifteen years (the Department of Agriculture never signed any contracts for longer than ten years, though). The government paid participating farmers for setting aside the land and paid up to 80 percent of the costs of the conservation practices. The act did not return to high, fixed price supports but still provided a somewhat flexible parity approach that would not permit a drop of more than five percentage points a year. Eisenhower was sufficiently satisfied with the compromise to sign it.

In the 1956 election campaign, the Democrats urged 100 percent parity for farmers with incomes of less than $7,500, and supports of up to 90 percent, depending on income, for all others. Eisenhower advocated a free market, unregimented farming, and broadened demand (the means by which broadening would be achieved were never well specified). While Eisenhower won by a landslide, it was not because of contentment in the farm belt, where again voters helped ensure Democratic control of both houses of Congress.

For Republicans, the worst was yet to come. In 1958, they lost disastrously in the farm belt, where even Republicans opposing the farm policies of the administration were turned out of office. The Democrats carried thirteen of the richest farm districts; they had carried three in 1952 and four in 1954. Eisenhower himself conceded that his efforts to recast programs had had "little effect," and at the end of his term he was disappointed over the use of "federal subsidies to create millionaires . . . under programs ostensibly devised to protect the little farmer." Surpluses were costing the government $3 billion to $4 billion a year, farmers' earnings were down, and more smaller operators were leaving the land.

In a special 1959 message, Eisenhower charged that the claim that price supports helped primarily the smaller family farmers was a myth, that the support level was high enough to encourage large operators to overproduce, and that acreage controls were offset by yield increases. He proposed that both the support floor and the parity concept be abandoned over a three-year period.

Reaction in Congress was predictable. Republican Senator Milton R. Young of North Dakota broke with his party and predicted a drop in wheat prices so sharp that it would "break every wheat farmer in the United States with the exception of the big ones." The Democrats decided to play politics. They passed a bill raising the price support of wheat to 90 percent and slashed acreage allotments by 25 percent, knowing that if Eisenhower vetoed it, the repercussions would be tremendous. Although advisers urged him to let it become law without his signature, he vetoed the bill and gave the Democrats an issue for the 1960 campaign.

The Soil Bank programs had not been implemented extensively by 1960, and to the extent that they were, their results were disillusioning; there was evidence that farmers retired their least productive land while harvesting the soils on which crops yielded most highly.

Benson, recalling efforts to put together a farm program in 1960 in his memoirs, described Vice-President Nixon as "one of the stumbling blocks. As the second ranking leader of his party and its probable candidate for the Presidency, his voice naturally became increasingly weighty. Again he seemed more interested in devising a scheme to capture the imagination of the voters, especially in the Midwest, than in supporting the Administration's sound proposals."

Benson made what he called a "last gasp assault" on the wheat problem in early 1960, basing his "solution" on "three pegs"— doing away with acreage allotments and marketing quotas on wheat, expanding the conservation set-aside in wheat areas, and relating price supports not to 1910–14 but to recent market prices. But several Republicans, including the powerful Senators Young of North Dakota and Karl E. Mundt of South Dakota, Benson wrote, "kept up a drum fire of pressure on the White House and the Republican National Committee to dilute the [President's farm] message until it would be practically meaningless." After sitting in on a meeting of Republican legislative leaders at the White House presided over by Nixon in February, Benson drafted a letter to the vice-president expressing disappointment in him, but never sent it. Benson (who favored Nelson A. Rockefeller for the nomination) felt that Nixon had been a strong supporter of Eisenhower farm policies in 1954 and 1956, but had begun equivocating shortly after on farm and other issues.

Eisenhower summed up the reasons for his failure in his memoirs:

Neither this law [1960] nor any other bill that we were able to get enacted into law during all the years of my Presidency could really get at the roots of the farm problem. This was impossible because the agricultural industry had been legislated into an almost complete separation from the necessary influence of free markets. . . . In the long run, the agricultural industry must look to the open market, the still operative laws of supply and demand, for its salvation.

There was talk that Eisenhower, in drafting his farm plan, had rebuffed Benson and yielded to Nixon's wish to collect rural votes. Confronted with this rumor at a news conference, Eisenhower said, "Well, this is the first that I have heard about him [Nixon] reshaping [the farm message]," and, added that he thought that Nixon would "be defending what I believe."

As vice-president, Nixon was identified with what were polemicized by the Democrats as the "Benson farm policies," and some of his associates felt that the secretary of agriculture should resign before the 1960 campaign. But Eisenhower publicly praised Benson, who stayed, and Nixon perplexed the President by setting up an independent advisory committee on agriculture. On the stump in Lincoln, Nebraska, Nixon conceded the difficulties with farm programs, and predicted that the solution lay in long-range land retirement combined with expanding sales and exports.

Meanwhile, the Democrats introduced a "family farm bill," providing for farmer committees which would work out programs commodity by commodity with the Department of Agriculture, subject to congressional approval. As for the 1960 Democratic platform, Benson interpreted it as a "rebaked Brannan Plan," plus greater subsidies, "unrealistic support levels, unworkable production controls, a costly and wasteful food stamp plan, and unbridled give-aways . . . without regard for domestic or world markets." John F. Kennedy, who as a senator from Massachusetts had favored flexible price supports, changed his position as he emerged as a leading contender for the Democratic presidential nomination. Questioned at a news conference about the switch early in 1960, he explained that he had previously represented the view of the majority of his constituents, but as a presidential candidate, he would reflect a national constituency.

The New Frontier on the Farm

Kennedy favored full parity of income for farmers and proposed strict limitations on production or sales—"barrels, bushels and bales" rather than acreage curtailment. If such measures turned out to be impractical, he said, then he favored price supports at no less than 90 percent of parity, acreage restriction, and direct payments. The core of Kennedy's concept was supply management, bolstered whenever possible by marketing quotas such as those established in the "Second New Deal" of 1938. He also intended to expand surplus giveaways to the needy at home and abroad. Congressional opposition to both the ideological and economic foundations of the supply management approach was so strong that it was defeated in committee.

Farm programs, as they evolved under Kennedy and Johnson, relied mainly on moving 41 million to 65 million acres of wheat, feed, other grains, and cotton in and out of production annually according to projected domestic and international market demands. What the government did in effect was rent land for roughly what farmers would have netted had they cropped, and keep it idle.

When Kennedy took office, the government owned $6 billion in farm surpluses, and held another $2 billion tied up in other programs. It was costing a million dollars a day just to store and handle them. Because there were not enough elevators and warehouses, some grain was stored in old freighters anchored at ports around the country. Farmers generally were earning only 55 percent of parity, when the mid-decade world food shortage brought the value of American reserves down to $1 billion and pushed farm income up 28 percent. But the food panic was over in a couple of years, and surpluses reaccumulated.

Secretary Freeman argued that the government should pay farmers to divert acreage to grassland or forest for conservation;

set planting allotments that would vary according to the projections of demand; and reduce price support under a two-tier system, giving farmers world market prices for what the government exported and more for what was used domestically. Johnson wanted price supports extended indefinitely and a national food bank established, but Congress was uncooperative.

By the time of the 1968 presidential campaign, about 60 million acres had been idled. Demand for soybeans had lagged in 1967, and in 1968 the National Soybean Processors Association predicted a surplus of nearly a billion bushels by 1971. In a single crop year, 1967–68, the corn surplus rose by 40 percent to 1.16 bushels, and from 1967 to 1970 the wheat surplus rose to nearly a billion bushels.

The Nixon Administration

During the 1968 campaign, Nixon spoke critically of the fact that 21 percent of farmers' net income came directly from government payments, giving "those who control the purse . . . the power to control farmers." He recommended that new programs "reduce this dangerous level of dependency on arbitrary political power" but did not disclose specifics.

Agriculturally, Nixon's first term was rather like a replay of Eisenhower's. His administration sought flexible supports based on world market prices, while most farm groups fought for higher parity guarantees. The debate went on for sixteen months, but finally, in November 1970, a deeply divided Senate passed a bill allowing wheat, feed grain, and cotton growers to divert a percentage of their acreage to conservation and to plant what they chose on the rest of their land. The aim was to return more decision-making power to the farmer and to let him judge the marketplace. To be eligible for loans, certificates, and payments, however, a farmer had to set aside or divert a specified acreage from wheat or certain other crops. The bill also authorized payments for diverting acres beyond those set aside for approved conservation purposes.

Congress did not prohibit the subdividing of farms for the purpose of making more units eligible for the subsidy ceiling, and a 1972 Agriculture Department report showed that acreage had been deeded or leased to members of farmers' families for just this purpose. Republican Representative Paul Findley of Illinois called the loophole "a cruel joke on taxpayers."

There were other abuses of the acreage limitations. Farmers owning cropland of both low and high quality would idle the poorer soils and collect payments computed on the basis of the yield of the better quality soil. Although the department officially held that the great majority of participants in the set-aside program idled quality land, it moved to close the loophole by computing payments according to the surveyed productivity of the acreage actually removed from production.

The consequences of the 1970 act, under these pressures, were becoming observable in 1971, when a majority of eligible farmers altered their cropping patterns. While corn farmers by no means deserted their main crop, they planted many more acres to soybeans, which were suddenly in demand; they were free to do so under the lifting of restrictions on acreage. The mid-South also shifted to more soybeans, and farmers on the southern plains, responding to the demands of an expanding livestock industry in their area, shifted to more sorghums. On the northern plains, many farmers shifted from oats, which were less in demand, to wheat and barley.

The 1971 corn harvest set a record and the wheat crop was huge. Fearing a farm-belt rebellion, the White House committed nearly a billion extra dollars to supports, though it would really have preferred low prices to expand exports. In mid-1972 as surpluses enlarged, nearly half a million unhappy farmers signed petitions requesting immediate government action. The Department of Agriculture, meanwhile, still insisted that the 1970 plan was "a major turning point."

The discontent climaxed when Earl L. Butz was nominated to be secretary of agriculture, after a time of good feeling toward Hardin. Butz, a former dean of agriculture at Purdue and once a candidate for governor of Indiana, sat on boards of major agribusinesses which, opponents charged, symbolized his lack of concern for the family farmer. Forty-four senators, including a number of Republicans, voted against his confirmation—an unusually large protest vote.

Butz set out to prove himself. His first major public act was maneuvering a billion-dollar boost in federal subsidies, mainly

for corn growers whose surpluses had depressed prices. Not surprisingly, most of the money went to areas carried by Nixon in
1968. He promoted the release of funds for rural development,
and was quoted as saying jocularly, "I'm spending money like a
drunken sailor."

Butz' initial difficulties paled beside the outcry raised against
the price controls of the New Economic Policy in 1971. Farmers
were earning about 75 percent of parity, so food commodities
sold from the farm were exempted from them. In February 1972
grocery prices rose by 1.9 percent—the largest single monthly
rise in fourteen years—and some of the rise was shared by
farmers. (The prices received by farmers between 1952 and 1972
had risen only 6 percent, while their debts had increased fivefold
and their taxes had tripled. At the same time, workers' wages had
risen 130 percent, and the proportion of disposable income spent
by consumers for food dropped from 23 percent to 16 percent.)

When retail food prices rose, political pressures naturally built
up to put controls on farm prices, and Butz picturesquely pledged
himself to fight control "like a wounded steer." The statement
set badly with the chairman of the Price Commission, C. Jackson
Grayson, who said, "The success of the President's program to
stabilize prices requires that everyone work to hold prices down,
not to push prices up, as Secretary Butz is advocating. What the
secretary is really advocating is a larger share of the national
income for farmers as a special group." Butz argued that the
farmers had a right to catch up, and warned that attempts to
control prices at the farm would cause "black markets, rationing,
under-the-counter favoritism, priorities, subsidies allocation, regulations, and a host of government officials checking prices,
weighing packages, and hauling people into court—and empty
meat counters." The President backed the secretary, who became
so popular that his invitations to speak were running 200 to 300
a week—third only to those of the President and vice-president
—and not long after he was given the first "Wounded Steer
Award."

But, though it was not foreseen, an inflationary holocaust was
beginning for food prices. Harvest failures in the Eastern Hemisphere enlarged the world market and decreased American surpluses. A rise in disposable incomes, particularly in the United
States, where it reached over 6 percent (adjusted for inflation),

increased demand for meat and especially for beef. This in turn increased demand for feed. An attempt to increase the production of cattle and hogs by cutting the number of females slaughtered meant less meat was being sold. Some experts suspected also the existence of a kind of self-fulfilling inflationary psychology, and Paarlberg cautioned, "The recent past probably is not the new normal."

The new situation appeared to the administration as the best chance since 1948 to move into freer marketing. A typical, efficient midwestern farmer could apparently pay his workers a fair salary and realize a fair return for his own management plus 6 percent return on his capital investment in his realty and machinery. While his recompense would be lower than that of a successful manufacturer, it would be higher than a skilled worker's wages. The timing also seemed propitious politically; the farm vote was fairly small in comparison to the urban bloc, the country appeared moderately conservative, and the people opposed government handouts.

The fear that unsound and irrevocable action would be taken by the administration brought warnings from conservative quarters, and in January 1973 John A. Prestbo, Chicago correspondent and agricultural writer for the *Wall Street Journal*, recalled the sudden renewal of surpluses after the mid-1960s food crisis and warned that another far-reaching decision might be based on a short-lived situation. "Two painful lessons emerged from the [crisis]," the analysis noted. "Don't build hard-to-change production plans on the fast-shifting sand of foreign demand; and don't base long-term changes in farm policy on short-term factors." The chief economist of the conservative Farm Bureau, Gene Hamilton, agreed. "The government has overreacted before," he said. "If the city congressmen get a chance to dismantle the farm program completely, we could have another surplus panic on our hands."

Appearing on NBC's "Meet the Press" in the spring of 1973, the chairman of the Senate Agriculture Committee, Herman E. Talmadge (D.-Georgia), was asked, why not eliminate all farm programs? He responded that he would favor it if it could be done, but added, "I haven't heard of anyone advocating eliminating the minimum wage . . . [or] collective bargaining. Subsidies are wage guarantees for the farmer." The farmer received 4 cents from a loaf of bread costing 28 cents, Talmadge pointed out, and less than 20 percent of the $116 billion spent for food. "Why hit the fellow who gets the least?" he asked.

Must American farmers overproduce? Some economists say that the termination of subsidies would force farmers to be more responsive to market needs as expressed by prices. We have seen how this holds true for cattle, swine, and poultry raising. But crop agriculture depends on more unpredictable factors. For example, during the year of the corn blight, the harvest was barely 4 billion bushels, and consumption was over 4.4 billion (the difference was covered by carryover surpluses). Prices rose, and the government loosened acreage restriction in anticipation of a recurrence of the blight. The blight did not recur, and farmers reaped a record 5.64 billion bushels. Within a year, surplus stocks had more than doubled, and in some areas prices were below production costs.

The agricultural establishment, despite its technological advances, remains antiquated in some respects, especially in marketing. Farmers have traditionally been oriented more toward production than marketing and are not likely to let their machinery and land lie idle to protect themselves in the future. However, farmers have become more interested in bargaining collectively with packers, processors, and retailers, and in hedging prices by selling future contracts guaranteeing a set price on delivery date.

"If the nation is to benefit from sharply increased agricultural exports—smaller trade deficits, increased employment, and so on," the Prestbo *Wall Street Journal* article argued, "then the nation should be willing to cushion some of the risk taken by farmers whose foreign markets may vanish between planting and harvest." And, while consumers anguish over inflated supermarket prices, their mood doubtlessly would be far more rebellious if they faced a chronic uncertainty of food supplies.

Though a free market for farm products did not exist in 1972, the Nixon administration was not defensive about its farm policy. Butz said in December 1972 that the policy was "helping farmers gear their production to profit opportunities in the marketplace," although he conceded "there's still a long way to go." "Manage your own farm," challenged an assistant secretary. "Make your own decisions. Grow what you want. Look to the market. Accommodate to change."

A radically altered world food situation in early 1973 persunded Nixon that it was time to do what he had always wanted to do. In his State of the Union Message on Natural Resources and Environment, he said:

> Farmers must be provided with greater freedom to make production and marketing decisions. I have never known anyone in Washington who knows better than a farmer what is in his own best interest. . . . Old-fashioned Federal intrusion is as inappropriate to today's farm economy as the old McCormick reaper would be on a highly sophisticated modern farm.

The administration planned to retain support loans to prevent prices from dropping to disastrous levels and still provide for direct payments when required to keep unneeded land out of production. It was, Butz frankly admitted, "a gamble on the side of plenty rather than scarcity." The farm bloc consists of a small minority in the House, but in the Senate, where membership is based on geography rather than population, such Republicans as Carl T. Curtis (Nebraska), Robert Dole (Kansas), and Milton R. Young (North Dakota) joined Democrats in an effort to extend farm programs with only minor revisions. There was the alarming possibility of a deadlock in conference committee, in which case program authorization would have reverted to acts going back as far as 1938.

After some wrangling, the Senate and House agreed on a farm measure, to be in effect for the next four years, which aims at supporting farmers' incomes rather than directly supporting the prices of commodities. Ironically, it embodies the principles of the Brannan Plan. The President signed the Agriculture and Consumer Protection Act of 1973, on August 10, 1973, and issued a special statement:

> Though it falls short of the high standards I have set for reforming farm legislation and eventually moving the Gov-

ernment out of agriculture, it does provide a constructive framework for encouraging the expansion of farm production. . . .

In the current period of unprecedented demand for farm commodities, it is essential to provide expanded production by allowing farmers the freedom to make production decisions.

The President then made reference to the concept of target prices for commodities, explained by an accompanying White House fact sheet:

Farmers are to receive their income from the marketplace normally, and *only* if prices fell below target prices would they receive any government payments. These deficiency payments would normally cover farmers' costs for production.

The national average prices which farmers receive for corn, wheat, and cotton for the first five months of the marketing year will be determined by the government; if the price falls short of the target, the government pays the farmer the difference—a "deficiency payment"—based on normal yields on allotment acreages. If the market price is above the target, the government makes no payment. The target prices were set as follows: corn at $1.38 per bushel, wheat at $2.05 per bushel, and cotton at $0.38 per pound. These targets are to be adjusted in 1976 and 1977 according to changes in the index of prices paid by farmers and modified for changes in yield per acre.

"Our long practice of holding United States' prices above competitive world levels, and shrinking our production in order to do so, appears suspended," said Paarlberg in an analysis of the measure. "Parity is no longer a goal. Friends and foes of parity have allowed the concept to expire in silence, the former out of grief and the latter out of charity."

The deficiency-payment technique raised questions as to whether price guarantees would be extended to nonstorable products, such as red meat, poultry, fruit, and vegetables—something that could not be done when the price-support techniques were nonrecourse loans and storage programs. The producers of hogs or potatoes who suffer from poor prices, for example, and press for price assurances enjoyed by the grain and cotton growers, would be demanding an equity denied to them under past programs. These demands will be politicized, and, says Paarlberg, "how [they] will be handled is a major unresolved issue."

Another unresolved question is what would happen if surpluses re-accumulate and depress prices again? Would deficiency payments mount excessively—perhaps several times as much as past price support costs? What would be the reaction of consumer-oriented urban congresspersons?

A final concern of farmers has been the target prices, which are not to be readjusted until at least 1976. Even since the law was enacted, their costs, especially for fertilizer and fuel, have risen steeply, and the target prices may already be unreasonably low. Should inflation make the target prices unprofitable before 1976, then the government is virtually without a program.

Though the government has various recourses, each of them would become an issue. The 1973 act provides for loans to farmers, but they are much lower than the target prices. The government would have to store any renewed surpluses it bought. The secretary of agriculture also still has the option of re-imposing acreage set-aside, and only farmers agreeing to the allotments would be eligible for deficiency payments or loans.

With the 1973 world food shortage, however, the secretary declared that no acreage limitations would be placed on the 1974 plantings of wheat, feed grains, and cottons. And, early in 1974, prices paid to farmers remained well above the targets. A further major provision in the 1973 law lowers the 1970 payment limitation of $55,000 per person for each crop to $20,000 per person, but the subdividing loophole remains.

When subsidies are mentioned, many people envision a farmer sunning himself on one of his many acres, perhaps out of cultivation, as he pats his wallet; and they recall that the bill for this sunbath, until 1973, was running $3 billion to $4.5 billion a year. Americans cannot be blamed entirely for this rather one-sided view, for the list of publicized outrages is long. Payments of hundreds of thousands and at times over a million dollars have been made to individual farmers.

"Hidden" subsidies also give government intervention a bad name. One of the largest benefits received by many farmers, particularly western farmers, is not received through direct subsidies but through government funding of irrigation projects. In 1902 Congress passed what is called the "106-acre law," which provided federally financed water supplies to 106 acres to local farmers (if a farmer who was benefiting from a government-financed water supply sold land in excess of the authorized 106 acres, he had to do so at what the market price had been before irrigation was brought in. These restrictions were made to preclude real-estate windfalls) residing either on the farmland or in the neighborhood. (This restriction was made to prevent absentee landlords from receiving benefits.) But within three years, landholders were agitating against these restrictions. By the late 1940s, farmers in the Central Valley of California were paying only 17 percent of what they were supposed to pay for water, and by 1971 there were charges that they were using subsidized water on unauthorized land. Trying to get remedial legislation passed, Representative Robert W. Kastenmeier (D.-Wisconsin) told the House:

> Hundreds of thousands, yes, millions of acres received subsidized water above the legal limit. The extent of the subsidy appears to range from $600 to $2,000 per acre, which remains unpaid to the public treasury.

Kastenmeier's bill, among others, would have provided that any land irrigated by government projects that was offered for sale could be purchased by the government at pre-project prices. (This was not provided for in the early legislation.) The struggle continues unresolved. Harold Ickes, secretary of the interior under Roosevelt, once observed:

> It is the age-old battle over who is to cash in on the unearned increment in land values created by a public investment. . . . Their [operators'] principal objective is to avoid application . . . of the long-established reclamation policy of the Congress which provides for the distribution of the benefits of great irrigation projects among the many and which prevents speculation in land by the few.

Considering the profits made by the cigarette industry and the unhealthiness of smoking, why does the government subsidize tobacco growers? The government subsidizes the major grains, but why does it not subsidize potato growers, who suffer from chronic surpluses in a free market? And why are our main protein sources, meat and poultry, not subsidized, although dairy products are. What is one to think of the 1971 White House order to increase the government price supports for milk—reportedly worth $300 million a year to dairymen—which reversed a ruling of the Department of Agriculture and was followed by a contribution totaling over $400,000 to the campaign to re-elect President Nixon? (On October 24, 1973, the *Wall Street Journal* reported that shortly before being dismissed, Special Watergate Prosecutor Archibald Cox obtained a 1970 letter to the President suggesting that he could have as much as $2 million in campaign contributions if he imposed import quotas on certain dairy products; Nixon set quotas on ice cream, certain chocolate products, animal feeds containing milk derivatives, and low-fat cheeses two weeks later. This was followed by his raising the government support price for milk by 27 cents a hundred pounds. Toward the end of the year, consumer groups were pressing for release of the tape recordings of the White House sessions.)

A Perspective on Subsidies

The outraged ought to bear two things in mind. The first is that, though the purposes of these subsidies avowedly were to help the "family farmer," the way they were administered was largely inequitable; it was mainly large operators who benefited from them, and many small farmers received nothing. To blame the farmer categorically, or to allow the horror stories to obscure the question of the value of a properly administered system of supports, is both simplistic and useless. Businesses not primarily involved in farming have benefited handsomely from farm subsidies. "Fat cat farmers aren't the only ones making tracks to the taxpayers' trough," said Representative Silvio Conte (R.-Massachusetts) in 1973. "The South Pacific Railroad whistled away with $32,000 in subsidies last year for two 'farms' in California."

The other point that bears consideration is that the rhetoric surrounding farm subsidies has been deceptive, creating the impression that food farmers are especially pampered. The government subsidizes virtually every segment of our national life, and what we pay to ensure our food supplies is not the biggest bill. In fiscal 1970, government social-welfare programs paid out over $100 billion, and veterans' benefits were running between $7 billion and $8 billion annually. Lockheed, after large cost overruns, received a credit guarantee of a quarter of a billion dollars from the government. In 1972, the Congressional Joint Economic Committee identified some 170 subsidy programs for airlines, urban renewal, oil exploration, and other projects which, it estimated, cost the public $63 billion annually (the Brookings Institution estimated the cost at around $77 billion). These subsidies take four main forms—direct cash, tax preferences, credit guarantees, and benefits in kind.

The controversy over subsidiaries and price supports has not wholly revolved around a cleavage of interests between the urban and rural blocs, since both have been rent by factionalism. Some farmers favor government subsidies and controls to ensure at least 90 percent parity, while others would prefer a free or open market in the belief that the play of natural economic forces would eliminate surpluses and ensure incomes. Federal interventionists feel that a free market would ruin thousands of farms and precipitate a depression, while non-interventionists argue that if growers were free to make planting and harvesting decisions in response to projected supply and demand, entrepreneurial farming would be preserved and become more efficient. The less extreme prefer government intervention only to prevent a collapse of farm income below a level that would be decided by the secretary of agriculture.

Since World War II, the major parties have generally been at odds on the farm question, and the parity issue has kept presidential candidates from appearing as Tweedledum and Tweedledee when undivided by other issues. Since 1933, the Democratic party has favored high levels of assistance and broad control, despite the necessity of additional taxes that make food less "cheap" than it appears to be. The Republican party has traditionally favored the principles of an open market although, until 1973, it never went so far as espousing "getting the government out of agriculture."

Yet neither party has been consistent, nor has either been able to hold its congressmen to the party line. Opinions vary with the type of farming and farm products that predominate in political districts and who gets the subsidy money. For the Democratic congressmen who formed the core of the post-World War II high-support bloc, the rallying cry was usually "90 percent of parity"; even the conservative southern Democrats take the "liberal" position on behalf of their agricultural constituencies when it means more money, though they ideologically oppose federal intervention. Republican representatives from the Great Plains states often voted for high supports because of the problems of the wheat market. Under normal conditions, domestic demand for wheat is inelastic—that is, Americans do not eat more bread, cereal, and macaroni when their prices drop or less when their prices rise. Therefore, when prices are so low that wheat cannot be grown profitably enough, or perhaps only at a loss, a farmer would not plant; in effect, he would go out of business. If enough wheat farmers go out of business, there would be a wheat shortage that would drive up the cost of wheat products. So government subsidy programs moved in two directions. First, a price level was set for wheat by offering loans based on the support price to farmers, who put up their harvests as collateral. If the price of wheat dropped below the support level, the farmer gave the government his wheat instead of repaying the loan; if the price equaled or exceeded the price-support level, the farmer marketed his wheat and repaid the government. To hold down surpluses, however, the government established an eligibility requirement: the farmer was allowed to plant only so much acreage and had to set aside the rest, for which he was also paid a direct subsidy. Nationally, it constituted an acreage allotment based on past planting, anticipated yields, and the desired level for carryover reserves.

Even Democratic corn farmers, however, have opposed supports for corn so high that they might encourage growers of other commodities to switch to it and lead to surpluses which, in turn, would cause the government to impose production controls. Because corn growers can produce at low cost, so the argument went, they preferred to protect their market rather than obtaining what they believed would be a greater gain for only a short term. Stockmen of both political parties opposed high supports because, accompanied by output restrictions, they might raise feed costs; lack of restrictions might lead to surpluses, lower feed costs, increased meat output, and a price break. To the extent that processors and other middlemen involved themselves politically, they preferred to keep prices low and usually opposed supports.

Since mid-1972, though, the altered world food situation has brought us, if Secretary Butz is correct, to a "hinge point" in agricultural history; and there is no reason to believe that political realignments will not occur as they have in the past.

The Question of Food Reserves

To ensure against food shortages, agitation has mounted in favor of a global buffer stock, what the FAO termed a minimum food-security proposal. Boerma said;

> The object would be for developed countries to build up stocks sufficient for their domestic requirements and for regular commercial exports, and also, where appropriate, for food aid to meet crop failures or natural disasters in other parts of the world. In the case of developing countries, the idea would be for them to build up reserves which would, over the long run, make them progressively more self-reliant and capable of withstanding crop fluctuations.

The FAO director-general warned that a world food-trade war would affect the lesser-developed countries more seriously than the richer countries. Henry Kissinger, in his maiden speech to the UN General Assembly as secretary of state on September 24, 1973, disclosed what appeared to be a favorable American attitude:

> A world community must assure that all its people are fed.
> The growing threat to the world's food supply deserves the urgent attention of this Assembly. . . . We now face the prospect that—even with bumper crops—the world may not rebuild its seriously depleted reserves in this decade.
> No one country can cope with this problem.

He proposed a UN World Food Conference "to harness the efforts of all nations to meet the hunger and malnutrition resulting from natural disasters." The conference date was for November 1974.

But others in the administration were less enthusiastic, including the secretary of agriculture. They feared the proposal could once again bring about more government involvement in agriculture and add such expenses as storage. "We seek to keep the government out of agriculture and place decision-making in the hands of rational entrepreneurs," Butz said, "Government-held surpluses no longer hang over the markets as the sword of Damocles." Paarlberg, who said, "My view is kind of different from the secretary's," argued that it is "risky" not to keep government reserves. "The commendatory word is 'reserves,'" he said, "the derogatory word is 'surplus,'" and pointed out that, historically, excess stocks have more often than not become a welcome cushion. In the past forty-five years, the government has accumulated large stocks several times under price-support programs, and in disposing of the surplus every time, did so only once by destruction—and that, unfortunately occurred during the depression. We needed those stocks during the droughts of the 1930s, World War II and reconstruction, the Asian food crisis of the mid-1960s, and the 1972 shortfall in world production.

If the government does not hold stocks, can we rely on private traders to maintain sufficient reserves for emergencies? Or should we assume that importing countries can and will build reserves? Indeed, what if by some twist of events, American agricultural output fell below domestic needs—as it threatened in the case of wheat in the spring of 1974—and surpluses did not exist abroad, would we be prepared to accept food rationing below our accustomed eating standards and perhaps below the recommended nutritional allowances? Ultimately, the question arises: does the government really have a *food* policy or only a farm program?

In the aftermath of new food shortages and price inflation, congressional opinion began shifting toward the reserve idea, not only as an emergency buffer but as a means of restraining prices—the opposite of what it had been in the past when surpluses had been accumulated as a result of support floors under prices received by farmers. Senator Dick Clark (D.-Iowa), in December 1973, introduced a "food bank" bill, authorizing the government to maintain "maximum reserve levels" of 300 million bushels of wheat, 25 million tons of feed grains (at least 80 percent to be corn), and 100 million bushels of soybeans, and declared, "A domestic reserve . . . would help protect American consumers from shortages and help stabilize the price of meat and other commodities for farmers and consumer alike." The bill also provided for American participation in an international reserve arrangement, and a similar measure was introduced in the House.

The legislation reflected fears of many farmers and economists that lack of sizable grain and soybean reserves accumulated during years of bumper crops would mean scarcity and gyrating prices when harvests fall below demand. Farmers with both large —thousands of acres—and small spreads—15 acres—told me in almost identical words during the summer of 1973, "I would like $3.00 wheat, but not $4.00 and $5.00 wheat when it throws the market and economy out of kilter." An Iowan who is both a farmer and a banker, Charles Ehm, told the New York *Times* in late 1973, "The farmers around here are doing great now, but they are worried. You've got to have some reserves. You know the private interests are not going to do it. What if we have a corn blight again; what do you do with our livestock?" And a neighboring farmer answered, "We'd just have to go out of the hog business. You know what would happen to meat prices then!"

In September 1973, Paarlberg offered this advice:

> My counsel to the professor who teaches a farm policy course is that he throw away his old notes and start out anew. That's a good idea in most cases anyway, and this year is an especially good one in which to make the change.

Epilogue / The Future of Agriculture

Despite the futility of predicting accurately, most of us are drawn to the exercise as the moth is to the flame; at any rate, agriculturists engage in prediction for planning purposes. In 1967, Lester Brown forewarned of persistent world food shortages, but in the following year concluded that the projections were out of date, that tropical agricultural breakthroughs forced us "to recalculate the future." Five years later, several diverse and largely independent episodes coincided in a statistically highly improbable way, prompting Don Paarlberg to remark, "Our analytical supply-demand models seem quite incapable of explaining what has occurred, let alone predicting it in advance." 1973 was described as a "mixed up year," and once again a time of famines was in prospect.

While past statistical patterns can be helpful in projecting, mathematical models often overlook the possibility of wide swings in mass behavior. Neither census analysts nor authorities on public health foresaw the sudden, massive acceptance of inoculation programs by the poor and illiterate, nor did agriculturists foresee the widespread acceptance of new technologies and practices based on superior crop varieties by simple village farmers.

Diverse social variables—birth rates, employment opportunities, income levels, health measures, technological advances, input prices, ecological factors, political reactions, and life styles founded on individuals' expectations—will influence the future of agriculture and the behavior of the food-producing class.

I present three possible scenarios.

Future A: Malthusian Apocalypse

When Athelstan Spilhaus was president of the American Association for the Advancement of Science, he ventured, "People are not only the greatest polluters in the world; they are the greatest pollutants." Pollution is too much of anything for the environment to support; as Walt Kelly's Pogo commented, "We have met the ENEMY . . . an' HE IS US."

Future A assumes that people will not curtail their birthrate sufficiently to bring population into balance with supportive resources, and that per capita food production will continue to drop. The labor force, increasingly malnourished and ailing, will become less productive, the green revolution will falter, and such improvements as irrigation schemes will deteriorate as they did in Mesopotamia. Effective commercial demand for food will drop, and, under these circumstances, the great food exporters will be unable to support the massive dole necessary to avert widespread famine. The proportion of preschool children afflicted by malnutrition (already two-thirds) will expand, they will be retarded for life, and the world majority will be socially subhuman.

The efforts to disseminate information about family planning and distribute the means of birth control widely, which one might prefer to think of as national actions against a distant possibility, will prove to be a desperate reaction to a future that is already upon us. Population control as a societal concept or a national policy—particularly in its contemporary thrust, the suppression of birthrates—is a new topic to many people, who will fail to grasp its need. This is not simply because effective contraceptives have been perfected for many women only in the last two or three decades, but because modern economic theory has postulated the desirability of a growing population as a labor force, market outlet, political constituency, and, spoken of mutedly, military manpower—the policy of natalism. It influenced the mores of the poor additionally in some cultures because children support their parents in old age in lieu of other social security, for some, because children seem necessary for self-fulfillment, and often among them few children survived to adulthood. "Death control," the prolongation of many more lives through public health programs, has moved us irreversibly toward the Malthusian specter.

Among lower animals, population crashes occur not only during famines, but also when they can no longer withstand environmental stresses. The best known are the suicidal marches into the sea by lemmings; en route they are irritable and pugnacious, quick to start fights, and finally they go berserk in their death throes. When a Sika deer population became excessive on a Chesapeake island, a massive die-off occurred, after which their number stabilized at a lower level. Examination, especially of their endocrine glands, by John J. Christian of the Albert Einstein Medical Center in Philadelphia, found that the dead deer suffered endocrinological and other physiological abnormalities and a lowered resistance to disease, which he associated with stresses of overcrowding. Ethologist John B. Calhoun of the National Institute of Mental Health, in "super density" experiments with mice, found that as crowding increased, "individuals of both sexes early in life lose the capacity to become involved in those social relations necessary for the survival of the species." Another population specialist who has worked with the UN Development Program, Ulla Olin, suggests that certain human behavioral response "is a direct parallel to animal behavior," that under stress "we have a tendency . . . to revert to instinctual behavior, which is governed by the 'animal' part of the brain," and that "population groups under extreme pressure become paranoid," foreseeing a doomsday.

During the 1960s, population pressures, specifically the need for food and livelihood, prompted many El Salvadorians, whose country is the densest in Latin America, to settle farmland in Honduras—until the Hondurans felt that the colonizing was jeopardizing their welfare. Emotions were enflamed when Honduras expelled about 75,000 settlers, and because of an incident involving the two nationalities on a sportsfield, the ensuing conflict was called the "soccer war." We will learn that it was a curtain-raiser for population wars to come, whose objectives will be living space and food supplies.

In Future A, the population over much of the world will be increasingly debilitated, diseased, aberrant, and violent. As massive agricultural breakdowns occur, the United States will finally have to apply triage in its food diplomacy; and there will be the touchy question of how much international dole the American people will be willing to pay for. Beyond that, farming will be carried out only to the extent of supplying those who can afford to buy commodities, the anxiety over surpluses will be chronic in this country, and billions will be spent to support target prices while keeping consumer food costs low enough to prevent serious political discontent. Globally we will be confronted with a situation not dissimilar to the domestic situation during the Great Depression when, despite hunger, we destroyed surpluses rather than subsidize the costs of distributing them.

Riots, revolution, and wars will be frequent—another Dark Age affecting most of the world—and it is dubious that the advanced countries will be able to immunize themselves. With hundreds of millions increasingly short of food, the United States will be more and more envied for its bounties. However much the teeming under classes will need additional *Lebensraum*, their mass leaders will be first of all interested in ensuring food supplies. Responsible governments will seek to negotiate; if they fail, demogogic leaders will seize control, converting their nations into military threats. The United States will contribute aid prophylactically, that is, to block a clear and present threat rather than for humanitarian reasons.

To the extent that population crashes occur, the danger of invasions by aggressive hordes, fighting suicidally if need be, will diminish. But in their wake will come epidemics imperiling healthy populaces. It will be the Age of Eco-catastrophe.

When I discussed the prospects of famine during the world food panic of the mid-1960s with Russell G. Schwandt, a successful farmer and then Minnesota commissioner of agriculture, he gave a typically American response. "Mass famines won't happen," he said, "because we won't let them." It is an article of faith that a Malthusian apocalypse will not come to pass.

Future B: Utopian Panaceas

Because we have seen Leonardo da Vinci's man-carrying balloons, Jules Verne's *Nautilus* submarine, and Buck Rogers' spaceships become realities, we tend to regard predictions of science-fiction writers and professional futurists credulously. Scientists are raising micro-organisms on petroleum for protein, converting gas escaping from wells into fuel, engineering new plants, synthesizing meats, and de-salinating water. Each of these seems like a panacea for some problem; Future B assumes that new technologies and practices will resolve the new world food shortage, restore diminished eating standards, stabilize prices, and most importantly, be the basis for population control. Societies would be governed along lines suggested by the technocracy movement of the 1930s, with control of industrial resources, reform of financial institutions, and reorganization of the social system based on the developments of scientists, technologists, and engineers.

Spaceships with their controlled environments will become food factories, and deserts and other wastelands will produce harvests as foreseen by a plan proposed by Glenn T. Seaborg in 1967 when he was chairman of the U.S. Atomic Energy Commission. Large, centrally managed farming complexes, called *nuplexes*, will be serviced by nuclear-powered de-salination plants and pumping stations, fertilizer and pesticide factories, and machine shops; each will feed up to 5 million persons, and support oasis-like habitats where people cannot now live.

The genetic engineering of new crops will raise nutritional quality, especially of the low-protein staples, and breed-in resistance to many more diseases and pests, tolerance to more weather variations, greater responsiveness to fertilizer, and better marketing properties. The proportion of fruit to leaf and stem will be much greater; gigantism, already an attribute of domesticated plants compared to their wild ancestors, will be much more observable; yet the plants themselves will often be much shorter

—Lilliputian in appearance—to facilitate harvesting, as so many fruit trees and the miracle grains already are.

The two most significant breakthroughs will be creating plants that will "harvest the sun" much more efficiently and alter nitrogen-fixing bacteria so that they will collaborate with non-legumes, mainly the cereal grasses. These increased capabilities will greatly increase the biological yield potential of plants with the above improvements. Much of this progress will be due to the International Biological Program Gene Pools Committee, founded in 1972, to reverse the genetic erosion of the mid-twentieth century and preserve in germ plasm "banks" most of the genetic stock accumulated over the past ten millennia.

In pest control, pheromones will be synthesized, new chemicals will be species-specific, mass birth control for more attackers will be perfected, and predacious beneficials will be relied on more. Pest-control specialists will monitor fields and recommend the integration of approaches; while the ideal of organic farmers will not be reached, many of their practices will be integrated, displacing pesticidal abuses.

With the genes of present-day "exotics," livestock breeders will improve some of our traditional animals, while in other instances the exotics themselves will become more important or be cross-bred to create new generations of exotics. Some animals, such as rabbits and bison, no longer eaten by many people, will assume more economic importance; and more animals will be slaughtered in the wild for commercial use under carefully guided game-management concepts, just as fish are harvested in the open seas.

Satellites and electronic sounders will teach us more about the spawning and migratory patterns of fish, their population dynamics, and the essentials of their food chains; with this knowledge we will take larger catches without depleting fisheries. More varieties will be eaten. Aquaculture will expand phenomenally in the United States, and cultured fish will be genetically improved. Some waters will be made more productive by the pumping of water rich in mineral nutrients from great depths that are "biological deserts."

We will return to the use of more manure and compost, and wastes will also be used as a culture medium for fertilizers. One of the greatest mechanical developments will be a machine that can fix nitrogen from the air for plant utilization; it will use solar radiation for energy, as will other farm equipment and buildings. Farm machinery will operate with more precision, safety, and comfort; it will be more automated; and computers will be used extensively for marketing decisions.

Farmers will be so specialized that the vocation will be glamorized; students will train and compete for available farmsteads, where they will have unusual managerial independence. The new technologies, including superior weather forecasting, will make farming life less hazardous and outdoor life pastoral.

Future C: Brave New World

Each major agricultural advance has transformed food production with great social impact; a hunter or a forager needed about 12 square miles to sustain himself, whereas the same area under cultivation can support 6,000 or more persons. The increased food-producing capability combined with labor needs of the industrial revolution led to greatly increased populations and natalist policies. Yet no agricultural advance completely displaced earlier methods—self-propelled tractors still draw plows—and each has caused new problems. There have been no panaceas. Scenario C assumes that many of the advances of the utopian future will occur, but however ameliorative, they will not prevent many misfortunes.

The tragedies that could lead to eco-catastrophe will take place —Sehal and Calcutta, for example, are observable as possible harbingers—but under this scenario, they will cause us to heed the advice of the Club of Rome study, *The Limits to Growth*;

If the present growth trends in world population, industrialization, pollution, food production, and resource depletion continue unchanged, the limits to growth on this planet will be reached sometime within the next one hundred years. The most probable result will be a rather sudden and uncontrollable decline in both population and industrial capacity.

It is possible to alter these growth trends and to establish a condition of ecological and economic stability that is sustainable far into the future.

We will reorient our criteria of development and progress, creating a new social ethic, which, however, we will live up to imperfectly.

That we have begun our reorientation is suggested in the first instance by recent vital statistics; the demographers appear to have guessed wrong again. Projecting population size is especially risky. Early in this century, demographers warned of a slowdown in population growth that would jeopardize economic progress, but after World War II birthrates began to climb. Demographers then predicted that the population would exceed 3 billion by the end of this century, straining the carrying capacity of the earth. This level, however, was surpassed during the mid-1960s, nearly forty years before the projections of little more than a decade earlier. UN demographers now project a world population between 5 billion and 7 billion for the year 2000, and American government spokesmen use this projection without dissent.

In 1970, demographers projected that the United States would have a high of 321 million or a low of 266 million people by the end of this century; the 1970 census showed the population of the United States at 205 million. A zero-population growth rate, much less a negative one, was not anticipated for many years because the very large postwar generation had reached prime reproductive age and because poor women were not expected to be efficient contraceptors until better technology was invented and their motivation stimulated.

In 1972 the American birthrate fell to, or perhaps slightly below, replacement level. Many of the new generation of middle-class couples were decidedly against bearing more than one or two children; increasing numbers wanted none. More surprising was the sharp drop in the birthrate among the poor, albeit they still had more children than the well-to-do. And more astonishing were unexplained drops in birthrates in some parts of India and the Caribbean. In China, more women now take oral contraceptives than in any other country—10 to 15 percent of eligibles—and Peking is believed by some authorities to be carrying out the most effective family-planning program in the world. In Saint

Lucia in the West Indies, though, family-planning workers told me, "We know our birthrate is falling, but we don't know why. It is not because of our program; it is too new."

Anti-natalist population control had been practiced successfully long before modern contraceptives were designed. Tribal societies reduced population growth when food supplies became limited; and in Japan from 1600 to 1850, the society maintained a zero-population-growth rate through the economic leverages of the dowry and inheritance customs. During the interwar period, the French government found that its incentives failed to bring about a desired increase in births; and the Soviet Union, with its different techniques of governing, could not increase family size in the European region of the country. It is significant that the Great Depression was characterized in the United States by a sharp decline in birthrates, but better times after the war witnessed the "baby boom." As the economy and much of the environment went out of kilter in the early 1970s, inflation, pollution, decline of services, rising unemployment, and escalating incidence of crimes against person and dwelling caused the birthrate to fall below that of the depression level.

Our brave new world will not expect automatic adoption of new contraceptive technologies and practices but will recognize that the underprivileged are afraid of risking the unknown; they live, as Roger Revelle puts it, "on the edge of the knife"—the reason why anemia-prone Indian women fled from the IUD when it increased menstrual bleeding. We will seek "points of entry" into behavior patterns for the purpose of persuading couples that birth control will move them further from the edge. The woman who has one more baby than she wants is more receptive to birth-control advice postpartum, especially when counseled by a woman successfully using a birth-control method; but if she does not begin then, she despairs after having several more births than she desired. Traditional methods, used en masse, slow birthrates, usually without side effects, and they will be offered as alternatives— the condom, coitus interruptus, and the rhythm method. Abortion will be made available to poor women at little or no cost as a woman's right. Institutionalizing the two-child family as a status symbol will encourage progressively men and women to adopt more effective contraceptive methods—more men will certainly be vasectomized, and more women sterilized with simpler procedures.

Declines in birthrates have not come soon enough to prevent localized and perhaps regional famine, and some population crashes will occur before living conditions are improved in the Third World cities and countryside. Particularly important will be the creation of more jobs, which will necessitate more labor-intensive approaches, specifically including farm mechanization. The brave new world will be acutely nutrition-conscious, and a sound diet will be human right and the basis of national food policies. We will rely on an international early-warning system to avert famines on humanitarian ground when they threaten.

Of the various prospects in the idealized future, genetic engineering probably holds more agricultural promise than any other. Yields will be higher, and most people will obtain more protein from staples. But they will bring with them more pest problems. Breakthroughs will change farming in many ways, but they will not redirect farming as radically as at times in the past; in some cases farmers will revert to abandoned practices, such as no-till or modified tillage and more manuring and composting. Monoculturing will be tempered through rotation and interplanting, chemicals will be used more discriminately, and water will be handled as a more precious commodity.

Farm machines will combine more services than those we have today, and may not increase so much in power as in degree of precision; more exact seeding will be needed for varieties genetically engineered to have a higher conversion index in using solar radiation, for example. The energy crisis will force manufacturers to produce machinery that either uses fossil fuel more efficiently or draws on other sources. Solar power may prove unable to move machinery fast enough to be economic, and batteries are a more likely source of power. Corn and some low-grade food crops are sources of an alcohol that is a high-grade fuel, and they will be utilized more extensively. Feedlot wastes will be recycled to produce both energy and feed.

Enclosed environments will become the major domestic food source for some arid areas, but open fields will remain the source of the grains. The ambitious nuplex approach will be adapted for some areas, but nuclear power is likely to be used more frequently for pumping the great aquifiers than for de-salination.

The new social accounting will take into special consideration ecological costs in agriculture, since damage to the agro-ecosystem affects the farmer financially. Similarly, the value of water-conservation measures such as protection or improvement of watersheds will be computed. Countering genetic erosion will be a major goal, and we will follow the advice of plant ecologist J. R. Harlan:

> Already a remarkable part of the human diet is supplied by four cereals: wheat, rice, maize, and sorghum. Imagine, if you can, the scope of the disaster if one of these should fail, if some new and virulent disease should appear with which we are unable to cope in time. Surely it is imperative that we know all that we possibly can about all of the germ plasm within genetic reach in our major food plants.
>
> Time and again we have reached out into the wild relatives of our crops to exploit a gene or a few genes for resistance to disease. Some crops have virtually been saved from discard by the process.

The National Seed Laboratory will have thousands more samples, and it will be emulated in all major regions of the world; we will see the greatest seed exchanges since the colonizing of the New World. Other scientific conservation work will probably include extending storage life of seeds.

New attitudes will prevail toward surpluses, and international machinery will exist for maintaining buffer stocks of food.

Agriculture will rely heavily on the Earth Resources Technology Satellite program and more advanced weather satellite systems. Photos from space will replace many time-consuming and expensive ground surveys of pest populations and detect threats of soil erosion. Meteorologists will be better able to predict episodic climate changes, and weather forecasts reliable for several weeks will make it possible for farmers to time plantings and, to some extent, harvesting and financing. A key component of the Earthwatch system will be the supercomputer center, which will use a computer now under development that promises to be ten times more powerful than any existing.

The overriding political-economic question of the last quarter of the century will be, Who will control agriculture? Will dominant firms, like holding corporations, keep the farmer in bondage under a contract system? Or will yeoman leading the pastoral life constitute our food-producing class? Under Scenario C, neither; the first is likely under Future A, the second under Future B. Considerable entrepreneurship will be left, based on the foreknowledge that the farmer, as an ecologist, needs latitude in making his decisions. But farmers will no longer be able to operate with individual independence; the marketing forces will be too powerful for them to compete in that fashion. In contract food production, some form of collective bargaining for farmers will evolve.

Agriculturists have made some projections for the year 1985, based on present trends. They foresee 2.1 million farms remaining, but more of them will gross $20,000 or more—about 830,000 compared with 618,00 in 1971; significantly, this group will produce 90 percent of our harvests. About 168,000 farms will sell $100,000 worth of commodities or more, and they will number 168,000 compared with 63,000 in 1971. Their share of the total sales is projected at 60 percent, which actually is a little below their 1971 share of two-thirds. About 2 percent of the population will produce food and fiber for the country compared with 4 percent now. Farmers will specialize to a greater degree, though not necessarily in only one crop; multiple cropping will lead to a limited diversification. Farmers will be much more heavily capitalized and recognized as businessmen with easier access to credit; and they will contract out more work, especially for customized harvesting with owner-operated and serviced machinery.

If the government remains out of much of agriculture, the fatuousness of the phrase "Get the government out of agriculture" will be fully revealed. It is more important to keep at least basic food producers in business than to support a giant aircraft manufacturer—though this assistance may not extend to all farmers. If the wheat economy is threatened by across-the-board injury to wheat growers, the government will have stand-by plans to intervene to ensure a harvest.

It will be recognized that a "farm lobby" has replaced the "farm bloc"; its influence will not be based on the number of votes it can turn out from its membership, but on the threat of decreased food supplies for the populace—something comparable to today's petroleum lobby. Farm programs will be oriented toward supply maintenance.

Trends leading into a brave new world are already established: environmentalism, consumerism, and nostalgia—in sum, humanism. Each is rooted in reaction against the failure to account for social costs in exploiting technologies and resources—including human—and against the discordance we have caused in nature. Confidence that we will create our brave new world assumes that we have yet to go beyond the point of no return in disrupting our environment, however rapidly we may be approaching it, and that we have the will and resourcefulness to change course, while resisting the Lorelei appeal of panaceas. Most of us will be willing to settle for less in material emoluments and to draw more upon our inner strengths. Man and woman will prevail, not by the conquest of nature, but by living harmoniously as another member of nature's realm. It will not be an issue of feast or famine, but of self-fulfillment reasonably in-between.

Index

Acetylcholine, 181–182
Adams Act, 300
Additives in foods, 194–195
Agribusiness Accountability Project,
287
Agricultural Adjustment Acts,
306–307
Agricultural colleges, 299–301
Agricultural experiment stations,
founding of, 296–300
Agricultural Marketing Act (1929),
306
Agricultural Marketing Act (1937),
307
Agricultural Museum, 270
Agricultural Research, 110
Agricultural revolution, 46
Agricultural Weather Wire Service,
93
Agriculture
as intervention in environment,
134–138
definitions of, 264
energy used in, 127–131

future of, 335–347
government intervention in,
295–301, 305–331
history of, 44–46, 264–270
mechanization of, 122–126
modern American, 270–284
New Deal measures in, 306–308
no-till, 126–127
pollution by, 146–150
pollution of, 144
Agriculture, U.S. Department of. *See*
U.S. Department of Agriculture
Agriculture and Consumer Protection
Act of 1973, 309, 322–323, 324
Agroclimatic regions, 81
Albright, Joseph, 28
Alkhinov, Vladimir, 37
Alekseeva, I. A., 163
Alfalfa, 47–48, 214–215
Algae, edible, 258–260
Alluvial soils, 71 (table), 72 (table),
77, 78
Alpha-tocopherol (vitamin E),
180–181

Altschul, Aaron, 159, 169
American Academy of Arts and
    Sciences, 270
American Farm Bureau Federation,
    293
American Farmer, 270
American Nutritional Survey (1970),
    171–172
American Philosophical Society, 270
Andrus, Leonard, 122
Anemia, 181–182
Aneurine (thiamin), 173–174
Angus, Thomas A., 109–110, 119
Animal-Plant Health Inspection
    Service, 98
Ants, driver (army), 101, 143
Aphids, grain sorghum attacked by,
    51–52
Apples, 227
Appleseed, Johnny, 227, 269
Aquaculture, 253–258
Aquatic plants, 258–260
Aqueducts, Roman, 84
Aquifers (*see also* Underground
    water; Water table)
    defined, 64
    excessive "mining" of, 141
    in India, 87
    levels of, lowered by
        channelization, 142
    rainfall drained off by, 83
    in Sahara Desert, 87
Arable land, 61–62
    defined, 61
Arsenic as insecticide, 102
Ascorbic acid (vitamin C), 177–179
Association of American Agricultural
    Colleges and Experiment Stations,
    300
Association of Land-Grant Colleges
    and Universities, 300
Athwal, Dilbagh S., 50
Atomic Energy Commission, and
    Hudson River pollution, 253
Atwater, Wilbur Olin, 70
Auxin, 48

Babcock, Stephen M., 248
Baby foods, excessive nitrate content
    of, 147
Bacon, defined, 243
Bacon, R. M., 117
Bacteria
    in insect control, 111
    role of, in nitrogen fixation, 67–69
    in soil, 67–69
Bananas, 229
Banks for Cooperatives, 303
Barbed wire, invention of, 270
Barber, Frank, 199
Barkley, Alben W., 310
Barley, 208–209
Barron's, 20
Beadle, George, 204
Beale, William James, 56
Beans, types of, 219 (*see also*
    Soybeans)
Beef, 234
    consumption, 232
    production, 237–240 (*see also*
    Cattle)
Beet sugar, 223–224
Benedict, Harris M., 145
Benedict, Murray, 308, 309
Benson, Ezra Taft, 311, 314–315
Beriberi, 173–175
Berries, 228–229
Bible, food laws in, 190
Binns, Wayne, 100
Biosphere, 134–136
    defined, 134
    element in soil genesis, 62
Birds
    control of insects by, 117–118
    as pests, 99–100
Birthrate since World War II,
    342–343
Blackwater River, 142
Blindness caused by Vitamin A
    deficiency, 171
Boerma, 38, 329
Bog soils, 77
Boll weevil, 103–104

Bollworm, 104, 111
Bontius, Jacobus, 173
Borlaug, Norman E., 45, 49
Brain sparing, 162
Brannan, Charles F., 309
Brannan Plan, 309–310
Breakfast cereals, 196
Breed, Bill, 141
Brezhnev, Leonid, 27, 28
Briggs, Porter, 256
Brown Chestnut soils, 78
Brown, Lester R., 21, 335
Brown Podzolic soils, 77
Brown soils, 71 (table), 72 (table), 77, 78
Bryson, Reid, 90
Buchwald, Art, 305
Buddhism, food laws in, 191
Budworm, 104, 105
Burr, George O., 167
Burr, M. M., 167
Butter, consumption of, 233, 249
Butterworth, C. E., 157
Butz, Earl L., 318–319, 321–322, 330

Cabbage looper, 111–112, 116
Calcium
    excess of, 187
    in nutrition, 184
California State Water Project, 86
Caltagirone, Leopoldo E., 104
Campbell, Hardy Webster, 87
Cane sugar, 223
Cannibalism, 189
Can We Solve the Farm Problem?, 308
Capillary water, 63
Capper-Ketcham Act, 300–301
Carbohydrates, 167
Carey Act (1894), 299
Carlson, Peter S., 55
Carrageen, 259–260
Carson, Rachel, 105
Carver, George Washington, 211, 220

Casal, Gaspar, 172
Cassava, 219–220
Catfish Farmer and World Aquaculture News, 256
Catfish farming, 256–257
Cattle, 235–242
Cattle rustling, 245
Cereal grains, 200–208
Chandrasekhar, Sripati, 155
Channelization of streams, 142
Chapman, John (Johnny Appleseed), 227, 269
Chavez, Cesar, 277
Cheese, 249–250
Chemical reactions in soil, effect of temperature on, 65
Chernozem, 71 (table), 72 (table), 77, 78
Chestnut soils, 72–73 (table), 77, 78
Chicken consumption of, 232
Chickens, 235, 245–246 (*see also* Poultry)
Chick pellagra, 175
Choline, 181–182
Chow, Bacon F., 161, 164
Christenson, Leo, 309–310
Christian, John J., 337
Citrus fruits, 226–227
Clark, Dick, 331
Clausen, Hjalmer, 243
Clay, 63, 64, 65, 66
Clement, Roland C., 117–118
Climate, 79–91
    cyclical changes in, 89–91
    defined, 81
    in soil genesis, 62
Climax environment, 134
Cloud seeding, 95
Cobalt in nutrition, 186
Coconuts, 221
Cod liver oil, 180
Coindet, Jean François, 185
Colorado River, diversion of water from, 140
Columella, 59
Colwell, Robert N., 152

Combines, 124
Commodity Credit Corporation, 307
Commoner, Barry, 135–136, 146–147, 148
Compacting of soil, 65
Composting, 69
Confinement approach to husbandry, 236–237
Conservation, soil, 297–298
    in Dust Bowl, 137–138
    soil bank, 312–314
Consumer Reports, 196
Containerization as means of pest control, 102
Convenience foods, 193–194, 195–196
Cool-temperate boreal zone, 79, 80
Cool-temperate zone, 79–80
Cooperative extension agents, 296
Cooperative marketing, 306
Cooperatives, farm, 293
Coordinating Research Council, 145
Copper in nutrition, 186, 187
Corn, 203–205
    breeding, 204–205
    drought-resistant, 51
    high-lysine, 52–54, 205
    history of, 203–204
    roots, length of, 47
    yield, 205
Corn belt, 198
Corn-leaf blight, 23
Corn-soybean belt, 199, 209
Corporate farms, 282–285
    definition, 283–284
Cotton, effect of pesticides on, 103–104
Cottonseed, 221, 222
Cotton wilt, 51
Cottony cushion, 106–107
Council on Environmental Quality, 146
Courtois, Bernard, 185
Cox, Archibald, 326
Cramer, H. H., 56
Cream, consumption of, 233
Credit for farmers, 301–304

Crickets, 98
Critchfield, Richard, 33
Crop belts, 197–199
Crop rotation, 46, 136, 270
Cyanocobalamin (vitamin B_{12}), 177
Cycles of change in climate, 89–91

Dairying, 246–250
Dairy products, 231
    consumption of, 247
    price supports and import quotas on, 326
Dakouré, Antoine, 29–30
Davy, Sir Humphrey, 60
Day, length of, and plant growth, 82
DDT, 102–105
    mutants resistant to, 103–105
DeBach, Paul, 118
Deciduous fruits, 227–229
Declaration of Santiago, 252
Deere, John, 122, 270
Demotion, 106
Desalination of water, 88–89, 299
Desert Land Act of 1877, 299
Deserts, 65
Desert soils, 71 (table), 73, (table), 78
DeVorkin, Donald B., 93–94
Dew, 83
Diet, balanced, 164–168
Diethylstilbestrol (DES), 239
Dokuchaev, V. V., 60
Domestication of animals, 233–234
Donaldson, Lauren R., 258
Drought, 25, 32, 81
    in Asia (1966–67), 19
    cycles in, 89
    in eighteenth-century France, 9
    in India, 14
    of 1934–36, 17, 136–137, 298
    in the Sahel, 29–30
Drugs, used in cattle breeding, 241
Dryland farming, 87
Dubos, René, 46, 131, 135
Ducks, 246

Dulmage, Howard T., 110
Dumas, J. B. A., 169
Dumont. René, 155
Dust Bowl, 17, 137–138
Dwarf fruit trees, 225

Eagles as pests, 99–100
Earth Resources technology satellite,
    150–151
Earthwatch, 150–152
Eating habits. *See* Food habits
Ecology, defined, 134
Education, agricultural, 299–301
Eggs, 231, 232–233
Ehm, Charles, 331
Ehrlich, Paul R., 20
Eijkman, Christian, 174
Eisenhower, Dwight D., 310–315
Electrolytes in nutrition, 186
Ellsworth, Henry L., 295
Emergency Committee to Save
    America's Resources, 252
Energy
    agricultural use of, 127–131
    nutritional, main sources of,
        167–168
Energy crisis, 34
Environment, defined, 134
Evapotranspiration, 65, 83
Excrement as fertilizer, 46 (*see also*
    Manure)
Excreta, animal, pollution by, 146
Extension agents, 296

Face fly, 107–198
Falcon, Louis A., 119
Family farm
    defined, 282–283
    racial aspect, 278
Famine, 32
    in Africa, 15–16
    in Britain, 9–10

in China, 13–14
in Egypt, 6
"ergot," 8
in France, 8–9
in Germany, 10–11
history of, 6–18
in India, 14, 33–34
in Ireland, 10
in Latin America, 14–15
during Middle Ages, 7–8
in North America, 17
in Roman Empire, 6–7
in Russia, 11–13
specific, 155
Famine in Soviet Russia, 1919–1923,
    The, 12
Famine 1975! America's Decision:
    Who Will Survive?, 20
Farm Bloc, 292–293
Farm co-operatives, 293
Farm Credit System, 303
Farmers as businessmen, 285–287
Farmers Home Administration, 303
Farmers' organizations, 291–295
Farmers Union, 290, 294, 310
Farm incomes, 275 (table), 276
    (table), 278–282, 289–290
    parity in: *See* Parity
Farming (*See also* Agriculture)
    part-time, 278
Farm loans, 301–304, 328
Farm mortgage banks, 302
Farm production regions, 199
Farms
    black-owned, 278
    collective, 286
    commercial, 286
    corporate, 286
    mechanization on, 124–125,
        276–278, 288
    size of, 271–276, 288–289
    subdivided for subsidy purposes,
        317–318
Farm subsidies, 307–308, 317–319,
    324, 329
    hidden, 324–325

Farm surpluses, 310–312, 316
  as reserves for shortages, 329–331
Farm Workers Union, 277
Fats, 167–168
  unsaturated, in fish, 250
Federal Farm Board, 306
Federal Farm Loan Act, 302
Federal Intermediate Credit Banks, 303
Federal Land Banks, 303
Feedlots, 236, 237
  pollution by, 149–150
Fertile Crescent, 265
Fertility of soil, defined, 62
Fertilizer, 69–70
  energy used in producing, 128
  excessive use of, 146–147
  excrement, 46
  manure, 130, 131
  nitrogen, interference of with symbiotic fixation, 68
  pollution by, 146–149
Fetal sparing, 161
Findley, Paul, 318
Fish, used in insect control, 108
Fisher, H. H., 12
Fisheries, 30–32, 250–258
Flaxseed, 222
Flood plains, farming on, 45–46
Floods, 32, 81
  in Mississippi valley, 24, 26
Flying piranha, 113–114
Folacin (folic acid), 176–177
Food Additive Amendment (1958), 195
Food and Drug Administration (FDA), 194–195
  vitamin dosage, regulations on, 170–171, 172
Food gathering, 44, 220
Food habits, 188–194
  American, 193–194
  and health, 189–190
  irrational group prejudices in, 192–193
Food prices and wages, 289–290

Foods
  additives in, 194–195
  considered medicinal, aphrodisical, or divine, 190–191
  convenience, 193–194, 195–196
  fortification of, 195
  inflation in price of, 319–320
  processing of, 194–195
  smuggling of, 36–37
  as a weapon in warfare, 4–6
Food-security proposal, 329–331
Ford, Henry, Sr., 211
Foreign Affairs, 23
Fortune, 90, 141
Fraser, H., 174–175
Freeman, Orville L., 19
Free Soil Party, 297
Froelich, John, 123
Fruit, 225–229
  defined, 200
Fruit moths, 101
Fuels, agricultural use of, 127–131
Funk, Casimir, 170
Fye, Paul M., 250

Gaines wheat, 50
Gast, Robert, 149
Gelperin, Abraham, 148
Genetic engineering in acquaculture, 258
Genetic improvement in plants, 52–56
George-Deen Act, 301
Gigantism in plants, developing, 50
Glenn Canyon Dam, 140
Goetsch, Ferdinand, 43–44
Goiter, 185–186
Goldberger, Joseph, 173
Goodrich, Philip, 149
Good Roads Act, 300
Gore, Albert, 310
Gossypol, 222
Guano, 70
Grafting, in fruit growing, 56
Grain, purchase of U.S. stocks by Soviet Union, 27, 28

Grain sorghum, 198, 207–208
   aphid attack on, 51–52
Grange, the 292, 293, 294
Grapefruit, 226
Grapes, 228–229
Grasshoppers, 98
Gray-brown Podzolic soils, 72 (table), 77
Gray Desert soils, 78
Grayson, C. Jackson, 319
Greenbugs. *See* Aphids
Greenhouse effect, 91
Greenhouses, 131–133
Green revolution, 22, 23, 32–39
Grijns, Gerrit, 174
Grimm, Wendelin, 215
Ground-water Podzol, 73 (table), 77
Grosser, Morton, 109, 118
Gyorgy, Paul, 164
Gypsy moth, 101

Hadley, Noah, 283
Haeger, Knut, 181
Hagan, Ken, 100
Hail, 83
Half Bog soils, 73 (table), 77
Hamilton, Gene, 320
Hariot, Thomas, 203
Harlan, J. R., 345
Harris, Marshall, 287
Hart, C. W., 123
Harvesting, mechanized, 124–125
Hatch Act, 300
Hathaway, Dale, 294
Hay, 214–215
Heat from irrigation water, pollution by, 146
Heimpel, 112
Helmont, Jon Baptiste Van, 59
Heredity, laws of, 49
Hesiod, 59
Hilgard, E. W., 61
Hill, F. F., 39

Hippocrates, 189, 190
Hoffer, Abram, 170, 175–176
Hoffmaster, Richard, 111–112
Hogs, 238, 242–244
Hollings, Ernest F., 159
Homestead Act, 235–236, 297
Honey, 225
Hoover Dam, 86, 140
Hopkins, Frederick Gowland, 169–170
Hopper, W. David, 264
Horan, F. E., 210
Horizons in soil, 62
Hormones
   in cattle feed banned, 239
   in pest control, 115–116
Huffaker, Carl, 120
Hughes, John T., 255
Humphrey, Arthur, 150
Humphrey, Hubert H., 19
Humus, 66
Hungry Future, The, 155
Hunting and fishing, 44
Hurricanes
   Agnes, 24, 25
   Camille, 93
Husbandry, 233–246
Hussey, Obed, 124
Huxley, Thomas, 251
Hydrocarbon insecticides, 102–106
Hydrodynamic numerical modeling, 92
Hydroponics, 131

Ice cream, consumption of, 233
Ickes, Harold, 235
Idler, I. R., 254
Illinois Pollution Control Board, 148
Immunity
   of plants, to pests, 51–52
Imperial Dam, 140
Infant methemoglobinemia, 148
Inositol, 182
Insect growth regulation, 115–116

Insecticides *(see also* Pesticides)
    Hydrocarbon, 102–106
    interference with control by
        natural pathogens, 109–110
Insect Pest Act (1902), 101
Insects
    beneficial, 103, 143–144
    control of, by pathogenic
        organisms, 109–112
    mutants resistant to insecticides,
        103–104
    nutritional requirements, 100–101
    as pests, 96–98, 101
Insolation, quality of, and plant
    growth, 82
Inspection as means of pest control,
    102
International Biological Program
    Gene Pools Committee, 340
International Brotherhood of
    Teamsters, 277
International Maize and Wheat
    Improvement Center, 54
International Water Development
    Year, 89
Iodine, 185–186
Irish moss, 259–260
Iron in nutrition, 182–184
Irrigation
    amount of water used for, 84
    cooperative, by Mormons, 85
    early systems of, 84–85
    questions involved in, 85
    subsidized, 325
    weather modified by, 94

Jackson, Henry M., 139
Jacob, E. H., 45, 200
Jaenke, E. A., 303
Japanese beetle, 110
Jaques, R. P., 112
Jefferson, Thomas, 121, 217
Jenkins, B. Charles, 54–55
Johnson, V. A., 53

Kaplanskaya-Raiskaya, S. I., 163
Kapper, Arthur, 292
Kariba, Lake, 142
Kastenmeier, Robert W., 325
Kellner, Irwin, 31
Kellog, Charles E., 58, 136–137
Kennedy, John F., 315–316
Kenyon, W. S., 292
Keratomalacia, 171
Kissinger, Henry, 329–330
Klamath weed, 108
Knapp, Seaman, 296
Knipling, Edward F., 113–114, 119
Koebele, Albert, 107
Kok, Bessel, 48
Konnerup, Nels, 98
Kwashiorkor, 168–169, 188–189

Ladybird beetle (ladybug), 103, 107
Lamb, 232, 244
Lamb, Hubert, 90
Land use, 138–139
    satellite photos used in planning,
        151
Lane, John, 122
Lard, 243
Law of the Sea Conference (1974),
    252
Leaching, 65
Legumes, 67–68 *(see also* Soybeans)
Lemmings, 337
Lettuce, 215, 218
Liebig, Justus von, 60–61
Lime, 60, 69, 70
Limits to Growth, The, 341–342
Lincecum, Gideon, 43
Lindbergh, Jon, 258
Ling, Shao-wen, 256
Lithosol, 71 (table), 74 (table), 77, 78
Livestock production, mechanization
    in, 125
Lobsters, grown by aquaculture, 255
Locust bird as pest, 99
Locusts, 97–98

Lomonosov, M. V., 60
Lunin, Nikolai, 169

McCabe, Robert A., 115
McCollum, Elmer V., 170
McCormick, Cyrus H., 124
McNamara, Robert S., 33
McNary-Haugen, Bill, 306
McQuigg, James, 90
Macrofloratin soil, 67
Macro-nutrients, 164–165
  in soil, 67
Magnesium in nutrition, 186
Maladjustment, social, 136–137
Malathion, 106
Malcolm X, 5
Malleanby, Kenneth, 146
Malnutrition
  among adolescents, 156
  effect of, on brain, 162–163
  in experimental rats and mice,
    161–162
  in infancy and childhood, 162–164
  and infection, 187–188
  in pregnancy, 161–162
  in U.S., 155–158
  among the well-to-do, 155–156
Malnutritional dwarfism, 155
Malone, Thomas F., 95
Manganese in nutrition, 186
Manioc, 219
Manure, animal, 130
  green, 131
  recycling of, 150, 242
Maple sugar, 225
Marasmus, 168
Margarine, 249
Mariculture, 253–258
Marine, David, 185
Market gardening, early, 265, 266
Marl, use of in fertilizing wastelands,
  69–70
Mayer, Jean, 156
Mead, Bill O., 36

Mead, Lake, 86, 140
Meany, George, 277
Meat, 231–246
Mechanization of farming, 124–125,
  276–278, 288
Megavitamin therapy, 170
Megovolastic anemia, 176–177
Mendel, Gregor, 49
Mercury found in fish, 252–253
Mertz, Edwin T., 52, 53
Mestranol, 115
Methyl Parathion. *See* Parathion
Mexico, water treaty with, 140, 299
Micro-climates, 141–143
Microflora, in soil, 67
Micro-nutrients, 165
  in soil, 67
Micro-organisms
  pathogenic, in pest control, 109–112
  in soil, 64, 66–69
Migrant farm workers, 277
Milk, 248–249
  consumption, 233
Milking, mechanized, 288
Minerals in nutrition, 182–187
Minimum Daily Requirement in
  nutrition, 165
Mitchell, J. H., Jr., 212
Mitchell, J. Murray, Jr., 90–91
Modest Proposal, A, 9
Moisture
  management of, 84–89
  modification of, 95
  and plant growth, 82–84
  in soil, 64–65
Molasses, 223
Molybdenum in nutrition, 186
Monoculture, 23–24, 143
Morelos Dam, 140
Morrill, Justio S., 300
Morrill Land-Grant Act, 300
Mrak, Emil, 119
Mulford, Stuart, 299
Mushrooms, 222
Mussen, Paul H., 163
Mutton, 232, 244

Myrdal, Gunnar, 39
Myxamatosis, 108

National Academy of Sciences, 95
National Agricultural Weather
   Service Program, 93
National Farmers Organization, 294
National Farmers Union, 290, 294,
   310
National Nutrition Survey, 156
National Plant Food Institute, 148
National Reclamation Act, 299
National Science Foundation, 259
National Seed Storage Laboratory,
   56–67
National Sharecroppers' Fund, 278
National Weather Service, 92
Navataeans, irrigation system of,
   84–85
Navel orange worm, 104
Nectarines, 228
Nelson, Oliver E., 52, 53
Newbold, Charles, 121
New Deal in agriculture, 306–308
"New Directions in World
   Agriculture," 21
Newland Act, 299
Niacin, 172, 173
Nickel in nutrition, 187
Nicotine as insecticide, 102
Nicotinic acid, 172
Nitrates
   pollution by, 146–149
Nitrites, 146, 147
Nitrogen
   in soil fertility, 60, 67–69, 70
Nitrogen-fixing bacteria, 67–69
Nixon, Richard M., 19–20, 314, 315,
   317, 322–323, 326
Noncalcic Brown soils, 71 (table),
   74 (table), 78
Norin, 10
   wheat, 50

No-till farming, 126–127
Nuplexes, 339
Nutrients
   of plants, 60–61
Nutrition, 155–156 (*see also*
   Malnutrition)
   education in, need for, 156–157
   public attitudes toward, 159–161
Nuts, 229–230

Oats, 208
O'Day, Dick, 87
Odell, Arthur R., 213
O'Harvey, Joan, 248
Oilseeds, 220–222
Olives, 221
Olive scale, 107
Oranges, 226
Ordinance of 1785, 297
Organic matter in soil, 62–63
Orthomolecular psychiatry, 170
Orton, William A., 51
Osmond, Humphry, 170
Overfertilization, 70, 146–147
Overfishing, 30–32
Overpopulation, 336–338

Paarlberg, Don, 37, 283, 288–289, 323,
   324, 330, 331, 335
Paddock, William and Paul, 20
Pantothenate (vitamin B_3), 175–176
Pantothenic acid, 176
Parakeets as pests, 99
Para-aminobenzoic acid (PABA), 182
Parathion, 104, 106
Parent material, in soil genesis, 62
Paris green as insecticide, 102
Parity in farm incomes, 279, 280,
   307–308, 310–311, 313
Parity price support, 308–309

Park, Arch, 151
Parr, C. H., 123
Partridge, Alden, 300
Part-time farming, 278
Pasteur, Louis, 247
Patrons of Husbandry, 292 (see also
    Grange, the)
Patton, James G., 290
Pauling, Linus, 164, 178
Peaches, 227–228
Peanut butter, 220
Peanuts, 220–221
Pears, 227
Peas, 219
Pedology, 60–61
Pellagra, 172–173
    chick, 175
Permeability, of soil, 63
Perosis, 182
Pest control, 100–120
    based on cost-benefit analysis,
        119–120
Pesticides, 102–106 (see also
    Insecticides)
    excessive use of, 104
    energy used in producing, 128
    fish poisoned by, 105
    mutant strains resistant to, 103–104
    persistent, 102–106
    poisonous to humans, 105
    pollution by, 146
Pests, 96–120
    birds, 99–100
    control of, 100–120
    encouraged by monoculture, 143
    insects, 96–98
    mutants resistant to pesticides,
        103–104
    plants, 100
    rodents, 98–99
Pheromones in pest control, 116–118
Philadelphia Society, 270
Phosphorus in nutrition, 184
Photosynthesis, 48
Pig, defined, 243
Pineapples, 299

Pistachio nuts, 230
Plants, 47–57
    immunity to pests, 51–52
    improvement of, 49–50
    nutrients of, 60–61
    as pests, 100
    response to care, 48–49
    repellent to pests, 116–117
Plantation system, 268
Plant nutrition
    elements of, 69
Plant Quarantine Act (1912), 101–102
Plow
    development of, 121–122
    steel, invention of, 270
Poage, W. R., 293
Podzols, 71 (table), 77
Poisonous Plant Research Laboratory,
    100
Polar zone, 79, 80
Pollard, William G., 83–84
Polyneuritis gallarium, 174
Pollution
    by agriculture, 146–150
    of agriculture, 144–145
    of fisheries, 31, 252–253
Population Bomb, The, 20
Population
    farms black, 278
    and food supply, 32
    growth of, since World War II,
        342–343
    world, increase in, 19
Population control, 336–337
Population crashes, 135, 337
Pore space in soil, 63, 64, 66
Pork
    consumption of, 232
Potatoes, 215–216
Poultry, 231, 245–246 (see also
    Chickens; Turkeys)
    processed, 236
    confinement, method of raising, 236
Poultry plants, pollution by, 146, 149
Powell, Adam Clayton, Jr., 5
Powell, Lake, 141

Power, 121–127

Prairie Chestnut soils, 78

Predators, natural, in pest control, 106–109

President's Science Advisory Committee, 53

Pressure, atmospheric, 81

Prestbo, John A., 320, 321

Price supports, 221, 307–308, 318–319, 324–329

Productivity of soil, 62

Prohaska, John T., 93

Protein, 165, 167, 168–169
   in barley, 208–209
   in beans, 219
   in cassava (manioc), 219
   complete, 168
   in corn, 205
   deficiency in, 168–169
   levels of, in corn, genetically increased, 52–54
   and Vitamin A, 171
   in oats, 208
   in fish, 250
   in peas, 219
   in potatoes, 216
   in rice, 206
   in sorghum, 208
   in soybeans, 211–213
   in sweet potatoes and yams, 219
   in wheat, 202

Psychiatry, use of vitamins in, 170

Peteroylmonoglutamic acid, 176–177

Pulses (*see also* Legumes; Soybeans), 218–219

Pure Food and Drug Act (1906), 194–195

Purnell Act, 300

Quarantine as means of pest control, 101–102

Quelea-quelea, as pest, 99

Rabbits
   as food, 244–245
   as pests, 108

Rainfall
   effective, 65
   and leaching, 65
   type of, as element in climate, 81

Rainmaking, 94–95

Raisins, 299

Rats as pests, 98

Reclamation
   beneficial organisms destroyed by, 143–144
   as interference with biosphere, 138

Recommended Daily Allowances (RDA)
   of nutrients, 165, 166 (tables)
   of vitamins and minerals, 166 (table)

Recycling of animal wastes, 150

Red Desert soils, 74 (table), 78

Red-yellow Podzolic soils, 71 (table), 75 (table), 77

Red Podzolic soils, 77

Reddish Chestnut soils, 74 (table), 77, 78

Reddish-brown soils, 74 (table), 78

Reddish Prairie soils, 75 (table), 77

Relief, in soil genesis, 62

Rendzina, 71 (table), 75 (table), 77

Revelle, Roger, 343

Reyniere, Grimond de la, 243

Rhizobia, 67–68

Riboflavin (Vitamin B$_2$), 175

Rice, 205–207

Rice belt, 198

Rickets, 179–180

Rivlin, Richard S., 175

Robbins, Paul, 283

Roberts, Lewis M., 55–56

Rodents as pests, 98–99

Roosevelt, Franklin D., 306–307 (*see also* New Deal)

Roots, 47–48

Rosier, Bernard, 155

Rotation of crops, 46, 136, 270

Ruffin, Edmund, 69
Runoff, 65
  agricultural, pollution of Lake Erie
    by, 147–148
Rural Credits Bill, 302
Rural Electrification Administration,
  307
Rye, 209

Sahel, drought in, 15, 29–30
St. Johnswort, 108
Saline seep, 136, 139–140
Salinity of soil, 65, 139–140, 299 (*see
  also* Desalination)
  in early irrigation systems, 85
Sanborn, J. W., 146
Sanders, Frederick, 93
Sandy soil, 63, 65, 66
San José Scale, 101
Satellite photos, 150–152
Schaefer, Arnold F., 159
Schmidt, Alexander M., 213
Scurvy, 178–179
Schwandt, Russell, 338
Screwworm fly, 113–114
Scrimshaw, Nevin, 187
Seaborg, Glenn T., 339
Sea farming, 253–258
Sea Grant Act, (1966), 258
Seaweed, 258–260
Second Morrill Act., 300
Seeds, germination of, 47
Selenium in nutrition, 186
Sen, B. R., 19
Separates in soil, 63–64
Sheep, 244
Shind, Annasaheb, 23
Sierozem, 75 (table), 78
Sika deer, 337
Silent Spring, 105
Silt, pollution by, 146
Simon, William F., 127
Single-cell protein (SCP), 150
Skinner, John Stuart, 270
Salama, Karel, 115

"Slash-and-burn" farming, 45
Slope, in soil genesis, 62
Smith-Hughes Act, 301
Smith-Lever Act, 296, 300–301
Smith, Ray F., 118, 220
Smog, 144
Snow as source of moisture, 83
Snowmelt, 83
Soil
  classification, 70–78
  conservation, 137–138, 297–298
  fertility, 59–61, 62
  genesis, 60–61, 62–64
  horizons in, 62
  permeability of, 63
  productivity, 62
  profile, 62
  salinity of, 65
  structure, 64
  temperature, effect of, 65–66
  texture, 63
Soil bank, 312–314
Soil Conservation Service, 298
Soilsphere, 58–78
Solar radiation, conversion of, to
  chemical energy, 48
Sorghum. *See* Grain sorghum
Sorghum belt, 198
Soslin, Morton, 36
Soviet Union, crop failures in 26–29
Soybean belt, 198–199
Soybeans, 200–201, 209–214
  and fertilizer, 213
  history, 210–211
  production in U.S., 214
  uses, 209–210
Specific famine, 155
Spilhaus, Athelstan, 336
Sprague, George F., 54
Stanton, A. T., 174–175
Starling as pest, 99
Strong, Maurice F., 152
Subpolar zones, 79, 80
Sugar, 222–225
Sugar Act (1934), 224
"Sugar diplomacy," 224

Sumptuary laws, 159–160
Sun, effect of on plant growth, 82
Sunflower seed, 222
Surplus farm products, 310–312, 316
Sweet potatoes, 219
Swift, Jonathan, 9
Symbiosis, 46
    of nitrogen-fixing bacteria and
        legumes, 68

Talmadge, Herman E., 221, 320
Target prices, 323, 324
Teamsters Union, 277
Technology in agriculture, 276–278
Temperature, effect of on soil, 65–66
Tennessee Valley Authority, 85–86
Terracing, 126, 127
Tetraethyl pyrophosphate, 106
Textured vegetable proteins, 212–213
Thaer, Albrecht van, 60
Thermal pollution of fisheries, 253
Thiamin (vitamin B₁), 173–175
Thompson, Ray, 144
Tippah River, 143
Tomatoes, 215–218
    history, 216–217
    mechanized harvesting of, 124
    vitamin content, 217
Torah, food laws in, 190–191
Tuberculosis and nutrition, 188
Tubers, 219–220 (*see also* Potatoes)
Turkeys, 246
Trace elements in nutrition, 186–187
Tractors, 122–123
Train, Russell E., 138
Trichinosis, 191
Trickleculture, 131
Triticale, 54–56
Trout farming, 255–256, 258
Truman proclamation of 1945, 252
Tsetse fly, 142

Underground water, 87–88

excessive use of, 141
polluted by feedlot wastes, 149–150
United Farm Workers of America,
    277
U.S. Department of Agriculture, 289
    established, 296
    pamphlet on soil erosion, 297–298
U.S. Weather Bureau, 92
Urbanization, agricultural land
    supply reduced by, 138

Van Itallie, Theodore, 157
Vavilov, Nikolai, 202
Vedder, Edward B., 174
Vegetables, 215–222
    defined, 200
Venkatachalam, P. S., 155
Viets, F. G., 150
Viruses in insect control, 110–111
Vitamin C and the Common Cold, by
    Linus Pauling, 178
Vitamins, 166 (table), 171–181
    A, 167, 170, 171–172
    in alfalfa, 214
    B complex, 172–177
    C, 177–179
    D, 179–180
    E, 180–181
    in fat, 167
    in fish, 250
    K, 181
    in olives, 221
    psychiatric, use of, 170
    Recommended Daily Allowances
        of, 166 (table), 72
    in tomatoes, 217
    in wheat, 202
Vocational Education Act, 301
Vrooman, Carl, 302

Wager, Robert, 36
Wages and food prices, 289–290
Waldheim, Kurt, 89

Wall Street Journal, 14, 284, 330, 321

Walnuts, 230

Walsh-Healey Occupational Safety Act, 126

Warm-temperate subtropical zone, 79, 80

Washington, George, and crop rotation, 270

Washington University Center for the Biology of Natural Systems, 148

Wasps, Parasitic, 107

Wasti, L. M. K., 158

Water
  agricultural use, percentage suitable for, 83–84
  farms and urban areas, proportions used by, 84
  gravitational, 63
  irrigation, amount used for, 84
  land supply reduced by demand for, 138
  movement of, in soil, 63
  nutrition, 187
  underground, 87–88, 149–150
  use, 139–141

Watercress, 260

Water rights, 298–299

Water-storage tanks, ancient, 84

Water supply in agriculture, 82–84

Water table, 84
  defined, 64
  lowering of, through excessive draining, 141

Water treaty with Mexico, 140, 299

Watershed, defined, 86

Watershed management program, federal, 86

Weather
  crop faliures caused by, 24, 27
  defined, 81
  modification of, 94–95, 125–126
  prediction of, 91–94

Weather Crop Bulletin, 92

Weather forecasting, 91–94
  history of, 92

Weather satellite, 94

Weber, Deane F., 68

Webster, Daniel, 296–297

Weeds, 100

Weekly Weather Chronicle, 92

Whaling, 251

Wharton, Clifton R., Jr., 23, 33

Wheat, 201–203
  Gaines, 50
  history of, 202
  Norin, 10, 50
  output and consumption, 37
  yield, 202–203

Wheat belt, 108

Wheat-rye hybrid, 54–56

Wheeler, Edwin D., 34

White, Theodore H., 13

Wild rice, 207

Willett, Hurd C., 93

William, R. R., 175

Williams, V. R., 61

Wilson, Woodrow, 302

Winds, as element in climate, 81

Wine, 228

Winick, Myron, 157

Wita, C. T. de, 49

Woods, Jethro, 122

Woods Hole Oceanographic Institution, 250

Woodward, John, 59–60

World Meteorological Organization, 91

Worms in soil, 67

Xerophthalmia, 171

Yams, 219

Yeutter, Clayton, 290

Yew, Man-Li S., 178

Yield, defined, 46

Yu, 59

Zayed, Sheik Shaikh, 132

Zinc in nutrition, 186, 187

ED EDWIN was raised in the farm and ranch state of Montana. His book on American agriculture and farm policy follows a long career in political reporting and analysis. He has been a political consultant for all three major TV networks and for educational broadcasting as well. Among his works are a series of political reference guides for CBS News, a biography of Adam Clayton Powell, Jr., and reports for *Life*, *Harper's*, *The New York Times* and the *Christian Science Monitor*. Mr. Edwin also conducts interviews for the Columbia Oral History Research Office, which has accepted *Feast or Famine* interview transcripts and personal communications for deposit in its collection.